> the tactical use of flame have been made, but are becoming less frequent as formation learns by experience (and casualties). The full value of Crocodiles can, however, only be fully realized when there are more of them, and they are employed in larger numbers.[1]

Mention has to be made of the ethics of using flame. As will be shown in these pages it was even questioned in the heat of battle on several occasions and one member of the regiment managed to write a book based on his experiences with the regiment without once describing a flame attack.[2] In addition, in an IWM interview[3] in the 1970s, Trooper Ellis denied they ever flamed with the intent of hitting German soldiers. On top of this, one high-profile officer of the regiment, already a pacifist by inclination, was court-martialled and served eight months in prison.

At the time, as indeed today, there were many who regarded flame-throwers, along with land mines, for example, as terrible inhumane weapons that should not be used. This complaint is often but certainly not exclusively made by Germans whose family members were on the receiving end of the Crocodile. It should be remembered, however, that Hitler's armies also used flame throughout the war. The adoption of flame by the British Army was not a tit-for-tat measure, but one of employing what proved to be an effective weapon system in a total war and a struggle for national survival. Though controversial, both land mines and flame-throwers are effective on the battlefield, and are today to be found in the inventories of quite a number of armies, particularly those with few scruples. As recently as the First Gulf War the British Army trialled a Spanish-manufactured manpack flame-thrower but rejected it; not for its effectiveness but for ethical and PR reasons.

A Churchill Mk I of 31 Army Tank Brigade on exercise on Salisbury Plain in early 1942.

moved reluctantly on to his secondary trade of gunnery. He eventually 'worked the system' by failing his gunnery test in order to be transferred to his preferred crew trade of driver-mechanic:

> Each day we went off to Walnut Tree Farm to learn the rudiments of the Churchill. The training was thorough; every minute part of the tank and its operation had to be known. The work was hard and dirty but it was never boring as service maintenance had to be learned word perfect. Back in our rooms at night, we would sit for hours quizzing each other; much of the drills were laid out in parrot fashion, learning by numbers.

Following absorbing all the detail of the mechanics and learning to drive a tank:

> Then came the day we all waited for: to take 40 tonnes of steel for a drive; we had done it all in the classroom, and now it was the real thing. The basic principles of driving applied: clutch, brake, accelerator, but no steering wheel; instead a tillable, something like an inverted handlebar on a bicycle, and once in the driver's seat you were on your own, no dual controls, instructor sat on the co-driver's flap outside the tank …
>
> Our training continued most days. It was spent on the tanks, in them or under them. Maintenance was always difficult, the way everything was

> squeezed in. Most parts were reached by laying between the engine hatches and reaching in. Other items were reached by a series of thirteen in all of bolted-on access covers of 3/4″ thick armour plate.

The Churchills had been rushed into production with a long list of known defects, but one by one they were recalled to the Bedford factory in Luton to be upgraded to Mk II A standard.[4] Trooper Cox recalled as the crews came back from their courses that 'The reliability of the tanks was improving; there were very few non-starters now our confidence in them grew. One could feel the increase in the unit's efficiency.'

The regiment's first encounter with the enemy was when they were moved to Brighton and, as autumn set in, into billets in the town. Trooper Cox recalled:

> Two Fw 190s at rooftop height flew over. We stood outside and watched. One dropped a bomb. It bounced in the road at the bottom of ours. We all seemed mesmerised. It happened so quickly. The nose of the bomb just caught the top of the wall, heading skywards again. By this time, we hit the ground and there was a huge explosion followed by a shower of bricks. No one was hit and we all got to our feet. A large railway viaduct had been hit. Travelling upwards, it had brought down a complete arch leaving the two sets of rails hanging there.
>
> We turned to go back inside our billet; what a mess, the sash windows were all blown in and the door was hanging off . . . We cleaned up as much as possible, but it beat sleeping out in tents.

The Tank, Infantry, Mk IV, V and VII (A22) Churchill

The General Staff issued the specification for the A20 infantry tank (I Tank) before the war, which was intended to replace both the Matildas and the Valentine. As with previous designs, the original A20 was based on the requirements of trench-warfare; i.e. it had to be long enough to be capable of crossing trenches and anti-tank ditches, as well as dealing with muddy and broken ground. The specification required the tank to be well protected with a gun capable of firing decent-sized high-explosive rounds. Consequently, for all these reasons, speed was not a major factor. Following the Polish campaign and the fall of France, a revised specification (A22) was issued to Vauxhall Motors in June 1940. This design maintained the role of an infantry tank, but reduced the requirements for trench warfare.

As with former specifications for previous 'I' tanks, the A22 was envisioned as being relatively slow, needing only to keep up with the infantry, but it needed to be heavily protected. Its armament was to be suitable for dealing with fortifications, so it mounted a low-velocity gun of a large calibre and a useful high-explosive round. The tank's length, however, still had to be sufficient to cross trenches and anti-tank ditches, plus have tracks that would crush barbed wire.

After difficulties with prototyping and hundreds of ongoing modifications, the Churchill Mk I was rushed into service with tank units during June 1941 and,

The Infantry Tank A22B Churchill Mk II.

as already described, was modified to Mk II standard. After trials in Egypt, the Churchill Mk III had its first operational use in the Western Desert in October 1942 at the Battle of El Alamein.

The Churchill Crocodile with which 141 Regiment RAC (The Buffs) would eventually to go to war in 1944 was a tank based on the latest version of the Churchill, the Mk VII.

Armour

Previous marks of the Churchill had weighed in at 39 tons, while the Mk VII and VIII were increased to 40 tons. The hull's frontal armour was increased from 4.5in to 6in and the side armour from 2.75in to 3.75in. Small increases were also made to the belly plate and turret roof. It is a credit to the design team that the significant increase in protection made the tank only 1 ton heavier than its predecessors. Even the German Tiger had less frontal protection!

Transmission

To manage the tank's considerable weight, the Merritt-Brown gearbox ratios were changed in the Mk VII, reducing its maximum speed from 15.5 to 13.5 mph. When towing the Crocodile's armoured trailer, speed was further reduced to 11.5 mph. This gearbox also provided a unique turning feature, enabling the tank to turn within its own length by one track driving forward and the other in reverse, but this was not recommended when the trailer was attached!

Suspension

The suspension system, consisting of eleven coil spring paired bogie wheels on each side, was likewise upgraded. Having so many road wheels improved the Churchill's ability to cross soft, muddy ground without bogging in and was aided by the track base being extended to the front of the hull, giving a comparatively low ground pressure of less than 14 lb per square inch. The track height as well as length contributed to the Churchill's almost legendary obstacle-clearing ability. So good was the suspension/running gear that the Churchill's cross-country speed was 11 mph faster than both the Sherman and the Panther.[5]

Engine

Power was provided by a Vauxhall Bedford Twin-Six petrol engine retained from previous marks and producing 350 hp. Being somewhat underpowered was not seen as a disadvantage in its role as a heavy infantry assault tank.

Crew Safety

The most important safety feature of the Churchill Crocodile was, as previously noted, its massive armour protection. It was unique in Second World War tanks in having access doors on each side of the hull in addition to the two hatches on the turret roof and those above the driver's and flame-gunner's positions. This gave crews a better chance of escape from the vehicle when knocked out. Additionally, the side hatches being much lower reduced the chance of crews being hit by enemy small-arms fire while escaping. However, it was found on earlier marks that the square side doors were very difficult to open when the tank was at an angle due to their weight. On the Mk VII the doors were smaller and circular in design, making them sturdier and more manageable.

A Mk VII Churchill with its distinctive circular escape hatch in the sponsons.

A tank crew's greatest fear was fire. The M4 Sherman had a particularly poor reputation for 'brewing up' after penetration by an AP or hollow-charge weapon. These intense fires were almost always the result of the tank's ammunition catching fire rather than the petrol engine as is often assumed. To address this, the Churchill Mk VII was fitted with armoured bins for its 75mm ammunition, which so reduced the likelihood of fire that it was retro-fitted to earlier marks of the tank. Similar arrangements were made for turret stowage of No. 36 hand grenades and 2in phosphorous mortar bombs.

Crew Comfort

The Churchill was popular with crews because of its relatively spacious interior. This was due to the unique design of having a sponson similar to First World War tanks taking up the space between the upper and lower track runs. When under artillery or mortar fire, leaving the safety of their AFV for essentials such as the call of nature could be avoided by using empty shell cases instead. Likewise, hot meals and tea could be prepared in the on-board cooker using tinned composite rations, with the flame gunner's position being the best for this task. One driver commented that there was a secure space behind his instrument panel where a whisky (or calvados) bottle could be stored! Likewise, precious sleep could be achieved within the tank's confines, although some contortion was often necessary!

When the tank was driven at speed the crew experienced excessive noise within the hull due to the eleven paired steel road wheels and no return rollers for the tracks at the top, with metal skids being provided instead.

Optics

Earlier marks of the Churchill gave the crews a very limited view of the world outside their tank. The commander's cupola, for example, had one or two periscopes fitted to his turret hatches, but during the Normandy campaign the Mk VII was retro-fitted with a rotating cupola with eight episcopes, one of which could be elevated. This essential modification was forced upon designers due to the high number of casualties being sustained by commanders having to remain 'head up' during action and being particularly susceptible to German small-arms fire. The gunner was also provided with an episcope, previously thought to have been unnecessary. The driver and flame-gunner had extended episcopes, necessary because their view ahead was restricted by the front of the tracks limiting their view to the left and right.

Armament

The tank's main armament was the QF 75mm gun, which was essentially a re-bored 6-pounder anti-tank gun that could fire a very useful HE or smoke round, but had a less impressive anti-tank capability. The 75mm HE ammunition was supplied by the US and was also used by the M4 Sherman, but although highly effective it had a thin brass case that was prone to damage or separation in the breech. Churchill crews found that unlike the Sherman's 75mm gun that an experienced crew could fire up to ten times a minute, this was not possible with the converted British gun as the Sherman breech loaded from above, while the Churchill loaded from the side. The Churchill carried eighty-five AP, HE and smoke rounds for the gun.

As a gun tank the Churchill was equipped with two Besa 7.92 belt-fed machine guns: one coaxial with the 75mm turret gun and a second that could be replaced by the Crocodile flame conversion kit. With a rate of fire of up to 850 rounds per minute, the Besa's high velocity was reported to be able to pierce the armoured gun shields of German anti-tank guns. It also had the advantage of being able to fire captured German ammunition. It tended to be prone to stoppages, especially in cold weather, so crews would often test-fire the guns before going into action to warm them up. On the other hand, it was capable of greater sustained fire, and was less prone to overheating than most other machine guns of its class.

More Changes

In May 1942 the brigade, now designated 31 Tank Brigade, joined the 53rd Welsh Division as a part of a short-lived trial of 'Mixed Divisions' which consisted of two infantry and one tank brigades. The organization of the regiment at this time is shown opposite. The Welsh Division's historian described the thinking behind this change:

> The new divisions were known as 'New Model Divisions'. They were designed to meet the anti-invasion role in which the main requirement was quick offensive action by a powerful force in order to dislodge any invasion troops while they were still off balance and before they could become firmly established. This it was thought could be achieved best by including a strong 'I' tank component in each division, rather than by concentrating the tanks centrally when they would obviously take longer to reach the Infantry with whom they were to co-operate – and indeed might not reach them at all. These arguments were valid so long as anti-invasion was the primary role. Later, when preparation for the assault on the Normandy coast was the main task of the troops in Great Britain, Infantry Divisions reverted to their original organization of three Infantry Brigades.[6]

During their time with the Welsh Division, the brigade took part in several large-scale divisional and XII Corps exercises. The former included live firing alongside the infantry and the latter in Kent practising the counter-attack role. This experience served to cement 141's knowledge and understanding of infantry co-operation. Trooper Cox, not always fully aware of what was going on, described one exercise during this period:

> The whole unit went off on an army exercise, Operation Tiger II. Nice to get away from that usual routine and use our tanks. We did a lot of road marches and a good deal of cross-country. Just going where and when we

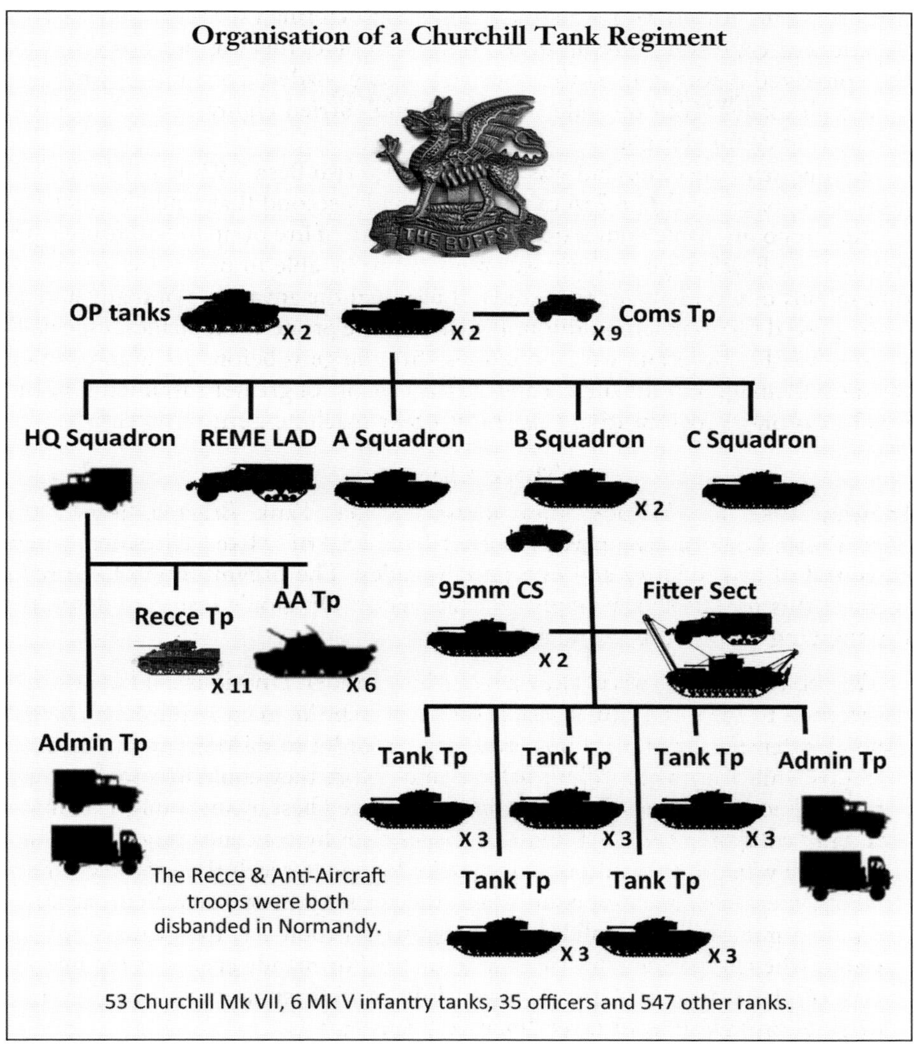

were told. The Army divisional commanders learned to move units about in a simulated war game. Wireless operators, radios on regimental networks, also on 'B' network between troops. Echelons had to keep up with our supplies, mainly petrol. Rations were handed out in bulk for us to prepare and cook ourselves, not always successfully. Most of the time we foraged off a village shop to see what was going on there, providing we hadn't been beaten to it.

In September of 1942, with the threat of invasion over, 31 Brigade became an independent tank brigade but remained with XII Corps. At the end of the year,

Vehicle Colours and Tactical Markings

The Churchill tanks issued to 141 RAC were factory-painted in a mid-khaki brown colour known as SCC2. It was only in October 1944 that the regiment's tanks began to be repainted in a dark green colour similar to the olive drab with which American and Canadian issue tanks were painted. This colour was known as SCC15. The painting process was somewhat haphazard, with one crewman stating that initially there wasn't enough paint available for all the vehicles and that there were no paintbrushes available either. This resulted in many tanks remaining brown and others only partially repainted.

All British vehicles carried a census mark equivalent to a civilian registration number. For gun tanks this would begin with the letter 'T' followed by six digits and another random letter, for example T173174H. This would be painted in white 3.5in high on the hull sides and lower front. ARVs would carry a similar mark, but beginning with the letters REC.

The census number can be clearly seen here on the example of a Mk VII Churchill at the Hill 112 memorial.

Each tank was also given a unique name painted on the engine air intakes on the vehicle side in the regimental colour of light blue. These names all began with the letter 'S' and included names such as 'Sultan' and 'Sandwich' in C Squadron (see Appendix I for other known names).

The sign of the 31 Tank Brigade, a green diablo, was painted on the lower front and upper rear hull on the left, although Lieutenant Wilson recalls being ordered to paint them out before D-Day. In September 1944 this was replaced by the 79th Armoured Division sign of a black bull's head within a yellow triangle. The unit serial number in Normandy was painted on the lower hull front and rear hull on the right. This was a green square with the number 993 in white with a diagonal white line. The tank's troop number was painted on the turret sides and rear in white paint within a blue squadron sign, A Squadron having a triangle,

B Squadron trailer en route to Brest in early September with a seemingly incomplete 79th Armoured triangle.

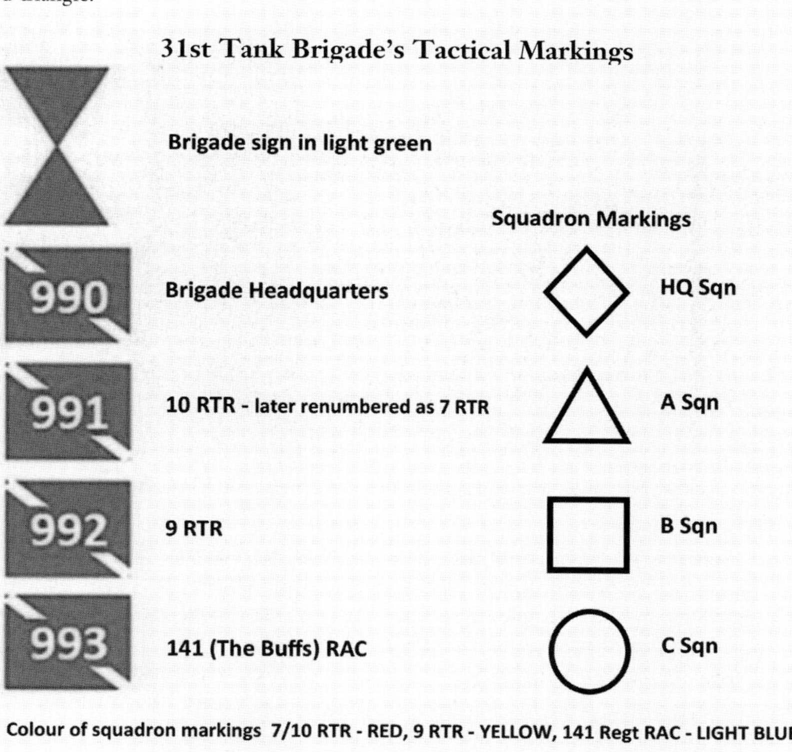

Squadron HQ and Troop Markings

HQ A Sqn

7

7 Troop B Sqn

14 Troop C Sqn

B Squadron a square, C Squadron a circle and HQ a diamond. An example number for a C Squadron vehicle would be 13B. The vehicle bridge classification should have been painted on the lower hull front. This was a yellow circle with the number 40 in black. There were also small signs indicating the position of the infantry telephone and first-aid kit.

Whether any or all of these markings were applied in Normandy is open to conjecture. If present they could be obscured by camouflage nets, spare track links or dirt. Also, painting or repainting of them depended on the time and materials being available, particularly on replacement vehicles. Many Churchills in action appear to have no markings at all.

The trailer often carried an air recognition panel draped across the top. This was a neon red or yellow panel with a reverse side in white on which messages or other identification could be drawn.

as orders of battle for the invasion of north-west Europe started to firm up, the brigade came under command of XXX Corps, with all three regiments still equipped with Churchill gun tanks.

Flame-Throwers

The use of flame in war is as old as warfare itself, or at least as old as flammable defensive structures. From flaming arrows, burning oils and the likes of Greek fire used in the siege of Constantinople in 1453, it was but a small step to the recognizable flame-throwers that were used by the Byzantines and Chinese more than a thousand years ago. Since then, a variety of flame weapons have almost always been present on the battlefield. In the modern age the flame-thrower saw its debut in German hands during the First World War against the French at Verdun and against the British on the Bellewaerde Ridge outside the Belgian city of Ypres, both in 1915. Though not a war-winning weapon system, the role of flame-throwers in battle became well understood, with the Germans using them on some 650 documented occasions on the Western Front. A British system, the Livens Large Gallery Flame Projector, was deployed for use on the Somme in 1916. It was a static system that had to be built into Russian saps dug out into no-man's-land and, using compressed air to drive a piston into a long container of fuel, it projected flame about 90 yards into the enemy's trenches.

The development of a flame-throwing tank for the British Army began in 1938 when the Imperial General Staff set out a requirement for a turret-mounted flame-thrower for the A12 Matilda Infantry Tank. The defeat in 1940, however, resulted in a focus on existing production to rebuild the army and flame weapons were sidelined. Even so, in 1941 the Canadian Army placed an order for seventeen flamethrowers mounted on Canadian built Universal Carriers, with this weapon system being intended for the Canadian Army. This early design eventually evolved into the highly successful Wasp Mk II Carrier which was only ready for prototype testing in the summer of 1943 and was issued at the end of June 1944.

A test run of the First World War Livens Large Gallery Flame Projector.

At the start of the Second World War, a manpack flame-thrower was in the inventory of the German *pioneers* and was first used at Danzig during the 1939 campaign, with a flame system being subsequently mounted in Sd.Kfz.251 Hanomag half-tracks. The US Army deployed is own system in 1942, but manpack weapons proved to be extremely hazardous for the user and therefore there was a reluctance to use the flame-thrower, hence the British move to put the weapon under armour.

Following the 1940 campaign the War Office showed little interest in further development of tank-mounted flame-throwers, preferring the agile Wasp and manpack solutions, but the Petroleum Warfare Department continued experimenting with flame at Moody's Down outside Winchester. The first flame-thrower they produced saw service as an airfield defence weapon, which being of substantial proportions was perforce mounted on an AEC Matador truck, weighing some 17 tons fully charged. This included 2 tons of flame fuel that was based on a mixture of tar and diesel, which in later versions achieved a not inconsiderable range of 200 yards.

One of the department's early decisions regarding armour was that mounting of a flame weapon would not prevent the vehicle from functioning as a gun tank and this was the case in the first prototype tank-mounted flame-throwers, code-named OKE.[7] Churchill Mk II tanks were converted for each to carry two units of Ronson Flame Equipment, which were fixed rigidly on the hull front with a range of just 50 yards, with the flame fuel being carried in an armoured tank mounted on the rear of the vehicle. The projectors were aimed by the driver by

A German *pioneer* manpack flame-thrower.

The flame fuel tank at the rear of a Churchill OKE flame-throwing tank.

steering the vehicle at the target. At a demonstration of the weapon system, Field Marshal Sir Alan Brooke, Chief of Imperial General Staff, suggested prophetically that it might be better to have one flame-thrower with a range of 100 yards than two rather inadequate projectors.

Three B Squadron Churchill OKE tanks (nicknamed 'Boar', 'Beetle' and 'Bull') with the single fixed flame projector mounted to the left of the hull machine gun were deployed with the Canadian Calgary Regiment during Operation JUBILEE,

A Churchill OKE abandoned on the beach at Dieppe. The flame projector can be clearly seen in this German photograph.

the Dieppe Raid in August 1942. They landed on White Beach from one of the new Landing Craft Tanks (LCTs) in the first wave, but all quickly came to grief without a flame action. One OKE was drowned, another was disabled on the beach by chert pebbles getting in the running gear and the final one reached the esplanade but minus its fuel tank. None of them came into action with flame and were either knocked out or captured.

Further development of a flame-throwing Churchill only took place against a backdrop of official disinterest in the project after Dieppe, with preference being given to the Wasp Carrier option. However, Major General Percy Hobart, commander of the forming 79th Armoured Division and its 'Zoo' of assault armour, saw a demonstration at Orford Ness in 1943 and rescued the Crocodile equipment from potential obscurity. He pressed the Ministry of Supply to put the Crocodile conversion kit into production, but it took the intervention of Field Marshal Alan Brooke to include flame-throwers in the brief for Hobart's division. Developing a production model was slow, and it was very late in the day that the first conversion kits were issued to 141 RAC under a veil of secrecy.

Initially it was decided that the Churchill Mk IV with a 57mm gun should be used for what was now code-named the Crocodile, with a flame gun capable of a

Major General Percy Hobart, commander of 79th Armoured Division.

range of up to 200 yards coaxial with the hull Besa machine gun. The 400 gallons of fuel was now carried in an armoured two-wheeled trailer with a very substantial tow bar attached to the rear of the tank weighing 6.4 tons. The trailer had no brakes, relying on the considerable weight of the towing tank to check its speed and, without suspension, it relied on its two huge run-flat tyres to absorb ground shock.

During a demonstration in March 1943, it was realized that the experimental flame gun was unsuitable, mainly due to the flame being easily deflected by side winds. With the Second Front looming there was too little time to develop a new flame gun so it was decided to adopt the already proven gun from the Wasp, although the range would be reduced to a maximum of 120 yards. It was also decided to exclusively convert the new Churchill A22 Mk VII tank to Crocodiles. It was considerably better armoured than its predecessors and its main armament was the 75mm QF gun with a better HE performance but reduced anti-tank capability. It was also possible to convert the Churchill Mk VIII to a Crocodile as the only difference between the tanks was the main armament which, in the case of the Mk VIII, was a 95mm gun. However, few of these conversions were carried out.

The Crocodile equipment only became available in early 1944. Consequently, a single squadron of 141 RAC was ready for deployment by the time of D-Day.

The Crocodile Conversion Kit

The flame gun replaced the hull Besa machine gun, a conversion that could be carried out by the crew in two hours. The sighting mechanism for the Besa was, however, retained. With a maximum range of 120 yards, flame was a fearsome weapon, with its fuel carried in a 6.4-ton two-wheeled armoured trailer. The key element of the Crocodile system was the 400 gallons of flame fuel known as 'FRAS' (Fuel Research Aluminium Stearate), which was a secret mixture of petrol, aluminium stearate and other chemicals, allowing the gel mixture to burn continuously and stick to any surface attacked. A trailer load provided enough fuel for bursts totalling 80 seconds of flaming. Trooper Joseph Ellis provides a simple description of the jelly-like flame fuel:

> The trailer contained 400 gallons of flame fuel. In simple terms, it was made of a mix of soap, petrol and rubber. The petrol burned, the soap spread, and the rubber stuck. The fuel was ignited as it left the nozzle and the burning petroleum jelly stuck to everything it touched. If it got on your clothes by accident and you tried to brush it off, it would stick to that as well. The only way to put it out was to roll you in something.

The composition of the flame fuel was a closely guarded secret, with crews once in Normandy being under strict instructions to destroy the tank rather than let it and its secrets fall into enemy hands.

The FRAS flame fuel tank was pressurized by five large gas cylinders. To bring the Crocodile into action took approximately thirty minutes, fifteen minutes

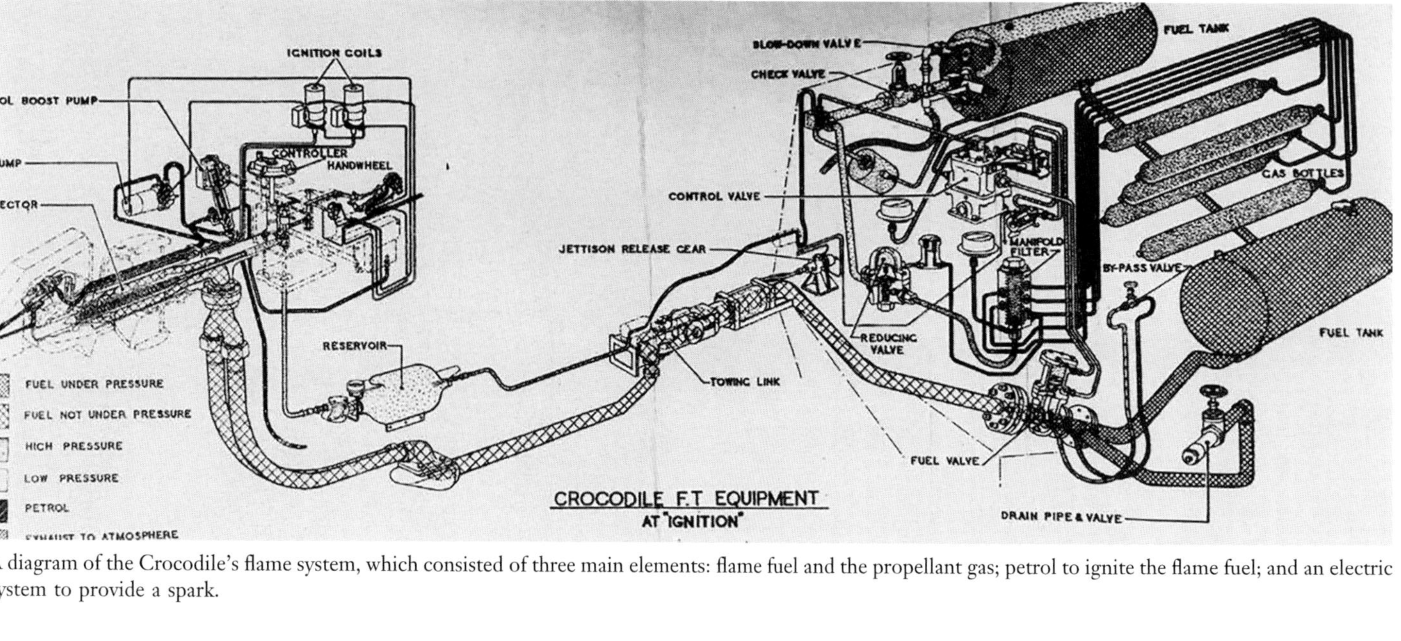

A diagram of the Crocodile's flame system, which consisted of three main elements: flame fuel and the propellant gas; petrol to ignite the flame fuel; and an electric system to provide a spark.

being required to bring the flame gun up to pressure, after which the pressure fell steadily. An early lesson learned in Normandy was the necessity of timely pressurization and going straight into action.

The Crocodile's trailer was connected to the tank by an ingenious attachment known as the towing link or elbow joint. This allowed the tank to turn in any direction without overturning or interrupting the flow of gas and fuel. The link also included a micro-switch that gave the driver a warning that he could turn no further by way of red/green warning lights on his instrument panel. The flame fuel was carried from the trailer by a steel pipe that ran beneath the belly plate and into the hull through an opening beneath the hull gunner's position originally designed for spent cartridge cases.

Until late in the Normandy campaign, the trailer pipes, flame gun and ancillary equipment for Crocodile conversion were sent to 141 RAC for their fitters to install and test. Subsequently, however, all Mk VII Churchills came with the Crocodile's elbow joint, pipework and the tank end of the elbow joint pre-installed, leaving only the Besa to be replaced by a flame gun.

Some 800 Crocodile conversion kits and trailers were produced and, in addition to two further regiments being converted in north-west Europe, several regiments worth were supplied to units in Italy and Burma during the autumn of 1944. A further 250 were held back in the UK for the invasion of Japan.

The towing link or 'elbow joint' connecting the tank and its armoured flame fuel trailer.

The assembly at the rear of the tank eventually became standard on Churchill Mk VIIs, making conversion to a Crocodile quick and easy.

Another Change of Role

After fourteen months training as an ordinary gun tank regiment, 141 RAC, as Trooper Cox recalled,

> … began to receive some new tanks, the Mk VII. They certainly looked formidable, with 7½ inches of frontal armour [*sic*], we were impressed. Nothing could go through that (so we thought). The side armour was thicker, and escape hatch doors now a circular shape instead of square with a small pistol port in the centre.

There were questions about why the junior regiment of 31 Tank Brigade received the newest tanks and not the two RTR regiments. The answer was not forthcoming, but the driver mechanics wondered:

> During routine maintenance, we notice quite a few fitting, drilled and tapped holes that seemed to have no reason for being there. Questions always draw blanks. No one seemed to know the answer. Various ones were suggested but none seem to fit; as it turned out none of us were correct.

All the regiment knew to start with was that they were detached from the rest of their brigade and ordered to paint out the brigade's diablo symbol. The conversion to the flame-throwing role was not revealed for some time due to the secrecy with which a whole variety of specialist assault equipment and vehicles were being developed for 79th Armoured Division. The unit responsible for trials and development of this equipment including the Crocodile conversion kit was 43 RTR based at the Orford Ness training area in Suffolk.[8]

Officers of C Squadron 141 RAC started to be sent away on courses, and on their return they would not talk about what they had been doing. At the same time, more and more heavily armoured Mk VII Churchills started to arrive at Eastwell. Lieutenant Andrew Wilson explained that 'By the end of February another batch of subalterns had come back tight-lipped from the course in Suffolk. All were from C Squadron.' Writing in the third person, he continued: 'Wilson did everything possible to find out. That is to say, he ceased to ask questions and merely listened. But all he heard was the name of the regiment that ran the courses – 43rd RTR – and the phrase experimental unit.'[9]

The arrival of field security police only added to the frustration of not knowing what was going on, but glances at documents on the adjutant's desk revealed 'a number of cryptic names' including 'Crocodile'. Armed with this information he posed the question to C Squadron officers in the mess: 'Can someone please tell me just what the hell is a crocodile?' Everyone stopped talking and the secret was revealed:

> The Crocodile equipment hadn't arrived yet. But they were expecting it every day. 'It's terrific,' said Benzecry. 'No one else has anything like it – even the Yanks.' Meanwhile the C Squadron boys were getting ready a disused farmhouse, away on the far side of the training area, where they were going to give instruction.
>
> A large stretch of the training area had been discreetly wired in, with the wire hidden behind bushes. The guards had been reorganized. The Field Security sergeant had taken up quarters in the village. From there he ranged about the countryside. He wore civilian clothes now. Once Wilson saw him in the Saracen's Head, listening in the background while a captain was talking to a girl.
>
> The equipment came, as the Mark VIIs had done, by night. The first Wilson saw of it was when he walked out to the squadron office one morning. There in the hard clear light on the training area stood a curious object with two enormous rubber tyres. It was shaped like the blunt prow of a boat, and in place of the bowsprit was a big steel pipe cased in armour plating. He went closer and saw that the pipe was meant to be coupled to the back of a tank.

It was not until sometime later that the commanding officer, Lieutenant Colonel Waddell, revealed the secret to his unit:

> The whole regiment assembled at Eastwell House to be addressed by the Colonel. 'I consider it to be a great honour. This regiment has been chosen to become the first flame-throwing regiment in the British Army, mounted on tanks.' He explained that over the next few months, an all-out effort would be expected of everyone to perfect our new weapon. So now we knew.

A Crocodile photographed during training at Eastwell Park in May 1944.

> Nobody said much. We all thought a lot. No one knew anything about flame-throwers. We all had to learn together. Everyone was sworn to secrecy. Anyone who mentioned the word outside the unit would be court-martialled.

Inevitably the locals had an inkling of what was going on. Peter Rainer recalled that much of the training area was screened by hessian for security. 'All the entrances were guarded and surrounded with barbed wire and sandbags, but we heard they were experimenting with tanks.' All the while the conversion kits arrived under the same veil of secrecy:

> We opened up our 'Christmas boxes' to find an assortment of pipes, valves, strange fittings of all shapes and sizes, long heavy steel pipes, slabs of armour plate all pressed into shape, nuts and bolts, seals and sealant. Each box had a number; the first box contained an instruction book for the assembly. Each crew would be responsible for assembling and fitting [the kit] to the time under the watchful eyes of the fitters and our own REME detachment, who had always done Trojan work with the unit.

After days of learning about the operation of the Crocodile with its pipes and electric circuits, the time came for the officers to see the regiment's single working converted Churchill in action for the first time:

> They were standing round the whole apparatus – tank and trailer linked up – while a demonstration crew manipulated a system of valves and gauges. There hadn't been a chance to see the tank since Wilson last saw it; instead of the co-driver's machine gun there was now an ugly little nozzle with two metal tongues above it like the points of a sparking-plug.
>
> While they stood there, there was continuous hissing and ticking from the trailer – the sort of noise a locomotive makes as it waits to take out its train. Then the noise ceased. The crew shut the trailer door and climbed into the tank.
>
> We began to find out what all those drilled and tapped holes that had baffled us from the time we had the Mark VII [were for]. We began the painstaking job of assembly, mostly by trial and error. Mostly the latter. Between us all, we put all the pieces together.

Meanwhile Lieutenant Wilson and the other officers were under instruction:

> 'First they'll do a run to show you everything,' said Benzecry. 'Trenches, dug-outs, pill-boxes, houses – the whole lot.' The spectators climbed onto a bank. They were looking at what the pioneers had built: a section of mock battlefield. The Crocodile lay below them, an impatient dragon licking its lips.
>
> It went towards the first target, a concrete pillbox. Suddenly there was a rushing in the air, a vicious hiss. From the front of the tank a burning yellow rod shot out. Out and out it went, up and up, with a noise like the slapping

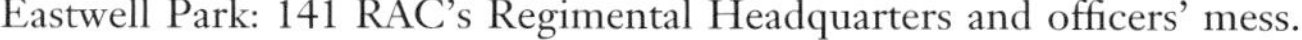

Eastwell Park: 141 RAC's Regimental Headquarters and officers' mess.

> of a thick leather strap. The rod curved and started to drop, throwing off burning particles. It struck the concrete with a violent smack. A dozen yellow fingers leapt out from the point of impact, searching for cracks and apertures. All at once the pillbox was engulfed in fire – belching, twisting, red-roaring fire. And clouds of smelling, grey-black smoke.

The final pieces to arrive at Eastwell Park for A Squadron were the coupling from trailer to tank made at the Lagonda London factory, 'a world of difference from their sleek prewar cars.' It was 'a masterpiece of precision engineering, it had to turn in any direction while still carrying high pressure fuel, also a jettison arrangement and shut of valve, plus being able to tow more than 6 tons across the toughest terrain.'

Finally, the squadron's Crocodiles were assembled and the squadron officers laid on a demonstration for their soldiers, at the conclusion of which:

> everyone stood mouths agape. It seemed ages before anybody spoke. 'Bloody hell.' 'Would like to be on then to that lot.' Tongues started to loosen. Underneath it we all secretly thought what a horrible thing to use on another human being. This attitude must have filtered through. We were reminded that the Germans had used them since the beginning of the war and were still using them and we had to get through the Atlantic Wall.

Preparations for the Invasion

On 17 March 1944 Lieutenant Colonel Waddell and his Intelligence Officer, Captain Harry Bailey, were:

> summoned post-haste to London and were informed that Crocodiles were needed for 'D'-Day. Plans were immediately made for four Crocodiles to go in the assault with 69 Brigade and three with 231 Brigade. Lack of shipping and our late advent prevented 30 Corps taking more, despite repeated requests to take at least a whole Squadron. For similar reasons I Corps would not take any – or perhaps they were 'not impressed'.[10]

A report stated that 'Although they had given demonstrations, not much was known of capabilities at brigade or battalion level.' Even if there was reluctance to use the Crocodiles, the fact is that with less than three months until D-Day, a major problem was that by the end of March the regiment still only 'had exactly nine Mark VII tanks and no [flame fuel] trailers.'

In the event, as D-Day approached, with Mk VII Churchills and conversion kits still arriving and training for the other squadrons just beginning, only C Squadron was anywhere near completing elementary training in Suffolk and was thus the only squadron likely to be ready for operations on D-Day. This, as it happened, was not a great problem as assault shipping was at a premium and with the Crocodile being a new and untried weapon system, XXX Corps was only able to make space in its landing craft for two troops, both now reduced to three Crocodiles. Consequently, 13 Troop commanded by Lieutenant Shearman and

A recreation of Lieutenant Shearman's Crocodile of C Squadron, 13 Troop, named 'Sandgate'. It is seen here aboard a preserved LCT.

15 Troop with Lieutenant Davies, both under command of Captain Barber, were earmarked for landing in the first hour of the invasion under command of 50th (Northumbrian) Infantry Division.

The two C Squadron troops joined the rest of the regiment in the long process of waterproofing the Crocodiles:

> The tanks could wade in up to 2 feet of water. Obviously not enough for leaving a landing craft onto a beach. As with our conversion to flame-throwers, we had a series of boxes just like a kit set, with all the instructions, so it was back under the tank to remove all the inspection covers. Every part of the tank had to be sealed. The gun, muzzle and mantlet, hatches, turret, ring, periscope; in fact, anywhere that water might get in. Bostik smeared on all the surfaces which had to be clean and dry. Then waterproof canvas over these areas and another coat of Bostik. The same process for the engine covers, where different types of Bostik were used because of the heat difference. Extensions of about 6 foot high were fitted to the twin exhausts and held by long stay rods. Fabricated steel ducting was fitted to louvres at the same height.

The late readiness of C Squadron and the secret nature of the Crocodile equipment both served to preclude the two troops from taking part in the final pre-invasion exercises and prevented the assault infantry battalions from gaining any knowledge of the capability of flame.

The two Crocodile troops and their 'miniature logistic echelon' left Eastwood Park for the short drive to Ashford railway station where they were loaded onto flats to transport them to the marshalling area around Southampton. On arrival at Cadlands Camp they started the process of briefing, waterproofing and testing its effectiveness in the wading pits before making the short journey from their camp on their tracks to the embarkation hard at Stanswood Bay near Calshot.[11] This particular hard was used for the loading of vehicles and equipment that were still listed as 'secret' onto their respective Landing Craft Tanks (LCTs).

Stanswood Bay, in common with the other four embarkation hards, had been built along the shores of the Solent and the rivers near Southampton for the embarkation of 50th Division and its supporting formations and units. These consisted of concrete approach roads and aprons (waiting areas), the hards themselves being made of preformed concrete slabs that looked like bars of chocolate. These were laid to enable the ramps of LCTs to be lowered onto a firm surface at any state of the tide and for armoured vehicles to drive down and onto the landing crafts' ramps without the need to negotiate a beach.

On D-Day the two troops of Crocodiles were to land behind the first assault waves of DD tanks, armoured engineers and infantry on GOLD Beach. 15 Troop were to land on JIG Sector with 231 Brigade at H-Hour +35 minutes aboard two LCTs and were to be under command of 1 Hampshires to clear Le Hamel. Meanwhile, 13 Troop would be approaching KING Beach with 69 Brigade, with a planned touchdown of H+45, as a part of the 7 Green Howards' battlegroup.

The embarkation hard at Staniswood Bay in Lepe Country Park on the Solent is one of the best-preserved examples that remain.

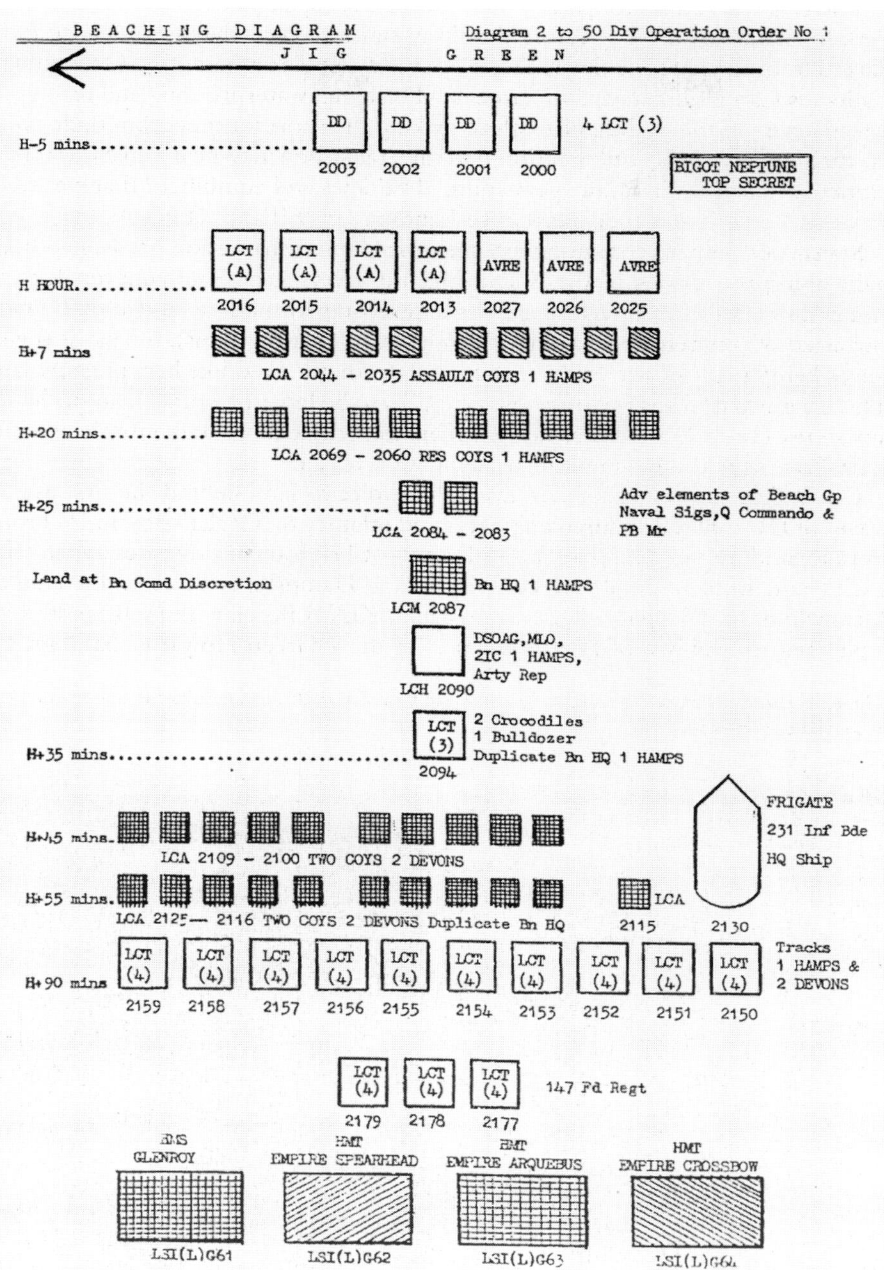

A part of 231 Brigade's Beaching Diagram for JIG Green.

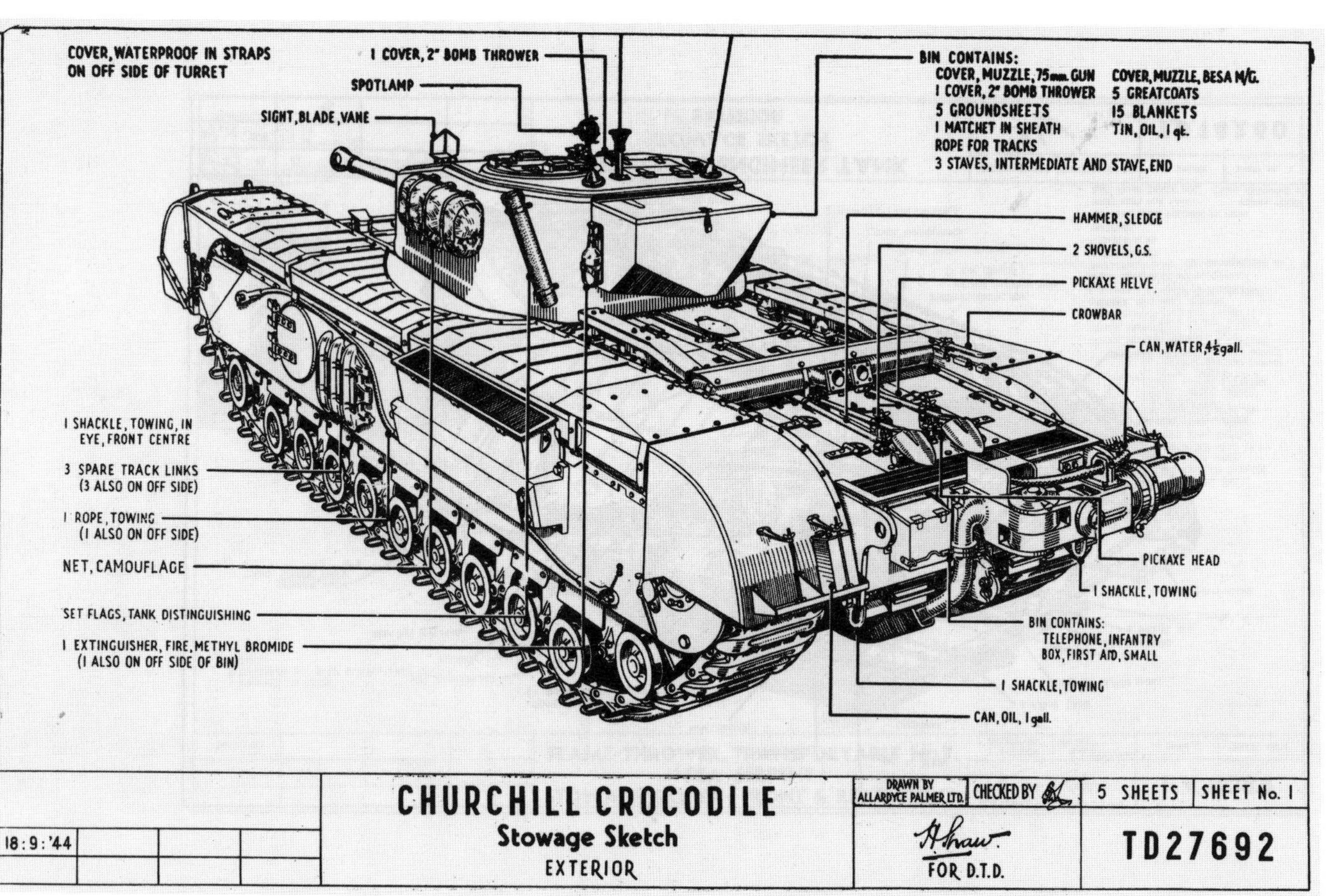

A drawing from a manual showing external stowage on the Crocodile for the myriad of equipment required by each tank.

Chapter Two

The Invasion and Early Days

After an uncomfortable night aboard the flat-bottomed LCTs on a sea that was still rough from the bad weather that had delayed the invasion by twenty-four hours, by 0530 hours on 6 June 1944, Force G was approaching the Normandy beaches. The craft bearing the two troops of Crocodiles of C Squadron 141 Regiment RAC were in the marked lanes swept through the coastal minefields, while ahead of them the preliminary shelling of GOLD Beach was under way by Naval Bombardment Force K. This forty-minute engagement of major coastal batteries was followed by flights of medium bombers. As the invasion flotillas approached the coast, every gun from destroyers, specialist assault craft and embarked artillery pieces 'drenched the beach with fire'.

Planned to lead the landing on GOLD Beach at H-Hour -5 minutes (H-5) were the Duplex Drive Sherman tanks of the 4th/7th Dragoon Guards (4/7 DG) and the Sherwood Rangers Yeomanry, but the sea conditions were such that the Combined Operations headquarters aboard HMS *Bulolo* off the beach ordered them to land behind the infantry. This meant that the first ashore on GOLD Beach at H-Hour were the dozen breaching teams provided by 79th Armoured Division, without the close support of the DD tanks. Five minutes behind the Funnies were the leading assault infantry battalions, which had to cross the fire-swept sands of GOLD Beach.

Touching down with the final landing serials of the leading assault infantry battalions, the task of the Crocodiles was to assist them with the clearance of their objectives inland. For both of 141's troops, these included villages of naturally strong stone-built houses and sundry German defensive positions where flame would be useful in subduing resistance.

D-Day

As the LCTs on their way to JIG and KING sectors threaded their way through the anchored Landing Ships Infantry and the bombardment force, some 6 miles out to sea most of the crews of the two Crocodile troops were seasick. Those that had better sea legs opened the valves of the gas cylinders and began the process of pressurizing the trailer ready for landing.

Lieutenant Davis's 15 Troop landing at H+37 minutes to support 231 Brigade did so at the height of the difficulty and confusion on JIG beach. A strongpoint at the eastern end of Le Hamel (*Wiederstandnest* (WN) 37) was where a particularly well-sited pillbox containing a Polish 1939-vintage 75mm anti-tank gun dominated the beach. The significance of this heavily casemated gun had been missed

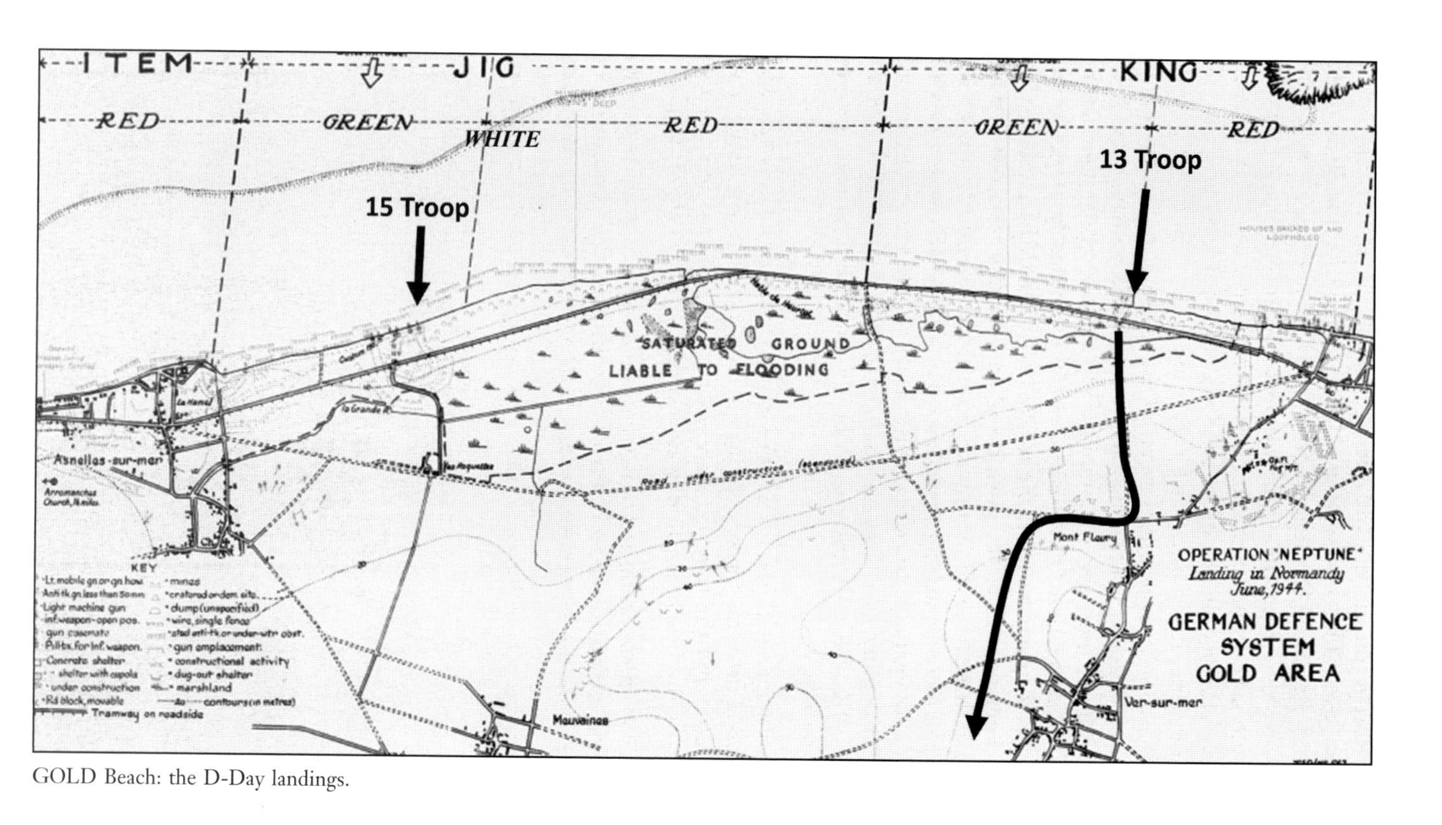

GOLD Beach: the D-Day landings.

by the air photograph analysts and intelligence officers of the 50th Division down to battalion level. This oversight was compounded by the breakdown of the motor launch bearing 147 Field Regiment RA's Forward Observation Officer. Consequently, the regiment's fire was directed further east onto WN 36 at Les Rocquettes. So from the outset, the DD tanks and the assault vehicles of the six JIG Beach breaching teams were being knocked out, and the infantry of 1 Hampshire were driven to cover by machine guns mounted in *Tobrukstands* in WN 37. These German defences survived the run-in shoot without being either neutralized or knocked, and their machine guns and anti-tank guns dominated the beach until late morning. A Combined Operations report noted at the time of 15 Troop's landing that 'The main trouble in the early stages came from a strongpoint at the eastern end of the sea wall at LE HAMEL; naval support could not be used against this as the position of our forward troops was not known.'

As the LCTs bearing 15 Troop approached the beach it was apparent that the Royal Engineer breaching teams and the RE and RN beach obstacle clearance teams had been able to achieve little and the tide was rising fast around the obstacles. Threading their way through wrecked craft, LCTs 2094 and 2095[1] grounded on JIG GREEN and JIG WHITE respectively, down went the ramps and the Crocodiles:

> 'parted company' with the LCTs. For with a delicious little gurgle of delight one subsided into the sea, one sat stolidly and comfortably down in a crater on the beach and the third creature, carried on by some unknown stamina right across the beach, straightaway collapsed with a broken track.

The first Crocodiles committed to battle had all come to grief in the sea or in the dunes before getting into action, fortunately with the loss of just a single crewman. This denied the support of Crocodiles that could have made 1 Hampshires'

Numerous armoured vehicles became bogged in the clay strips on GOLD Beach as well as being knocked out by the anti-tank gun in Le Hamel.

The air photograph used by 13 Troop in briefings for the invasion is marked with the troop's route inland. (*Courtesy of the D-Day Museum, Portsmouth*)

clearance of Le Hamel and WN 37 easier. Eventually, a Churchill Armoured Vehicle Royal Engineers (AVRE) firing demolition rounds into a defended sanatorium and the rear doors of the 75mm casemate broke resistance, but it took eight hours to finally subdue the defences of Le Hamel.[2]

Landing with 69 Brigade, some fifteen minutes late at 0830 hours on KING Sector, Lieutenant Shearman's 13 Troop[3] was more fortunate, perhaps because 'Lieutenant Shearman was on the ramp checking the water's depth.' This was a process not without its danger, 'with the odd sniper's bullet pinging against the bow'. Just as he gave the OK to drop the ramp another craft cut in front of them and his LCT had to go astern and approach again. Once the ramp was down, Shearman aboard 'Sandgate' led the way across the beach, with the Crocodile ['Sandling'] of Sergeant Warner 'on his tail'. Although the beach was still under fire and the infantry were clearing the defenders, the situation on KING was far better than on JIG, but the troop's third Crocodile was drowned in a shell hole before it reached the beach. Thus 'Of the six Crocodiles which set out with such glorious hopes and the entire regiment's thoughts, only two remained to carry on the D-Day battles.'[4]

Landing sometime after H+120, Captain Barber went ashore with his jeep and driver, having been diverted from JIG to KING Beach thanks to the WN 37 anti-tank gun. A half-squadron 'skeleton' logistic echelon landed sometime later to support the Crocodiles with stores, spares, etc. that could not be procured from other armoured units. These stores included flame fuel, spares and nitrogen propellant cylinders that were unique to the Crocodile.

A Regimental Mention by Colonel Waddell for one of the C Squadron clerks provides some information on the echelon's D-Day activities, starting with their landing on KING Beach:

> Cpl Hart landed in France at H+60 [*sic*] on D-Day. His job was to help the organisation of the echelon, attend to returns, etc., and if necessary, contact 13 and 15 Troops in the forward area.
>
> On landing his Jeep became bogged and the engine stalled. Despite shell fire Cpl Hart dismounted in about 3 feet of water, restarted the engine and directed the driver ashore. Having done this Cpl Hart followed the leading infantry through VER-SUR-MER, and as the vehicle park had not been established he set up a harbour for the rest of the party.
>
> From then until the arrival of the rest of the squadron, Cpl Hart, working under the most difficult conditions contacted the clerks in 30 Corps, 50 Div and 231 Bde, arranged the various returns and ensured they were rendered on time. By his excellent work Cpl Hart did much to assure the smooth running of the detachment.[5]

The Advance Inland from KING

With two Crocodiles across the beach, Lieutenant Shearman's 13 Troop was quickly heading inland with 7 Green Howards. They went straight up a road from the beach and over a still intact crossing of an anti-tank ditch, and before turning right went through the Mont Fleurie Battery, which had already been cleared by 6 Green Howards. The troop's initial objectives were around Ver-sur-Mer, which the infantry found to be unoccupied, as was the headquarters location of 441 *Ost* Battalion[6] at the village's southern end. Their next objective was the *Batterie Vera*; La Marefontaine or WN 32 to the south-east of the village. This was the position of 6 Battery, 1716 Artillery Regiment, and although its 100mm guns were not in action, an air observation post Auster reported movement around the casemates.

As a part of the softening-up process WN 32 had been heavily bombarded, as explained in an official account of operations:

> ... there were four roomy concrete casemates, all open at the back, and instead of large-calibre [coastal defence] guns they were occupied by four 10cm split trail gun-tows. The battery had been a target for heavy bombing from H minus 30 to H minus 5. The bombing was good but the main concentration fell 50 yards to the rear on ancillary buildings.[7]

A marked air photograph showing detail of the WN 32 casemates and the battery's ancillary buildings.

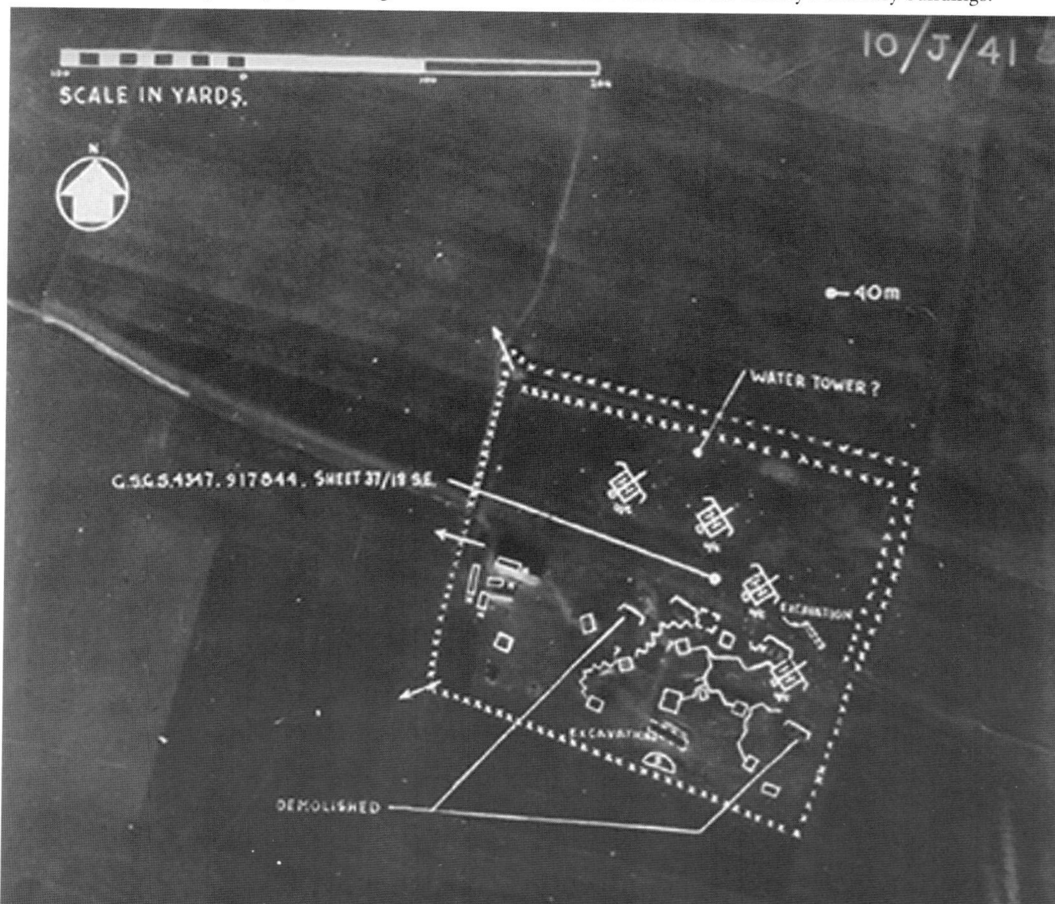

The battery had also been engaged more successfully by the cruiser HMS *Belfast* with her twelve 6in guns firing 224 rounds. The account continues: 'Though no casemates had been hit, the gun crews must have had an unpleasant time from blast through the apertures and openings at the back.'

The task of taking the battery fell to C Company 7 Green Howards, while the remainder of the battalion advanced on Crépon with the Shermans of 4/7 DG. The company, having threaded their way through the narrow streets of Ver-sur-Mer, was joined by the Crocodiles that had taken a more open route further to the west. After 'quick orders', 13 Troop and the infantrymen advanced to attack the enemy position. The original plan had been for the Crocodiles to flame the battery from the rear before the infantry attacked from the front. Lieutenant Shearman covered C Company's advance, engaging the German defences with their coaxially-mounted Besa machine guns and two rounds of 75mm high explosive, but not with flame. There is no explanation for not using flame, but it is possible that in the time between landing and the attack on WN 32 pressure could have been lost, with the trailers lacking the necessary pressure. It could also be that the enemy were surrendering before the Crocodiles got within range: 'The enemy were quick to surrender and 40–50 prisoners of war were collected in the locality.' Nonetheless, two tanks of 141 Regiment RAC were in action for the first time.

An air photograph taken on 24 May during a bombing raid by Mitchells of 226 Squadron RAF. Three of the casemates can be seen north of the bomb strikes, along with craters from a previous attack.

Two of the Vera Battery casemates.

The battle-damaged interior of one of the M669-type artillery casemates at WN 32.

Leaving C Company to secure WN 32, the Crocodiles followed 7 Green Howard's advance south towards Creully, where they would support them while the tanks of 4/7 DG were committed to the right, clearing the Meuvaines Ridge:

> At this point Shearman's two Crocodiles represented the only armour up with the forward companies and as such their popularity with the Green Howards ... was absolutely sky high. For them these two hulking Crocodiles clattering amiably along, bearing sometimes as many as forty infantry, were pausing here and there to pepper with BESA or HE the fleeing Hun backsides fast disappearing over the skyline.[8]

At the Tierceville crossroads, just to the north of Creully, the significantly faster Shermans caught up and took over the lead, providing close support to 7 Green Howards' leading companies. The rest for the Crocodiles was brief, before being summoned west shortly after 1500 hours to support 5 East Yorks and 6 Green Howards, which were halted north of the village of Villers-le-Sec:

> ... where everybody came under long-distance shelling from tanks [StuG IIIs of *Kampfgruppe* Meyer] south-west of Creully. The Shermans were out of it in a flash but 13 Troop, with its cumbersome trailers, had time while negotiating the corners to indulge, a little hopefully, in an armoured gun duel with no loss to either side.

At this point 13 Troop was redeployed back east; this time to the south-east of Creully to help cover 50th Division's left flank as the 21st Panzer Division was reported moving to counter-attack. In the event 22 Panzer Regiment's attack fell further east between the 3rd Canadian and 3rd British divisions. The troop, however, watched a squadron of Shermans of 4/7 DG attempt to continue the advance only to see four of them 'brewed up almost instantaneously by Panthers lying up in the woods'. These 'Panthers' were StuGs of the aforementioned *Kampfgruppe* Meyer. There were no Panthers facing the British sector until the arrival of the 26th SS Panzer Grenadiers *Kampfgruppe* of the 12th *Hitlerjugend* and Panzer *Lehr*, both on D+2.

'The day's peregrinations were, however, not yet over. Later the troop was to go [forward] to COULOMBS.' There was no sign of the StuGs making an offensive move, consequently the troop was sent back to support 7 Green Howards who were halted at a 'fortified farm'. This was a potentially good target for a flame attack, but headquarters 69 Brigade ordered the battalion to pull back. At this point Lieutenant Shearman met the commander of the flail tanks of C Squadron, Westminster Dragoons and they agreed to drive back and rally for the night near the village of Crépon some miles inland from King Beach.[9] Here they met Captain Barbour and the Crocodiles were able to replenish fuel, 75mm HE and Besa ammunition and gas cylinders during the short hours of a summer night. Thus ended D-Day for the Crocodiles: they had seen plenty of action as ordinary gun tanks, but there was no flaming.

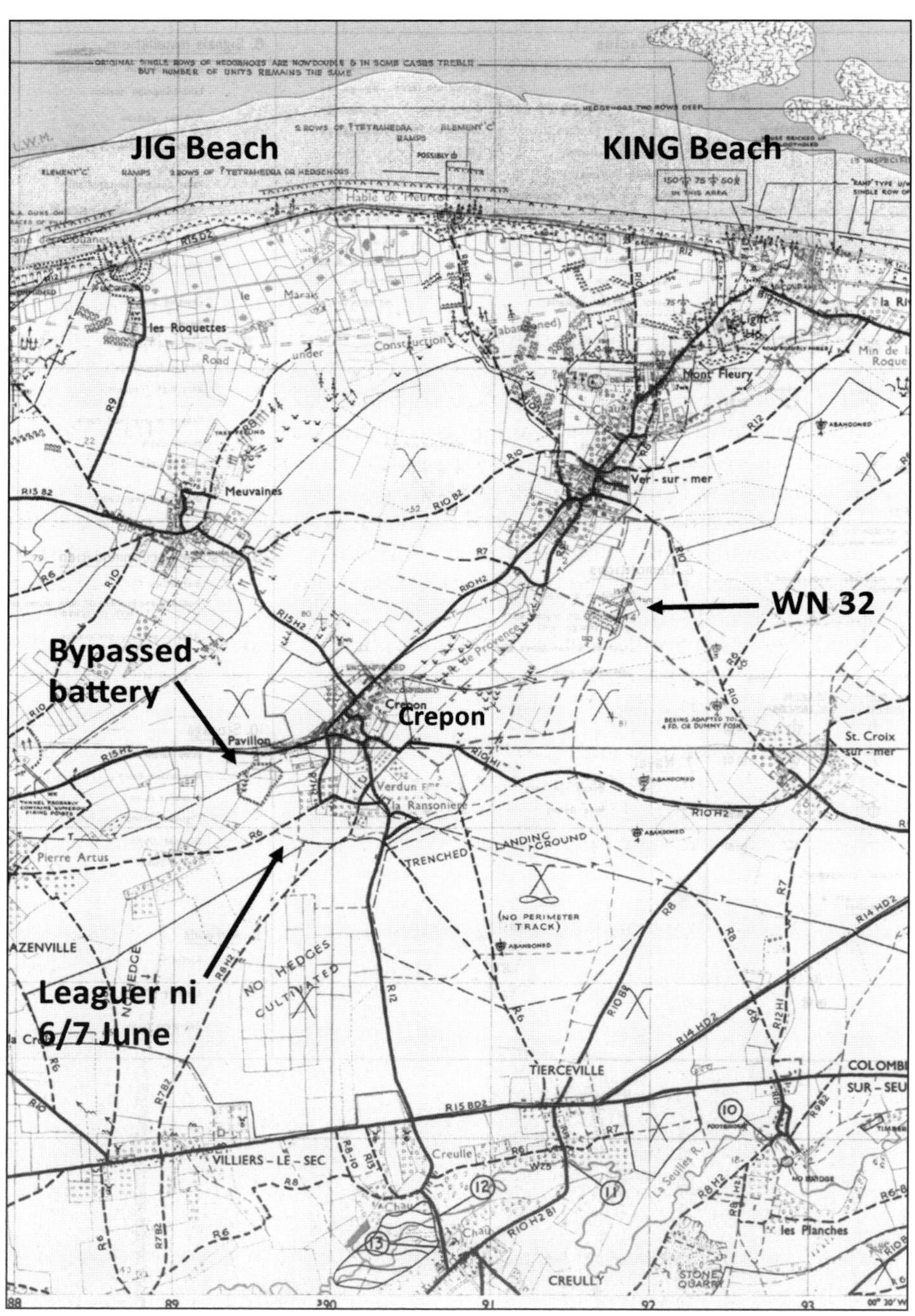

An extract from the defences overprint map showing 13 Troop's area of operations on D-Day.

The D-Day casualties suffered by the thirty-eight men of 141 Regiment's two troops of C Squadron were one man drowned and one man missing.

D+1: The Flame Action at Crépon

The war diary of 86 Field Regiment RA opens its account of operations on 7 June as follows: '05.35 AVREs [*sic*] of 8th Armoured Brigade coming into harbour by 462 Bty. 462 battery's gun positions are fired at by infantry guns positioned in wood outside of battery area. AVREs withdraw.'

This enemy position was marked on the defences overprint map and the previous day a platoon of D Company, 6 Green Howards had come under small-arms fire from the hedgerows behind Le Pavilion Farm. In extricating his soldiers pinned down in a cabbage patch, Sergeant Major Hollis earned his Victoria Cross. The enemy was then bypassed during the battalion's advance inland. The enemy, in the form of four 100mm guns belonging to 5 Battery, 1716th Artillery Regiment had remained quiet during the evening as British tanks had parked up to the south of Le Pavilion in a more open area.

At dawn the following morning, as far as 13 Troop was concerned, there was 'a rude awakening in the shape of a salvo from about 100 yards in rear of their overnight leaguer.' One of the German guns was promptly knocked out by a flail of C Squadron, Westminster Dragoons and the chaos among the troops who believed they were 5 miles behind the line can be imagined. They were 'breakfasting and all unwitting of the target they presented to the Bosche guns'. Lieutenant Shearman and

> [Lieutenant Shearman and] two Crocodiles covered the withdrawal of the thin-skinned flails and succeeded in keeping the enemy guns quiet with an area shoot of 75mm HE. But as he rolled out in the wake of the flails, Shearman caught sight of a whole array of artillery and transport in the growing light.

A Sherman Crab, better known as the flail tank, in action.

Having withdrawn by some 400 yards southwards, with no infantry in the area, gunners from 462 Battery and assorted soldiers from the Royal Signals were organized to attack the enemy battery and were issued with grenades. The war diary of 86 Field Regiment recorded that at '09.30 2 Shermans, 1 flame-thrower Churchill and drivers from 462 Battery led by Lt IA Carpenter enter wood.' With artillery and mortars shelling the position and the more heavily-armoured Crocodile leading, the attack was under way:

> This was a great moment in Crocodile history: the first use of flame against real live Germans. Supported by the fire of two of the flails, the Crocodiles assaulted [one leading and the second following in reserve]. Some eight shots of flame [plus HE and Besa] and the position was white with flags – 150 prisoners of war walked out, and a party went in to deal with the killed and wounded. This then was the baptism of Crocodile flame and a very successful one too. Perhaps too successful, for it helped to build that early impression that Crocodiles were the one and only answer.

In addition to the four artillery pieces, an anti-tank gun was also captured and among the German wounded were four officers.

During the course of D+1 one of the 15 Troop Crocodiles was recovered from the area of JIG Beach, presumably the one that had broken its track, and joined 13 Troop along with the other 'de-horsed crews' in the Crépon area.

A Pause in Operations

Over the next few days, the Crocodiles were not involved in active operations. 50th Division spent most of D+1 to D+2 closing up to its D-Day objectives, linking up with the US V Corps from OMAHA Beach and clearing the vast area behind the front line. Consequently, the planned dash by 8th Armoured Brigade 15 miles inland to form a patrol base on the high ground at Point 213 east of Villers-Bocage was delayed. It should have been completed by nightfall on D-Day, but eventually got going on the afternoon of D+2. By then, however, the 12th *Hitlerjugend* Panzer Division had arrived and the 24th Lancers ran into them and the Shermans were halted in their tracks. The 4/7 DG fared a little better, having tangled with the *Hitlerjugend*'s recce battalion, but 24 Lancers reached Point 103 where they too were halted, this time by the advance guard of Panzer *Lehr*. While the fighting continued on and around Point 103, 50th Division's focus moved further west to the thick bocage country south of Bayeux. Here on the road to Tilly-sur-Seulles, the division, along with leading elements of the 7th Armoured Division, fought to get south, while advancing in the opposite direction, Panzer *Lehr* struggled to develop any momentum in Hitler's drive to the sea.

Meanwhile, with plenty of crew but only three Crocodiles, the half-squadron moved a little further south to Brécy with the Westminster Dragoons, while their skeleton echelon established itself at Sommervieu. Shortly afterwards, the Crocodiles were called west to support an advance by 231 Brigade south to the

Tilly-Balleroy road on 11 June. This would extend the right flank of the Second British Army into a gap between them and US V Corps created by the collapse of the battered German 352nd Infantry Division. This was the beginning of the bocage or hedgerow country of small fields and orchards, which became steadily thicker further to the west.

With 1st Hampshires at Bernières-Bocage

The Crocodiles joined 1 Hampshires at St Paul-du-Verdon during 10 June and when the battlegroup was relieved by the 8th Hussars[10] they moved to 231 Brigade's left flank for the advance through thickly-wooded bocage country to the important lateral road at La Senaudière.

Lieutenant Colonel Howie led 1 Hampshires forward to the area of Bernières-Bocage where there was what was reported as a 'persistently troublesome pocket of enemy that needed mopping up'. 2 Essex of 56 Brigade had spent the night of 10/11 June and the following morning were halted in the area by what proved to be rather more than a 'pocket'; it was in fact the tip of a broad enemy salient that stretched south to La Senaudière. Taking over from the Essex during the afternoon, the Hampshires' first objective was to clear the pocket. The battalion's war diary records that:

> Arriving at the start-line NW of the village of BERNIÈRES-BOCAGE the bn launched an attack on the enemy pocket of resistance SW of the village where our supporting tanks were held up by a well-camouflaged 88mm gun firing point-blank at the sharp bend 500 yards south of the village.

The part played by the Crocodiles is not recorded in detail beyond the fact that they were the tanks mentioned above. Captain Bailey, however, wrote that 'through the woods and hedgerows they edged towards the [Tilly-Balleroy] road with a caution born of a thousand schemes and all the trepidation nourished by

231 Brigade's operations on 11 June 1944.

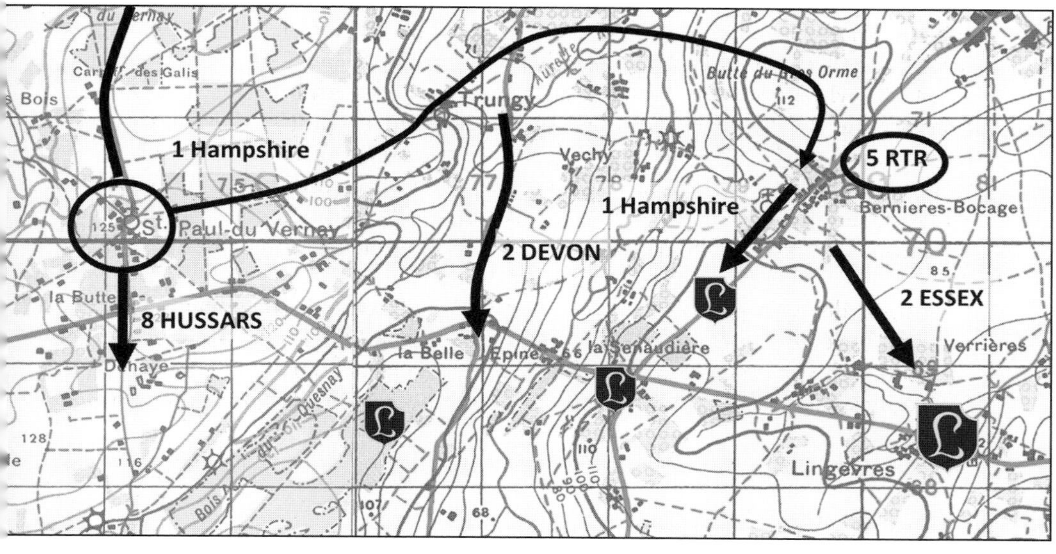

the sight of Sherman brew-ups [*sic* 5 RTR Cromwells]. The moment had come to break cover onto the only road.'

On this road they encountered anti-tank fire from a 75mm gun covering this open flank. Who, what or where the Crocodiles were being shot at from in the bocage country was often a matter of guesswork, but German documents confirm that the fire was from a platoon of Panzer IVs that had been sent to reinforce Panzer *Lehr*'s recce battalion. This was the first time that the Hampshiremen had come up against stiff resistance in the bocage and they, like virtually every other unit, complained in their war diary about the difficulties of dealing with a 'well sited position with all approaches and tracks covered by Spandaus'. The battalion's war diary concludes:

> The enemy mortars from the security of their natural concealment bombarded the village [Bernières-Bocage], the road, the tracks and the fields via which our mopping-up coys had to advance. In spite of these natural advantages, our rifle coys gained ground and dug-in in a defensive area SW of the village.

The 'mopping-up' had in fact only been partly completed, with the Hampshires halted well short of La Senaudière. They took up a tight defensive position in a

The Panzer IV with its highly effective L48 KwK 40 gun which, firing the *Pzgr* 39 AP ammunition at a velocity of 750 m/s, could knock out any Allied tank. With its long barrel, distinctive muzzle brake and rounded *shurzen* 'bazooka plates' on the turret, the Panzer IV was often reported as a Tiger.

Having not been dug in, this German 81mm mortar crew succumbed to counter-battery fire. In common with the rest of the Allied armies, many of 141 RAC's casualties were inflicted by mortars.

wood and, feeling vulnerable with very short fields of fire out into the hedgerows, the Commanding Officer Lieutenant Colonel Howie 'invited the Crocodiles to stay in the same wood for the night'. Captain Bailey describes the 'first of many fanciful plans' put to Crocodile commanders:

> Should the Germans counter-attack the Crocodiles were to make a rampaging circuit around the whole battalion position, setting up a defensive belt of flame in much the same way primitive man kept off the wild beasts of his day. Shearman said, 'Not on' and was temporarily released to JUAY MONDAYE for replenishment. But the fun had only just begun.

Counter-Attack at La Belle Épine

Meanwhile, during 11 June, 1,000 yards to the west, 2 Devons had reached the hamlet of La Belle Épine on the Tilly-Balleroy road against lesser opposition. They were, however, counter-attacked at 1730 hours and B Company was driven out of La Belle Épine back onto the battalion's main position. For a time the Devons were in serious difficulty.

The latter were also very much on their own as they had advanced beyond the range of their radios in rolling, wooded country and were out of touch with both Brigade Headquarters and their supporting artillery. The first 231 Brigade knew about the attack on the Devons was when an officer ran 3 miles back to report what was going on. At the time, however, Brigadier Stanier was away visiting the Hampshires where Corporal Richards, the brigadier's driver and operator, was monitoring the radio net. He recalled that

> While at the Hampshires' headquarters, which was under mortar fire, we picked up a message intended for Brigade HQ from the Devons, stating that the Germans had counter-attacked and cut the road behind them. We stopped when we saw one of our tanks and the Brigadier spoke to the officer in charge, whilst I stayed in the Jeep listening to the radio. The Brigadier decided that we should return to Brigade HQ but I said that I could hear the Devons, but Brigade HQ couldn't.
>
> As we drove back some soldiers of the Devonshire Regiment came up and told us that the Devons' Battalion Headquarters had been wiped out, the Colonel was dead, and the Second-in-Command had been killed. I explained to them that they were mistaken as I just had been speaking to those persons on the radio. The soldiers said that they were out of ammunition, but, having plenty, I supplied them, and Lt Montgomery got them together and called on the tanks to help the Devons out.

These tanks were seven of the surviving Crabs of the Westminster Dragoons' B and C squadrons.[11] They had been placed under command of 231 Brigade and were holding the Butte du Gros Orme (Point 112) along with C Squadron's two Crocodiles. Despite their specialist roles, they were the only armour available as 5 RTR, the only other tanks in the area, was at the time supporting 2nd Essex.

The German attack had been halted for some hours by the Devons before the armoured help finally arrived. The day culminated at 2200 hours just before dark with a determined counter-attack by A Company supported by the Westminster Dragoons and two Crocodiles. Sergeant Hills' vehicle did not take part in the counter-attack. The flail's war diary reads:

> This composite Sqn was ordered to the assistance of the 2 DEVONS who, having fought continuously since D-Day, had been repulsed from LA BELLE ÉPINE, and the task of the composite Sqn was to support the 2 DEVONS back into the village. The Sqn arrived in the forming-up area just before dusk and in the failing light it was impossible to distinguish any definite enemy points as the information was also scanty. It was therefore decided as the objective was only some 300 to 400 yards from the start line that the flails be used as ordinary tanks would bring maximum fire to bear on the village, all the hedges and likely enemy-held positions. In the dusk it was a terrific sight. Tracer streaked through the gloom, and fires caused by the 75mm shells from the tank's guns lit the scene with a red glare.

The war diary of 141 Regiment RAC records simply that 'In the evening jettisoned [flame fuel] trailers and participated in counter-attack on LA BELLE ÉPINE firing 75mm and BESA into the buildings.'

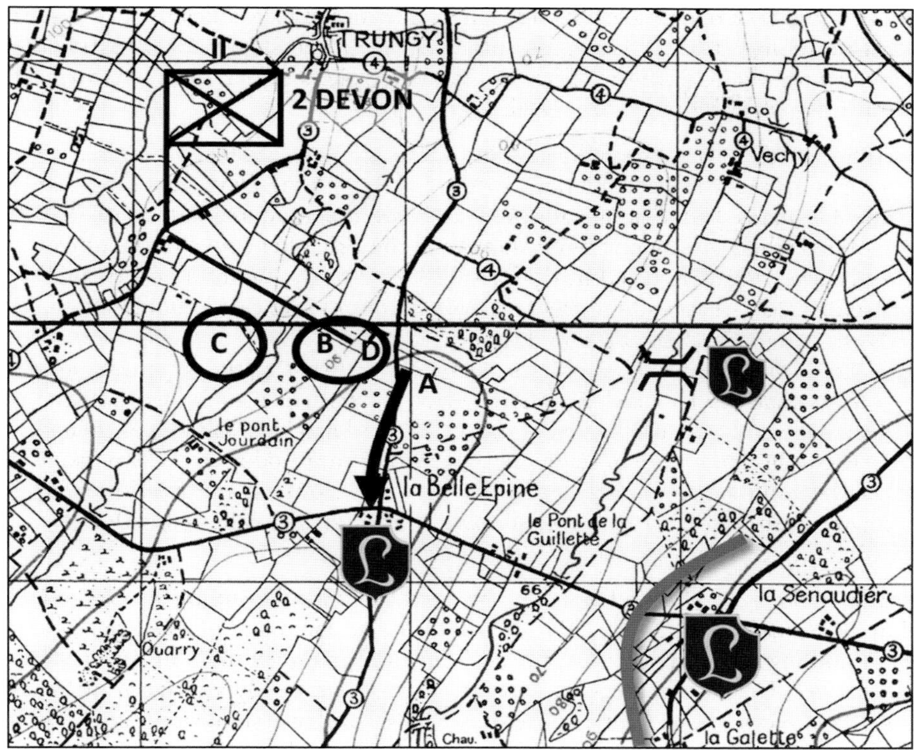

The counter-attack on La Belle Épine and the situation overnight.

In more detail, the heavily-armoured Crocodiles were to carry out the assault with, as indicated above, support from two flails and 'By the time he [Shearman] reached La Belle Épine it was getting dark.' On reaching the hamlet 'The tanks turned left at the crossroads and took alternate sides plugging every house with 75mm and BESA and even the woods beyond. It apparently made a magnificent sight in the dark and the Germans dead in the houses testified to the thoroughness with which they did their job.'

The counter-attack on La Belle Épine was over in thirty minutes. A factor that could have helped were the operations further east being mounted that same evening by the Essex on Lingèvres and the Gloucesters on Tilly, which presented a threat that precluded Panzer *Lehr* sending reinforcements west to La Belle Épine. By 2300 hours word reached the headquarters of 50th Division that '2 Devons restore sit with coy counter-attack, tho' enemy penetrate and hold woods at 7869.' With the situation restored, the armour was duly released back to leaguer. The war diary's account concluded that

> By midnight they had finished and once more the Crocodiles set off for JUAY MONDAYE, only to be sent back immediately [mid-way through

The Belle Épine crossroads have changed little, but all signs of the battle have long since gone.

> refuelling] to LA BELLE ÉPINE to be in readiness at first light in the anti-tank role against possible armoured counter-attack. In this role they stayed all day and were reluctantly released that evening (June 12th), after dark and after argument to JUAY MONDAYE.
>
> The crews had now done forty-three hours without respite and Captain Barber sent up 15 Troop to take over the two Crocodiles. They also brought with them Sergeant Hills and his Crocodile, thus putting the Crocodile strength up 50%.

La Senaudière

The 1st Hampshires had resumed their advance south to La Senaudière on the 13th but, although they had made progress south, they had again been rebuffed. Elsewhere, 7th Armoured Division's advance into the Caumont Gap had culminated at Villers-Bocage in an encounter with Michael Wittmann's SS Tigers. For the 14th, XXX Corps planned a far better resourced attack south to the Tilly-Balleroy road by 50th Division, employing both 151 Durham and 231 brigades, with the latter being supported by the composite squadron of flails and Crocodiles.

To help blast the soldiers of Panzer *Lehr* out of the entrenched bocage hedgerows, an impressive fire-plan was developed, including the guns of six British field regiments, three medium regiments and a US 155mm battalion, plus naval gunfire and close air support, all timed just before the 1130 H-Hour. No. 83 and 84 Groups RAF were to carry out strafing attacks and bombing of the enemy defensive line in the villages and along the Balleroy road with 120 tons of ordnance. This, however, required the Hampshires to withdraw for safety reasons to the northern end of Bernières-Bocage.

The Hampshires' war diary describes the mechanics of the attack that the Crocodiles were to support and the effect of the safety withdrawal:

> Arty barrage covering 100 yds in three minutes was laid on. Spting [supporting] arms consisted of a troop of Crocodiles and a troop of M10s of the NH [Northumberland Hussars]. The Bn moved off already deployed and opposition was met N of LA SENAUDIÈRE, showing the enemy had occupied same ground which we had given up when the air attack began.[12]

Captain Bailey describes in his account how for 13 Troop it was all rather rushed and poorly coordinated:

> At the last moment [Lieutenant] Davies was called forward to meet the CO a little way inside BERNIÈRES-BOCAGE, where his battalion was being heavily sniped. In the confusion and hurriedly shouted orders, Davies was left with the impression that he was required to advance to LA SENAUDIÈRE flat out where he would meet the leading companies. As it transpired, they were still in BERNIÈRES-BOCAGE.

The Hampshires' war diary describes how the Crocodiles went ahead of the infantry into the village flaming, and although the adjutant concedes that they did considerable damage, 'all except one were knocked out and again provided no immediate assistance to the Bn.' The battalion, however, did not do justice to the bravery of the Crocodiles of 15 Troop in leading the attack! Fortunately a fuller account is available. With the Hampshires looking on, the Crocodiles advanced on their own towards the buildings of La Senaudière grouped around a crossroads: 'At full speed 15 Troop shot off on its 1½-mile mission to LA SENAUDIÈRE, laying a colossal smokescreen on the left for the whole

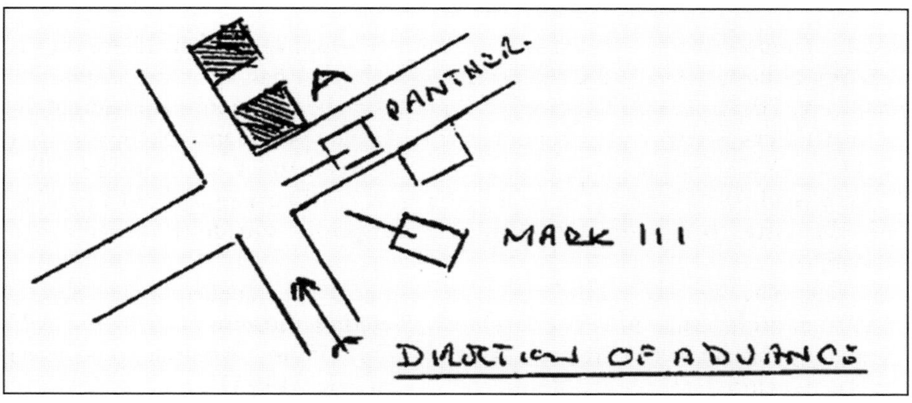

Captain Bailey's sketch map of the action at La Senaudière.

length of the advance. Fifty yards from the cross-roads Davies spotted a Pz Kw III just off the road to the right.'[13]

The Crocodile was advancing so fast that it was difficult to lay the gun and before Lieutenant Davies' gunner could fire, the second Crocodile drove in front of him and almost in front of the barrel of the panzer as it fired, fortunately missing. In a return of fire that ricocheted off the panzer's turret armour, 13 Troop 'winged the Mark III before it made off', reversing at speed:

> By now Davies was busily engaging a window in the house marked 'A' [see Bailey's sketch map] and as he crossed over the cross-road failed to see a Panther tucked up against the side of a house on his right. Nor strangely enough could the Panther have seen him, because all three tanks were now across the cross-roads without a shot being fired [at them] and only Cpl Gates' trailer protruded onto the cross-roads itself. The Panther holed the trailer twice but it did not burn. But both Cpl Gates and Sergeant Hills were now aware of the Panther's presence and in no time put it out of action.

Of the two Crocodiles, one engaged the Panther with its 75mm main armament and even at a close range the AP round failed to penetrate the German tank's frontal armour, while the second, appropriately enough, flamed the Panther and set the whole vehicle on fire. Lieutenant Wilson, however, recalled that on his arrival in Normandy he saw the knocked-out Panther and was told that the 75mm round fired by Lieutenant Davies had ricocheted downwards off the Panther's mantlet and penetrated the thinner armour above the driver's position. The tank kill credit, with both main armament and flame, should, therefore, probably be shared between Davies and Sergeant Hills.[14]

The Crocodile's armoured trailer containing flame fuel and nitrogen cylinders.

Nitrogen Propellant

The Crocodile's trailer, along with the 400 gallons of flame fuel, contained five heavy cylinders of nitrogen gas. It took between fifteen and thirty minutes to pressurize the flame system with this gas before action. Fully pressurized, the gas projected flame at the rate of 4 gallons per second.

The procedure for pressuring up and into action is described by Trooper Cox:

> 'Pressure Up' came the command from our flame gunner. Beach jumped down and ran to the back of the trailer. It was my job to help him with the trailer door. Quite heavy. Turn the five cylinders on, then close the door. Beach then had to climb on the trailer to open the pressure and fuel valves and switch on the electrics. We both then returned to the tank. 'Driver advance' and I moved off in low gear.[16]

A 'Special Brief' to Headquarters Royal Armoured Corps from 21st Army Group dated 16 June reads as follows:

> Expenditure of Nitrogen (excluding tanks lost on beach):
> 58 bottles; i.e. approximately 5 bottles a shoot. This is due to leakage in keeping trailers standing by pressured up with no specific target.
> The percentage of bottles to fuel must be increased.

Consumption of nitrogen was, however, reduced as the campaign progressed by the expeedient of pressuring up at the last moment before action and subsequent modifications that reduced leakage of gas.

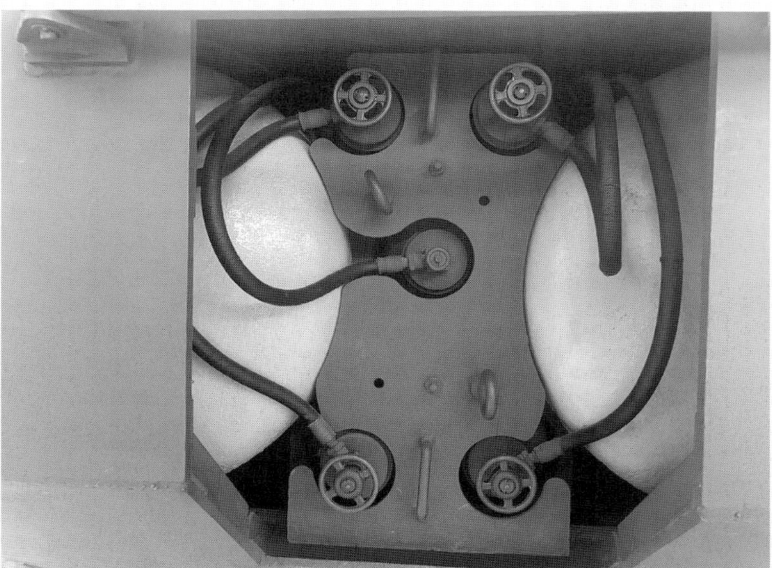

Inside the Crocodile's trailer the nitrogen cylinders are secured by a steel plate. Visible are the four regulator valves which are opened to pressurize the flanking flame fuel tanks.

Meanwhile, the winged Panzer III had worked around to the right and scored a mobility kill with a shot to one of Corporal Gate's tracks, but Sergeant Hills knocked it out in turn. Another Panther arrived on the scene and at close range engaged Corporal Gates' stranded Crocodile which was hit again by a high-velocity 75mm round that 'penetrated his front plate and brewed up the Crocodile. This was our first casualty and cost us one Crocodile, two missing believed killed, and two wounded. Davies and Sergeant Hills returned and were released back to SOMMERVIEU.'

A Regimental Mention records that Captain Barber came forward on foot at the conclusion of the action, located the wounded crew members and returned with a medical officer and stretcher-bearers to evacuate them.[15]

Although two Crocodiles survived the action, they had lost their flame fuel trailers while manoeuvring at speed and had sustained damage to their tracks, and one had damage to its turret from enemy fire.

The Crocodiles of Lieutenant Davies' 15 Troop had, at the cost of one tank, driven those of Panzer *Lehr* out of La Senaudière and within hours the village was in the hands of the Hampshires.

Reflecting on the first actions of the Crocodile, Captain Bailey wrote:

> It is said that in the last war the tanks sold their birthright because they were not initially launched in large numbers. Circumstances such as production, the lateness of our coming and the prior allocation of shipping, all these and many more factors meant the Crocodiles sold their birthright too. Nine days of highly unorthodox fighting cannot help but establish habits and precedents which, although possibly correct and successful in the scattered and confused fighting before the German reserves arrived, do not work against Panzer Divisions with plenty of 88mms & 75mms, Panthers and even Tigers.

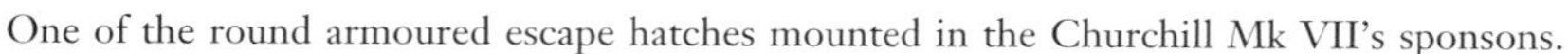
One of the round armoured escape hatches mounted in the Churchill Mk VII's sponsons.

Chapter Three

Into Battle

While the two troops of C Squadron were already in Normandy, the remainder of 141 RAC was continuing with training, last-minute conversion and preparations for deployment to France. Another task was sundry modifications to the equipment to remedy defects that had been revealed during training. With the 200+ hours needed to waterproof the Churchill, most tactical training was, as a result, theoretical.

While the main body was waiting to move from Eastwell Park:

> We had visits firstly by Mr Churchill, for whom we laid on a flame demonstration. He was obviously impressed. His hatred for the Nazis, he rarely referred to them as 'Germanism', left him with no scruples regarding the use of the weapon. He inspected the parade, marched throughout our lines, puffing his cigar with a satisfied grin. He didn't address us, but the written report on orders displayed his pleasure. A short time later, Montgomery came to inspect the unit, a more military affair, and we were rehearsed for a couple of days to make sure we did everything in top form.
>
> He inspected the parade, speaking to the odd soldier here and there, then went off to his famous Jeep routine. 'I want everyone to "bweak wanks" and gather "wound me".' He couldn't pronounce his Rs. We all gathered 'wound'. He stood on the bonnet of his Jeep, so we could all see him. He expounded how long months waiting would be over and we would soon have a crack at Jerry, driving him back out of Europe.[1]

For the deployment to Normandy, 141 RAC was reaffiliated to 31 Tank Brigade for movement under VIII Corps. It had been planned that the brigade would cross the Channel between D+7 and D+13, once the initial build-up of I and XXX Corps was complete: '141 RAC less one squadron [*sic*, two troops] has been phased in [allocated to shipping] by 8 Corps with 31 Tank Brigade on D plus 10. It is under command 8 Corps but will revert to Army control on concentration in FRANCE.'[2]

The regiment left Eastwell Park for the VIII Corps armoured concentration area in the region of Aldershot, where they heard the announcement of D-Day on the BBC. Lieutenant Wilson recalled:

> Then one evening there was the sound of friendly aircraft going south. The sound went on all night. Once I went out and looked up, and up against the stars I saw the long bodies of gliders.

> Early next morning William came into the room. 'Get up,' he said, 'the invasion has started.' 'I know,' I replied. 'Where?' 'Normandy.'

With warning orders for the move to the ports received, RASC transporters arrived on 12 June to take A and B squadrons' tanks to transit camps in the woods around Blackdown, 12 miles north of Portsmouth and the embarkation hards. The all-important flame fuel trailers with only marginally less security than before were loaded three to a transporter.

The process of embarking had been thoroughly rehearsed by the assault troops, but well down the list for crossing to Normandy it was a new experience for 141 RAC. An officer described the drawn-out process and the waiting to go:

> When you reached the transit camp you knew you were at the end of the conveyor belt. They issued you with forty-eight hours' rations and a big box of maps, and reminded you to fill the will form in your officer's book ... Next afternoon, when everything was ready, we attended to a few last details and went to the camp cinema. All through the film a sergeant kept coming into the hut to call the numbers of different serials, and men would get up with a grumble, casting their shadows on the screen. At last the film ended and we walked out into the daylight.

An earlier version of a Churchill aboard a Diamond T tank transporter following a demonstration.

> In a draughty marquee, there was tea in enamel mugs and thick uneatable slices of bread and jam. Sherrif was there, and the Scotsman, dressed in overalls for the journey. They swallowed some tea and picked up their kit and walked out to the road, where the drivers were warming up the tanks.
>
> The tanks clattered into the port. The trailers were fixed now; there was no more secrecy. People came out of their houses and stood watching them. Many of them waved and sometimes an old soldier with envious eyes would shout 'Good luck, boys.' They moved on. The people were still watching; you couldn't see them any longer, but you sensed them. Then it started to rain, and there was only the dim red tail-lamp of the vehicle ahead in the drizzle. Stops became more frequent. Noisy dispatch riders went fussing along the column, and presently there was the dark, portending odour of docks. 'Get on to the pavement and don't show lights.' They switched off engines. Somewhere in the silence, water gushed from a broken drain-pipe. It was a mean street. Nobody lived there. The houses had all been bombed ... Forwards, the road led to a loading-ramp – and beyond that? You just didn't know.
>
> 'Serial 56?' Beneath a blue lamp the Embarkation Officer was ticking off the vehicles on a list. Ahead was the landing-ship – an enormous tunnel of light heaving gently on the water. The driver let in the clutch. The tank slewed round on the concrete and backed up the steel flap.

Once aboard the tank landing ship the final stage of waterproofing the tanks and trailers was completed, which would otherwise cause the tank to overheat on the

A convoy of trucks being reversed onto a Landing Ship Tank during the build-up phase of the invasion.

final drive to the port. Tall steel boxes were added to air intakes, extension to exhausts, and hatches etc. received their final sealing.

In the event, thanks to delays in the landing programme, principally due to the storm that raged between 19 and 21 June, it was not on D+10 but D+16 that 141 Regiment RAC started to arrive in Normandy. On 22 June Lieutenant Colonel Waddell's tactical headquarters and A and B Squadrons arrived off the coast and after a rough crossing, the three Crocodiles of A Squadron aboard a Royal Navy LCT were approaching JUNO Beach. Trooper Cox recalled:

> The tanks were unshackled from the deck moorings ... The tide was high and the time late morning, the beaches a mass of men and material, and we wondered if there was a place to land. Over to our left a battleship, the *Nelson* I think it was, fired off a broadside. A belch of flame and black smoke followed by the roar of the shells, the ship rolled back and forth from the recoil.
>
> On all sides, landing craft were going in and down went the ramp and out went the troop leader's tank. The lightened craft moved in closer, then away went the Sergeant and now it was our turn. Down the ramp into two feet of water! All that waterproofing – weeks we had been at it and the Navy put us in high and dry. The beach was sandy and quite firm. There was a small railway station on the top of the bank; it was Bernières-sur-Mer. In peacetime no doubt a pleasant little spot but now a shambles ... we moved inland, orders came to jettison the waterproofing gear. Dickie pulled the lever, the rear louvre fell off, the exhausts fell across the engine deck and the other two louvres just sat there; a quick jump out of the turret, a good kick from my boot and both louvres fell off followed by the exhausts. Once inside it was time to blow the rest of the waterproofing. Dickie fired the charge; a mighty bang filled the tank with smoke, dirt and dust everywhere, so we switched on the fans which soon cleared the air.

Leaving the de-waterproofing area, A Squadron drove through the already congested beachhead to their assembly area 6 miles inland at:

> a small village called St Gabriel and there formed a leaguer something like the Wild West, substituting covered wagons for tanks. The village had fallen quickly and was little damaged; a few of us went into a café and ordered some Vin Blanc we'd heard so much about; it was awful stuff.

With the arrival of the balance of the headquarters and three remaining troops of C Squadron, on 24 June the regiment was complete. However, C Squadron minus two Crocodiles that had drowned on JUNO Beach while offloading, having de-waterproofed, in darkness were directed straight to Sommervieu in XXX Corps' area to join the remaining two tanks of the 'D-Day Boys'. This foreshadowed the end of the unit's vain hope that the squadrons would fight together as a regiment as within days they were split up. A Squadron joined VIII Corps, B Squadron went east to I Corps at Cresson and C Squadron was soon motoring to Juaye-Mondaye behind the centre of XXX Corps' front:

> The regiment was thus spread along the whole of the Second Army Front. This enforced separation was a great disappointment to the Regiment which for four years had trained and lived together for the moment when it would go into action against the German Army as a single, well-trained and homogenous body, 141 RAC, the Tank Battalion of The Buffs. No-one was more disappointed than the Commanding Officer. Nevertheless, this was the situation and it had to be cheerfully faced. There thus began a period of learning the hard way; a costly series of penny packet experiments over which the Regiment could have little or no control.[3]

Each squadron took its squadron quartermaster sergeant and fitter section, with its Armoured Recovery Vehicle (ARV).[4] Away from the regiment the squadrons

Each squadron deployed with a Churchill Mk I ARV. A fourth ARV was held by the regimental REME.

received their routine logistic support from the corps to which they were attached, but they relied on their own quartermaster and REME section for specialist Crocodile support.

Meanwhile, Lieutenant Wilson and D (Reserve) Squadron were left behind in Aldershot to pack up and waterproof the regiment's reserve Crocodiles and take them to a transit camp near Eastbourne, where they would await their turn to join 'Movement Control's sausage machine'. From there they were taken by transporter to one of the embarkation camps near Southampton. Wilson recalled:

> For a week the war and the invasion seemed to have passed us by. Then one evening as we came back to our billet, an anti-aircraft gun started firing. Another took it up, and quickly they were firing from all round the town.
>
> 'What are they after?' said Sherrif. 'There isn't even a searchlight.'
>
> We looked out to sea, where the streams of tracer converged. Presently, from out of the snow-storm, six red dots appeared. They passed across the sky with a curious droning sound, and when they were gone there were another six. The guns fired often during the night. Next day everyone learned about flying bombs, and the [embarkation] serial was put at six hours' notice to move.

Lieutenant Wilson, the D Squadron tanks, and eleven other establishment and replacement officers arrived with the regiment just as Operation EPSOM was

The situation on the British front at the beginning of the last week of June 1944.

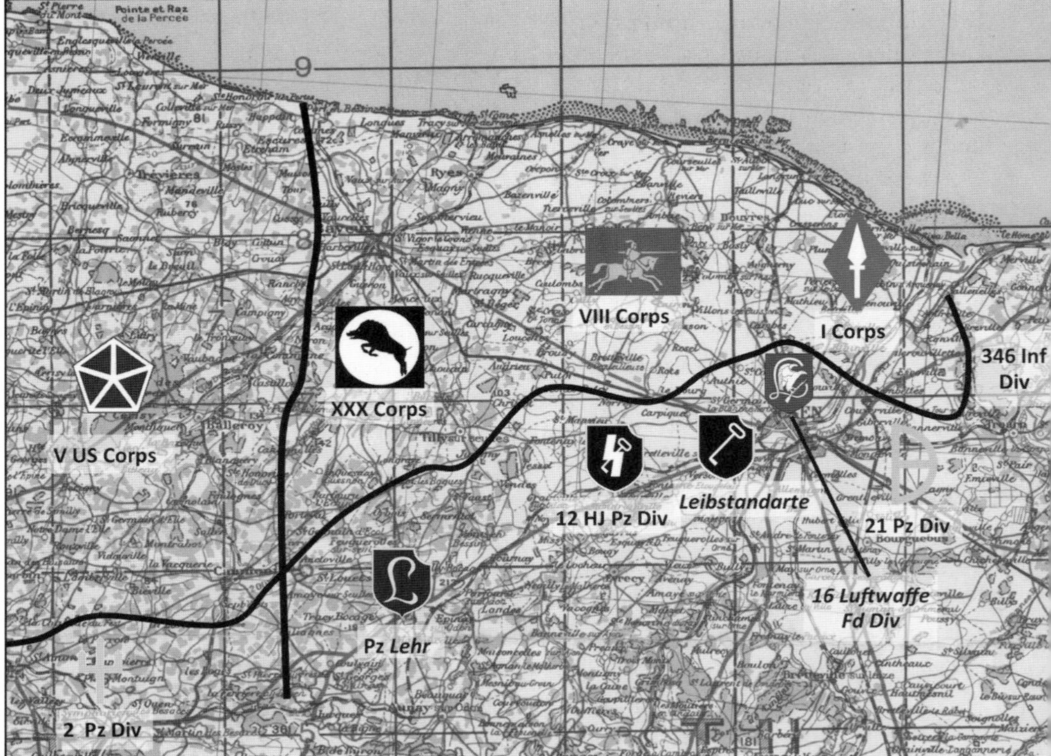

getting under way. Other than an armoured unit's first replacement, RAC battle casualty replacements normally came up with the tanks of the armoured delivery organization. In the case of 141 RAC, as they needed specialist Crocodile training, the regiment held a significant number of crewmen as well as officers in D Squadron.

Operation EPSOM

Major Cooper's A Squadron was the first to take part in a large-scale offensive, almost as soon as they arrived with VIII Corps. The nodal city of Caen had not been captured on D-Day thanks to delays in getting off the beach, but above all the presence of 21st Panzer Division. Over the following days the Germans 'roped off' the British lodgement with the arrival of the 12th *Hitlerjugend* Panzer and Panzer *Lehr* divisions. While Lieutenants Shearman and Davies were fighting at La Belle Épine and La Senaudière, 7th Armoured Division had attempted to exploit a gap to envelope the Germans containing the British along with the city of Caen, but was halted at Villers-Bocage.

Operation EPSOM, launched on 26 June by the newly-assembled VIII Corps, was again designed to break through the extended lines of the *Hitlerjugend* Panzer Division, cross the rivers Odon and Orne, envelope Caen and put armour onto the more open country that stretched south to Falaise. EPSOM would be preceded by Operation MARTLET, which was designed to draw the *Hitlerjugend*'s reserves west and fix them in the Rauray Spur area. The break-in battle was to be fought by the 15th Scottish Division, supported by the Churchills of 31 Tank Brigade and the assault armour of 79th Armoured Division, along with the Crocodiles of A Squadron. This would take VIII Corps through the German defences to seize crossings of the River Odon. In the next phase, 11th Armoured Division, in action for the first time with the Shermans of 4 Armoured Brigade under command, were responsible for breaking out across Hill 112 to the River Orne and exploiting beyond. Elsewhere, on EPSOM's second day, B Squadron, under command of I Corps, was to support the 3rd Division in an attack north of Caen (Operation MITTEN) designed to extend the frontage and draw further reserves away from 15th Scottish Division and the main effort. The operations of B Squadron will be covered later in this chapter.

The attack by 15th Scottish Division was to be delivered on a frontage of two infantry brigades, each supported by a regiment of Churchills and a squadron of flail tanks. On EPSOM's left flank, with villages and hamlets being encountered early in their advance, 44 (Lowland) Brigade was allocated A Squadron's Crocodiles. The plan as far as A Squadron was concerned was simple:

> The Squadron split into two efforts, Major Cooper on the right under [A Squadron] 9 RTR through [LA GAULE to] CHEUX with three Troops and Captain Strachan ... with 4 and 5 Troops on the left under [B Squadron] 9 RTR. In both cases the Crocodile's role was to tag along with the reserve squadron for use as and when required.

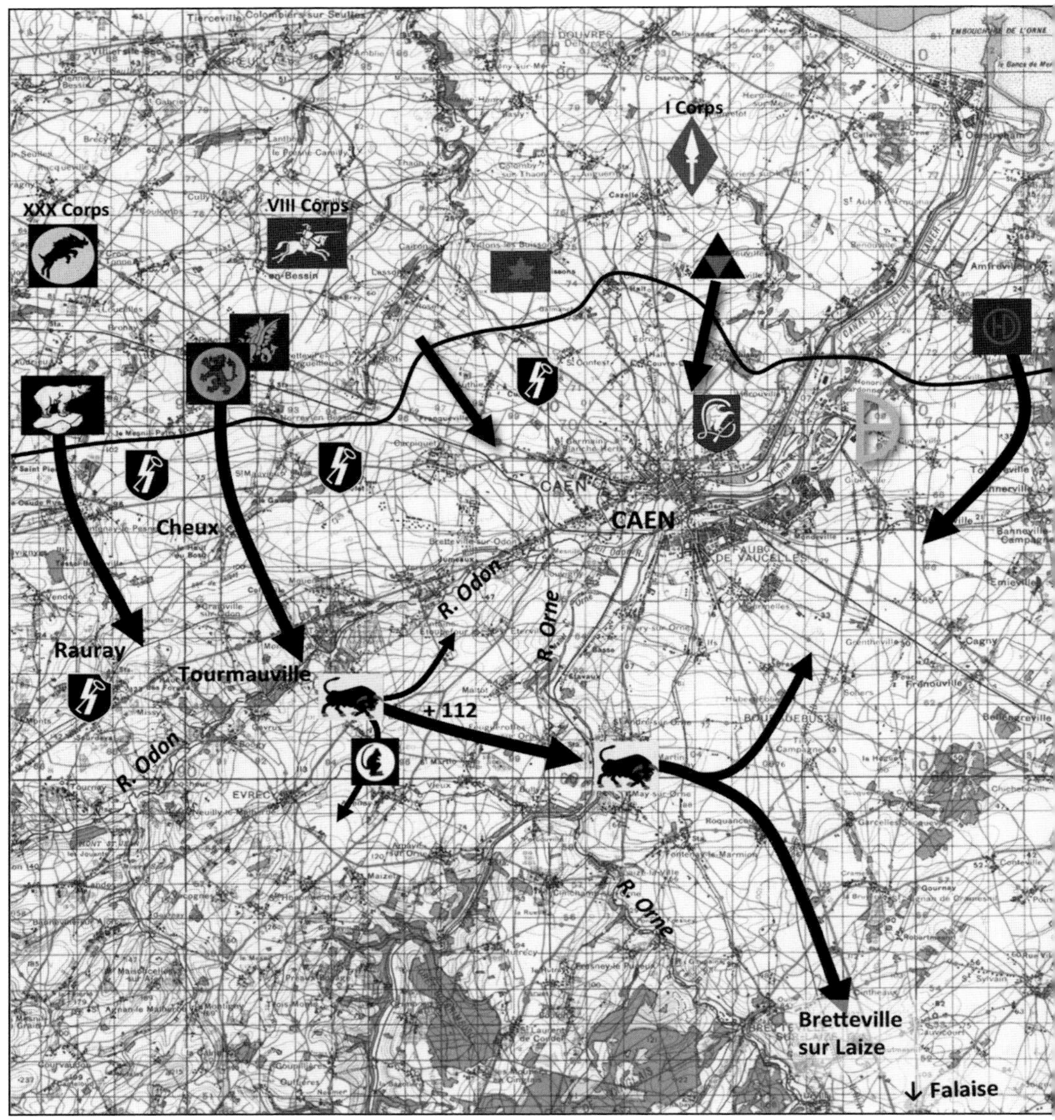

The outline EPSOM plan and supporting operations.

This plan would inevitably commit the Crocodiles to unplanned action at close range, which became a common feature of 141 RAC's operations in the early days of the campaign.

The attack was launched on a wet and misty day that precluded the pre-H-Hour strike by aircraft of 2nd Tactical Air Force (2 TAF). Most were grounded in the UK and those based in Normandy were only able to fly during breaks in the weather. According to the official history:

> On June the 26th flying weather was so bad in England that the large programme of air support for the opening of EPSOM had to be cancelled [at

0645 hours] and, for the first time since D-Day, practically no aircraft based in England left the ground. Only 83 Group, stationed in Normandy, would be able to help VIII Corps, and though they flew over five hundred sorties their support was handicapped by low cloud and mist.

General Dempsey's Second Army had assembled more than 600 field, medium and heavy guns under VIII Corps or sixty-four guns per kilometre, plus the 15in guns of a battleship and 6in guns of two cruisers belonging to the Naval Bombardment Force. The historian of 15th Scottish Division recalled the opening of the battle:

> As H-Hour approached the suspense was extreme. At 7.29 A.M. the orders came over the Tannoy speakers to the waiting guns: 'Stand by to fire Serial 1 [of the fire plan] – one minute to go – 30 seconds – 20 seconds – 10 seconds – 5, 4, 3, 2, 1, FIRE.' With an ear-splitting crack hundreds of guns hurled their

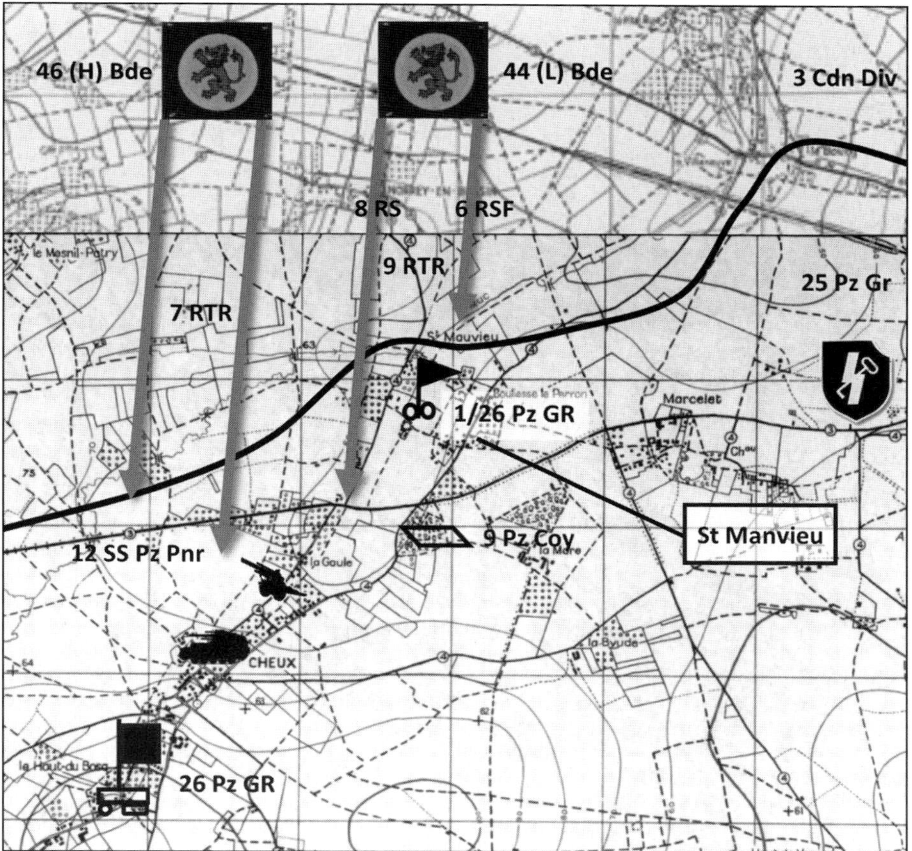

The attack of 15th Scottish Division on the *Hitlerjugend*, 26 June 1944.

> shells overhead, the infantry and tanks advanced to close up to the opening barrage line, where our shells were bursting 500 to 1,000 yards ahead. It was the moment for which the 15th Scottish Division had been preparing for five years.

As the defenders, 26th *Panzergrenadiers* of 12th *Hitlerjugend* SS Panzer Division, were well dug in, few were killed or wounded, but this was the heaviest bombardment to which they had been subjected. Their divisional commander *Standartenführer* Kurt Meyer described what it was like:

> The earth seemed to open and gobble us all up. All hell had been let loose. I lay in a roadside ditch listening to the noise of battle. There was no let up to the artillery barrage. All telephone lines had been destroyed and communications with Divisional Headquarters and units at the front no longer existed . . . My ears tried unsuccessfully to analyse the sounds of battle and all I heard was the permanent spitting, cracking and booming of the bursting shells, mixed with the noise of tank tracks.[5]

The barrage 'stood for ten minutes on the opening line', which coincided with the forward companies of the *Hitlerjugend*'s outpost, while the attackers crossed the start line into battle, following the wall of exploding shells.

The advance of 8th Royal Scots (8 RS or '8 Royals'), with A Squadron 9 RTR, to their first objectives astride the Caen-Fontenay Road and around the hamlet of

Shrouded in mist and smoke, the soldiers of 15th Scottish Division advance in single file through the fog on a track cleared through a minefield.

La Gaule went well, despite the tanks and infantry becoming separated thanks to the sundry Canadian and German minefields and the fog that filled the Mue Valley. Major Cooper's three troops of Crocodiles were not called on during this initial advance and followed on behind the Churchills. Trooper Cox, a crewman aboard 'Stallion' of 3 Troop, recalled:

> A large area of wheat fields had to be cleared, our job was to support the Infantry. We crossed the start line, the Infantry plodding through the high wheat almost ready for harvest. It was the Germans doing the reaping, hidden machine guns cutting down our infantry. We spent most of our time

An air photograph taken on 24 June of the St. Manvieu area.

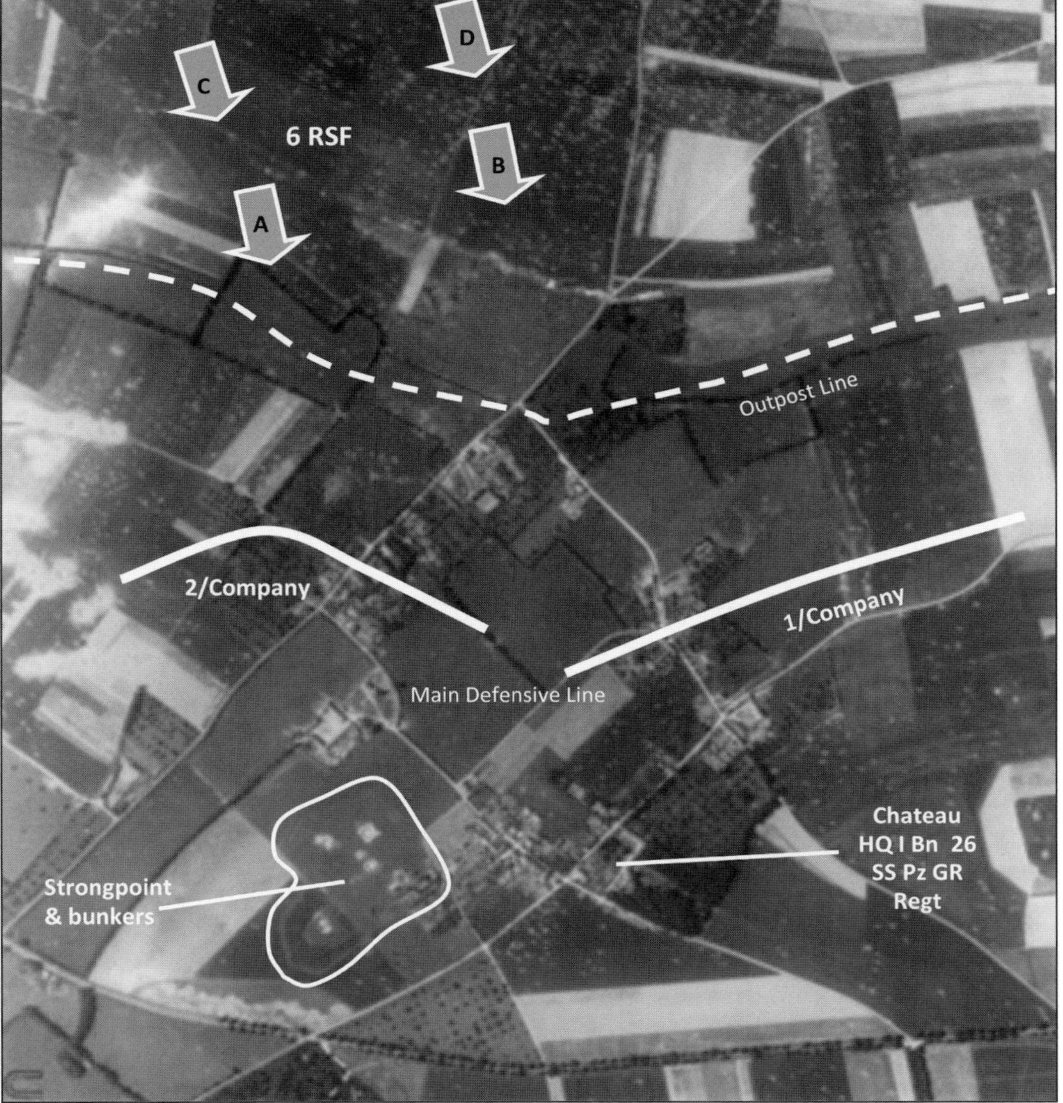

> looking in front of us for the wounded laying in the wheat; we had the dread of running over them. Added to this mines had been laid at random in the fields. Two of our tanks found them and no casualties though but both were out of action.

The two A Squadron Crocodiles lost tracks on anti-tank mines near the start line, which had probably been laid and poorly marked by the Canadians.

St. Manvieu

On 44 Brigade's left flank 6th Royal Scots Fusiliers (6 RSF), the same battalion that Winston Churchill commanded during the First World War, accompanied by the tanks of B Squadron 9 RTR, advanced on St. Manvieu. They had the same problem with the minefields, but in the fog they lost cohesion, with companies and platoons losing direction from the outset. Consequently, as they fought through the German outpost line on the line of the Mue stream, the fighting degenerated into a series of uncoordinated infantry platoon and section attacks. The Anti-personel mines added to the loss of coordination and the attacks on the various parts of the village stalled. Captain Strachan, with the Crocodiles of 4 and 5 Troops, was called forward to assist the infantry in breaking into St. Manvieu. The intelligence officer, Captain Bailey, who normally travelled with the CO to visit the squadrons in action, wrote of Captain Strachan: 'Quite early he was given the job of helping 6 Royal Scots Fusiliers of 44 Brigade to clear St. MANVIEU. For a time everything went well, flaming the houses one by one and producing most gratifying reactions from the Germans inside.'

Even though the stone-built houses and farm buildings had been prepared for defence, the flame fuel slapped against the walls and found its way into buildings. Terrified, the young SS *Panzergrenadiers* abandoned their positions and fell back into the southern and eastern parts of the village. By 1130 hours, the westernmost portion of St. Manvieu was reported as being 'taken', but the Crocodiles at that time were in action helping the mopping-up until 1430 hours. VIII Corps' war diary records that 'Two houses, in particular, were defended with great determination and were finally cleared by flame-throwers.'

At 1600 the rest of the village was attacked, but with minimal information on the enemy's location. A walled château complex that housed the headquarters of *Sturmbannführer* Krause's 1st Battalion, 26 SS *Panzergrenadiers* resisted capture. Captain Bailey wrote:

> But one strong-point jiggered the contract – a large house and courtyard surrounded by walls, shrubs and trees. Basically, this was a problem of getting flame tanks to within 80 yards of their target. There was only room for one tank [approaching from the west] to flame whilst the rest covered him with fire.

The war diary entry by 6 RSF's intelligence officer reads: 'The operation of clearing the village ... proved a slow and costly procedure, and it was not until

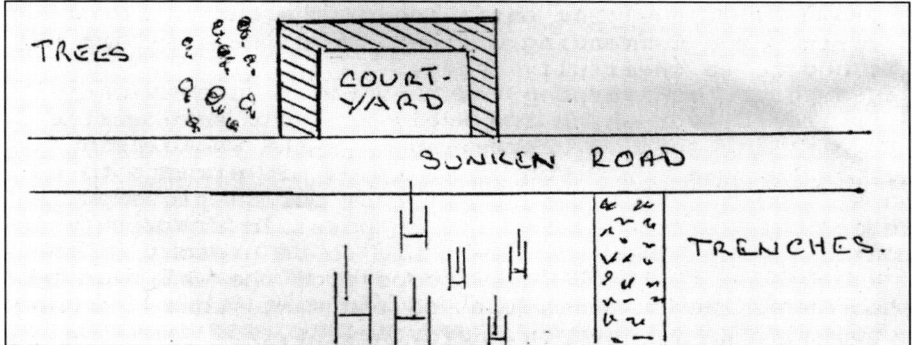

The sketch map of the action at St. Manvieu Château by Captain Bailey.

1700 hrs that the northern end of the objective was finally cleared by which time the Bn was very thin on the ground as the result of cas.'

During this attack, with the other Crocodiles firing into the château complex, Lieutenant Harvey led his troop forward, flaming as he went. Directing his Crocodile into the château area, presumably due to rubble getting into the running gear, his tank threw a track. Without the RSF infantry that had disappeared into the undergrowth, Lieutenant Harvey and his crew were on their own. Clearly Harvey's flaming had successfully chased the SS *Panzergrenadiers* from the buildings as the tools to break and refit the track were later found neatly laid out on a groundsheet.

Meanwhile, 'Captain Strachan was ranging around pumping 95mm into the houses and bushes'[6] and was joined by Colonel Waddell in his tank. The CO had been invited to accompany the advance as an observer and had hitherto been with Major Cooper and his half-squadron. However, 'As the CO leaned out of his turret to have a word with Strachan a runner [from the infantry] came up: "They've got the company commander now, and that's about the last of us." It was patent that without Infantry the strongpoint could not be cleared.' In addition, Captain Strachan failed to find any infantry to help as 'Each time he succeeded in this and made a plan the Infantry were whisked away.' The lack of infantry is explained in the RSF's war diary:

> [Enemy] Counter-attack was launched about 1800 hrs on the left flank but was beaten off and no penetration was made except to an orchard at the northern end of the village. Later a further counter-attack on the right flank was seen to be developing and the CO, in order to avoid the posn being infiltrated, had to call on Bde for the assistance of two Coys 6 KOSB. Bde Comd however decided in view of the cas incurred by the Bn in the operation to date to send up 6 KOSB complete less one rifle coy to take over from 6 RSF. This relief was completed with difficulty as counter-attacks were in progress during a portion of the time, and it was not until 2300 hrs that the final elements of the Bn were withdrawn from the posn to reserve.

With the infantry busy holding their gains in St. Manvieu, 141 RAC was left to manage with its own resources. Trooper Cox recalled:

> The Colonel arrived to see how things were going; hearing the news [that Lieutenant Harvey was missing] he grabbed our troop leader's tank and took us back into St. Manvieu to find the missing tank. The village was only partially in our hands and it was almost dark when the tank was found in a courtyard with its track broken. No one could be found, all the maps and codes had been torn up in little pieces, then the Jerries spotted us and we got out fast, a hail of shells following us.

The fate of Lieutenant Harvey and the award of the Knight's Cross to 24-year-old *Unterscharführer* Emil Dürr referred to in German accounts have been linked, but an exact sequence of events is impossible to establish with any certainty. It would appear, however, that having prepared to replace his track, the SS soldiers returned, having realized that the attack by the Crocodile had not been followed up by the Scottish infantry. The account written up by an SS *Kriegsberichter* has a different version of the story,[7] in which *Unterscharführer* Dürr, who commanded an anti-tank gun[8] in 4 (Heavy) Company, 1st 26 SS *Panzergrenadiers*, reacted to the arrival of a tank/Crocodile:

> Then, suddenly, there was a shout of alarm within the doggedly defending troops. A flame-thrower tank had set up at the entrance to the park, dominating the path to the command post, and able to harass any movement.

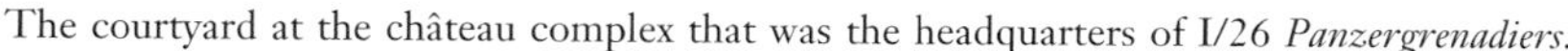

The courtyard at the château complex that was the headquarters of I/26 *Panzergrenadiers*.

Unterscharführer Emil Dürr. The Knight's Cross of the Iron Cross was posthumously awarded to Dürr, and was the first awarded to the 12th *Hitlerjugend* Panzer Division.

'That tank has to go,' the commander ordered. He said it as he was walking by; he had no time to stop ...

Unterscharführer Dürr had heard the order. He did not hesitate. 'I'll go,' he said, and was gone. He took a *Panzerfaust* and went to scout the situation. It was difficult to get close to the tank. It was sitting in a position that dominated the terrain on all three sides. *Unterscharführer* Dürr did not calculate for long. He jumped across the inner wall of the yard and ran straight at the tank. But the *Panzerfaust* did not pierce the tank. Maybe he did not aim accurately in his excitement.

Then Dürr felt a blow to the chest, and immediately a warm substance was running down his thighs. Hit! Shot in the chest! Angry, Dürr pulled himself up and ran back up the path he had come. He picked up another *Panzerfaust* and ran up to the tank a second time. This time, since the distance was unfavourable, he aimed at the tracks. The tank rattled; the track ripped. But again, Dürr was covered by violent machine-gun fire. Crawling, he worked his way back. With one jump he scaled the wall, out of the range of fire. He spotted a magnetic charge and quickly grabbed it. A comrade wanted to hold him back: 'you're bleeding ...' Dürr did not let himself be stopped. The tank had to go ... For a third time he had set out on his dangerous journey. For the third time, already quite weakened, he jumped across the wall. He ran, stumbling, toward the tank, paying no attention to the bullets. Now he was

> very close, one more jump, attached the charge. He was about to get away when he heard a rumbling sound behind him; the charge had dropped to the ground ... Not even seconds were left for him to consider, no time to contemplate his duty, desires, wishes ... the tank had to go. And once again he was at the flame-thrower tank like a flash. He grabbed the charge with a strong fist, pressed it against the tank, staggered once, pushed, gasping, against the diabolic dynamite ... Then came the bang ... He crawled back down the path, now open, to the command post. The comrades spotted him, pulled him in, took him to the medic. Four hours later his life came to an end. Not a word of complaint had come across his lips.[9]

Arguably the German soldier's dislike of flame had motivated *Unterscharführer* Dürr and, whatever the sequence of events, he was awarded the *Hitlerjugend*'s first Knight's Cross of the Iron Cross.

The fate of the missing crew was resolved as the war came to an end, when Crocodiles of 141 Regiment RAC 'found some British soldiers [prisoners of war] hiding in **a** ditch at a place called Woezer' as they advanced to the Baltic:

> They had been in a working party, one of them a member of the missing crew. He said the SS had captured them, put them against a wall and shot

The Bayeux CWGC Cemetery and Memorial to the Missing. The names of Lieutenant Harvey and three of his crew are engraved on the memorial.

> four of them. For some reason he was sent to a prisoner of war camp; they said he looked so young. Another of my mates Henry Prince was in that crew ... At the time no one knew their fate. I don't know what it would have done for our morale; our ignorance must have been fortunate for any SS prisoners coming in.[10]

The assumption is that the Crocodile crew was summarily executed by the SS and their bodies buried to conceal the crime. There is, however, little evidence that the murder of Crocodile crews was commonplace, but at a time when the murdering of both Canadian and *Hitlerjugend* prisoners was rife, this may have been just another manifestation of that struggle.

German Hollow-Charge Munition

In late 1942 Germany introduced, no doubt with some desperation, the magnetic hollow-charge munition: the *Haft-Hohlladung* 3kg nicknamed the *Panzerknacker* ('Armour Breaker'). The tank threat on the Eastern Front came as a massive shock to them as they found themselves struggling against large numbers of tanks that were superior to anything they had, in particular the T34 and KV series. The German infantry with their anti-tank rifles, rifle grenades and 37mm anti-tank guns were almost powerless against them. Calling in the support of medium and anti-aircraft artillery was often the only means they had of halting a Soviet armoured attack. This had also been the case in 1940 when they encountered the heavier French and British armour, but victory had obscured this fact.

A German soldier demonstrating the use of the *Haft-Hohlladung*.

The *Haft-Hohlladung* 3kg (3kg *Haft-H13*) was a hand-held cone-shaped mine weighing 3kg with a handle at the narrow end containing the fuse. At the broad end were three pairs of magnets. It had to be attached to an enemy tank by hand, and then the small igniter at the base of the handle was pulled. The fuse had a 7.5 second delay before exploding, giving the brave soldier very little time to get clear. With a penetration through armour of 140mm, it was replaced later by a more powerful version, the *Haft-H13* 5kg. In this munition the original cone-shaped body substituted for the head of the *Panzerfaust* 60, which gave an armour penetration of 180mm.

A Royal Engineer with a *Haft-Hohlladung*.

With the introduction of the *Panzerfaust* in spring 1944, the *Hohlladung* was no longer produced; however, sufficient stocks were available to cause problems to Allied tank crews in Normandy.

Several contemporary accounts by British tank crews during the campaign mistakenly mention the use of 'sticky bombs' by German infantry. These were, of course, *Haft-Hohlladungen*. During the dark days of 1940, the British Army had developed, in desperation, an anti-tank mine that relied upon a glue adhesive to attach itself to the surface of an enemy tank: the 'Sticky Bomb'. The Grenade, Hand, Anti-Tank No. 74 was not, however, a hollow-charge device, but was packed with nitro-glycerine, relying on the potency of this somewhat unstable explosive to damage the tank. This required as much selfless bravery by the user as its German equivalent, with the added risk of the grenade attaching itself to the attacker's battledress!

More than 2 million sticky bombs were made; being used, no doubt with some trepidation, in the Mediterranean theatre.

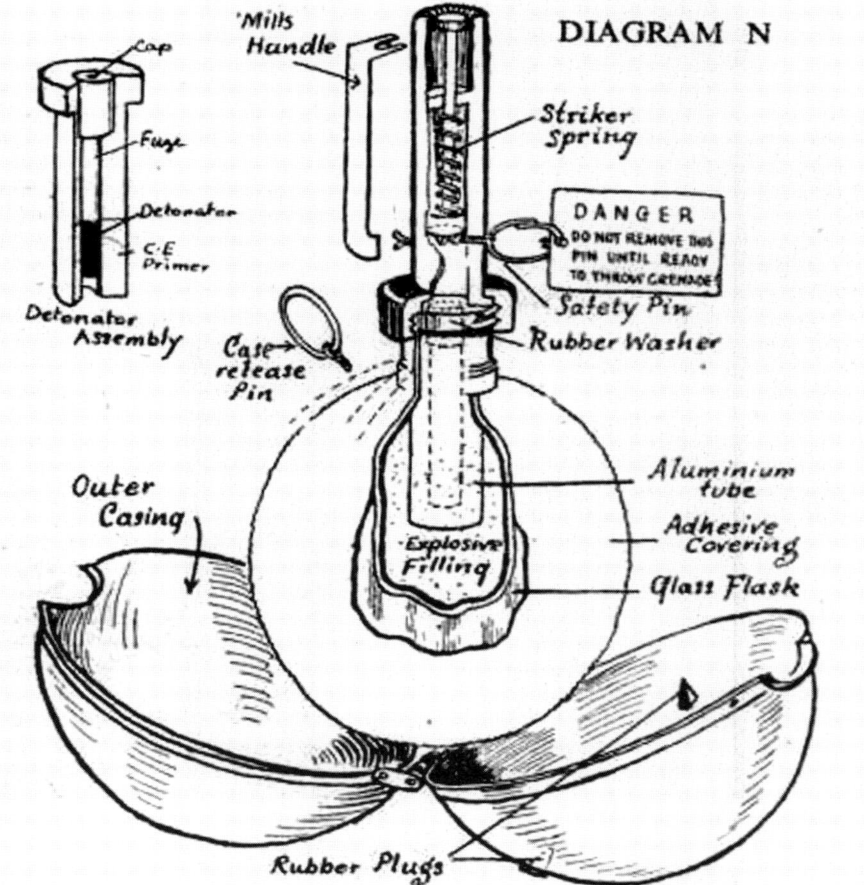

A diagram of the Grenade, Hand, Anti-Tank No. 74 'Sticky Bomb' from a Home Guard manual.

Having carried out a 'nightmare relief in place' of 6 KOSB overnight, the following morning at 0930 hours 4th Wiltshires of 43rd Wessex Division completed the capture of the eastern part of St. Manvieu with a fire plan and the support of flame. The remnants of I/26 *Panzergrenadiers* had, however, mostly exfiltrated to the east during the night. In the first two days of EPSOM Captain Strachan's half-squadron was involved in three separate attacks around the village and used half a trailer of fuel each. The war diary recorded that 'HE, AP and Besa were also used in large quantities' by A Squadron.

Cheux

While Captain Strachan's half-squadron was in action at St. Manvieu, on 44 (L) Brigade's right flank the advance of 8 RS had slowed and 2nd Argyll and Sutherland Highlanders (2 A&SH) took over the advance towards Cheux:

> The infantry held up at a farm, we moved in, a voice came over our field telephone fixed to the back of the tank, a Scots accent: 'Can you hear me in there?' 'What's your problem?' Dickie asked. 'A bloody sniper up in that barn giving us bother.' We swung the gun round to the gable end of the farmhouse where there was a small hole about a foot square, Ray lined it up, we waited. Sure enough, a rifle was poked through; we could see his arm then his face. Ray pressed the foot-operated pedal from the BESA. A shattering burst of fire, that's for my mate Jim, I thought. By late afternoon the village was in our hands, we pulled back to rearm and refuel. We had lost one driver from sniper fire; the other troops had not done so well, one tank was knocked out by a Panther. The crew bailed out. Another fell into a dugout but the crew escaped with acid burns from the batteries.

6 Troop were themselves subject to sniper fire when the echelon vehicles came forward to replenish the Crocodiles:

> Our fuel was now in Jerrycans and the driver of the tank in front saw two small jets of petrol coming out of the jerrycan held between his legs. He dropped it quick and took cover, 'a bloody sniper', we looked to see where it came from, in time to see a German soldier come out from a stand of elms. He stood for a moment then levelled his rifle and shot dead one of the gunners then threw down his rifle in surrender. A gunnery Sergeant emptied a full magazine of his Sten into him; we didn't blame him.

Despite the much slower than planned pace of the battle, Major Cooper and his three troops of Crocodiles remained on call throughout 26 June. However, that is not to say that the Crocodiles were entirely passive observers from the high ground north of Cheux:

> The CO [who had joined them] lazily potted at a Panther way over in the HAUT DU BOSQUE area.[11] Sgt Wheatcroft took in three 88 mm shots [*sic*] through the engine and was, not unnaturally, put out of action with no

> injury to the crew. Hours after schedule, CHEUX was 'declared taken' (in actual fact four days later snipers were still being cleared away) and Crocodiles and tanks rallied just north of the main road LA GAULE-FONTENAY.

The following day any armoured crewman who had his head out of his hatch continued to risk being shot. Even though overrun, the fanatical young soldiers of the *Hitlerjugend* lying up in the bocage hedgerows south of Cheux or concealed in the rubble of the villages sniped at the British. Captain Bailey recalled that 'These were the days when you stood quite calmly chatting to someone and turned around to find him dead. The air fairly buzzed with vicious little cracks.'

As the campaign progressed, it was common practice in Churchill regiments for a plate to be welded behind the commander's cupola to prevent silhouetting of his head for German sharpshooters. Even so, as in this photograph, commanders kept their heads low.

During the night of 26/27 June a troop of A Squadron was called forward to help deal with the stay-behind snipers. The order was given to Trooper Cox's 'Stallion' to 'Pressure up':

> Two troops of us went in dousing the area with flame, quite a few came running out and many who were not quick enough would not be coming out at all. They were Hitler Youth ... completely brainwashed they fought like demons but cried when they were caught mainly because they thought they would be shot.

Trooper Les Arnold, a crewman in one of 9 RTR's OP tanks, wrote:

> Later in the evening some 141 RAC Crocodiles set fire to woods and buildings close by which held snipers and other enemy troops.[12] These burned most of the night and the enemy concentrated artillery and mortar fire on them; so we stayed in the tanks or dug in under them.

Flaming, however, was not always the answer according to Captain Bailey:

> Captain Storrar ... flamed the hedgerows and still they fired. Finally, the 2iC of 7 RTR, Major Fleming (later killed by a sniper himself) took out the Recce Troop of 7 RTR and rounded up some forty young Nazis. Always it was snipers and God knows they took their toll. Yet, in effect, it was nothing more than the professed German tactics of a strongpoint fighting on long after the attacking troops had passed by. To walk the streets of London in the nude is to feel fully clothed as compared to standing on a tank manoeuvring an unwieldy jerrican and presenting your posterior to a host of aggressive German snipers.

This flame action is recorded as using one-eighth of a trailer of flame fuel. For the remaining three days of EPSOM:

> Still under command of 31 Tank Brigade for Operation EPSOM, A Squadron continued to operate from a forward base north of CHEUX daily, providing a quota of Crocodiles to the 7 RTR and 9 RTR in their swoops south of CHEUX towards the River ODON. Their job was to follow the advance ready for action should a suitable role occur. In actual fact it did not. Nevertheless, this continual activity did impose a considerable strain in regard to maintenance (especially the special equipment) and lack of sleep, and it soon became obvious that such allocation could not continue indefinitely. The monotony of this procedure was occasionally relieved for the command tanks, moving along with squadron HQs, in an occasional brush with the enemy armour.
>
> On one occasion whilst holding a dismounted conference with Major Howard Jones of the 7 RTR, a particularly heavy 'stonk' began to arrive. Without undue deliberation they both took refuge underneath a tank. To their horror and disgust at the very peak of everything, the tank moved gently off.

A Churchill of 31 Tank Brigade during Operation EPSOM, with a jeep and a section of 6-pounder anti-tank guns.

When the 11th Armoured Division took the fighting beyond the River Odon to Hill 112, A Squadron remained with 31 Tank Brigade supporting the infantry keeping the narrow 'Scottish Corridor' open. Trooper Cox's Crocodile 'Stallion' was undergoing forward repair when tanks of 12th SS Panzer Regiment moved east from the Rauray Spur to prevent a widening of the salient:

> We took up our position at the end of the hedge. The noise of the engine was creating an ear-shattering noise without the exhaust or engine covers. We felt quite good; let them come to us for a change, it would be a nice surprise for them. We cut branches, placing them round the tank with just the gun poking through. We wouldn't be using flame, so Beech [the flame gunner] set up the Bren and he stood up in his hatch. I said 'Look behind you.' The turret Besa was pointed at the back of his head. 'Oh well,' he said, 'I might as well go to sleep', and he settled himself down. It all seemed quiet; then we spotted a Mark IV crossing our front; we could see clear across some flat ground for about a mile. We fired five AP shots as he passed the tracer and seemed to be going straight for the target. He finally made it to cover; I doubt if we hit him. Nothing else happened, the artillery hammered away in an endless barrage, the noise was incredible . . . The German infantry were cut to threads by the artillery who had caught them in the open, the attack ground to a halt. The fitters came back and soon had our tank fixed and running again.

Finally, VIII Corps went over to the defensive when the powerful II SS Panzer Corps approached the western side of the Scottish Corridor with the 9th *Hohenstaufen* SS Panzer Division. Again, A Squadron fought as gun tanks:

> We were on a ridge code named 'Piccadilly' [the southerly extension of the Rauray Spur] … To our front a wooded area some 2,000 yards away. Five Panthers and two Tiger tanks [possibly Panzer IVs] left the wood heading straight for us. There were two troops of us plus a regiment of Shermans [from 4 Armoured Brigade], at least fifty tanks including some Fireflies, Shermans fitted with 17-pounder guns. We held all the cards, hull down on a ridge, the Germans out in the open. We just let them come. At about 800 yards everyone opened up. Ray lined up on a Panther and fired. I watched the tracer, bang on the front; I saw the tracer go skywards, it had bounced off. We fired off seven shots, each one a hit, each one bounced off and they were still coming; it was incredible, one shot from an 88 and any tank we had was a goner. Yet here we were pouring shell after shell with no apparent effect, and they were getting pretty damn close.
>
> Then the 17-pounders began to prove their worth: first one Panther went up in flames, the rest turned to go back exposing their weaker sides. I watched as a Tiger stopped, and the crew bailed out making for the drainage ditches. One by one they succumbed to the relentless barrage of

Soldiers of the 10 DLI of 49th Division inspecting an abandoned Tiger near the Rauray château.

> fire. Two of the Panthers almost made it, both going up in flames. In essence quite a victory, seven tanks destroyed and we hadn't lost one; had we not been hull down on the ridge and met them in the open as they had been, they would have cleaned the lot of us up. No wonder they hadn't told us about Panthers and Tigers. In comparison our tanks were a bloody disgrace and our 75mm guns were even worse; not even a dent could we make under 400 yards. One hit from an 88 at 2,000 yards and you were history; it was not a happy thought.

For the remaining days of EPSOM 'Each day we would go out on call and sit up "The sharp end" as we termed the front.' Eventually A Squadron was ordered back to Bernay to rest and refit. As the tanks reversed out of their forward positions in daylight, they stirred up clouds of dust and as they left the infantry were shaking their fists at them:

> The tanks were not allowed to travel on roads because of the damage they caused. Tank tracks crisscrossed the beachhead. With the dry weather they had two or three inches of dust over them, created by the constant passing of the tanks grinding down the soil. It was almost impossible to see, with the air louvres blowing the dust many feet into the air. It got everywhere, our tunics buttoned to the neck, scarves over our mouths, goggles and hats pulled down. The progress was quite slow and drew some shellfire. At one point we passed a row of seven Honey tanks belonging to 7th Armoured (the Desert Rats), they had all been knocked out. The 7th took quite a hiding, as all they'd learnt in the desert meant nothing here. We continued on our way for quite a while when suddenly through the dust appeared the same row of knocked-out tanks. No doubt about it, we were lost, the column stopped, and we got down for a leg stretch. The Captain [Storrar] shot off in a scout

One of the many signs imploring drivers to keep their speed down.

> car, after an hour we were on our way again, this time we made it to Bernay, our rest area. We never let the Captain off and his 'Cooks Tour' of the beach head became legend.

During EPSOM, the squadron is recorded as losing two Crocodiles with broken tracks and one overturned: 'All three recovered.'

Operation MITTEN

> Failure. Bad plan – bad tie-up with Inf. Far too few Crocodiles for large objective. Good job for a Sqn, which would have saved many Inf lives.

While EPSOM was under way, I Corps had been tasked to extend the pressure on the Germans with an attack to the north of Caen in order to prevent the movement of reserves from 25th SS *Panzergrenadiers* or 21st Panzer Division's front to the support of their sister regiment facing EPSOM. The front here had been static for three weeks since 3rd Division's strike inland between D-Day and D+2 had been halted. British and German defensive positions were at close quarters and, despite two previous attempts to eliminate it, a German-held salient dominated by the Château de la Londe remained firmly in the hands of 192 *Panzergrenadiers* of 21st Panzer Division.[13]

The tactical aim of General Crocker's I Corps was to advance the front towards the ridge overlooking Caen by some 2 miles. In Operation MITTEN, 8 Brigade of 3rd Division was to capture Château de la Londe, which would be followed in phase two by an attack to the west by Brigadier Orr's 9 Brigade and Brigadier Cunningham's 9 Canadian Brigade of 3rd Canadian Division in Operation ABERLOUR. The objectives were the capture of St. Contest, Authie and Cussy.

On the afternoon of 27 June, the de la Londe salient was to be taken by 1st South Lancashires (1 S Lancs), supported by two troops of Shermans from the Staffordshire Yeomanry, flails of 2 Troop, C Squadron, 22 Dragoons and the Crocodiles of 8 Troop of B Squadron under Lieutenant Raymond Brooke. Operation MITTEN, however, did not start well. While the attackers were forming up there was 'very severe shelling and mortaring on Le Landel, and the forward command post was hit and the Commanding Officer, Lieutenant Colonel J.E.S. Stone, was wounded but continued at duty.'[14]

With the divisional artillery doing its best to suppress the German defenders, C and D companies advanced at 1530 hours across the cornfields under heavy mortar and machine-gun fire to deliver a frontal attack on the château. The Crocodile's role in the attack was to flame the northern edge of the château's park. 'Heavy defensive fire was still falling, however, and the ground was swept by fire from dug-in tanks and concealed machine guns which slowed the pace of the advance.' D Company 1 S Lancs on the right reached the edge of the park but could not break in, while C Company was pinned down in the open. The Crocodiles had advanced with the attackers but, according to the regimental war diary: 'Seeing his other two tks going too far right [possibly the hamlet of

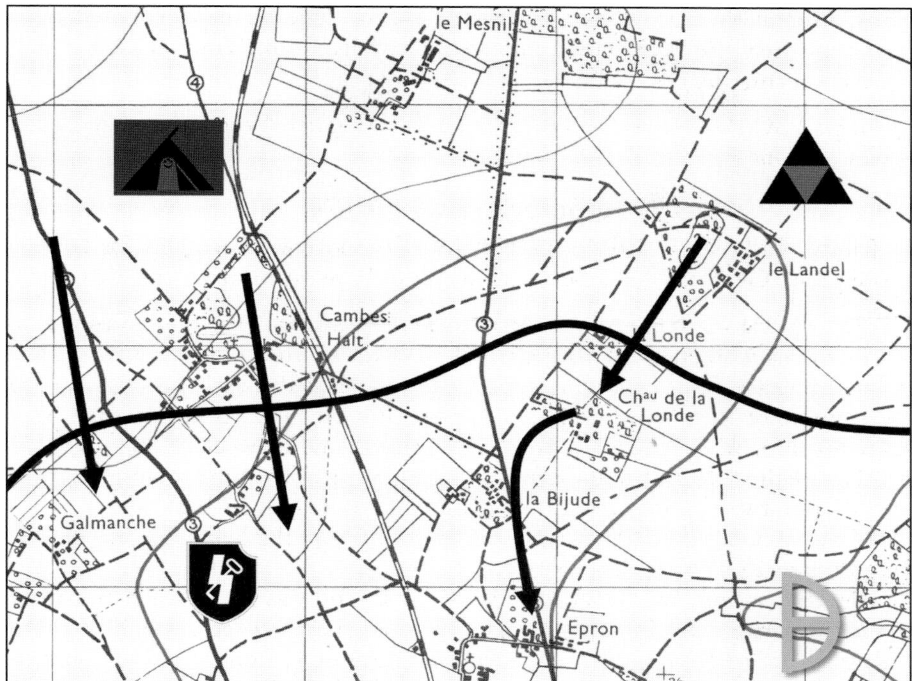

The line held by the Germans and I Corps' plans for MITTEN and ABERLOUR.

La Londe], Lieut RC Brooke made a dash himself for the correct objective and was knocked out by a 75mm A tk gun at 20 yards range. Lieut RC Brooke and gunner killed.'

The Pak 40 responsible was 'prettily concealed behind an ornamental grille in a wall' and there were not only anti-tank guns, but a significant number of panzers dug in in and around the park. The result was that while the Staffordshire Yeomanry perforce duelled with the enemy tanks, they were unable to provide meaningful support to 1 S Lancs or the Crocodiles.

With the defenders well prepared and the attackers lacking close support, casualties in both infantry companies were heavy and their frontal attack ground to a halt. Consequently, A and B companies were deployed around the left flank in the belief that there was a better chance of success in that direction but, as Lieutenant Jones of A Company explained, they fared no better:

> We were subjected to intense MG fire from both flanks and the front, and at the same time we were heavily mortared. Many men became casualties at once, others took refuge in the ditch and crawled back ... We were in a shallow ditch, blocked a few yards ahead by the bloated corpse of a cow, whilst the hedge-junction to our rear was continually raked by machine-gun fire. A heavy concentration of mortar shells was falling to our left, on the

> other side of the hedge/bank, and a Crocodile ... was burning there, with its turret blown completely off. One of the two riflemen with me was struck in the shoulder by a bullet which seemed to pass through his body and he died within seconds ... The fire seemed to come from every direction and it was impossible to locate its source. We kept expecting troops and tanks to follow us up in support and relieve the pressure, but none came. When dusk came on we were able, under cover of darkness, to return to Le Landel and report to Bn HQ where we learned that our attack had been called off and that a Brigade attack was planned for a few hours ahead.

Captain Bailey concluded:

> The Sergeant's turret jammed and in the end both he and the Corporal were driven back by anti-tank gunfire, having accomplished precisely nothing at all. Two troops in a frontal attack might well have pulled it off. But young Brooke was dead to prove that an assault must have a clear and simple plan with simple signals and infantry who are fresh and free to plan. The more Crocodiles the merrier – there was no doubt about that.

The battle came to an end for the S Lancs at about 1900 hours, with the depleted companies withdrawing to La Landel.

The salient around Château de la Londe was clearly too strongly held for a single battalion to capture and hold. Major General Whistler was, however, not going to let matters rest and had ordered 8 Brigade to renew the attack at first light on 28 June. This time Brigadier Orr would attack with both 1 Suffolks and 5 East Yorks, but the Crocodiles of B Squadron did not feature in the plan and remained on call. This was probably because in their first operation with the brigade a single troop had, as Bailey said, contributed 'precisely nothing at all'. 141 Regiment RAC and those they would support were having to learn on the job how to use flame to best effect and save infantry lives. It is worth recalling the post-war Staff College verdict that 'Although they had given demonstrations to senior officers, not much was known of the capabilities at the battalion or brigade level.'[15]

The renewed attack on Château de la Londe began at 0430 hours with 1 Suffolks on the left and 5 East Yorks on the right. For both battalions it was a bitter, protracted and costly fight. Only late in the day were the Crocodiles called forward, but again they were too few and poorly integrated into the plan to make much difference and barely get a mention in war diaries or accounts.

Some 300 casualties were suffered by 8 Brigade on 28 June, so added to those of previous attacks, it is with some justification that 3rd Division referred to the Château de la Londe area as 'the bloodiest square mile in Normandy'.

General Whistler called off Operation MITTEN and ABERLOUR was cancelled. The Germans, although they had lost the La Londe salient, held firm at La Bijude and would do so for another ten days until Operation CHARNWOOD and the fall of Caen.

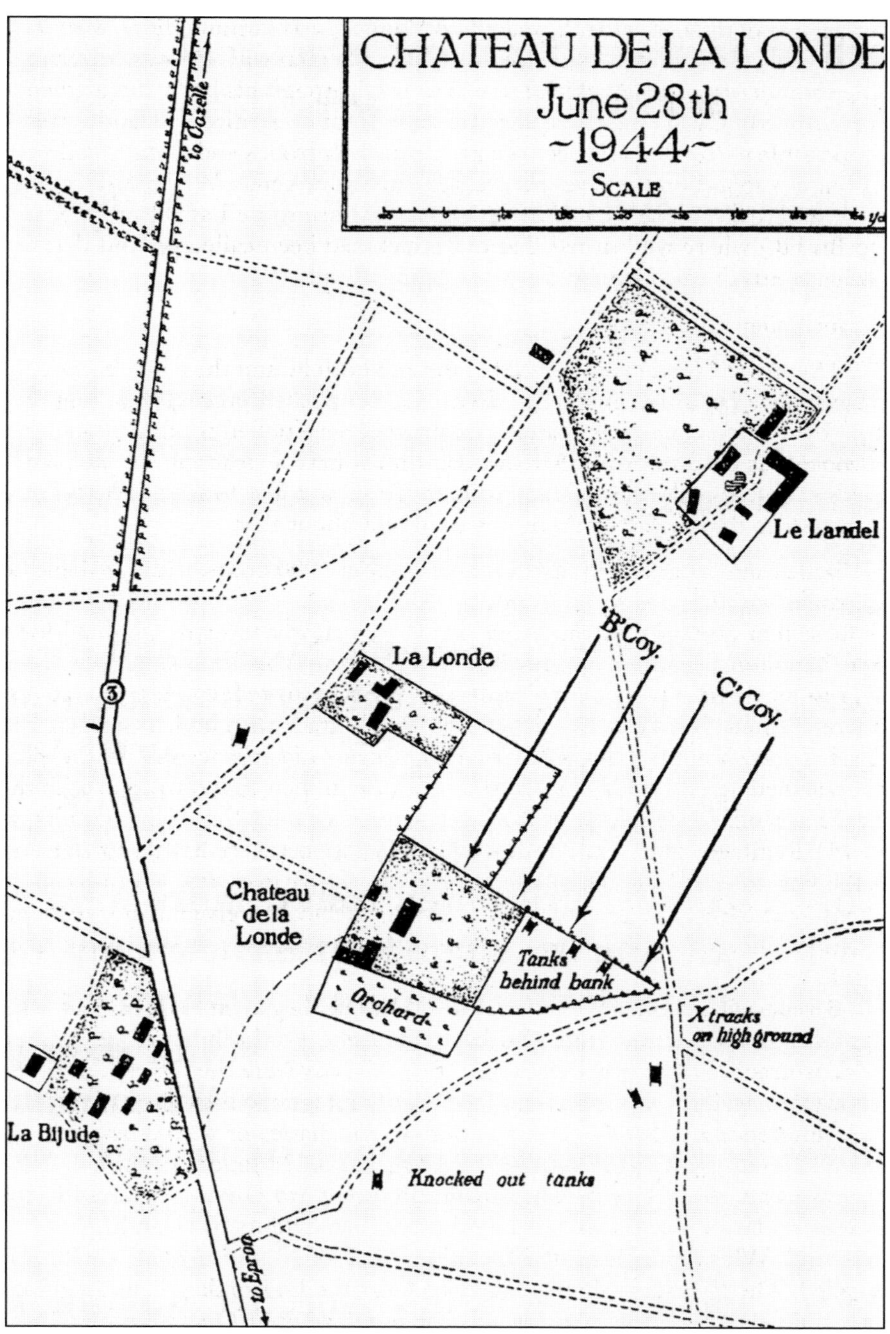

The attack by 1 S Lancs on Château de la Londe on 27 June 1944.

The first of two photographs of Château de la Londe following its capture by 8 Brigade.

At the end of their first week in action, the adjutant summarized the lessons learned at St. Manvieu and Château de la Londe, in particular on the tactical employment of Crocodiles in battle:

> The whole of this period presented a process of learning the hard way; a process in which the Regiment has very little control – a series of penny packet experiments. From these small actions, however, the necessities of adhering to the following principles were very forcibly brought out:
>
> (a) The first essential of any plan entailing the use of Crocodiles is to ensure they are got to within 80 yds of the objective to be flamed – this entails armour protection to the flanks, arty and smoke.
> (b) Very clear signals must be laid down between the inf and supporting Crocodiles.
> (c) The inf must follow the Crocodiles in or the enemy will return immediately.
> (d) If the Crocodiles are held back until required any given strongpoint should be attacked by FRESH inf (reserve pl or coy) as it is impossible to make proper plan with the inf pinned to the ground.
> (e) A wood should be attacked if possible on the fwd edge with the flanks well screened by smoke or covered by armour and SPs with smoke on the objective and demoralising smoke behind. The flaming should be done at angles (especially if the Crocodiles are few in number), and into the wind so that the flame smoke is blown back and forms a protection to the tank's rear.

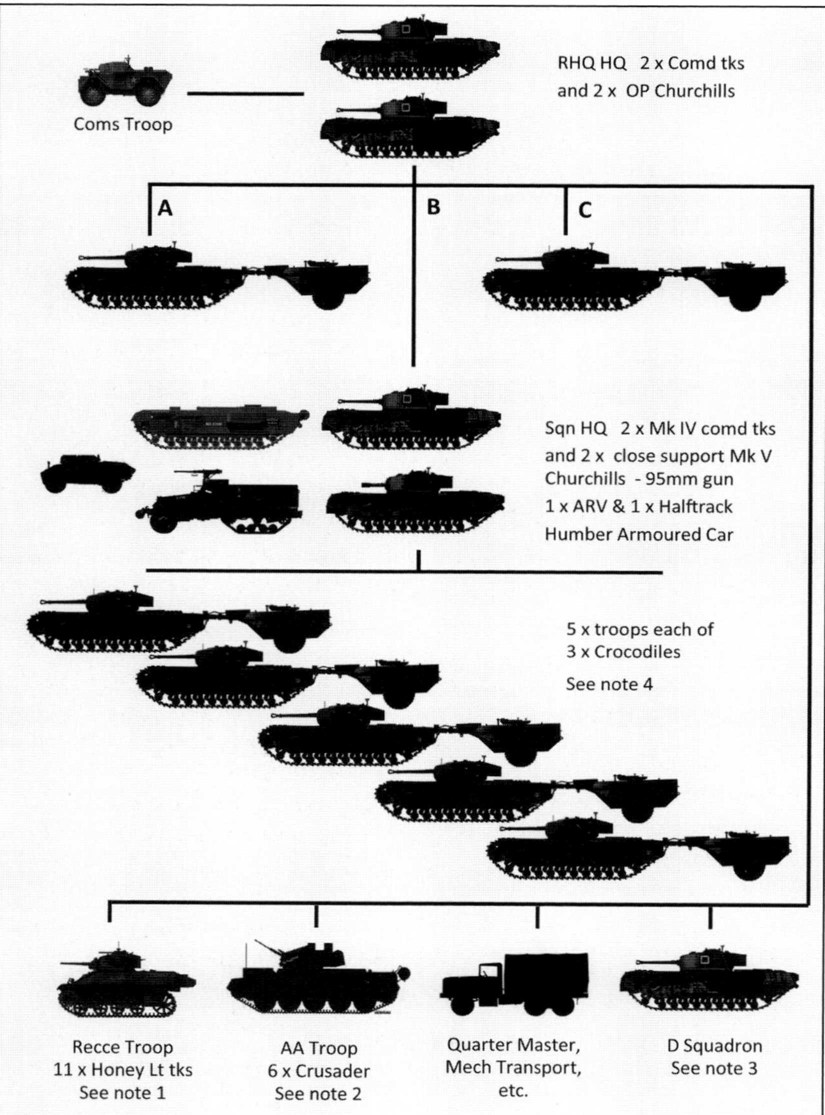

Notes:

1. The Recce Troop was disbanded during the Normandy Campaign as the regiment in practice did not fight as a unit but as squadrons attached to formations for specific tasks.

2. AA troops were also disbanded in most tank and armoured regiments due to the reduced air threat and increasing manpower shortages.

3. In Normandy D (Reserve) Squadron was in effect a bespoke armoured replacement squadron, supplying Crocodile vehicles, equipment and manpower.

4. In October 1944 the sabre squadrons were formerly reorganised into three troops of four Crocodiles reflecting developing practice.

Even after conversion to Crocodiles, 141 RAC reflected a tank regiment. However, this changed as the tactical employment of the Crocodile developed.

Chapter Four

D (Reserve) Squadron

Lieutenant Wilson and elements of D (Reserve) Squadron, having undergone the de-waterproofing procedure, were en route to RHQ at Brécy when they pulled over to let a column of tank transporters pass:

> As the transporters came near, you could see there was something wrong with the Churchills. Several had their turrets and guns askew. Closer and you could see the holes where the shots had gone in. I counted the tanks ... eleven, twelve, thirteen. They belonged to a regiment that had been in the same brigade at Ashford [31 Tank Brigade, 7 and 9 RTR]. After that no one spoke much.[1]

The following day the adjutant explained the vulnerability of the Churchill to the newly-arrived officers. He told Lieutenant Wilson that:

> ... the flame-thrower was terrific, but the tank itself a death trap. There followed a little catechism about British and German tanks:
>
> 'What do the Germans have most of?'
>
> 'Panthers. The Panther can slice through a Churchill like butter from a mile away.'
>
> 'And how does a Churchill get a Panther?'
>
> 'It creeps up on it. When it reaches close quarters, the gunner tries to bounce a shot off the underside of the Panther's gun mantlet. If he's lucky, it goes through a piece of thin armour above the driver's head.'
>
> 'Has anybody ever done it?'
>
> 'Yes. Davis in C Squadron. He's back with headquarters now, trying to recover his nerve.'[2,3]

Trooper Smith arrived in Normandy in an LCI (Landing Craft Infantry) near Ver-sur-Mer (KING sector of GOLD Beach) with a draft of armoured crew replacements at the beginning of July. He was a trained Cromwell crewman, but like many he had an idea of which regiment he wanted to join. In his case it was The Buffs, in which his father had fought during the First World War. Arriving at a Reinforcement Holding Unit (RHU) in Normandy, it was apparent that it was Sherman crews that were in greatest demand at the time, but after questioning about his regiment and a confident answer '141 RAC', after several days he found himself bound for Ryes, where D Squadron was at the time. Like all 141 RAC's replacements he had two crew trades out of three from driver, gunner

A British truck loaded with jerry cans of fuel on the bypass built by the Royal Engineers around medieval Bayeux.

and radio-operator, but not the Crocodile and he had to undergo training on the flame system:

> During the day most of my time was spent on the flame course. It took ten days, mostly devoted to the mechanics of the weapon and the attendant drills but eventually we all had our turn in sending a jet of flame 80 yards to cascade onto a pile of oil drums. Lastly there was the written test. The pupils had been one Captain and two Lieutenants, myself and two other men. Obviously, the sergeant instructor knew his business because when the results were announced the captain was top.[4]

D Squadron was co-located with or at least in proximity to the Main Regimental Headquarters, the quartermaster, the technical adjutant and the REME Light Aid Detachment (LAD). From here in a jeep, Humber armoured car or tank, Lieutenant Colonel Waddell would go out as a tactical HQ to visit the squadrons, particularly those preparing for battle. Increasingly his role was to ensure that the Crocodiles were being used appropriately.

Also making daily runs forward were the trucks of the Motor Transport Troop taking fuel, ammunition and food to top up the squadron's echelons or on occasions directly to the harbour. Most of these journeys to the front were at night, but by day or night in the increasingly crowded rear areas they were mainly via slow-moving traffic circuits. Long one-way routes were strictly enforced in the tight confines of the beachhead, which made routine visits and admin runs time-consuming for the CO and QM; miss the turning and around they went again.

With regard to replacement tanks, the first stage in preparing a Churchill Mk VII for issue to squadrons was for the REME to fit the Crocodile conversion kit, but after that it was for the men of D Squadron to 'bomb-up' the tank for battle. Trooper Smith who remained with D Squadron for some time recalled:

> These had to be taken up to a fighting squadron at a moment's notice. The first task ... was to stock them with ammunition. This was productive work for us. The sunlight glistens on the brass rounds, piled on the track guards ready to be handed into the turret ... Another man is halfway through the pannier [door] stowing the green smoke rounds. Another sits by himself in the shade priming grenades. Around the tank is a litter of wood, wire and cardboard, a tin box containing [yellow] smoke bombs, cylinders that have housed the HE rounds, bits of yellow and white adhesive tape, paper torn from the Besa boxes, split Sten ammo shining in the grass. The temporary commander trying to force the tail smoke charges into position.[5]
>
> By the time we had the tank ammoed up, the engine cleaned and fuelled, the trailer charged, and all the miscellaneous kit checked and stowed there was usually a demand for a tank from one of the squadrons and we had to go through the whole routine again.

Initially 141 Regiment RAC had the organization of a standard Churchill regiment, but by the time they were fully deployed it was obvious that the air threat posed by the Luftwaffe to tanks was minimal and the Anti-Aircraft Troop was

A pristine Crocodile flaming. Once in battle they quickly became battered, typically losing track guards.

disbanded. At the same time, as 141 RAC did not in practice fight as a unit, the Recce Troop was also disbanded, the regiment lost its Stuart light tanks and recce troop crews were trained as Crocodile replacements.

While there may have been little threat from the Luftwaffe by day, it was, as will be revealed later in these pages, certainly not the experience of the squadrons by night, all of whom suffered air attacks on at least one occasion. Being in the increasingly cramped beachhead and well to the rear, D Squadron received the attentions of the German bombers on a regular basis. The Luftwaffe crews on dark nights dropped illuminating flares and when the moon was bright they could roughly identify likely targets, but anti-aircraft fire could indicate the location of something worth bombing:

> ... the Luftwaffe kept our AA gunners busy, flak being our principal weapon at night. AA guns were rarely to be seen in daytime, but they were everywhere after dark. The drone of aeroplanes was smothered by bursts in the distance. If we were dressed, we would crawl under the tank. If we were in bed someone would say the canvas bivi could withstand the [falling] shrapnel. It could be heard pattering through the branches of the apple trees while the sky glowed red with balls of tracer from countless Bofors, the rosy spray of Oerlikon adding to the confusion. No burst to be seen – just lazy curving tracer vanishing at its apex. If we were on guard I would go around to the

Anti-aircraft guns were often near neighbours in the crowded beachhead.

> officers' marquee and throw apples on the roof to make them believe shrapnel was hitting.

Hygiene was another issue in the rear area, but certainly not exclusively there. The number of dead cattle and horses was a problem across the battlefield, and in the rear area were open latrine pits and, more innocuously, fruit knocked from orchard trees and subsequently squashed, all of which were a breeding ground for flies. As static armies have found out over the millennia of warfare, such conditions are ripe for disease, which once it gets a hold can spread through a unit very quickly. Smith recalled an attack of diarrhoea in D Squadron that stopped virtually all activities:

> It was so bad that some barely dared put their trousers on and wandered around, shirt tails flapping. The woods adjoining the orchard held convenient, and soon reeking, foxholes, and were swarming with every kind of

Every time D Squadron moved to a new location, they had to dig slit trenches, dugouts and latrines.

Recovery and Repair

The regiment's Light Aid Detachment (LAD) and squadron fitter sections were made up of a combination of tradesmen from the RAC and craftsmen of the Corps of Royal Electrical and Mechanical Engineers (REME). Repair and recovery was controlled by Captain Drysdale commanding the attached LAD, which was part of the regiment's rear echelon. It consisted of a total of twenty-five tradesmen of all ranks. Their function was to carry out minor repairs, but not the replacement of major assemblies or other time-consuming tasks. These were the responsibility of the second line or brigade workshop. Likewise, the more challenging tasks were referred to brigade with their heavy recovery equipment and tank transporters.

The LAD was equipped with five 15cwt trucks, two motorcycles and two 6 × 4 breakdown vehicles. These were normally Scammell Explorer and Ward LaFrance trucks. The former had superior cross-country performance and a powerful winch, but the latter had an excellent jib for towing and lifting tasks during repair.

Each of the three Crocodile squadrons had a fitter section with a Churchill Armoured Recovery Vehicle (ARV) attached to the HQ troop. This vehicle was essentially a turretless Churchill tank equipped with Hollebone drawbars, tow ropes and shackles, etc. It also had a detachable frame, and a block and tackle with a lift capacity of 7.5 tons which when fitted to the vehicle front or rear could be used for the removal of major assemblies. This earlier ARV was not fitted with a winch, relying on its engine pulling power for recovery. The crew of three was led by a REME sergeant, the other two being regimental tradesmen. The ARV retained the hull Besa machine gun and was also armed with a twin Bren on an anti-aircraft pintle. The fitters carried pistols for personal protection.

A Mk I Churchill ARV was found in the LAD and in the fitter sections.

Sherman flail tanks of the 22nd Westminster Dragoons. Although not yet officially a part of the 79th Armoured Division, as the campaign progressed the Crocodile squadrons increasingly found themselves under the wing of the division's officers.

> insect. Work was suspended for several days, during which we lived on biscuits and tablets distributed by 'Aspro Joe' the MO.

Although Trooper Smith remained with D Squadron for the best part of a month, most replacements completed their flame course only having had a few days' wait in the rear area before they were called forward. They would either go up with the trucks during a routine replenishment or as a part of the crew of a replacement Crocodile.

As the campaign lengthened and German resistance prevented the gaining of much ground, along with the arrival of more and more troops and the establishment of temporary airfields, real estate management in the rear area became a real issue. Consequently, D Squadron was repeatedly moved during July into smaller areas with less cover as the army's build-up progressed.

21 ARMY  **GROUP**

PERSONAL MESSAGE FROM THE C-IN-C

(To be read out to all Troops)

1. After four days of fighting the Allied Armies have secured a good and firm lodgment area on the mainland of France.

2. First, we must thank Almighty God for the success we have achieved and for giving us a good beginning towards the full completion of our task.

3. Second, we must pay a tribute to the Allied Navies and Air Forces for their magnificent co-operation and support; without it, we soldiers could have achieved nothing.

4. Third, I want personally to congratulate every officer and man in the Allied Armies on the splendid results of the last four days.
British, Canadian and American soldiers, fighting gallantly side by side, have achieved a great success, and have placed themselves in a good position from which to exploit this success.

5. To every officer and man, whatever may be his rank or employment, I send my grateful thanks and my best wishes for the future.
Much yet remains to be done; but together, you and I, we will do it, and we will see the thing through to the end.

6. Good luck to you all.

B. L. Montgomery

General
C.-in-C.,
21 Army Group

France, 10 June 1944.

General Montgomery's message of 10 June to 21st Army Group at the conclusion of the first phase of the invasion.

Chapter Five

The Battle for Caen

My broad policy, once we had secured a firm lodgement area, had been to draw the main enemy forces into battle on our eastern flank, and to fight them there, so that our affairs on the Western flank can proceed the easier.
[Montgomery: 30 July, Directive M 505]

The end of June and early July saw all three squadrons of 141 Regiment RAC (The Buffs) becoming more heavily committed to the fighting across the Second Army's front. Following EPSOM, however, the focus was now in the east and the capture of Caen by direct attack rather than envelopment. During this month the regiment and those they supported continued to learn lessons, in some cases the hard way, on how to use flame effectively.

The beginning of July saw the fighting with II SS Panzer Corps around the EPSOM salient continuing, with A Squadron remaining in support of VIII Corps. They were regularly deployed, but were not called forward to flame. Further west, Major Duffy's C Squadron had remained with XXX Corps and after a period of inactivity 'awaiting replacements for the D-Day Boys', was rushed to support 49th (West Riding) Division. The recently captured area of the Rauray Spur was on 1 July being very heavily counter-attacked by the 9th *Hohenstaufen* SS Panzer Division and *Kampfgruppe* Weidinger of the 2nd *Das Reich* SS Panzer Division.

The attack had fallen most heavily on 11 Durham Light Infantry, 1 Tyneside Scottish and 24 Lancers and, despite some positions being overrun, they managed to halt the German attacks with increasingly heavy artillery fire. The engagements progressed from a MIKE (regimental) shoot of twenty-four guns, through a divisional UNCLE target (seventy-two guns) to calling on all the available guns of the corps in a VICTOR shoot. The 49th Division claimed a total of thirty-four Panthers knocked[1] out by the Lancers and the guns of the anti-tank regiments, so that by the time the Crocodiles arrived in Cristot at 2000 hours, the situation had been stabilized.[2]

The following morning, however, two troops were called forward to help the infantry deal with SS infantry left behind in the ruins of the village and hedgerows following the withdrawal of the panzers. The squadron war diary noted:

On the next day 14 Tp (Lieut. Grundy) moved to mop up snipers in the area of RAURAY with 11 DLI – they were really small German parties which had succeeded in infiltrating through the British posns, in the general

A knocked-out Panther Ausf.A. The waffle-pattern Zimmerit anti-magnetic mine finish shows that it was probably built by Alkett in Berlin.

> German counter-attack which was going on at that time. The troop flamed a few hedgerows and flushed about five Germans.

The report on the operational use of the Crocodile records that in this type of operation the coaxially-mounted turret Besa machine gun was 'always' used in addition to flame and HE. With a heavy barrel, the Besa was able to sustain a high rate of fire that made it a very useful suppressive weapon in the Crocodile's arsenal when approaching to within flaming range.

The war diary entry for 2 July continued: 'Meanwhile 11 Tp in sp 1 Tyneside Scottish were moving up to the Start Line for a similar show when the Tp Comd's tank was hit and "brewed up" – three killed, Lt Benzecry and L/C Huzzey badly burned. It is believed that this was done by a British SP.' Fratricide has always been a factor in war, and on this occasion the large turret of the Churchill and the relatively long 75mm gun with an obvious muzzle brake may have been the cause. The war diary concluded that this incident 'emphasises the need for very careful tank recognition by the other arms (the MK VII has several recognition features formerly taught as being exclusive to German Tanks).' There was another factor: the older version of the commander's cupola had recently been replaced by one with a greatly enhanced set of eight periscopes providing all-round vision, but it was not dissimilar to the distinctive German cupola.

The loss of a Crocodile was a security problem for the regiment as the trailer and the composition of the flame fuel were still secret. Lieutenant Wilson, who was with D Squadron at Brécy, had taken to visiting the squadrons with Captain Drysdale, the regiment's REME officer. During one of these trips they were tasked to go forward and carry out a demolition of Lieutenant Benzecry's trailer:

> Wilson went up to the tank which was lying in an Orchard with an ugly charred hole in the driving compartment.
>
> 'I wouldn't look inside,' said Drysdale.
>
> They opened up the trailer, which for some reason hadn't caught fire, and packed it with slabs of guncotton against the flame fuel tanks. When it was ready, they finished the job the M10 had started.[3]

Major Duffy and C Squadron remained at Cristot under command of 8 Armoured Brigade until 6 July, ready to support 49th Division when necessary.

Operation WINDSOR: 4 July

The city of Caen that 3rd Division had planned to have captured on D-Day or shortly afterwards was still in the hands of I SS Panzer Corps, held by the now badly depleted 12th *Hitlerjugend* Panzer Division. *Obersturmbannführer* Mohnke's 26 SS *Panzergrenadiers* held positions to the west of the city around Carpiquet airfield and village, while 25 SS *Panzergrenadiers* was deployed around to the north of Caen.

Defenders of Caen: a signed photograph of Mohnke (right), his divisional commander Kurt 'Panzer' Meyer (centre), and *Sturmbannführer* Olboeter, commander of III/26 SS *Panzergrenadiers* (left).

The three troops of B Squadron that were not in action with the 3rd Division at Château le Landel had been due to support 7 Canadian Brigade in the capture of Carpiquet village and airfield in Operation OTTAWA. This, as one of the operations supporting EPSOM, had been cancelled due to pressure from the west by II SS Panzer Corps. The Carpiquet objectives were to be reinstated as Operation WINDSOR once Second Army was in a situation to be able to return to the offensive. In the meantime, B Squadron remained based at Cresserons with the Sherman flails of 22 Dragoons, but on 1 July four troops moved to Bretteville-l'Orgueilleuse for Operation WINDSOR.

Under command of General Keller's 3rd Canadian Division, they were to support the infantry of 8 Canadian Brigade in the attack on Carpiquet, possession of which was an essential prerequisite for the subsequent attack on Caen by I Corps. Once again, the Crocodiles had no specific role, but were in reserve for use by the assault infantry battalions in the event of difficulty. Major Sydney Spearpoint commanded 6 Troop (Lieutenant Mike Henderson) and 9 Troop (Lieutenant Peter Sanders) on the right, where the Royal Winnipeg Rifles (RWR), attached from the 7 Canadian Brigade, were to capture the airfield's southern hangars. On the left, Captain Ryle led 7 Troop (Lieutenant Beck) and 10 Troop (Lieutenant Mason), which were to be ready to assist the North Shore Regiment and *Le Régiment de la Chaudière* in their attack on the northern hangars and Carpiquet village respectively. Once these objectives were secure, the area of the control tower and barracks was to be captured by the Queen's Own Rifles of Canada.

Armour for the attack was provided by the Shermans of the Fort Garry Horse, the flails of 22 Dragoons and AVREs of 80 Assault Squadron RE. No fewer than twenty-one regiments of field and medium artillery regiments were to fire in support. In addition, there were the two 15in guns of the monitor HMS *Roberts* and the nine 16in guns of the battleship HMS *Rodney*. The latter fired fifteen broadsides at the airfield buildings and village at a range of some 26,000 yards during 3 July to soften up the *Hitlerjugend*'s defences. That was a total of 135 shells, each weighing 2,375lb.

Sheltering in the village and the pre-invasion concrete bunkers of the airfield defences were the 200 surviving soldiers of *Sturmbannführer* Krause's I Battalion 26th SS *Panzergrenadiers*. The 3rd Company held the village, while the 1st, 2nd and 4th (Heavy) companies held the airfield and the southern hangars and buildings. In among the infantry were a small number of panthers of 4th Panzer Company, while further back the five surviving Panzer IVs of 9th Company were deployed in the area of the barracks. Behind them were 88mm guns of the *Hitlerjugend*'s anti-aircraft battery. These guns were deployed in the anti-tank role.

The divisional commander *Oberführer* Kurt Meyer outlined the plan to defend the village, although possibly with a degree of hindsight:

> The defenders of Carpiquet no longer had any anti-tank weapons, as they had been destroyed several days earlier. There were, however, minefields to

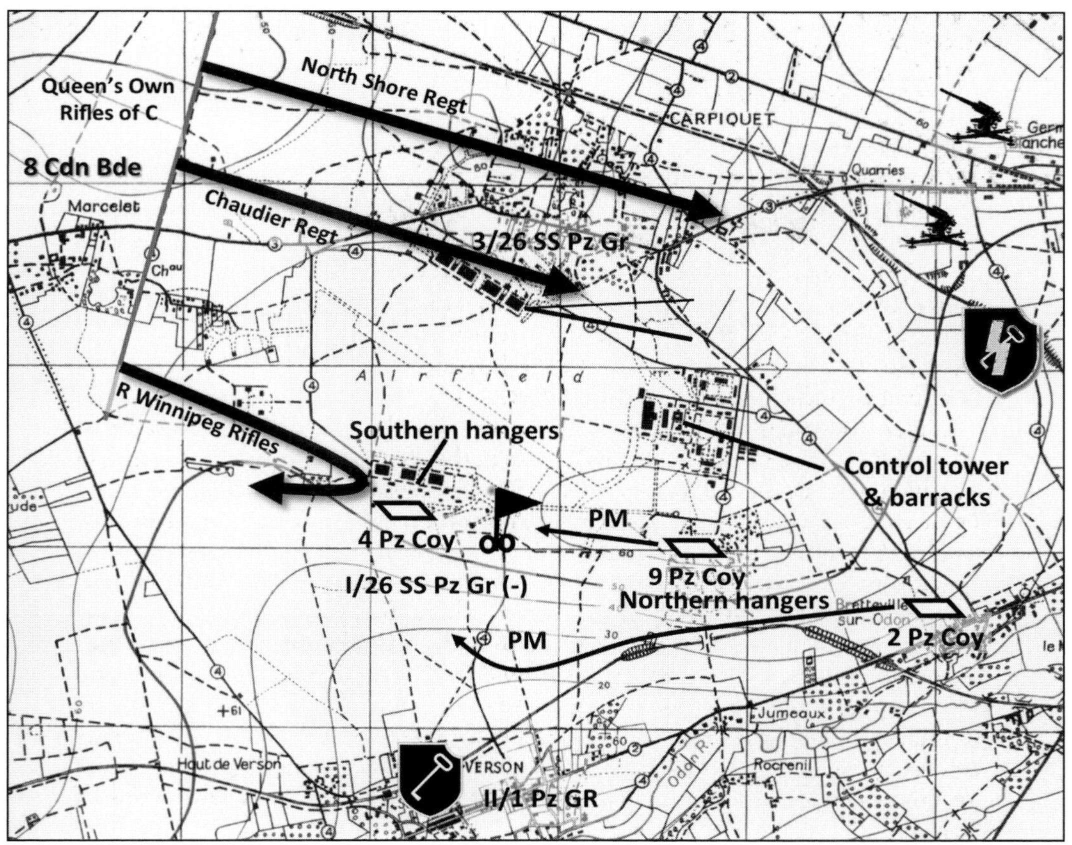

The Canadian attack on Carpiquet, 4 July 1944.

> the front of the village. The *Panzergrenadiers* were to tempt the enemy into the village and conduct a fighting withdrawal to the eastern edge where the 88mm guns were in ambush positions.[4]

The defenders were alerted to the imminence of the attack when they noted increasing enemy activity during 2/3 July and by the divisional radio intelligence section in eastern Caen. As was often the case, they intercepted a growing volume of Canadian radio chatter during the night of 3/4 July. Patrols also brought back information and finally, a member of the division who had been lying up in enemy territory since being overrun during EPSOM, brought back the location of Canadian assembly areas, which were promptly shelled.

The battle began at 0500 hours with the by now customary massive bombardment of known German locations and battery positions, with the young SS soldiers sheltering in their trenches or in the heavy concrete bunkers. Advancing behind the wall of exploding shells, the Canadians were able to close on the SS positions, but fighting through the fire-swept ground was another matter. On the left of the Canadian attack the main weight of two battalions fell on the SS 3rd Company in the village and a platoon of 1st Company in the northern hangars.

One of the concrete Carpiquet airfield bunkers being used by the Canadians after the attack.

Rather than sheltering behind the ridge at Marcelet in hull-down positions until needed, Captain Ryle's Crocodiles had been ordered to follow behind the infantry:

> So in the bright sunshine, naked as newborn babes, over the top they came. Fanned out in the flat cornfields and landing ground this side of Carpiquet. Where the mortars blossomed orange and the black plumes of earth shot skywards from the shells. Where the Messerschmitt played vulture overhead. They fanned out and waited tensely – a rendezvous with death.[5]

They did not have to wait long before they were called on to provide support to the *Chaudière* on the approaches to the northern hangars. Lieutenant Henderson's 6 Troop successfully flamed a pair of bunkers with a single Crocodile in a 'small action with no casualties'.

Next in action was 10 Troop supporting the North Shore's attack on Carpiquet village. However, thanks to bombing and shelling the ground was badly cratered and Lieutenant Mason, having crossed the railway line, possibly to outflank the village, became 'hopelessly bogged. Sergeant Vernon ditched his tank and could only extricate himself by jettisoning the trailer.'[6] Lieutenant Mason took over Sergeant Norrington's tank, taking with him the maps, leaving the sergeant unable to provide the squadron's ARV with a grid reference for recovery.[7]

Meanwhile, on the right Lieutenant Henderson was ordered forward to assist the Winnipeg Rifles:

> The infantry were held up just short of a bunker the other side of the St Manvieu-Caen Road. Mike bowled over with his troop, had a chat with the infantry captain some fifty yards away from the bunker. He decided that he could only get his own Croc on to it and went in giving the hot squirt for all he was worth. Whoever was in there didn't stand one earthly – ammunition went up inside and the whole thing was a blazing conflagration for hours.

The next call came to help clear the tenacious SS soldiers from the southern hangars:

> Another urgent call came over for flame on a hangar some 500 yards to the S.W. of this bunker and Sydney slipped the leash on Peter [Sander, 9 Troop] to go bull-headed for the object of his disaffection giving everything he had the whole way, 75mm, Besa, flame, his own revolver and a vocabulary as voluble as it was extensive ... The rest of the Squadron forgot the battle and turned in their cupolas to watch this fire-raising display by Peter and Sgt Decent – Sgt Decent of course was not to be outdone in ferocity, not even by Peter. Not satisfied with brewing it up from the front they brewed it up on both sides – by the fortune of heaven they did not go round the back where, all unknown then there lurked a dirty 88.

On the left, Lieutenant Beck's Crocodiles were in action successfully flaming SS infantry positions dug into the railway embankment north of the village. Meanwhile, with Carpiquet having been cleared, the infantry continued following the barrage:

> A nearby Sherman suddenly spied a nest of Germans in a quarry by the Caen-Bayeux road, which said monstrosities showed unmistakable signs of vicious life now that our infantry on the tail of the barrage had swept on. The Sherman asked [Captain] Nigel [Ryle] to 'fix em' ... There were no infantry so Beck with 7 Troop just went in without support. He poked his own nose in the quarry and gave them hell, burning some and flushing more as target practice for the other tanks.

As described in the squadron's war diary:

> On the left 7 Tp (Lt. Beck) then went into action flaming trenches and dugouts in the Quarry at 966701. Lieut Beck unfortunately went right into

Carpiquet airfield before the attack, having at this stage 'only been lightly shelled'.

> the Quarry and could not extricate his tank. An AP shot pierced the link and set the trailer on fire, whereupon the crew were evacuated from the tank by another tank from the Tp. Casualties: One Offr (Lieut Beck) and a gunner badly burned.[8]

Lieutenant Beck 'was in a pretty hot strong-point with no infantry to clear it and unable to do a thing', being unable to turn tank and trailer. In an attempt to escape from the quarry he had Sergeant Brandi fire 75mm armour-piercing shot at the link with his trailer. Captain Bailey provides more detail, commenting that:

> Crocs are tricky things and they didn't shut off the Hopkinson Valve. The first shot made a hole straight through the neck and in a split second the whole issue was covered in blazing fuel, pressure fed. The heat was so intense that there was no alternative but to bail out, Germans or no Germans. The co-driver Bards looked out through the pannier door, saw the flames, decided it was impossible to get out that way and hopped it straight through the hatch. Simpson the driver looked out through the hatch, saw the flames, decided it was impossible to get out that way and hopped it straight through the pannier door. In the turret Davenport with his usual sangfroid waited till everyone was out, picked up his pipes, coolly traversed the turret to reach the driving compartment and through the pannier door made an

The Hopkinson valve was protected by the steel casing of the elbow joint.

> 'exit' . . . Sgt Brandi dashed in to collect the crew whilst Sgt Maddock gave them covering fire.

'At this point,' the war diary noted, 'the real fun started' again on the left with further SS infantry that had been bypassed by the Canadian infantry. Captain Ryle, aboard 'Standard', a Mk V Churchill mounting a 95mm gun, was watching his half-squadron to the east of Carpiquet village 'and letting off the occasional round' when

> He glanced casually down from his cupola over the side and saw a German some ten yards away drawing a bead with his rifle, just on his first pressure in fact to take a pot right at Nigel's head . . . He popped down momentarily in the turret and [was heard] on the 'A' [radio set]. 'Give the bastard the f****** 95.'

Having blown the SS rifleman apart at a range of 10 yards, 'The next minute all hell was let loose around Captain Ryle's tank':

> Nigel suddenly discovered that he was sitting right in the middle of a well-camouflaged company position left almost untouched by the advance. Literally dozens of Germans sprung out of concealment in the long grass. They stalked his tank, climbed on his tank, did everything except knock it out. Bloodthirsty Mulvaney, his gunner, followed up his 95mm with a Besa burst of 50 [rounds] which began on a Hun's backside and crept up the body which was found later in two clean halves. The Shermans joined in and shot

Captain Bailey's sketch of the Operation WINDSOR action. Captain Ryle in his tank 'Standard' is portrayed shooting a German off the back of his tank, while body parts fly across the battlefield.

> them down [and Lieutenant Colonel] Waddell joined in ... 'Shoot the ruddy bastards down Sgt Dallman, shoot the bastards down.' Nigel performed feats of agility. With one hand he was dealing with Germans on the engine deck, with the other holding the microphone and yelling to Sydney [Spearpoint] for assistance, forgot to switch over and exhorted Mulvaney on the 'A' set to 'Give the buggers hell.' About twenty-five were accounted for by Besa fire alone.

The personal weapon of the Crocodile's three-man turret crew was the .38 Enfield pistol, as shown in Harry Bailey's sketch of the action. Also stored in the turret of the Mk VII were nine No. 36 grenades for keeping the enemy at bay in similar circumstances. The squadron war diary adds some further detail:

> A hectic session ensued under the auspices of Capt Ryle with 7, 6 and 10 Tps called in one by one to assist. The Germans were so close that the turrets could not be rotated quickly enough. Nevertheless, Besa fire accounted for about twenty-five of these ... Capt Ryle appealed strongly for infantry, one coy would have seen the whole posn cleared up, but none were available.

On the left flank the Canadians had taken the northern hangars and the village, but the 88mm guns and the arrival of I SS Panzer Corps reserve, a battalion of the *Leibstandarte* which deployed in the barrack area, prevented exploitation by the

Queen's Own Rifles of Canada. On the right, despite a good start the Winnipeg Rifles had not taken the southern hangars and a final attempt at 1600 hours with Major Spearpoint's Crocodiles in support failed when reserve panthers and Panzer IVs arrived to throw the Canadians back. General Keller's failure to take these hangars and the high ground to the south of the airfield that overlooked the Odon valley and Hill 112 has been much criticized as it limited the options, as did MITTEN, for the attack on Caen that I Corps was preparing.

> The day's work was not yet quite complete. Over on the right one Canadian Battalion was having a sticky time in one particular spot, and it was decided to give them an indirect shoot [with HE] from the northern part of the ridge.

The Enfield .38 revolver, personal weapon of the turret crews, and the Sten gun was issued to Crocodile drivers and flame gunners.

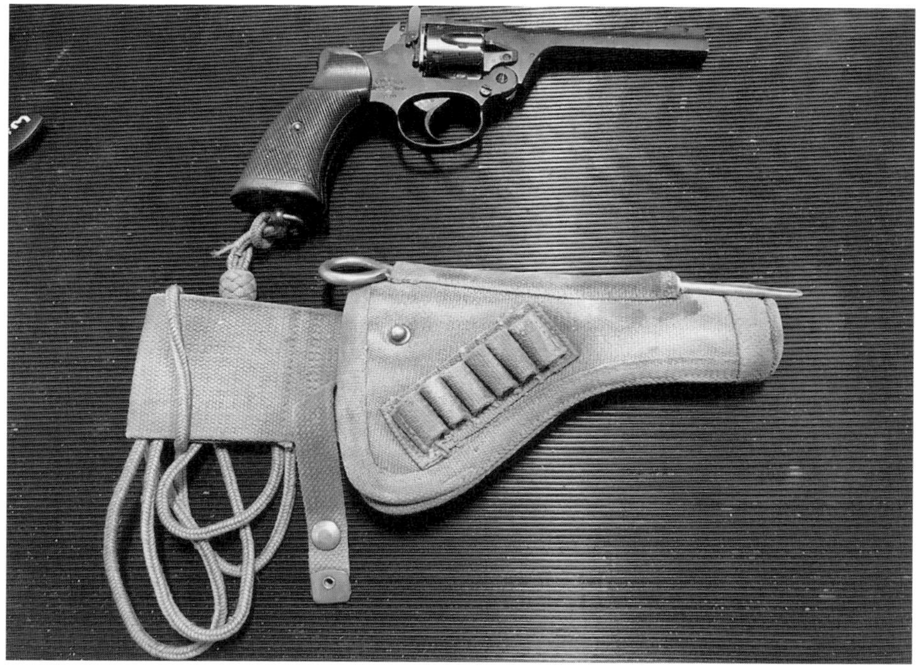

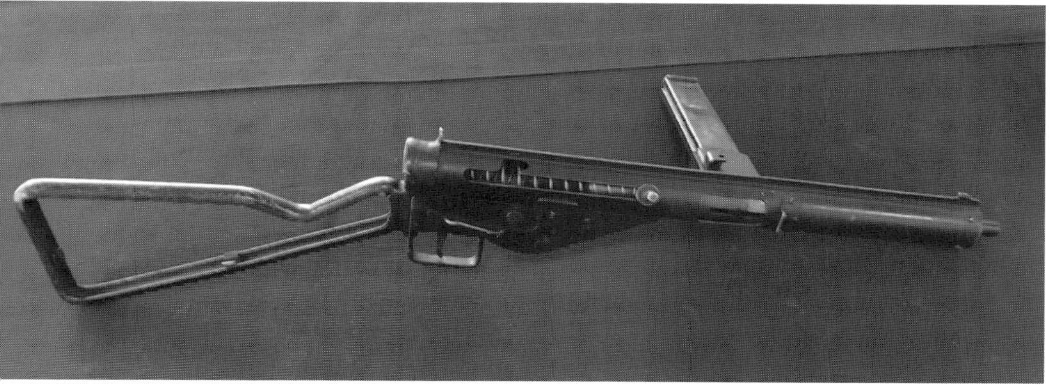

> Rapid calculations with protractors and landmarks for range and direction. Then all opened up together. Out of the setting sun Mike [Henderson, 6 Troop] was bowling a good length ball and keeping it up – some of the best airbursts ever seen. And on this note Carpiquet ended for the Crocs.

The war diary concluded: 'The Sqn harboured the night at NORRY EN BESSIN 927707 and was released next morning from the operation, returning to CRESSERONS at 052802 but not for long.'

Operation CHARNWOOD: 8–9 July 1944

A month after D-Day Caen was still not in Allied hands and criticism of Montgomery's conduct of the campaign was mounting in Eisenhower's headquarters and the American press, even though the city had lost much of its significance. It did, however, need to be in Allied possession if the ground south to Falaise was to be exploited.

The task allocated to I Corps was to clear Caen of its German defenders, and importantly to seize the bridges across the Orne in the southern part of the city before the Germans could blow them. To achieve this and deliver much-needed ground for the army's growing infrastructure and the RAF's airfields, Lieutenant General Crocker had under his command three infantry divisions, each with an armoured or a tank brigade to deliver the assault.

Defending Caen against 120,000 Allied soldiers were just two weak German divisions. Of the now greatly reduced *Hitlerjugend*, 25 SS *Panzergrenadiers* stood in the path of the 3rd Canadian Division and a brigade of the 59th (Staffordshire) Division. To the *HJ*'s right was the newly-arrived 16th Luftwaffe Field Division, which had finally relieved elements of the 21st Panzer Division. They were to be attacked by another brigade of the 59th and the 3rd British Division. Holding the Carpiquet barracks to the west of the city was 1 SS *Panzergrenadier* Regiment of the *Leibstandarte*. The defenders may have been few in number, but their positions were well-developed as much of the front had been static since the aftermath of D-Day. Due to the loss of nearly all the *HJ*'s towed anti-tank guns to Allied artillery, half the sixty-one Panzer IVs and Panthers of 12 SS Panzer Regiment were dug in forward alongside the trench systems.

As General Eisenhower was increasingly concerned about 21st Army Group's lack of progress, it did not take much persuasion for Montgomery to secure the full support of Bomber Command in a heavy bomber raid on the northern suburbs of the city. As dusk fell on 7 July, 457 aircraft dropped 2,363 tons of bombs on Caen.[9] Following the Lancasters were the medium bombers and rocket-firing Typhoons, but much of the ordnance fell too far south and the level of destruction wrought on the city was terrible. Meanwhile, however, the Allied artillery including naval gunfire was falling on the outlying villages still held by the Germans.

The effect of the aerial firepower has been hotly debated. With the majority of the bombs falling just to the north of the city centre rather than on the northern

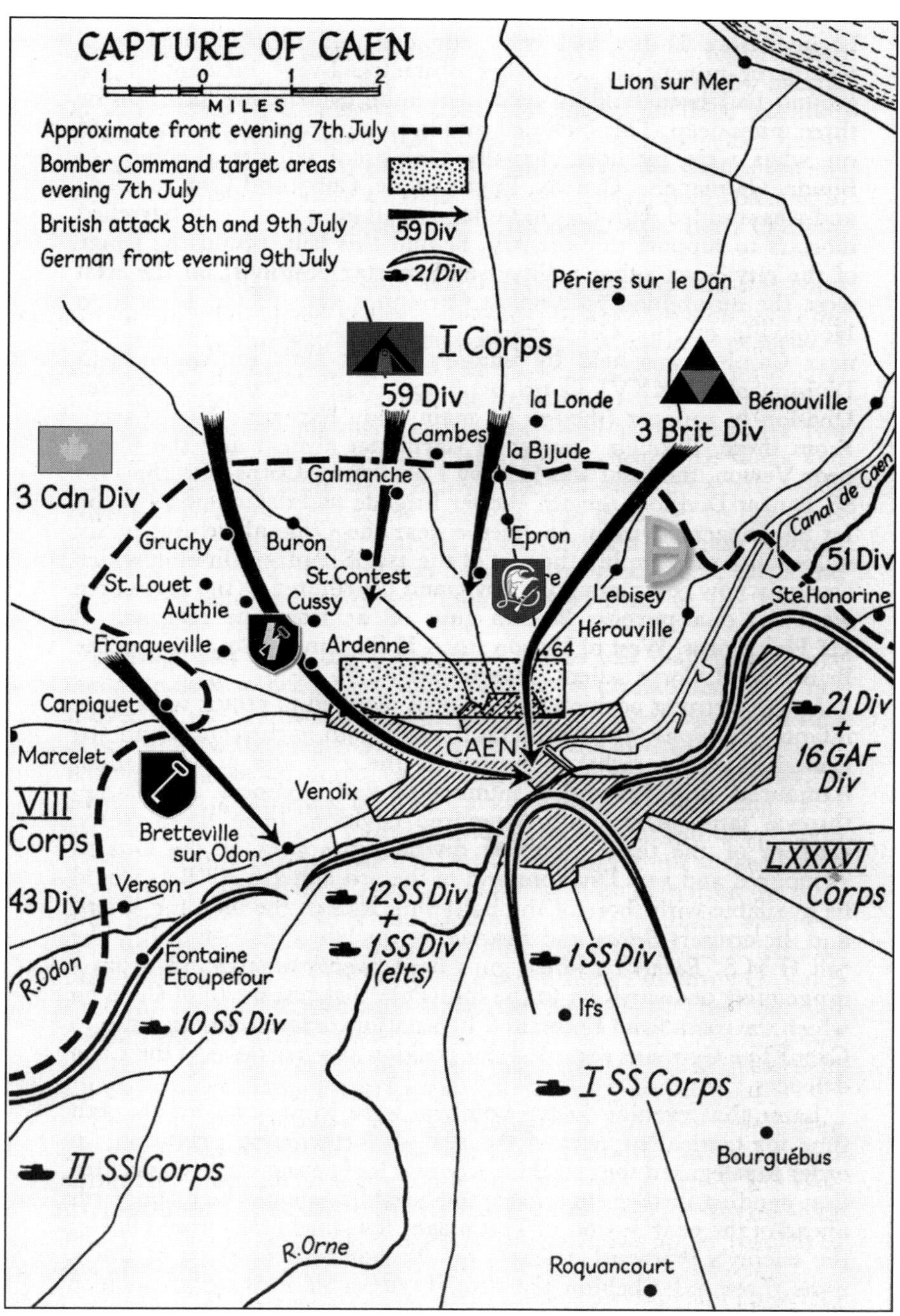

The battle for Caen.

Panzergrenadiers watch the bombing of Caen from the Ardenne Abbey.

extremity as intended, there were few casualties among the defenders. Two of the *Hitlerjugend*'s Panzers were hit and another two turned over, while further back in reserve, III Battalion 26 *Panzergrenadiers* suffered only seven casualties, but the Divisional Escort Company was more seriously hit. The only other casualties were a handful of logistic units passing through the city at the time. *Oberführer* Kurt Meyer, whose headquarters was located in a 'barracks' inside the medieval castle just north of the city centre, summed up the impact on the division:[10] 'The front line was so sparsely manned that a bomber attack couldn't cause much damage. Two thousand five hundred tons of bombs had merely succeeded in overturning a few SPW [half-tracks].'

The Crocodiles were on the move to the FUP at 0400 hours and at 0420 hours, ninety minutes before sunrise, a bombardment by 632 guns opened with 'artillery fire of unimaginable intensity'. Kurt Meyer continued describing how shells:

> from both the land and the sea fell on our front line. The divisional headquarters cellar shook, and plaster and dust fell on the candlelit map table. Our artillery and mortar batteries laid down final protective fires. We had been procuring ammunition for days and were trying to give it to our heavily engaged infantry. Fighter-bombers were diving down on our artillery batteries and attacking every vehicle they could see.

The 3rd and 59th divisions advanced behind the curtain of exploding shells, while the Canadians waited for the second phase before attacking from the west. Major Spearpoint was, however, not happy with the deployment of the four troops of

An RAF aircraft photographed during the bombing of Caen on the evening of 7 July 1944.

B Squadron: despite protests, they had been penny-packeted out to various brigades, in each case being held as a reserve as follows:

- 6 Troop: Lieutenant Moss – 3rd Division. Objective Lebisey.
- 8 Troop: Captain Dean and Lieutenant Beechey – 176 Brigade, 59th Division.
- 9 Troop: Major Spearpoint and Lieutenant Sanders – 197 Brigade, 59th Division.
- 10 Troop: Captain Ryle – 7 Canadian Brigade, 3rd Canadian Division.

On the left 3rd Division captured Lebisey from 16th Luftwaffe Field Division and pressed on towards Hérouville and the ridge overlooking Caen. Consequently, 6 Troop was not called on, but the 59th Division faced much sterner opposition in the form of I and II Battalions, 25 SS *Panzergrenadier* Regiment. Fighting their way past Galmanche, 197 Brigade pressed on towards St. Contest but also without calling on 9 Troop. On the left, 176 Brigade and 13/18 Hussars had by 1045 hours failed to capture La Bijude, thanks to determined resistance by the SS *Panzergrenadiers* in the village and surrounding trenches. Captain Bailey wrote:

> The infantry had got no further than the forward edge of Cambes. After enormous casualties from mortaring and shelling they ran straight into heavy fire from an extensive trench system of some 200 yards, strongly and fanatically held across the open fields just west of La Bijude and south of Cambes.

In the resulting conference at headquarters 176 Brigade:

> It was seriously suggested (and agreed to by Comd of a Sqn of 13/18 Hussars of which 8 Tp were under Comd) that the posn be attacked by 8 Tp alone supported by sixteen infantry personnel. The wiser counsels of Capt Dean fortunately prevailed. He pointed out that the posn demanded at least an infantry battalion and that the enemy anti-tank situation was most dubious.

Captain Dean argued that to 'put the Crocodiles in without adequate infantry to kill the enemy and occupy the ground was merely to risk the Crocodiles to no purpose whatsoever'. This was a sound assertion summed up by the credo 'No infantry, no show'. Even so, Captain Dean had to radio for Colonel Waddell to drive over from 9 Troop to clinch the argument with the 59th Division in what was their first acquaintance with Crocodiles.

With Colonel Waddell present, a better plan was produced by the commanding officer of 7 Norfolks and approved by the brigade commander. The

A Panzer IV dug into a hull-down position. The *schurzen* 'bazooka plates' surrounding the turret and the long gun barrel with a prominent muzzle brake led to numerous misidentifications as Tigers.

battalion's reserve company and a 13/18 Hussars' squadron of Shermans along with 8 Troop's Crocodiles were to advance on La Bijude from the north and from the area of the Château de la Londe. Fire support was to be provided by the Hussars and by the 95mm gun of Captain Dean's command tank. H-Hour was at 1400 hours:

> 8 Tp crossed the Start Line (East of Rly Line at 023737) sp by the fire of 13/18 Hussars. Almost immediately Cpl Hischier's Crocodile lost a bogey assembly from a German 'Bazooka' and was then penetrated by a 75mm through the flame gun ball mounting. The tank brewed up with two killed and three badly burned. Right from the start Lt. Beechey could only get unignited [flame fuel] shots from his gun and shortly afterwards had his gear-box compartment penetrated by a 75mm which almost completely dislocated his steering. Nevertheless, moving in wide circles, he continued to give fire support and direct his Tp Sgt. Shortly afterwards the Sgt's pressure failed and he came out of action. To crown everything the infantry had not followed up the attack.

Lance Corporal Roberts and Trooper Pitt in the hull of Corporal Hischier's Crocodile were killed outright, but the turret crew 'lay doggo for a time then, very badly burned, managed to crawl to an RAP'. With the ignition system of his flame projector not working, Beechey had fired wet shots which had been ignited by his troop sergeant until he was hit. Then, having evacuated his tank, he used a CO2 bottle to put out the fire and alone climbed back into the immobilized Crocodile to provide fire support. His was not the only tank with mechanical problems this time in the flame system: 'Sgt. Decent's pressure gone – these were the early days when Crocs were just about as constant as fickle womankind but making up for it with Besa, which he liberally applied.' The war diary continued: 'At this moment 9 Tp (Lt. Sanders) [and Major Spearpoint], tardily released from its Bde [197 Brigade], appeared':

> Without any knowledge of the ground or plan the tp rushed into action. The flaming was magnificent – never before had such a colossal 'rod' appeared as that which now issued forth from Lt. Sanders tk. HE and Besa liberally applied also helped and this time the infantry went on and through the enemy posn.

The lessons of the day's fighting were that without infantry support, closing to flaming range was extremely dangerous and that penny-packeting wasted the full effect of massed flame that could have made all the difference to the 59th Division. Just three Crocodiles were an easy target for the still plentiful Pak 40 anti-tank guns of the 16th Luftwaffe Field Division and without the timely arrival of 9 Troop the attack on La Bijude would have failed.

With the enemy pushed back from La Bijude, B Squadron could look to recovering Lieutenant Beechey's Crocodile and Corporal Hischier's trailer that

A dug-in Pak 40 manned by an SS gun crew wearing oak-leaf pattern smocks and helmet covers.

had not burned with the rest of the tank. Captain Dean set out on foot with Sergeant Rowe:

> Except for the light from three burning tanks which necessitated them crawling, it was now completely dark. Then, on answering a call from a wounded man, Capt Dean released an 's' mine and died shortly afterwards . . . Before he died Sgt Rowe first attempted to lift him, then went back and brought up the tank. As the crew dismounted, however, the silhouetted tk brought down such a hail of mortars that Sgt Rowe decided to take it back and try another effort on foot. Lt Beechey now took charge of the party and set off once again, and then he too making his way towards a wounded soldier stepped on a mine and received severe leg injuries. No RAP could be found nearby but he himself, carried on a tank, directed the crew with great fortitude to an RAP some miles back. He died the next day, a brave officer. If it accomplished nothing more, this unfortunate episode showed how vital it was from an admin point of view not to split up a Sqn into small fragments because we cannot rely on the inf to be able always to deal with our casualties.

By the end of 8 July, the three assault divisions of I Corps had made significant advances, particularly 3rd Division, and were closing in on the defenders. Overnight on the 8th/9th the *Hitlerjugend* were ordered to withdraw into the suburbs of Caen south of the River Orne. The following day the three Allied divisions completed their advance through the rubble of the city and with the defenders gone did not need the services of B Squadron, which returned to Cresson where they remained until 16 July.

Chapter Six

The Bocage

Following the capture of Caen, the campaign in Normandy was entering a new phase as German infantry divisions started to arrive from further afield.[1] The enemy's aim was to extract the panzer divisions from costly line-holding deployments in order to form an operational reserve. This they were starting to do, and were also beginning to transfer armoured formations west to confront the US First Army. Therefore Montgomery needed to redouble his efforts to draw the Panzer divisions east and fix them there. To this end, he directed the Second British Army to 'immediately operate strongly in a southerly direction, with its left flank on the Orne.' The army objective was a line from Thury-Harcourt via Mont Pinçon to Le Bény-Bocage.

As far as 141 Regiment RAC was concerned, while the rest of the regiment was fighting on the plains around Caen, to the west C Squadron was involved in a very different set of actions. They were under command of the desert and Mediterranean veterans of 50th (Northumbrian) Division on the right flank of the Second British Army around the village of Granville.[2] For Major Duffy's squadron, now in the thick bocage country south-west of Bayeux, the fighting was of a very different character amid the hedgerows and orchards.

The bocage country in this area was a maze of small irregular-shaped fields, most being less than 100 yards wide. They were surrounded by thick embanked hedges, with the knotted roots and stone of the bank providing protection from fire and an effective obstacle to movement. The whole area was laced with narrow sunken tracks and country roads that were barely wide enough for a tank and were invariably covered by fire. To carve a route across country for 1,000 yards invariably involved breaking through ten or more hedges.

Fighting in the bocage was almost always at close quarters, sometimes very close. The *Official History* summarizes the essence of the problem:

> The enemy's small infantry detachments, each with a tank or anti-tank gun or two and a couple of 'eighty-eights' lurking in the background, were able to cause considerable delays by skilfully exploiting the close country. Some, hidden in the hedgerows, tried to lob grenades into the tanks' turrets or to fix 'sticky' bombs on them as they moved through the deep lanes.[3] Fortunately ... their bombs were not lethal enough to cause major damage, but it was clear that our tanks must have infantry to work with them.

The desert campaigns had a considerable influence on British armoured tactics. In the bocage country it was clear that very close infantry support was required.

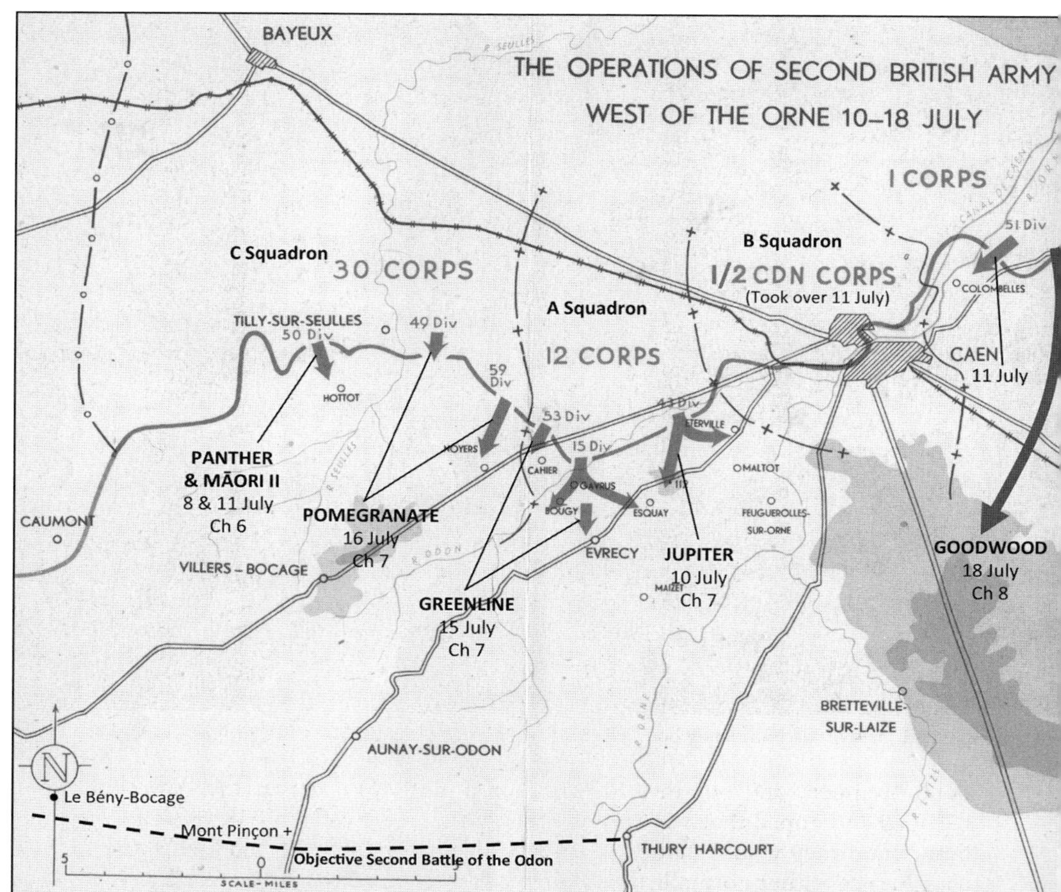

The operations of the Second British Army west of the Orne, 10–18 July. 'Some days must elapse while troops were being regrouped for these twin attacks [US attack towards St. Lo and the British Operation GOODWOOD], and meanwhile the pot was to be kept boiling by a limited action to hold the enemy armour in the east and to round off the ground won in the Epsom battle …' [Author's emphasis] (Essame, *The 43rd Wessex Division at War*).

It wasn't just the terrain that inhibited the advance, as explained by a veteran tank gunner of 4th County of London Yeomanry, Trooper Leslie Dinning:

> Poke your nose round corners and sitting a few yards up the road was a bloody big Tiger, Panther or a self-propelled gun, literally waiting for you and BANG! You had no chance. It only needed one shot from an enemy tank or SP, whereas we had to put multiple shots in the side or the rear of the Tigers or Panthers. We hadn't a hope in hell of penetrating the front of a Tiger with a [lowish-velocity] 75mm gun.

For the infantryman the experience of fighting at close ranges was equally intense, as explained by Rifleman O'Rourke who recalled:

> We'd break cover from a hedgerow, which we'd bashed our way through avoiding gates if the enemy were around as they'd probably be mined or

An oblique view of the Normandy bocage: a patchwork of small fields divided by hedges and banks.

> booby-trapped, and out into the next small field. We hardly ever saw a German and hoped they were not waiting in the hedge only 100 yards away. Sometimes they would shoot as we broke through the hedges, and we'd go back into cover but normally they waited until we were out in the middle and then opened fire with their Spandaus. The NCOs had smoke grenades [white phosphorus] which made an instant cloud and we would drag our casualties back and thank our lucky stars we had survived.

The battle in the bocage had begun with a drive south from Bayeux on D+2 by XXX Corps, but a meeting engagement with the powerful Panzer *Lehr* Division north of Tilly-sur-Seulles brought the advance to a halt. Since then, 50th Division had fought amid the hedgerows, latterly against the newly-arrived 276th Infantry Division[4] and the supporting tanks of Lieutenant General Freiherr (Baron) von Lüttwitz's 2nd *Wien* Panzer Division. At the western end of the divisional area, they were proving to be redoubtable opponents to the battalions of 56 Infantry Brigade. In a report on his operations up to 14 July, von Lüttwitz made it clear that his men were also used to fighting in open country and were struggling with the bocage as well:

> The country in which the fighting is taking place consists of meadow and brush land enclosed squarely by hedges, with embankments and sunken roads. This does not lend itself to engagements over large areas. All engagements soon resolve themselves into shock-troop and individual engagements. The possession of 'dominating heights' is often not as decisive as

the possession of traffic junctions. Often, the former cannot be exploited because hedges and trees limit visibility and field of fire, whereas road traffic arteries are essential since it is only by roads that the heavier weapons, artillery and tanks can be brought forward. Nevertheless, certain features always retain their dominating role, whereas, conversely, some traffic junctions can be dispensed with.[5]

After four days in reserve to 49th Division at Cristot, on 6 July two troops of C Squadron were summoned to La Senaudière in order to support 56 Brigade, to whom they were attached for most of the following week. The squadron's other two troops were warned for different operations. Thus once again the Crocodiles were farmed out in penny packets; this was especially bad as the troops could each muster only two Crocodiles. However, Major Duffy and Captain Hall had four command/support tanks between them. The fighting in which Captain Hall's troops were to be involved ranged from small local actions to a full-scale brigade attack, which the regiment's report on the analysis of action described as 'Well-planned and carried out. Inf followed up well. Tank support good. Small operations showing how Crocodiles can be invaluable to Inf (50 Div).' For Major Duffy, in the view of Captain Bailey:

. . . perhaps it was the most dis-satisfying time of all. True, 'C' Squadron was to get a number of shows but almost without exception these were small

The Panther – a dangerous opponent in the bocage country.

> affairs of very little account, a drain on men and equipment for little gain either in tactical experience or profit to the infantry.

In the forthcoming operation on the right flank of the Second British Army, Major Duffy was acting as little more than a troop leader. The report continued:

> They were of course unfortunate in being on the west where the country was just sheer hell for tanks – ditches, banks and woods. How much more so for the Crocodile with its delicate trailer. Not once but many times was the trailer suspended in mid-air as the Mk VII mounted a bank.

Crossing banks was one of the major contributory factors to damage to the Crocodile's flame system, as to get into action the driver had to ignore the warning lights that towing tolerances had been exceeded.

Operation PANTHER

On 7 July Major Duffy and Captain Hall joined the throng of officers heading to battalion headquarters of 2 Essex and 2nd South Wales Borderers (2 SWB). The intelligence officer of the Essex wrote that the 7th was 'a day of preparation for big battle. Stream of visitors of various sp arms all day as attack was laid on at very short notice. Orders to sp arms 1200 hrs.'

In addition to a troop of Crocodiles each, both the Essex and 2 SWB were to be well supported. They each were allocated a squadron of Shermans from 4th/7th Dragoon Guards (4/7 DG), but without the hedgerow-cutters that were being developed by the US Army, help through the hedges was to be provided by D7 armoured bulldozers and a troop of AVREs. Also from 79th Armoured Division were flail tanks, which were to work alongside a company of the divisional engineers to clear German mines. From within 50th Division there were self-propelled M10 tank destroyers and heavy mortars. In addition, medium guns of an AGRA were on call. It can be readily appreciated that the two Crocodiles allocated to each assault battalion were a small part of a fully supported battlegroup in the attack. It is, therefore, not surprising that commanding officers, who had extensively trained with other supporting arms prior to the invasion, were slow to learn the characteristics of the Crocodile and how to use them to best effect: 'Major Duffy with 11 Tp moved into the area 7565 [La Butte] where he remained all day prepared to assist the 2 SWB. Capt Hall with 13 Tp (Lieut Sherman 'rides again') moved to a RV at 765684 in sp of 2 Essex.'

Captain Bailey recorded 'a strange coincidence' and that was that 2 Essex 'had been flamed in Tilly by the Boche and had suffered very heavy casualties' at Essex Wood near Verrières. It had been a night attack by Panzer *Lehr*'s flame-throwers mounted in Sd.Kfz.251 Hanomag half-tracks. 'One company commander in fact had been so horrified that he refused to utilise the Crocodiles, but another was very much intent on giving back the same medicine in stronger dose.'[6] It would seem that by the end of the operation the whole battalion had put scruples aside and was grateful for the help provided by the Crocodiles.

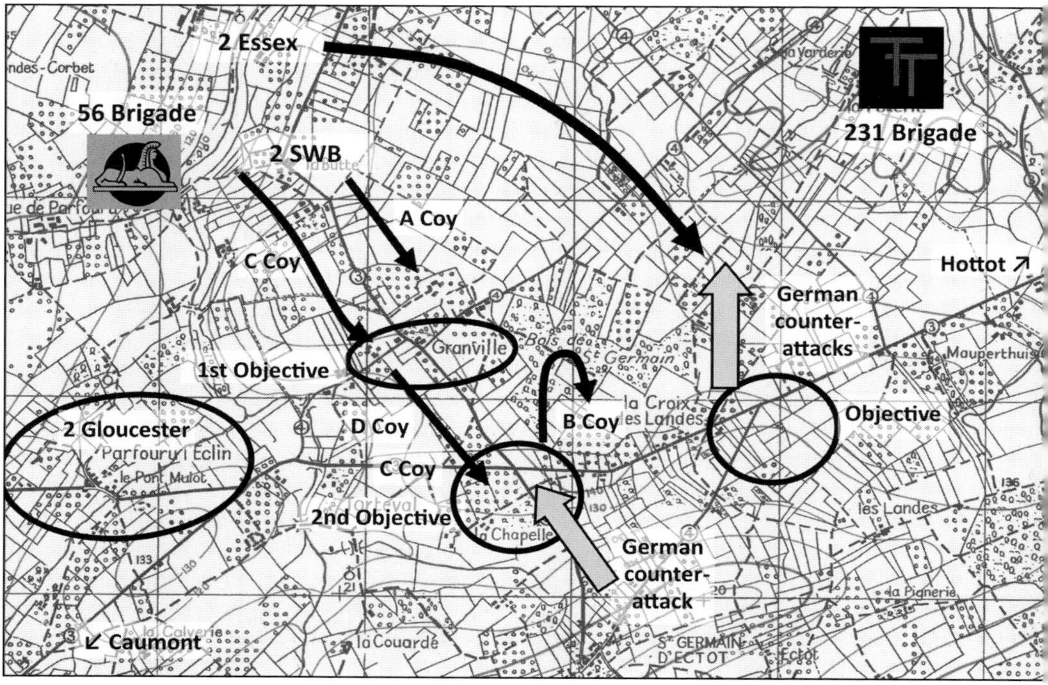

Operation PANTHER.

The German Sd.Kfz.251/16 Ausf.D *Flammpanzerwagen*, an unpopular and ineffective weapon system.

The attack on the morning of 8 July got under way with the infantry slipping through the hedgerows surrounding fields, which in some cases were recorded as being 'little bigger than a tennis court'. However, the armour, waiting for the D7 bulldozers to carve a way through, was soon lagging behind. On the far right of the attack, C Company 2 SWB was doing well, and having reached the village of Granville, continued the advance, but machine-gun fire from the Bois de St. Germaine had brought A Company to a halt. This wooded area in the centre of the attack was believed by Brigadier Ekin to be unoccupied by the enemy, but at the insistence of Colonel Elliot of 2 Essex he allowed one platoon of C Company to be diverted to secure it. Inevitably they found this ideally placed wood, from the defenders' perspective, full of Germans, effectively separating 2 Essex on the left from 2 SWB.

Up to this point 2 Essex had been making reasonable progress, with the leading company having reached the battalion's third objective. A head-on encounter with the Germans who were intending to attack at midday was narrowly averted. Their plan with three battalions of 276th Infantry Division supported by Panzer IVs was to attack east of the Bois de St. Germaine, but fortunately the Essex spotted a build-up of enemy movement. Colonel Elliot pulled a company back to form a defensive line just in time to avoid a bombardment that fell on the position they had just vacated. The two Crocodiles of 13 Troop were now in action alongside the Essex in a close-quarter battle during the afternoon and evening against at least two enemy battalions. The A Squadron war diary reads:

> Capt Hall with 13 Tp (Lieut Sherman 'rides again') moved to a RV at 765648 in sp of 2 Essex from which place they were soon driven out by shelling. However, somewhat later in the day (at 1300 and 2015 hrs) 13 Tp flamed out M.G. post as 775646. Again Germans fled.

On the other flank Major Duffy with 11 Troop had moved forward to La Butte 'where he remained all day prepared to assist the 2 SWB.' This battalion had, however, reached its final objective, but now that 56 Brigade realized that the Bois de St. Germaine was occupied, it was ordered to attack the wood from the south, but was driven back.

On the following day, the 9th, the close-quarter defensive battle on 2 Essex's front continued with repeated German attacks and infiltration: 'On four occasions [Lieutenant] Shearman flamed up MG posts, killing quite a number of Germans with flame and Besa, routing others and "persuading" some to take the line to Div PW Cage.' It was in one of these small actions, which broke up a German company counter-attack, that a wireless intercept was picked up in which the German company commander was appealing for help: 'The *Flammenwerfer* are here and if help did not come immediately all was lost.' With the Essex dug in and the Germans out in the open, subject not just to flame but artillery and small arms as well, despite their strength the Germans were forced back. Neither side had sufficient combat power to prevail, despite 276th Infantry Division

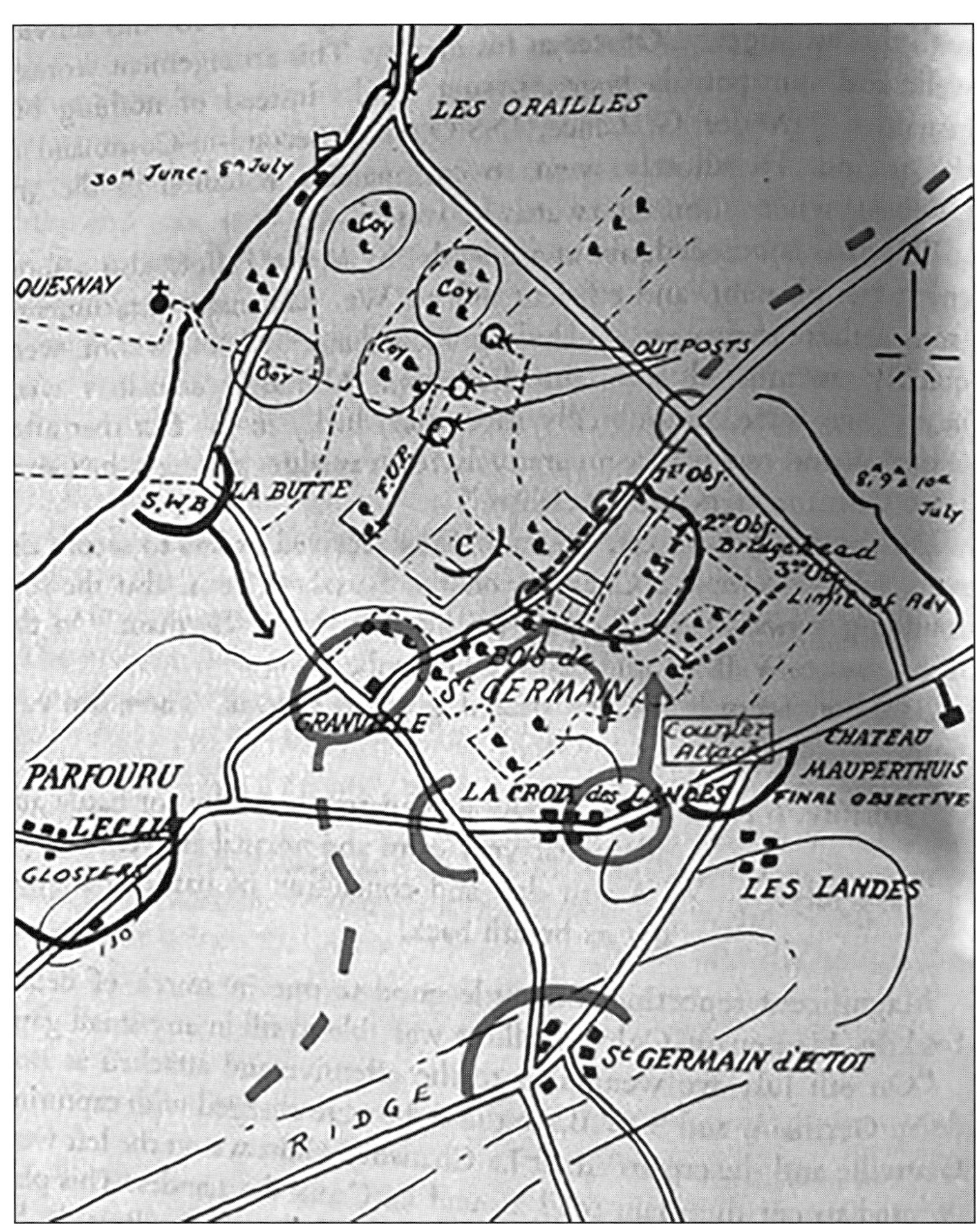

A map from Essex Regiment's history showing their fighting during July up to Operation PANTHER on 8–9 July.

employing a force ratio that suggests they should have won. For 141 the fight was not without cost:

> The whole affair concluded with a bang; a 'Bazooka' on Shearman's mantlet which temporarily stopped the engine, stopped the wireless and jammed the gun ... Desperate and repeated pressure on the starter motor accompanied by prayers to all the Saints at last produced results and no casualties were suffered.

Both the Crocodiles and the command tank involved in this close-quarter action amid the bocage were 'holed' by *Panzerfausts*, but none of them were knocked out. The Essex Regiment's historian concluded that 'Except for a few patrols that tried to probe for weak places the battle was over. Our casualties were not light but those of the enemy must have been extraordinary, including 100 prisoners.'

The *Panzerfaust*

In the bocage, where engagements were normally at short range, the hand-held *Panzerfaust* anti-tank weapon in the hands of committed German infantry was highly effective and no doubt contributed to keeping the Crocodiles from closing with the enemy.

By 1941 it was realized by the warring armies that the anti-tank rifle was now obsolete due to tanks having thicker sloped armour. This was highlighted during Operation CRUSADER in November/December 1941 in the Western Desert. A post-combat report conducted by the British Army showed that of the 1,700 Axis armoured vehicles destroyed, virtually none were the result of anti-tank rifle fire!

The *Panzerfaust* ('Tank-fist') was the first infantry anti-tank weapon to combine the principle of a recoilless weapon with that of a rocket, using these principles to

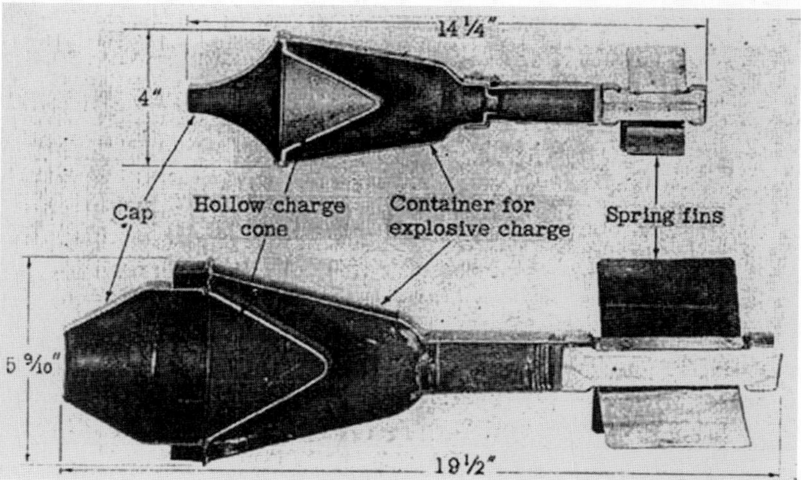

A diagram of the *Panzerfaust*'s warhead.

project a hollow-charge bomb using the Munroe effect to burn a hole through armour plate.

The four models of *Panzerfaust* broadly followed the same basic layout and operation, named the 30, 60 and 100 indicating their maximum range. The oversized projectile contained a hollow-charge warhead containing a shaped charge with a cone-shaped copper lining, which on detonation produced a self-forging fragment of molten metal that bored its way through armour plate. Behind this was a tail tube that fitted into the launcher tube. Around the tail tube were wrapped four tail fins. These deployed when leaving the launch tube to stabilize the projectile in flight. The launch tube was discarded after firing.

In the case of the 30m (*Klein*), the charge contained 0.4g of explosive. This gave a penetration of up to 140mm of armour at 30 degrees from the vertical. The 30m (*Gross*), 60m and 100m all contained 0.8g, giving a penetration of up to 200mm. This compared favourably with German heavy anti-tank guns of the period.

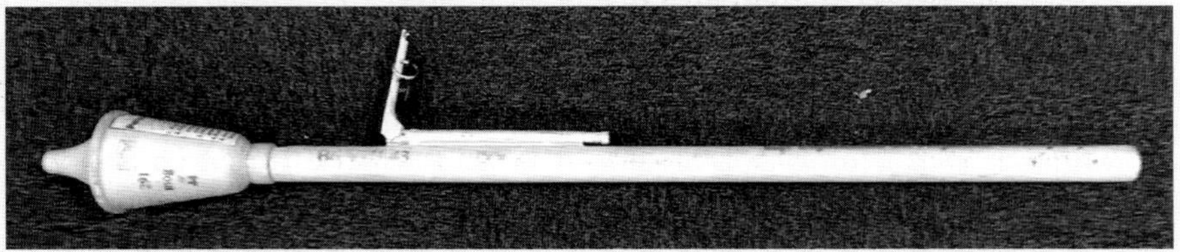

The *Panzerfaust* 30, nicknamed *Klein Gretchen.*

The launch tube contained the firing mechanism and the sight. The sight folded flat, and by raising it to the vertical the weapon was primed and ready for firing after the removal of a safety pin. In the case of the 30m (*Klein*) and 30m (*Gross*) there was a red-painted firing button. The 60m and 100m had a simple firing lever behind the sight.

A sketch of aiming and firing the *Panzerfaust* and its dangerous back-blast.

Unlike the bazooka and *Panzerschreck*, the *Panzerfaust* used an explosive charge (*Patrone*) to propel the projectile out of the launch tube. Back-blast in the form of a 2m jet of flame was always a safety and tactical issue. Anyone positioned behind the weapon when fired risked serious injury. Firing from a confined space like a building or trench was also an issue. The smoke and flame generated also gave a 'signature' in that the firing position could be clearly seen. This, along with its inherent inaccuracy, highlights how much courage was required to use this weapon effectively.

The *Panzerfaust* was designed to be used even after very little training. Instructions on its use were printed on a label pasted onto the projectile so that even an untrained soldier could use it with some effectiveness.

Development started in the summer of 1942 on the *Panzerfaust* (*Klein*) 30m, followed soon after by the more effective *Panzerfaust* (*Gross*) 30m. Both weapons were demonstrated to the HWA (*Heereswaffenamt*)* in March 1943 and troop trials were conducted on the Eastern Front. The results were highly successful and full production of 100,000 (*Klein*) 30m and 200,000 of the larger (*Gross*) 30m per month was ordered in July. However, these figures were not reached until the following April.

The *Panzerfaust* 60 began to be issued to troops in August 1944 so is pertinent to the story of 141 RAC in Normandy along with the earlier two models. The *Panzerfaust* 100 didn't appear until December.

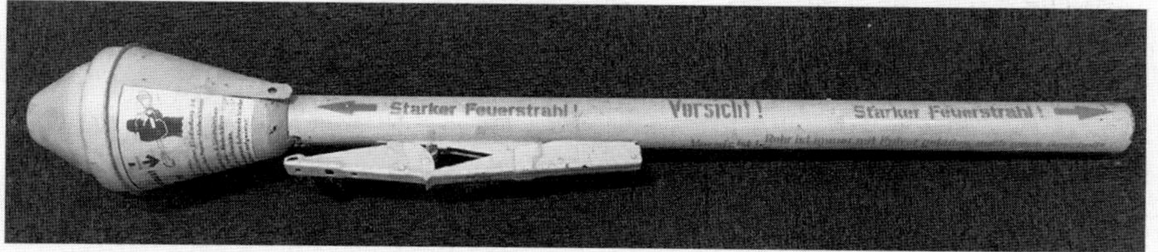

The *Panzerfaust* 100.

The *Panzerfaust* in all four versions was produced in colossal numbers in the last two years of the war, estimated in excess of 8 million. This enabled units to be lavishly equipped at all levels. During the Normandy campaign around 6 per cent of British and Canadian tanks were destroyed by hand-held infantry weapons. By the autumn this figure had increased to 34 per cent, partly due to fewer AFVs and anti-tank guns being available to German units, but also to the increased availability of the *Panzerfaust*. In common with other armament production, slave labour was used extensively in the Reich, resulting – in common with other arms manufacture – in a very high percentage of defective weapons.

In the bocage country and urban areas, the *Panzerfaust* in the hands of the German infantryman made a very good close-quarter ambush weapon.

*HWA (*Heereswaffenamt*): This was the agency responsible within the German Army for the procurement, development and quality control of military equipment including weapons and AFVs.

Operation MAORI II

On the evening of 9 July all four troops of C Squadron were located together at La Senaudière and spent the following day repairing battle damage and preparing for another two half-squadron operations with XXX Corps:

> 11th July once more found the Squadron split up in small packets, under command of 231 Brigade for an attack on HOTTOT, 12 Troop in support of 2 Devons and 14 Troop in support of 1 Hamps. Over on the left, under command of 10 DLI of 70 Brigade [49th Division] Lieut Wareing with 11 Troop had excellent armour support from the Sherwood Rangers.

Hottot, a linear village on the Juvigny-Caumont road, was by this stage in the campaign little more than a set of ruins, defended along with Château Cordillon by II Battalion 986 Grenadier Regiment and dug-in panzers. The second attempt by 231 Brigade to capture the village began with the usual fire plan at 0700 hours. Fired by all field and medium guns within range and thickened up by the mortars and Vickers machine guns of 2 Cheshires (MG), the three infantry battalions, each supported by a squadron of the Sherwood Rangers' Shermans, crossed their start lines. The barrage they followed only moved forward at the rate of 50 yards in two minutes. Consequently, with the aid of field engineers and the 'Funnies' of 79th Armoured Division, no doubt with improved procedures following experience gained during Operation PANTHER, they blew and carved gaps in the bocage hedgerows, enabling the tanks to keep up with the infantry. The Hampshires reached their objective within an hour and the 2nd Devons in the centre were advancing on Hottot, but at about 1030 hours the Westcountrymen were

Operation MAORI II.

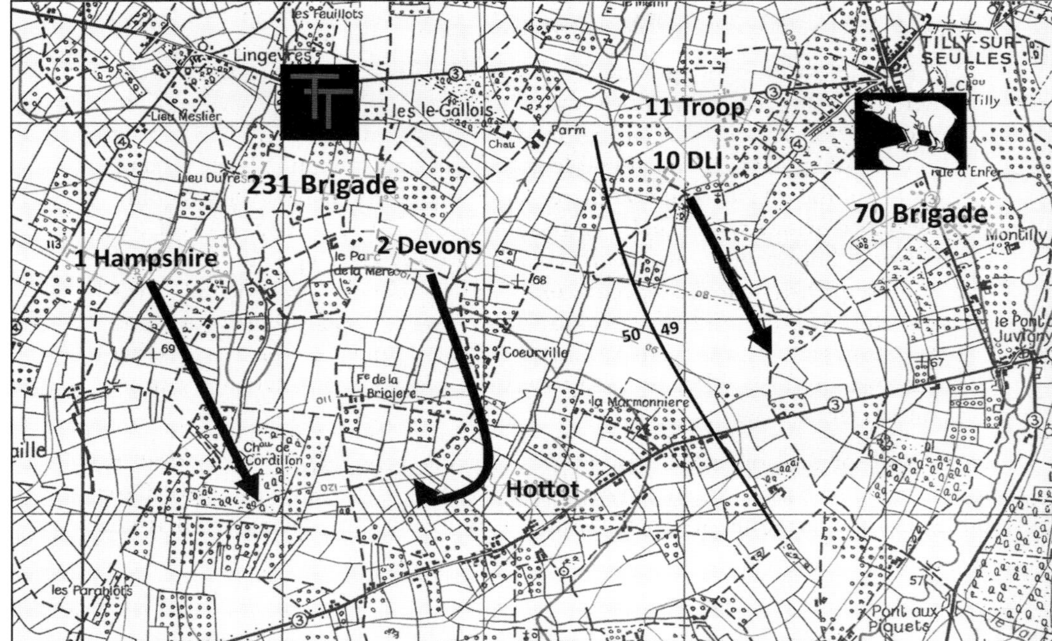

A dug-in and well-camouflaged Vickers machine gun of 2 Cheshires in the Hottot area.

counter-attacked by infantry and thirty panzers. C Company, somewhat forward of the other companies and disorganized following clearing hedges and banks during their advance, was driven back, losing an entire platoon in the process.

As was the case with 56 Brigade during 8–9 July, fighting was at close quarters throughout the day, but there is no record of 12 or 14 troops being called on to flame. With, however, no further progress being made against the heavily-defended village of Hottot, 'something "had got to be done"' and at 231 Brigade's insistence 'the Crocodiles had better do it':

> So, as the shadows lengthened over HOTTOT, the Crocodiles were ordered to prance madly down the main street 'flaming all the way' in demonstration as it were. A strong protest naturally ensued. HOTTOT was infested with enemy tanks. Crocodiles can flame only straight ahead.[7] And to what end if the infantry did not intend to occupy the village? Who was going to ensure that our secret fuel and gun did not fall into enemy hands if the infantry did not propose to occupy the village? 30 Corps upheld the protest and subsequently issued a directive on the use of Crocodiles. The C.O. was fortunately present and on very obvious grounds managed to avoid this senseless gesture by appeal to 30 Corps, who subsequently issued a directive on the use of Crocodiles. By such threads do the lives of Crocodile equipment sometimes hang.

In an echo of the comments made by other squadrons during this period, the report concludes that 'This was typical of the many fantasies designed for Crocodiles in their early history by Crocodile "know-alls".' In defence of Brigadier

An oblique air photograph of the bocage country looking south towards Hottot.

Stanier's 231 Brigade, it should be recalled that charging into villages is exactly what the Crocodiles had done in the early days of the invasion at La Belle Épine and La Senaudière while under his command.

On 70 Brigade's front, where Lieutenant Wareing's 11 Troop was in support of 10 DLI, the Crocodiles were employed during the Durhams' attack rather than being left to follow on behind and be, one suspects, forgotten. Being committed to Phase 3 of the attack, they waited alongside the DLI infantry and tanks of C Squadron of the Sherwood Rangers for most of the day before the attack began on hedges and orchards north of the road, halfway between Le Pont de Juvigny and Hottot. At 1630 hours they moved forward over more open country and approached the hedgerows and orchards around an enemy-occupied farm building at a track junction. Trooper Reddish joined the Shermans in brassing up the hedges with his Besa machine gun. Wareing's Crocodiles, with the tanks providing suppressive fire, drove forward to flaming range and 'pulled off three small but very satisfactory shows, flaming the edges of the woods and bringing in a bag of 24 prisoners.' The Durham infantry followed closely and were in the orchards clearing the buildings and enemy trenches. It is tempting to suggest that if the Crocodiles had been used by the 231 Brigade battalions in the same way as 10 DLI, they may have been able to break into Hottot, but that is conjecture.

Operationally, neither Operations PANTHER nor MAORI II made anywhere near as much ground as intended, but they did contribute to fixing the panzer divisions where Montgomery wanted them, and the Crocodiles played their part in 'writing down German forces'.[8] Infantry manpower was becoming a problem for the British with unexpectedly high casualties, but for the Germans, losses in

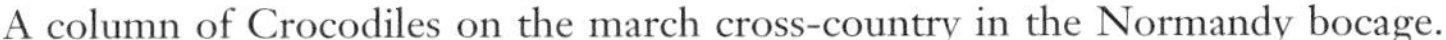

A column of Crocodiles on the march cross-country in the Normandy bocage.

armour, men and supplies were virtually irreplaceable. On 15 July, after less than two weeks in action, 276th Infantry Division was reporting that its losses totalled 1,000 men.[9]

The entry in the C Squadron war diary for 12 July is brief: 'Released from MAORI II. C Sqn returned to LA SENAUDIERE, where Major Duffy made valiant and indeed successful efforts to make his camp the smartest this side of the ORNE.' However, with losses in battle, mechanical issues with the tank and technical problems with the flame system, C Squadron was effectively 'non-operational' and was pulled back to RHQ in Brécy for repair and reorganization. The sundry mechanical issues with the Churchill were normal for tanks, but with the squadron having been deployed away from the regiment's workshop and relying on its own fitter section, there was a backlog of work to be done. There were also numerous technical failures with the Crocodile system, which as a new weapon in action for the first time were inevitable. Consequently, both repairs and modifications were needed. Back in Brécy they also had the services of 31 Tank Brigade's REME workshop.

The Besa Machine Gun

The Churchill and the Crocodile conversion, in common with other British-manufactured tanks, were equipped with the Besa. This was a Czechoslovakian-designed medium machine gun adopted by the British Army in 1938. It had 7.92-calibre ammunition with a × 57 cartridge, identical to that used universally by the Wehrmacht!

The hull Besa as fitted in a Churchill Mk VIII tank. It could be removed and replaced by the flame gun in less than two hours.

Being designed as a medium machine gun capable of sustained fire, it was ideally suited for the Churchill tank in the infantry support role. Even though the hull Besa had been replaced by the flame gun in the Crocodile, a second Besa co-axially mounted alongside the 75mm gun could provide a considerable weight of suppressive fire at the vehicle approached to within flaming range. This capability was particularly useful in the bocage country.

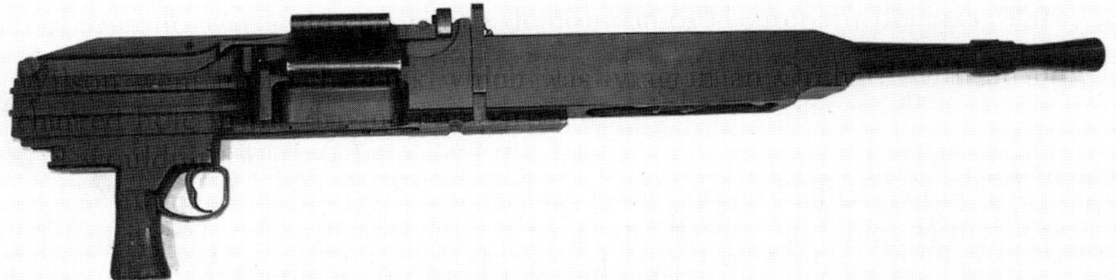

The Besa machine gun removed from its mounting.

Depending on which version of the Besa was mounted, it could fire between 450 and 850 rounds of belted ammunition per minute in direct support of infantry. In the sustained fire role this would be limited to the lower figure to avoid the weapon becoming overheated. The Besa was capable of a much higher rate of sustained fire than the .30-calibre Browning machine gun mounted in the Sherman, which was essentially a light machine gun.

One of the other advantages of the Besa was that it was issued with three types of ammunition:

- Ball – normal rifle/LMG ammunition.
- Tracer – used for target indication and incendiary against buildings, etc.
- Armour-piercing – capable of penetrating up to 13mm of armour plate. This had been impressively demonstrated by a Churchill unit in Tunisia in 1943 where the shields of German anti-tank guns proved to be no defence for their crews.

Typically, the 225-round belts of ammunition would be mixed according to tactical requirements.

The turret-mounted Besa mounted co-axially with the main armament was fired by the gunner.

The last burst of flame: the residue is still burning on the hull.

Chapter Seven

Hill 112 and the Second Battle of the Odon

Following the capture of Caen by I Corps on 9 July 1944, General Montgomery needed to maintain pressure on the Germans and noted in his directive M508:

> Some days must elapse while troops were being regrouped for these twin attacks [US attack towards St. Lo and the British Operation GOODWOOD], and meanwhile the pot was to be kept boiling by a limited action to hold the enemy armour in the east and to round off the ground won in the Epsom battle. [Author's emphasis]

The resulting operation was given the code-name JUPITER. This was in essence a continuance of EPSOM, with the aim of seizing a bridgehead across the River Orne. If successful, this would significantly aid development of Montgomery's next 'colossal crack': Operation GOODWOOD.

Operation JUPITER: 10 July 1944

Major Cooper's A Squadron of 141 RAC remained to the west of Caen based at Bernay, but with VIII Corps' headquarters moving to take over the sector to the east of the River Orne, the Crocodiles came under command of the newly-arrived XII Corps. This corps was to oversee the renewal of the attack on Hill 112, which was to be delivered by 43rd Wessex Division and the two Churchill regiments of 31 Tank Brigade. The two assault brigades, 129 and 130 Infantry, each had the by now usual half-squadron of Crocodiles under command.

The troops under Captain Storrar were to support 129 Brigade's advance up the Roman road to Hill 112 where 4th Somerset Light Infantry (4 Som LI) faced SS infantry dug in in a hedgerow on the forward slope. The task of flaming this position was allocated to the Crocodiles of No. 3 Troop commanded by Lieutenant Tonbridge, supported by two of the squadron's command tanks and Churchills of C Squadron 7 RTR.

During EPSOM, Major General Thomas, commander of the Wessex Division, had successfully conducted a night assembly and a dawn battalion attack on the village of Mouen with 1 Worcesters and hoped to replicate this in his first divisional attack. The SS defenders of Hill 112, however, deduced from the registration of artillery targets and the volume of armoured movement towards the Odon valley that an attack was imminent.

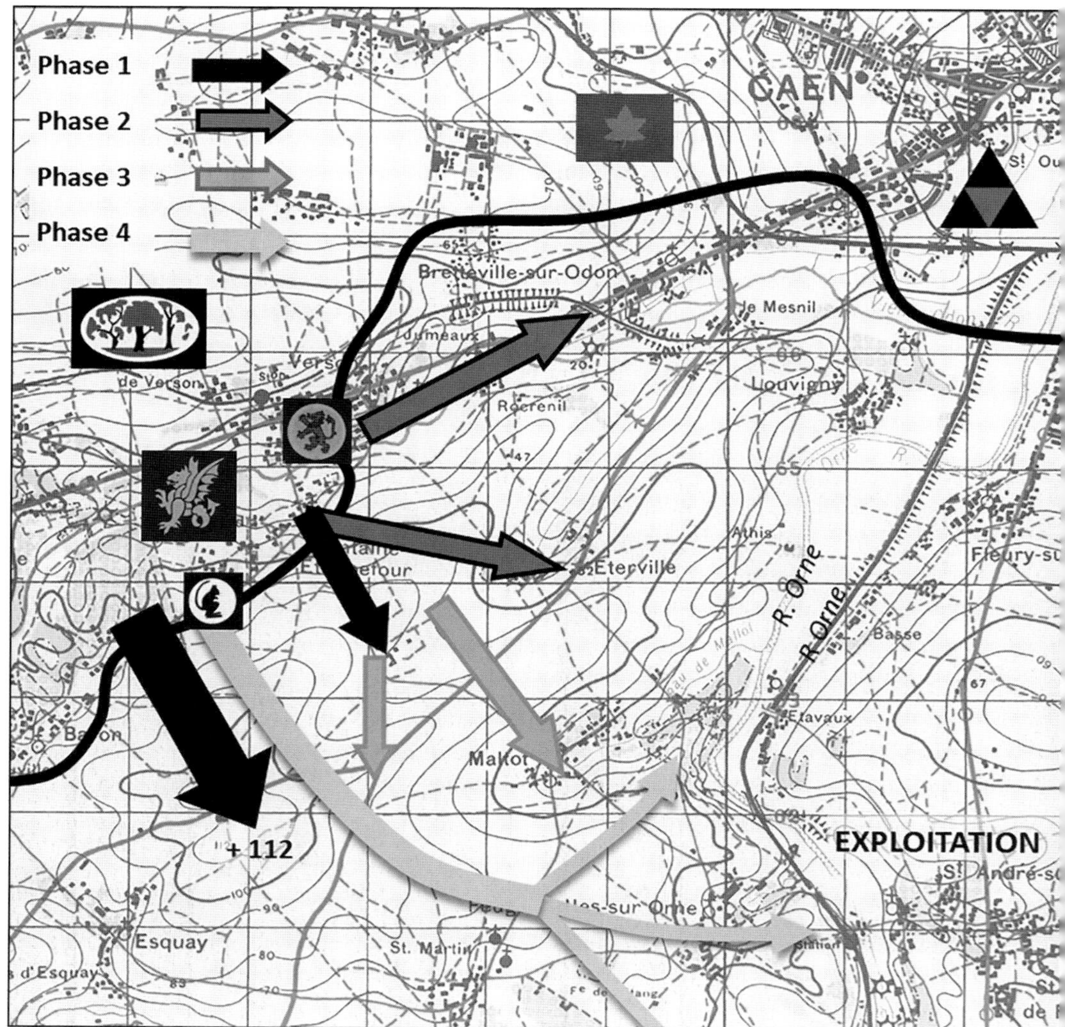

The 43rd Wessex Division's plan for Operation JUPITER.

Despite the British artillery's creeping barrage helping to keep the defenders' heads down during the initial stages of the attack, as 129 Brigade group advanced up the concave slope of Hill 112, the enemy could see them as they left their FUP at the foot of the slope. Consequently, as 7 RTR and 4 Som LI crossed the start line in the first light of dawn, they were almost immediately under direct enemy fire. This took its toll on both infantry and the supporting armour, as described by Trooper Cox who was motoring up behind the Churchills and infantry in 'Stallion'. He passed through a line of knocked-out tanks that had taken:

> an awful beating and shattered crews were running back. Their CO gallantly tried to rally them, flying an umbrella from his cupola so the crews could see him. He was only yards from us when a sniper killed him. Their RSM was in tears as they lifted him down.

As 129 Brigade closed on the enemy position, casualties continued to mount among both men and armour. Sergeant Hole of the Somersets' Mortar Platoon, looking up the hillside from the area of the FUP, described what he saw as dawn rose:

> The whole scene was illuminated by burning carriers and tanks. Flame-throwers were in action. The enemy, using *Nebelwerfers*, was mortaring the advancing troops. Practically every weapon was in use – rifles, grenades, phosphorous, machine guns and tanks – and casualties were extremely heavy.[2]

An air photograph of the northern approaches to Hill 112.

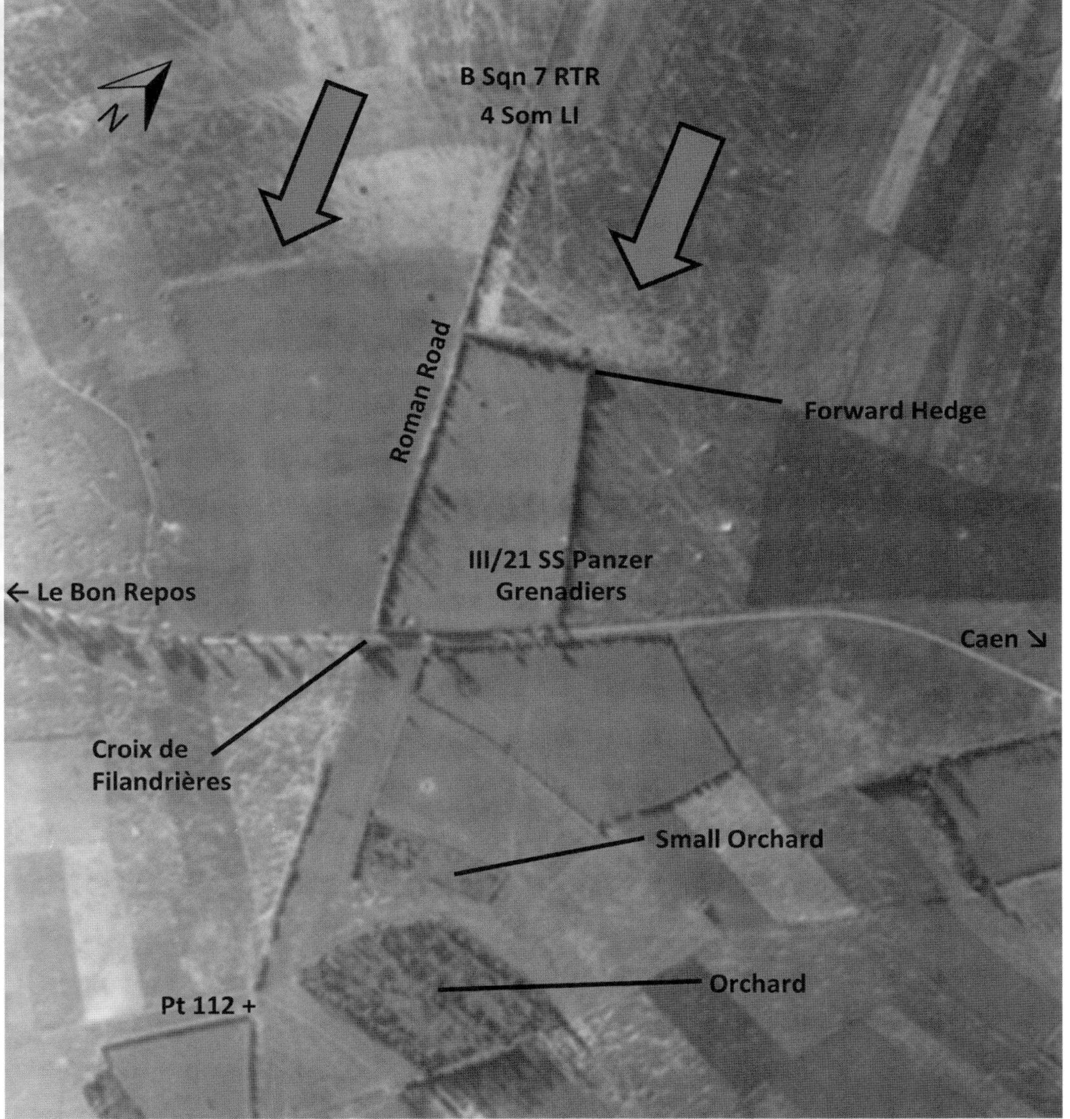

Under artillery and now small-arms fire, the Somersets approached the Germans' main defensive position held by *Sturmbannführer* Sattler's III Battalion 21 SS *Panzergrenadiers* dug in in the hedged bank around the rectangular field immediately north of the Caen-Évrecy road. To do their job amid shot and shell coming from the crest of Hill 112, the Crocodile troops had to close to within 100 yards of the hedgerow to help the infantry of B Company clear the defences to the east of the Roman road. Thanks to lessons learned, they were able to approach to within flaming range with smoke that covered the troops' immediate flanks. A report in A Squadron's war diary records that:

> in this case an excellent screen was laid by the two comd tks assisted by 7 RTR and it is the considered opinion of this regiment that smoke is a major weapon for [flame] attack and escape. Judging from the badly shaken PW and the great impression on our own infantry, this was a very successful show indeed.

In addition to the artillery firing smoke, both the Churchills and the Crocodiles, in a standard ammunition load of eighty-five rounds, had ten smoke rounds. The tanks also had a white phosphorous instantaneous smoke round that was fired from a 2in mortar in the turret and a pair of 4in smoke dischargers on the rear to help cover the Crocodile's withdrawal.

Trooper Cox describes how, with the infantry having gained a toehold in the forward hedgerow, the Crocodiles were summoned to flame the flanking hedges:

> Now it was our turn to 'Pressure up'. I went round the back of the trailer to give Beech a hand with the door; we wasted no time out there. As we drove along a track [the Roman road] we were well exposed to our right, we felt naked and waited for the bang from an 88. 'Pull left,' said Dickie. We went down a ditch, then up crashing through the hedge, then dropped into the field. I looked to my right and my heart stopped ... The field was square about 200 yards each side a thick hedge all round. Our infantry held one side, the German the other three; neither side could make a move. We split into pairs to take on the hedge giving it a good dowsing, just about emptying our tanks of flame fuel.

Unfamiliar with flame, however, the Somersets held back, afraid to enter the burning area, and Captain Storrar had to dismount from his command tank. He led the infantry through the residue of flame fuel to the hedgerow to mop up the SS who were surrendering in significant numbers or had been badly wounded. Trooper Cox commented that the Somersets' CO, Lieutenant Colonel 'Lippy' Lipscombe:

> was delighted he had lost too many men already, but this bit of the attack hadn't cost him a man. As the flames died down, he went to have a look, came back full of smiles and asked if we would like to go and see our handiwork. He estimated 300 Germans dead, but we declined. Taking up a defen-

The attackers' eye view of the forward hedgerow that A Squadron's Crocodiles flamed, which overlooked the concave slope and the axis of advance.

> sive position, we had to wait until nightfall before going back down the hill to re-arm and refuel.

At this stage of the introduction of the Crocodile the effect of flame on the enemy was very much of interest to the analysts at HQ RAC, 21st Army Group. The numbers of wounded could, of course, be identified as victims of flame, but not many of the dead. The RAC war diary concluded that 'Owing to previous shelling the number killed by flame could not be properly estimated ... We suffered no casualties in this action apart from two wounded (mortar casualties) in the forward rally.'

Captain Storrar commented 'that on a target of this nature the effect was moral rather than lethal, thus once more emphasising the necessity for a quick follow-up by the infantry to winkle out the temporarily demoralised enemy and occupy the ground against enemy return.'

The role of flame in taking the SS *Panzergrenadiers*' main defensive position in the forward hedgerow cannot be ignored. It enabled 4 Som LI to gain a toehold on the plateau rather than being pinned down on the concave slope under observation.

The other half of the squadron under Major Cooper supported 130 Brigade in its attack on the low ground a mile to the east, where a troop of Crocodiles supported 4 Dorsets' attack on the village of Éterville. To break into the village, A Company on the battalion's right was confronted by a series of substantial hedges that surrounded a château. Major Symonds, OC A Company stated that 'The plan to shoot us into Éterville was that the tanks would engage the enemy in

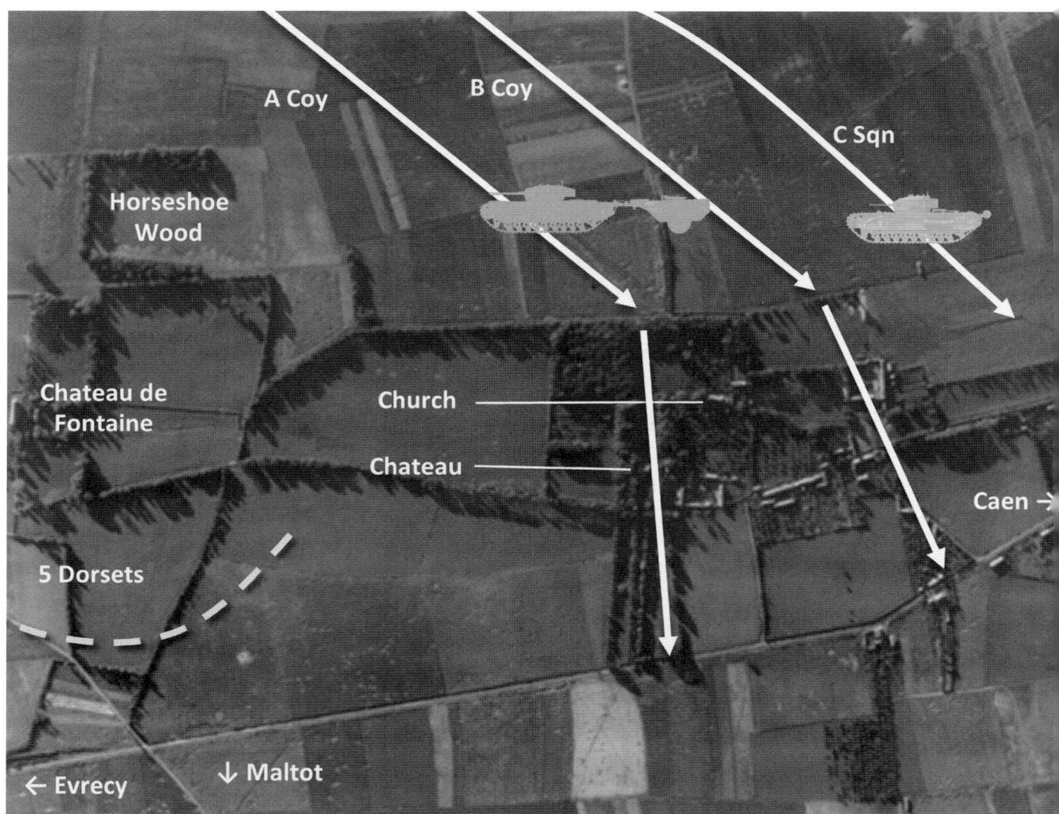

A marked air photograph showing the attack by 4 Dorsets on the village and château of Éterville.

the hedgerows with HE and Besa, covering ourselves and the Crocs forward to within assaulting range.'

Coming up the convex slope that in this instance provided a reasonably covered approach for the attackers, Private Alfie Brown of A Company was sheltering 'somewhat hesitantly behind the bulk of the Crocodile's fuel trailer'. He recalled that as they advanced to within 100 yards of the edge of the village:

> there was a rushing sound like a train and a loud wumf as the hedge burst into flames … black oily smoke was everywhere. I don't know if any Jerrys were caught but I saw some further along, running back from bunkers in the hedge to the mansion. As a result, we got into Éterville fairly easily but that's when our problems really began.

The SS infantry positions were not the only ones taken on by the Crocodiles. To the right of A Company, between Château Fontaine and Éterville, SS Mann August Bauer, a member of the 8th (Heavy Weapons) Company, II Battalion 22 *Panzergrenadiers*, witnessed the Crocodiles in action:

> We shot at the advancing tanks with everything we had. Suddenly a great cloud of black smoke emanated from a *flammpanzer* and hit the cannon of SS *Rottenführer* Theopil Hauth situated to our right. The Pak was put out of

> action and the commander and crew were killed or wounded. We knocked out several English tanks before we were forced back into the village [Éterville].

One of the frequent occurrences that Crocodile commanders had to learn to deal with was manifested later in the day when the Wessex Division's infantry were in trouble at Maltot. In the second phase of JUPITER, 7 Hampshires and 4 Dorsets had entered the village, but had been heavily counter-attacked and were in the process of being overrun. Captain Bailey reported that

> Major Cooper on the left emphatically resisted insensitive and wild suggestions for the remaining two troops to be dispatched into MALTOT for their valueless destruction where 9 RTR had lost tanks to dug-in Tigers and Panthers at a rapid rate. They would have been grist to the enemy mill.

Photographed during pre-invasion training, the black smoke referred to by British and German soldiers is apparent.

As night fell, A Squadron went back a mile across the Odon, but in Mouen they were 'under constant arty and mortar fire until they were released on 13 July. This was not the first time that Crocodiles were to be kept needlessly exposed too far forward.' Notes on the tactical use of the Crocodile concluded that:

(a) Flame was most effective against houses and fortified buildings. These were invariably set on fire and gutted.
(b) Open defences among woods, hedges and undergrowth provided good targets as the vegetation was easily set on fire.
(c) As would be expected, flame was least effective against pillboxes and the like; only if it could be projected through apertures to the inside did the occupants suffer.[3]

Tactics for the use of the flame gun against a dispersed or area targets required a different approach; one that was governed by it being located in the front armoured plate. Here it had an arc of fire of just 25 degrees due to the extension of the Churchill's tracks forward, and a further limitation was that being on the left, the Crocodile's arc of fire in that direction was just 5 degrees. To engage targets that were 'spread out defences like bunkers and trenches required an approach to the left of the target, flaming and pulling right to drench the area in flame. Each tank using the same technique would avoid passing in front of the other.'

The flame gun and the track guards that limited its arc of fire to the left.

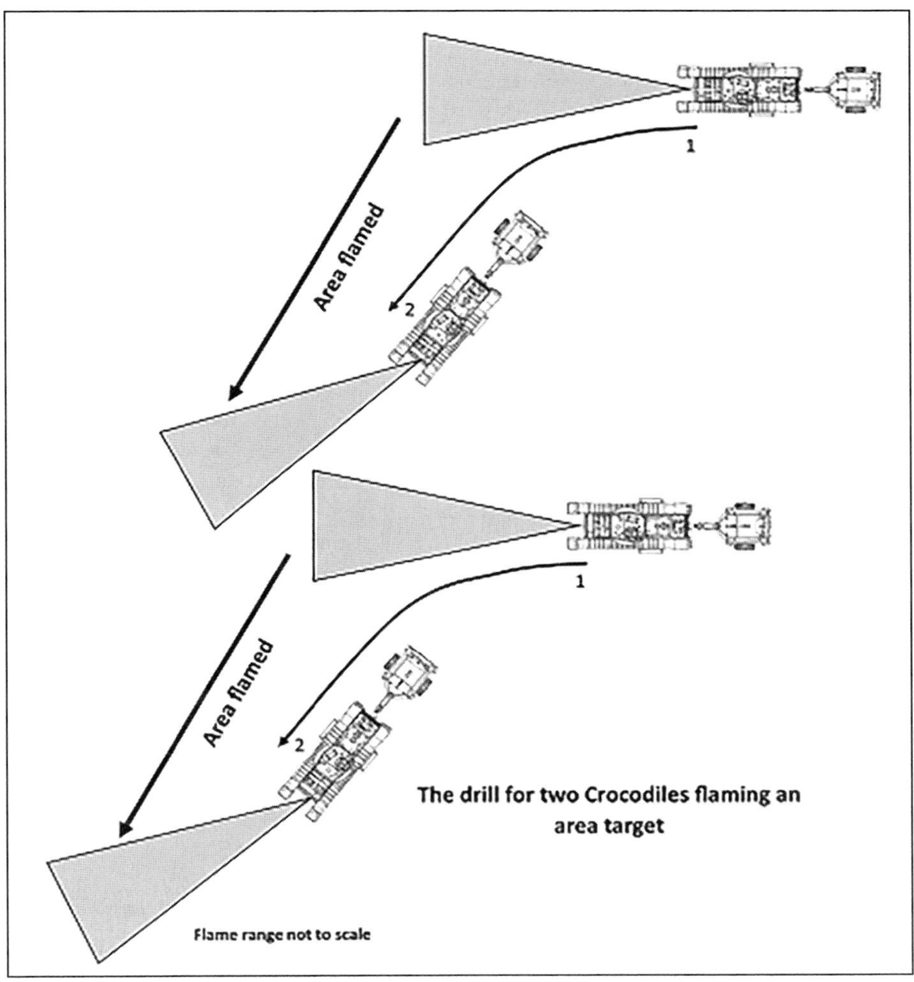

The Second Battle of the Odon

Operation GOODWOOD was to be Montgomery's next major operation and in the same way that he set the entire British front in action both before and during Operation EPSOM, C-in-C 21st Army Group would do the same again. In his words the aim was 'to make the Germans think we are going to break out across the Orne between Caen and Amayé [sur Orne].' Although planning a significant advance, GOODWOOD and its supporting operations' aim was to draw and fix enemy armour against Second British Army while the US First Army broke out on the western flank during the third week of July. Meanwhile, the squadrons of 141 Regiment RAC were throughout the month mainly in action supporting attacks to the west of the city of Caen and the River Orne.

This Second Battle of the Odon was a series of operations fought by Lieutenant General Ritchie's XII Corps (GREENLINE) and by Lieutenant General Bucknall's XXX Corps (CORMORANT and POMEGRANATE). As indicated above, they were intended to draw and fix German armoured reserves away from VIII Corps' attack east of Caen (see map on page 110).

By mid-July German infantry divisions were arriving in Normandy, having been held at other likely invasion points thanks to Operation FORTITUDE and then marching on foot and by night thanks to Allied air interdiction. On the front to be attacked in GREENLINE, the 277th Infantry Division had taken over Hill 113 from 9th *Hohenstaufen* SS Panzer Division and the 271st Division was in the process of relieving the 10th *Frundsberg* SS Panzer Division on Hill 112. The German aim at this point in the campaign continued to be the extraction of the panzer divisions from the line to create an operational reserve with which to respond to Allied attacks or to launch their own counter-offensives. At the insistence of Hitler, *Oberkommando des Heeres* (*OKH*, Army High Command) continued to demand unrealistic counter-offensives by the now much-reduced panzer divisions.[4]

The tactical aim of XII Corps' GREENLINE was with an attack at last light from the Odon bridgehead on 15 July to seize the high ground south-west of Hill 112 and the village of Évrecy. This would secure start lines for subsequent operations towards either Aunay-sur-Odon or to Thury-Harcourt 'as the situation dictated'. On subsequent days, XXX Corps in Operation POMEGRANATE was to advance towards Noyers, and eventually to the elusive Point 213 to the north-east of Villers-Bocage.[5]

Operation GREENLINE: 15 July 1944

The XII Corps' attack was to be delivered by Major General MacMillan's 15th Scottish Division, reinforced by a brigade of 53rd Welsh Division and 34 Tank Brigade. The operation was to begin at 2130 hours without the standard preliminary bombardment, but 450 guns were concentrated to engage known enemy positions and using the Royal Artillery's considerable flexibility at other targets as the operation developed.

The two troops of Major Cooper's A Squadron were to provide support to 2nd Glasgow Highlanders of 227 Highland Brigade in their attack on the hamlet of Le Bon-Repos, which was defended by III Battalion, 21 SS *Panzergrenadier* Regiment. The hamlet stands where the Éterville to Évrecy road drops down from Hill 112 and had an outlying strongpoint centred on a farmhouse. The attack on Le Bon-Repos in which the Crocodiles were involved was only the first phase of an operation to secure Esquay and the left flank of the main GREENLINE attack, which was directed towards Évrecy.

In contrast to previous operations where the Crocodiles were held in reserve, in GREENLINE they had a well-defined role, and thanks to the 'use of air photos and ground observation a very thorough plan was made'. In addition, contributing significantly to success, a rehearsal was carried out for the infantry 'to

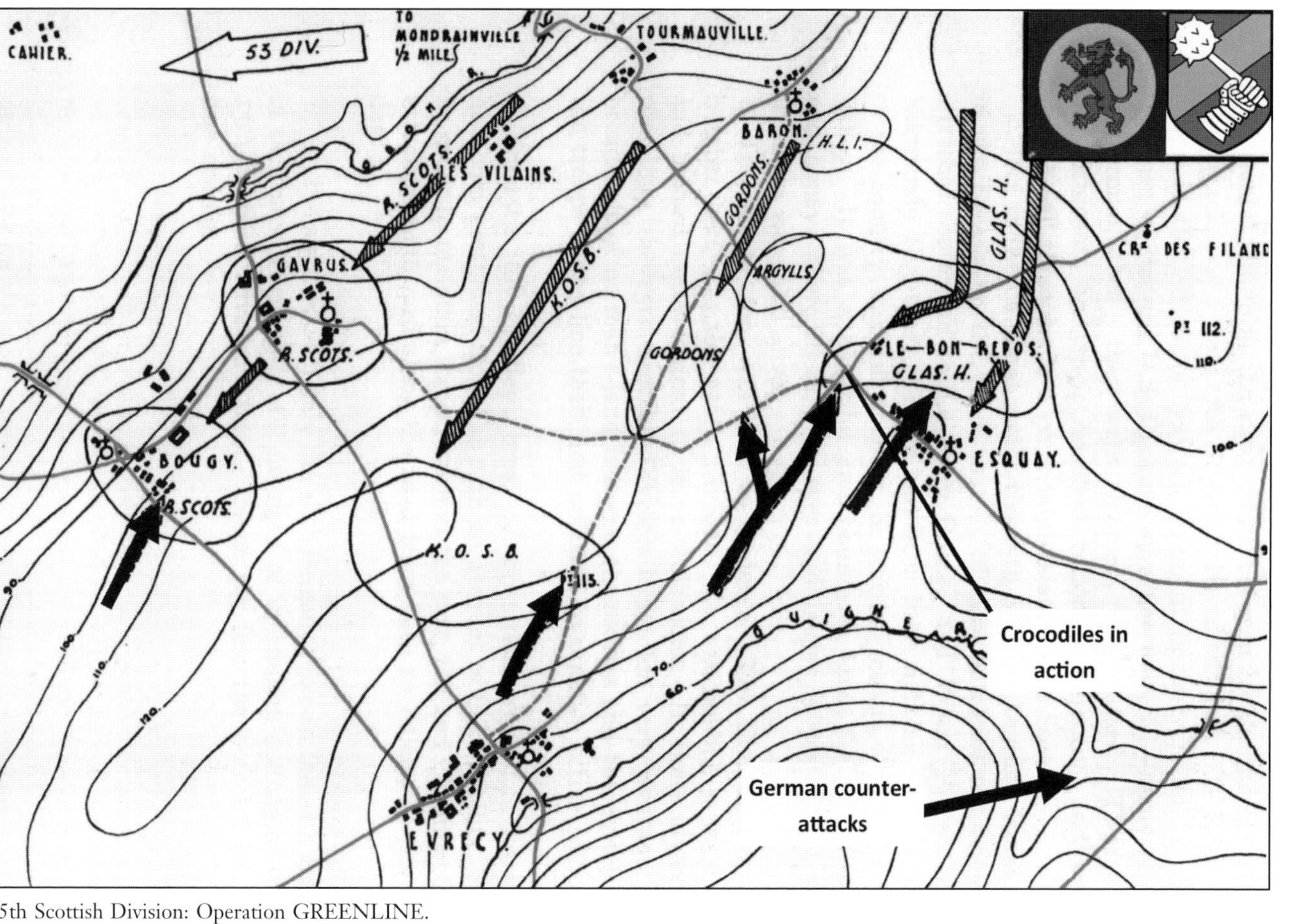

15th Scottish Division: Operation GREENLINE.

demonstrate the safety of walking through the flame once it was on the ground.' Nos 2 and 3 troops (Lieutenant Playford and Tonbridge) under Captain Storrar's control joined A and B companies of the Glasgow Highlanders, along with two troops of Churchills from A Squadron, 107 Regiment RAC.[6] They were to advance from the area of Baron south-west across the shoulder of Hill 112 and finally astride the road into Le Bon-Repos from the east. The plan is described in some detail in the squadron war diary:

> Two tps 107 RAC were to precede the Crocodiles' advance, one TP each side of the road. Next the Crocodiles, also one Tp each side of the road, flaming the fire posns in the hedgerows *en route* to LE BON REPOS. The Tp Sgt in each case was to lead, the Tp Offr moving behind filling up the gaps in the flame and the Tp Cpl to a flank ready to replace the Tp Sgt as he exhausted his flame. Immediately behind each Tp of Crocodiles a platoon of infantry with one section actually detailed to follow immediately behind the flame tk. The whole object was to be 'stonked' as part of the Div Arty Programme up till H plus 20 and smoke laid on and beyond the objective.

Battlefield smokescreens are notoriously difficult to get right and for their effect to be maintained. In this case, as dusk settled the smoke covering Hill 112 billowed down into the Odon valley and the two infantry companies became mixed up as they struggled to find their FUPs. However, as tank engines roared, they followed the Crocodiles. When 107 RAC's Churchills reached the forward enemy strongpoint, so thick was the smoke that they were unwilling to advance into it. Trooper Cox was listening in to the radio net:

> We moved up to the start line; it seemed almost peaceful, down came the smoke on cue, a nice bit of shooting, only one problem, the wind had dropped, not a breath of it; a London Pea Souper would sum it up. On the radio we could hear our Squadron Leader talking to the new tank unit. Their commander was not happy to go forward into that lot. Well, we did have the advantage of knowing the ground but not at night in a thick smoke screen. A few more tart remarks over the air and we were off on our own.

The war diary continued: 'Finally, the Crocodiles advanced without them [the Churchills], although in a better light this lack of armour support might have been serious. By now it was almost completely dark but the drill worked to perfection.'

Trooper Cox described the approach route to the objective:

> We pushed on; driving on a compass bearing we knew would bring us to the road that ran from left to right across our front. We kept the Besa chattering away, no telling if Germans could stalk us in the murk and found the road, at least we had a landmark and we were right where we should be. Our troop was to cross the road and turn right towards Bon-Repos about half a mile distant.

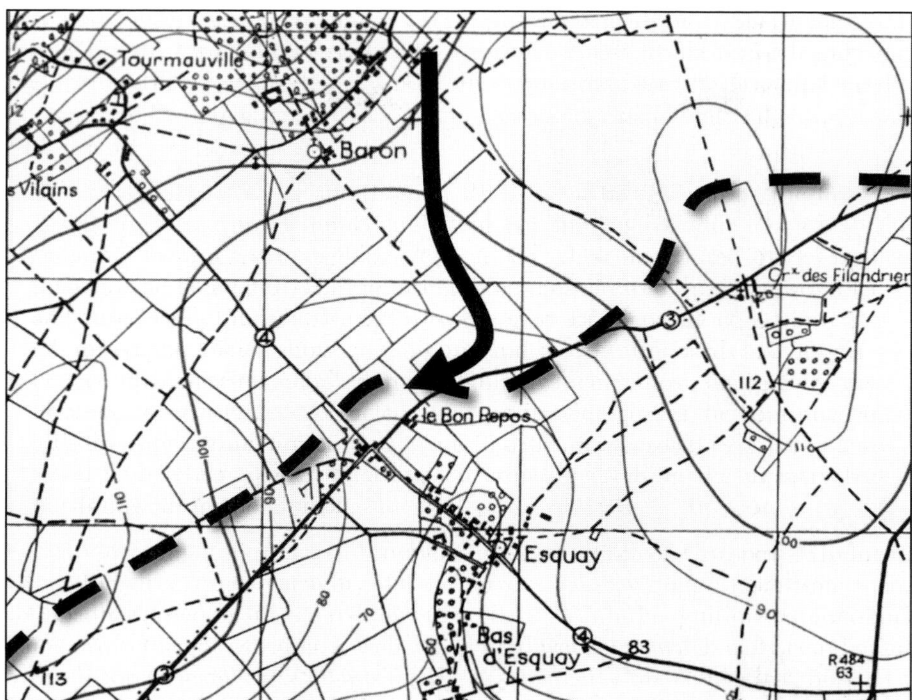

The route from the FUP near Baron across the shoulder of Hill 112 and down into Le Bon-Repos. The direction of attack from the east rather than from the British positions to the north provided some surprise.

The road that the attackers were looking for was at the time lined with poplars that had been damaged by shellfire:

> Our other troop would take the other side and burn out Bon-Repos ... In the murk we could see one of the other tanks flaming, the flames showing through a dark red. We ran parallel to the road and Dickie told Beech to use flame in short bursts. A burst of flame shot out, it splattered on the trees and kept going. 'I said short bursts!' shouted Dickie. 'I've got a runaway gun,' came the reply. An electrical malfunction had stopped the cut-off valve from working. We sped along the line of trees hosing the flame up and down, a terrifying volume of fire, it dropped off the trees into the ditches ... Then

The squadron war diary's diagram of the attack on Le Bon-Repos, 15 July 1944.

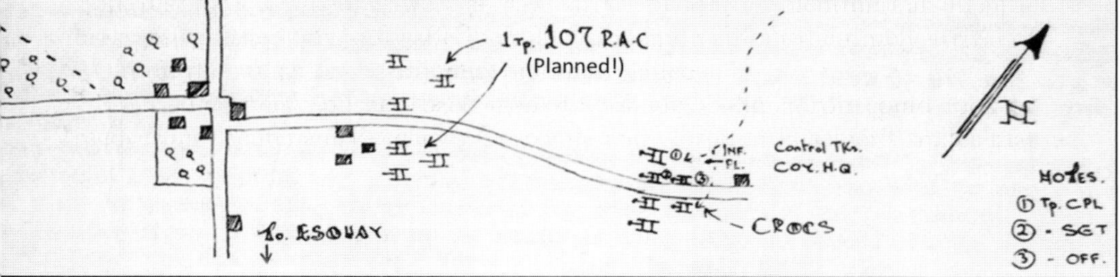

> suddenly it stopped; everywhere the black smoke mingled with the artillery smoke, vision was almost zero. Then we saw Bon-Repos, it was ablaze from end to end; obviously our other troop had done its work.

The squadron war diary concluded that 'The enemy were flushed out of their posns. Tp Cpls automatically replaced Tp Sgts until in turn their flame was exhausted.'

Lieutenant Foley commanding 5 Troop of 107 Regiment RAC had a slightly different account:

> Also taking part in the battle were the flame-throwing tanks of another regiment, and after pushing 'Alert' out to the right a bit to fill the gap … [created by the divergence of another troop] I halted the troop while the flame-throwers squirted their frightening cargoes at the remains of the cottage.
>
> The infantry were silhouetted against the flickering flame, moving purposely about with fixed bayonets. Then I saw them regrouping for the second half of the attack.
>
> I took off my headset and listened to the noise. A fierce crackling came from the burning ruins where the flame-throwers had somehow found some unburned debris; a cacophony of small-arms fire came from all directions …
>
> By now it was quite dark and the only illumination came from the flame-throwers still squirting fire all over the place, the occasional shell bursting in the mud.[7]

The two troops 'quickly burned the enemy garrison out of the entrenchments between Le Bon-Repos and Croix des Filandriers.' The infantry followed up and:

> slaughtering *en passant*, were put into LE BON REPOS without casualty either to themselves or to the Crocodiles. A polite 'Thank you – we're O.K.

Le Bon-Repos crossroads: the axis of the GREENLINE attack (right) and the subsequent raid (left).

> now' from the platoon commander to Lieut Playford, the Crocodiles turned about and the infantry continued on their way.
>
> This after all is the acid test of any plan or application of a particular weapon – an objective won; no casualties lost.[8] This was up to date the best laid on and successful show and it amply bore out the points brought ... up on the use of Crocodiles by Lieut-Col H. Waddell ... which the C.O. has been plugging from the beginning of ops.[9]

The six Crocodiles, each having used a full tank of flame fuel, had by 2300 hours helped the Glasgow Highlanders and their supporting Churchills on their way to securing Esquay, earning the personal thanks of the corps commander.

Despite 'Monty's Moonlight', searchlights playing on the clouds, having lost their night vision thanks to the flame, Cox commented that 'All we could see was an eerie glow':

> We had no idea where the rest of our tanks were, only that we had to cross the road but at what angle to get back to our lines was anyone's guess. Against the flames we could see half a dozen soldiers. Dickie said 'Give them a shout; they may know the right direction.' I put my head out and could see they were Germans. They seemed bewildered and no wonder; probably hoping to be taken prisoner and be out of it. Taking a guess at the direction we headed into the gloom, just catching a glance of our sergeant's tank as he passed going flat out. We carried on at a steady pace not knowing what we may run into – one tank did fall into a bomb crater.

The war diary noted that:

> The cross-country journey back to rally was not without incident amidst smoke and darkness. Capt Storrar, with his genius for falling into situations, this time managed to fall well and truly, tank and all, in a bomb crater. Not before he had gathered his force, however, by a series of Verey Lights, signals which the Germans invariably repeated.[10]

'Stallion' was one of the lost tanks that needed guidance back to rally in the Odon Valley:

> We pressed on, eventually finding a group of tanks including one of ours from 4 Troop; how he got there we could only guess, they hadn't been in the attack. They had decided to stay put until morning; it was our opinion daylight would see us exposed in an unhealthy spot. I called up on the air for a flare, hoping someone was out there. Sure enough, the Squadron Leader came on air saying he would fire a red verey [light]. We saw the flare go up but almost at the same time another went up from another direction. The Germans were listening to our network. The Squadron Leader had seen both flares; he came back, firing green now. We spotted it and off we went; soon we came out of the murk and could see the searchlights and picked up landmarks and back to our harbour.

An artist's impression of 'Monty's Moonlight'. The angle of the searchlight had to be carefully adjusted to avoid illumination of one's own troops.

For the squadron, their first night attack had seemed 'chaos and confusion', but thanks from the infantry were received the next morning.

At 2330 hours the previous evening, with the aid of Monty's Moonlight, the main attacks by other Scottish brigades had begun further west. These attacks made ground, but by the afternoon of 16 July the *Hohenstaufen* and the Tigers of 102 *Schwere* Panzer Battalion had been sucked back into the battle and had contained the Scots' advance.

While this fighting was under way, A Squadron returned to its 'home in a field' to the north of the Odon where they were shelled and mortared seemingly continuously, with the crews not daring to leave the safety of the Crocodiles or the sleeping scrapes dug under their bellies for all but the most essential reasons. Eventually, having suffered casualties to the unpredictable enemy fire, the squadron was moved back to one of the few vacant fields near St. Manvieu. The explanation for this was six deeply buried bombs, but with a choice between exploding shells and 'harmless unexploded bombs', they took up residence.

A Squadron was not long out of the firing line. While preparing food there was a whine of diving aero engines: 'four ME 109s coming straight for us':

> I always kept the Bren leaning against the tank, cocking lever out. I grabbed it and got a good bead on the one following the leading aircraft as they went very low overhead. A cry went up. 'You've got the bastard.' Sure enough, I saw ball on fire. Then suddenly the ball left the plane and he flew on as his drop tank fell to the ground. Well, I bet that scorched his arse anyway. The Germans were having to fly from bases a long way off. The RAF saw to that.

Taking the chance to wander a little, several A Squadron troopers went foraging around what they thought was a nearby abandoned farm where they had spotted some chickens. While attempting to catch the chickens to vary their diet, a very

A Churchill gun tank has a broken track repaired with the aid of the squadron fitters and their ARV.

angry farmer appeared amid a scattering of feathers and much squawking. Attempts to apologize were met with a torrent of French, the gist of which was 'The Germans come and go but the British come and my chickens go.' A donation of compo cans, however, placated the farmer.

Trooper Cox recalled the couple of days out of the line:

> Back to the camp, a bit of tank maintenance and just lounging around relaxing. The following day the trucks took us to a mobile bath house. Such luxury we could have stayed in there all day, but we were moved on. On handing in our clothes, they gave us a clean shirt and underwear and socks, we began to feel human. After lunch off we went to see a film. The choice of venue could have been better; a barn with half the tiles missing, the brilliant sunshine making it difficult to see. [ENSA] Stage door, canteen and the film, it was the sort of diversion we needed. Two full nights of undisturbed sleep saw the red rings round our eyes fading, the next morning pack up, prepare to move, our rest was short-lived.

Operation POMEGRANATE: 16 July 1944

On 15 July, Major Duffy's Crocodiles of C Squadron, having refitted following their time in the bocage with 50th Division, were on the move for the short distance from Sommervieu for their next operation, this time with 59th Staffordshire Division. Following its part in the capture of Caen on 8–9 July, the 59th, after a few days of licking their wounds, headed west from I Corps north of the city to join General Bucknell's XXX Corps. Having completed a difficult road move, the division arrived in an assembly area north of the Rauray area ready to be inserted between 49th West Riding and 53rd Welsh divisions for Operation POMEGRANATE. This attack was designed as a second blow twenty-four hours after GREENLINE. The Crocodiles of C Squadron were also organized in four troops rather than five due to repair problems and sufficient replacement Crocodiles not being available to meet the demands of all three squadrons in the few days between operations.

The war diary recorded that:

> On 15 Jul the Sqn came under command of 59 Div thence u/c 33 Armd Bde and moved to LOUCELLES for 59 Div operation to capture LANDELLE-NOYERS. Could 'C' Sqn remain together? No. 11 Tp (2/Lt. Wareing) with 12 Tp (2/Lt. McFarland) under Capt Barber were placed in sp of 177 Bde, 14 Tp (Lieut Grundy) under Capt Hall were placed in sp of 197 Bde whilst 13 Tp (Lieut Welch) were in Div res.

Having waited with D Squadron at RHQ for almost three weeks, Lieutenant Wilson was finally posted to a Crocodile troop, replacing Second Lieutenant Macfarlane in C Squadron. In his enthusiasm, Wilson ran to the transport lines and later recalled:

> You'd never dare tell anyone that you had rushed to get into action. But it was true. To get into action was an imperative urge you never questioned. The war in the bridgehead had lasted four weeks. You couldn't foresee that it was going not to last six more. When it collapsed you wanted to share the triumph and relief of those who'd been in it.[11]

The attack by 59th Division on 16 July was to capture the line Landelle-Haut des Forges-Noyers and the orchard south-west of Missy by 1800 hours and 'destroy all enemy up to this line'. At the same time, 49th Division on the right had the more limited task in Operation CORMORANT of capturing Vendes. These operations along with GREENLINE were the precursor to an advance by XXX Corps towards the high ground north-east of Villers-Bocage.

The Crocodiles were just a small part of the corps and army troops grouped to support the Staffordshire Division in the attack:

> 33 Armd Bde (less 148 RAC)
> C Sqn 141 RAC: 12 Crocodiles
> A Sqn W Dgns: flails
> Two tps 6 ARE: AVREs
> 198/73 A Tk Bty (SP M10): 3-inch guns
> 234/73 ATk Bty (SP 17pr)
> 86 Fd Regt RA (for sp of 33 Armd Bde): 25-Pounders
> 84 Med Reg: in direct support

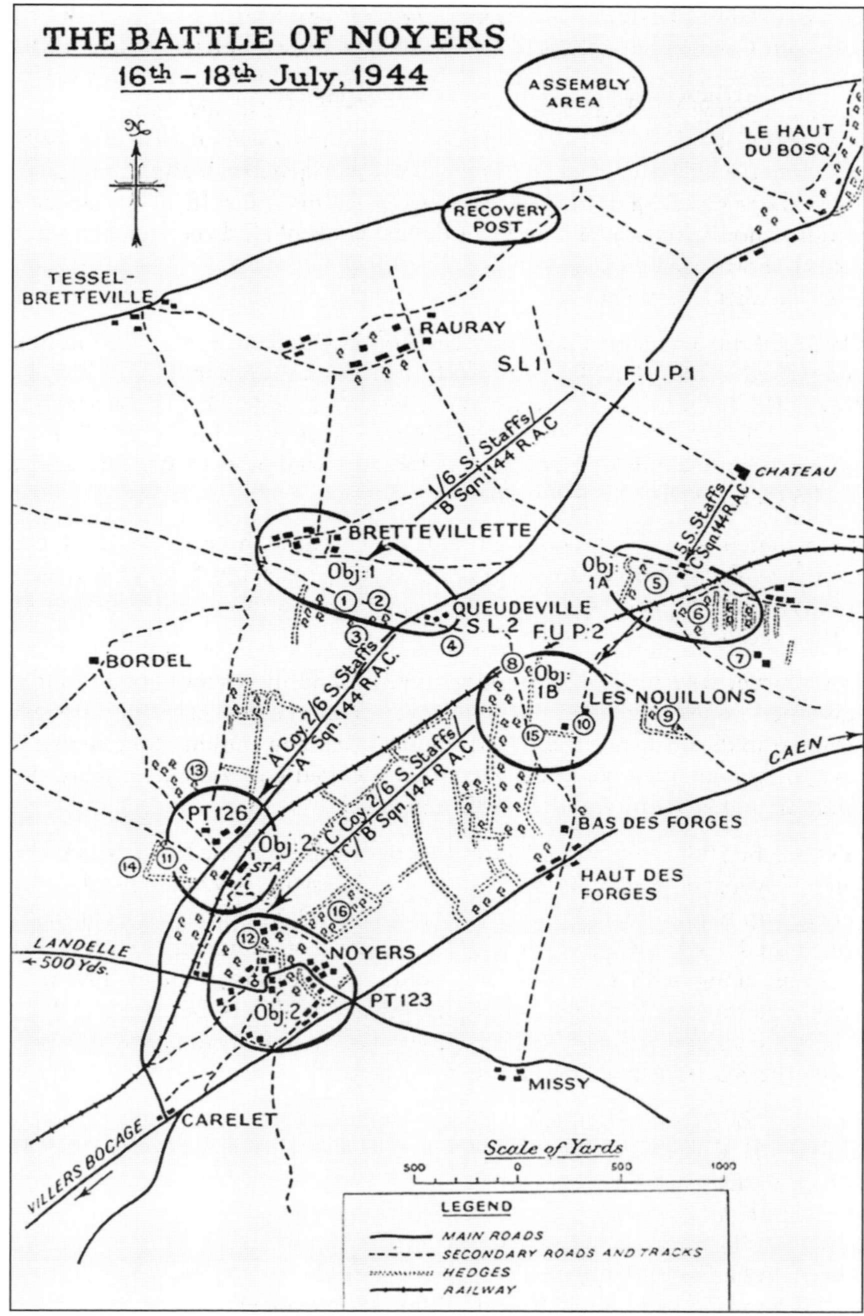

59th Division's advance to Noyers: Operation POMEGRANATE.

Lieutenant Wilson arrived to take over 12 Troop as their third troop leader since arriving in Normandy:

> In England there had been elaborate formalities when you took over a troop; an inspection of the tanks and guns; a check of all the tools and equipment; half a dozen papers to sign. Now there was nothing. He waited while Macfarlane took out his kit from the troop leader's tank and carried it away to one of the supply trucks. Then he threw his own kit on the engine deck.

The troop sergeant had been among the squadron's D-Day boys and, looking at his new troop's faces as he was introduced: 'He knew that the only questions that mattered to them were the ones they would have liked to ask for themselves: whether he could read a map properly, and if he could tell a Panther from a Bren-gun carrier.'

The divisional plan – in less thick bocage than their previous country around Hottot – was to attack with three battalions. On the right, 197 Brigade with 5th East Lancashire Regiment (5 E Lan R) was to take ground just to the east of Vendes and 177 Brigade with on the left 1st/6th South Staffords (1/6 S Staffords) which were to secure Brettevillette and Quetteville, while 5th South Staffords (5 S Staffords) was to advance on orchards west of Grainville-sur-Odon, and then Les Nouillons.

At 0500 hours, after a short and fitful night's sleep, Lieutenant Wilson led 12 Troop forward following 'the three long forms of the other troops' Crocodiles ... and tailed in behind them':

> As we reached the road, the artillery started firing. The guns were positioned all around. Their flashes lit the darkness, and the blast came unnervingly over the hedges. Standing up with my head and shoulders above the turret flaps, I suddenly felt grateful for the encircling armour and the warmth which began to seep from the engine.

The infantry of 177 Brigade moved off, leaving the Crocodiles, as so often before, waiting in the FUP. Wilson's experience must have been typical:

> From time to time there were long bursts of machine-gun fire. Then came a new noise – a long low moaning then a series of crumps, which we knew were mortars. They began to explode in small angry bursts among the Crocodiles and I closed the flaps, pleasantly conscious that I was now under fire and that the fire could do me no harm.

The Crocodiles of C Squadron sat in the FUP all day, but no call came for their services. Despite capturing almost 400 prisoners and throwing in three fresh battalions including in a night attack, 177 Brigade was stalled before Noyers and 197 had been driven back to their start line by heavy counter-attacks. Of the tanks, B Squadron of 144 Regiment RAC lost thirteen Shermans to mines and one to a *Panzerfaust*.

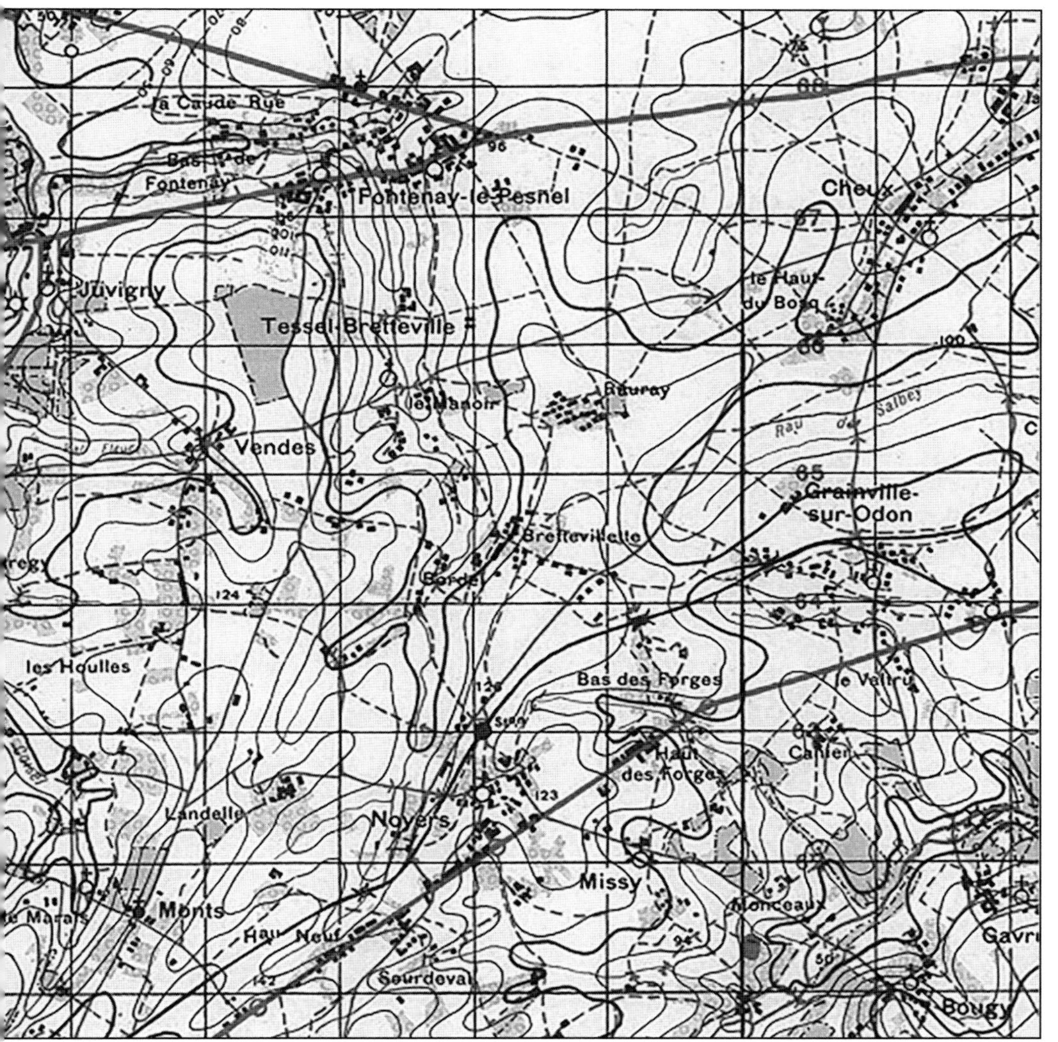

At troop level most map-reading was done using a 1:50,000 map that did not have a lot of detail to work on in difficult bocage country. Extract of GSGS series 4250, Sheet 7F/1 Caen covering the POMEGRANATE battle area.

On the 17th the call to action finally came. With Captain Barber leading, 11, 12 and 14 troops went forward to join 1/7 Royal Warwickshire in renewing 197 Brigade's attack. They were supported by the Shermans of 1 Northamptonshire Yeomanry, with the aim of recapturing the previous day's Phase One objective that had been lost to counter-attack. Lieutenant Grundy's 14 Troop were first in action helping the infantry break into an area of hedges and orchards. It was noted in the war diary that 'it was a complicated operation tied up for an H Hour of 1230':

> 14 Tp (Lieut Grundy) was the first in action assaulting the woods and orchards at 871646 [a wood and hamlet between Le Bordel and Vendes] with

A Sherman of 144 RAC (number on right mudguard) of 33 Armoured Brigade (green-over-blue diablo on left mudguard).

> 'C' Coy of the Royal Warwicks, and very well sp by 'B' Sqn. 1 Northants Yeomanry. Further sp was provided by a battery of SPs, the Div Arty and inf mortars. Although small it was in every way a successful action. The plan was well tied-up, the infantry moved some 20 yds only behind the Crocodiles and Besa was used in addition to flame but owing to the proximity of the infantry 75mm HE was off. Several PoW were captured. The Crocodiles were released beyond mortar range immediately after the action.[12]

The Crocodiles did their job and the attack was a success. Elsewhere on their divisional front, 177 Brigade resumed their attack on Noyers. That afternoon it was to have been the turn of Lieutenant Wilson's 12 Troop, but mechanical issues intervened:

> At the same time plans were going on for the use of Crocodiles on the outskirts of NOYERS in four separate phases. 12 Tp were destined for Phase I but owing to the difficult country two of the Crocodiles developed mechanical defects and could not get to the Start Line. In Phase III 11 Tp (Lieut Wareing) successfully flamed houses first knocked down by the AVREs at 883627 but the inf did not follow up – in fact Lieut Wareing claims that he did the operation in magnificent solitude, neither Germans nor British being anywhere nearby.

This attack and a second later in the afternoon made little progress against determined enemy resistance in Noyers. The Yeomanry noted that 'five of our [gun] tanks were knocked out, the squadrons having been already seriously depleted by mine casualties in the previous days' fighting.' As darkness fell the infantry again withdrew and Noyers was subjected to another night's shelling by the Royal Artillery.

On the 18th C Squadron was committed to battle on three separate occasions, during which Lieutenant Wilson was finally in action for the first time, flaming in support of 197 Brigade:

> Suddenly the hum in the headphones cut out. It was Barber calling them forward. They were going into flame. The other troop [11] led. They ran along a path marked by tapes. Beside it was something black, swarming with flies, beneath a German camouflage cape. Further on were the first dead British.
>
> At the start of a rise Barber was waiting with the infantry C.O. He made an up and down movement with his clenched fist, which was the sign for opening the nitrogen bottles on the trailers. Wilson jumped down.

Captain Barber delivered brief orders to flame an orchard and a hedgerow beyond. 'There are some Spandaus there. Flame them out. The infantry will follow you. A Sherman troop's waiting to cut off the enemy at the back.' With the other troop leader, Wilson ran back to the Crocodiles where the crews were closing the trailer doors and shouted 'Mount!' and once they were aboard 'Driver, advance. Gunner, load H.E.' 'The troops moved forward in line abreast, Wilson's on the left. As they came through a hedge, mortaring started. Everywhere infantry were crouching in half-dug foxholes, trying to protect their bodies from the bursts of the bombs.'

A Crocodile and its flame fuel trailer.

With mortar bombs exploding around them, the six Crocodiles went through several hedgerows, with commanders looking through the periscopes scanning for the orchard:

> Suddenly it came into view: a bank of earth, another hedge, and beyond it the orchard. 'There you are. Dead ahead, driver.' The driver slammed down into second gear. The tank reared up for a moment, so that you couldn't see anything but the sky; then it nosed over the bank, and through the periscope he was looking down, a long, empty avenue of trees ... The sergeant and corporal moved their tanks into the avenues on each side of him. The other troop started firing their machine guns, and Wilson took the cue: 'Co-ax, fire!'

As was more often the case than not, there was no visible target to indicate, just an open field where the avenue through the orchard ended a couple of hundred yards away. Opening fire, the Besa 'broke into a roar, filling the turret with bitter fumes ... details of the field became visible, not so much a field as a wilderness of scrub. A hundred yards to go. The forward edge was in range now.' Lieutenant Wareing's 11 Troop was flaming to the right and Wilson ordered 'Flame gun, fire!'

> There was the well-remembered hiss, the slapping like leather. The fuel shot out, spraying the trees, paving the ground with a burning carpet. The tank ran on through it. 'Slap it on, flame-gunner, all you've got!' The flame leapt out with an almost unbroken roar. The driver was slowing up, uncertain where to go. Suddenly the leader of the other troop called across the wireless: 'Hello, Item Two. Don't go into this lot. Let them have it from where you are!'

Lieutenant Wilson recalled that he could only see blazing undergrowth, but he kept his Crocodiles flaming at the edge of the field 'till the fire rose in one fierce, red wall':

> Then the gun gave a splutter like an empty soda-water syphon. He looked round. The other troop had finished. They were already heading back through the smoking orchard. He turned his own tanks and followed. Beneath the trees with smouldering leaves, the British infantry were coming in with fixed bayonets.

Other than some dead Germans several days old, Wilson had not seen any sign of the enemy and asked Lieutenant Wareing 'But where were the enemy?' 'Don't worry about the enemy,' his fellow troop commander replied, 'all you've got to do on these jobs is to get in and flame.' In the bocage country and the hedges and orchards surrounding villages the enemy was seldom seen. This was a matter of discussion in 12 Troop: 'Some said that as soon as the Germans saw the Crocodile trailers, they pulled out; others that they lay low, hoping that the flames would go over them.'

That day C Squadron was in action four times in the same area: 'The pattern was always the same. A call to pressure up; a quick conference with the infantry; a run across some fields to flame an enemy you never saw.' The war diary commented that they were all 'affected by mechanical troubles which have a high proportional effect on the efficiency of a single troop effort.'

From the Crocodiles' point of view their flame actions were successful, but indecisive because the infantry did not come in quickly enough and the infantry of 277th Infantry Division, still full of fight, counter-attacked. They were supported by a *Kampfgruppe* from 9th *Hohenstaufen* SS Panzer Division, consisting of the pioneer battalion and a company of Panzer IVs of 7/II Battalion, plus anti-aircraft and conventional artillery. The squadron's last flaming during 18 July was with 177 Brigade, whose attempts to capture the ridge centred on Noyers were in their third day, and it was a disaster. This attack was on an orchard and hedges to the north of the hamlet of Haut des Forges, which stood on the Caen to Villers-Bocage road (see map on page 145: 'Obj 1b'). The squadron's war diary recorded:

> Finally, an attack on the orchards and buildings to the N.E. of NOYERS ... with 1/6 Staffs, 2 AVREs and the sp of one field regiment. The inf did not

The country around Noyers is similar to the thicker bocage to the west but has larger fields.

in fact reach the start line, nor did the Inf Coy Comd keep his RV with the Armd Comd and the Crocodile Comd (Capt Hall). Nevertheless, the armour assured Capt Hall that the inf could be there and both AVREs and Crocodiles (13 Tp under Lieut. Welch) went in.

13 Troop was in support and Lieutenant Wilson's 12 Troop was following behind. He later wrote:

> The division they were working with was fighting forward a few hundred yards at a time. The troops were going into action in pairs, and it was the turn of the Argentinian [Lieutenant Welch] and Sherrif. Squadron Headquarters and the other troops were lying under cover behind a small ridge, waiting to hear the wireless message which would mean that Sherrif and Argentine were crossing the start-line.
>
> At last it came. For a minute there was nothing but the mush of atmospherics in the headphones and the sound of shelling and mortaring all around. Then suddenly someone shouted across the net: 'Look out – in the clearing!' Immediately there was heavy firing. It was over to the left.
>
> The Argentinian called: 'Hello Item Three …' But the message never finished. There was a terrific crack.
>
> A few yards away, [Major] Duffy stood in the turret of his headquarters tank, clutching his microphone, trying to find out what had happened. But the net was jammed with a confusion of calls. The tanks were caught in the fire of a Panther, and the infantry were being cut down by Spandaus.

The squadron war diary records:

> All four [two AVREs and two Crocodiles] were 'brewed up' by two 75mm guns (this was deduced many days later when it was possible to examine them). Two Mk VIIs and trailers were thus completely destroyed with no hopes of recovery as the inf had not occupied the ground. Lieut Welch was killed in bailing out (although Sgt Warner gave him smoke protection), the gunner was killed by the 75mm and the other three badly burned. Sgt Lamer's crew were evacuated by the remaining Crocodile and he himself made valiant efforts single-handed and on foot to go to Lieut Welch's assistance. Futile losses, these.

Lieutenant Wilson concluded his account of the action north of Haut des Forges:

> At last the tanks were ordered to withdraw. The artillery put down a smokescreen, and the Crocodiles came in, one by one, across the ridge. There were only five of them. Argentine's had been hit. He had bailed out with his crew, but a few yards from cover a Spandau had got them.

Lieutenant Colonel Waddell instituted a system of 'Regimental Mentions' partly because gaining awards under General Montgomery's command was notoriously difficult and slow. Regimental Mentions provided a more immediate recognition.

Even though the Germans were by this point in the campaign fully aware of the Crocodile, the composition of the flame fuel was still secret. Trailers that had to be abandoned in the battle area were blown up or in some cases 'attacked' by the RAF to burn off the fuel.

Sergeant Warner was Lieutenant Welch's troop sergeant during the attack on Haut de Forges:

> Sergeant Warner J in action saw his troop commander's tank hit and 'brewed up'. He immediately put down smoke to cover the crew while they 'bailed out'. Shortly after his own tank was hit and put out of action. Having seen his crew safely back he returned to look for his Troop Leader and tried for upwards of two hours to get forward. Eventually he was sent back when an artillery concentration fell on the area. He brought all codes back with him.
>
> By his action he showed loyalty, courage, calmness and leadership which are an example to the Regiment.

Operation POMEGRANATE was called off by XXX Corps, with the attacks by 59th Division south towards Noyers being stalled on the outskirts of the village, but Point 126 was in their hands. The operation had cost '1,250 killed, wounded and missing in the division during three days' fighting.' As far as C Squadron's flaming role was concerned, they had lost two Crocodiles knocked out and suffered significant battle and mechanical damage. The lessons recorded in the war diary were as follows:

> From the 16–18 Jul then 'C' Sqn had thus found themselves committed to six single tp actions, many of which had been seriously affected by mechanical defects. The main lessons from all these actions were:
>
> 1) That an allotment of a single troop is fatal as mechanical defects (which are relatively high for the Crocodile Special equipment) have a high proportional effect on a single fighting tp's strength.

2) It is absolutely vital for the Crocodiles to do their OWN planning with the infantry and have a close-tie-up.
3) Without infantry following behind the whole effort is completely wasted and at far greater risk to the Crocodiles.

Before leaving the operation, a word must be said of the very good sp given by 144 RAC under Lieut-Col Jolly in the actual fighting. It was first class [support to 177 Brigade and Captain Barber's half-squadron].

When the operation was finally called off, C Squadron returned to La Senaudière where they were to again support 50th Division, but their part in an attack was cancelled and the squadron returned to RHQ and the LAD at Brécy for further much-needed maintenance.

The Raid on Le Bon-Repos: 23 July 1944

Very well-planned 'shock' raid. Good artillery and tank support. Inf. followed up well. Fine flaming a big success. [141 RAC report]

Back on XII Corps' front, 53rd Welsh Division was subject to a series of German counter-attacks during the afternoon and evening of 21 July, one of which had retaken the hamlet of Le Bon-Repos from 1/5 Welch. The battalion had suffered badly during the fighting with 116 casualties. In order to regain a moral superiority over the enemy, 53rd Welch Division mounted a 'reprisal raid' which, following their previous success, included seven of A Squadron's Crocodiles:

53 Welsh Division is to stage a very carefully planned attack with a view to demonstrating their superiority over the SS and taking prisoners. Thus as Capt Storrar was enjoying a fitful afternoon nap and dreaming what he would do to a pint of beer in the rear later ('A' Sqn were due for a rest) he was rudely awakened and once again asked to co-operate [in an attack]. On this occasion the raid was to be done with the 4 Welch and again the 107 RAC as per diagram.

So as not to repeat the direction of attack, this time the road from Tourmauville was used as its axis, but the concept was similar with the Churchills of Colonel Cottis' 107 RAC forward and to the flanks, with the infantry of Lieutenant Colonel Williams' 4th Battalion the Welch Regiment following.

'There was very little time for the tie-up with the infantry and had it not been for the young and very able CO of the 4 Welch the whole thing might have been a glorious MFU – as it transpired it was again a great success.' The inclusion of a seventh Crocodile under Lieutenant Griggs to provide a confidence-building demonstration to the infantry must have been a factor in the raid's success.

The sketch map from the squadron war diary showing the raid on 23 July 1944.

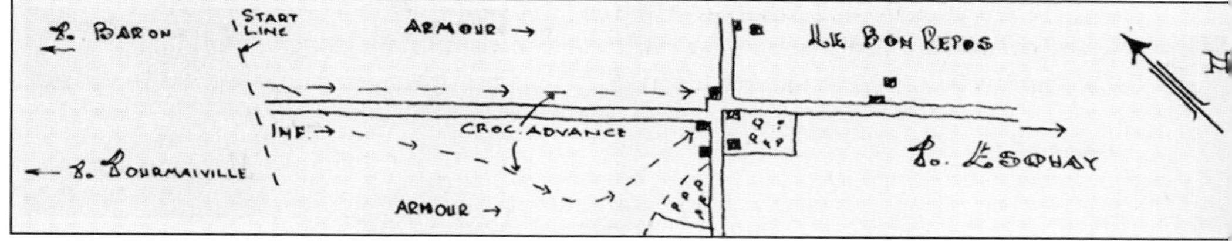

A photograph of a Crocodile flaming taken during one of the demonstrations laid on for commanders and assault troops.

Captain Storrar and Lieutenant Andrews commanded the headquarters tanks and the troops by Second Lieutenants Tunbridge and McCulloch (3 and 2 troops respectively). On crossing the start line four of the Crocodiles, supported by tanks and artillery, 'flamed their way madly to the objective, saturated it with flame, Besa and HE, watched the infantry in, turned and came straight back to their Sqn without a casualty.' Major Lewis, one of the 4 Welsh company commanders, wrote that in the darkness:

> The Crocs arrived and fired large squirts of flame at one of my platoons. The Germans and my own troops ran away from those hellish flames. The Crocs then turned their attention to a house on a corner where some twenty Germans letting out agonising screams were sizzled to death. My lads appear to have dodged the flames but God knows how. Our infantry continue to knock hell out of the enemy and they are soon on the run.

The raid passed on through to Esquay with a 'goodly number of PW taken, a large number of the enemy killed, and the infantry informed us that sixteen men were killed in the house at LE BON-REPOS alone.' This time Major General Ross wrote a letter congratulating the Crocodiles on their effort and

> I also wish to acknowledge the assistance of the two troops of 141 RAC. I agree with Lieut-Col WILLIAMS that it would have been preferable to have had longer time to arrange the co-operation of the Infantry and the Crocodiles but it was only known at 1500 hrs that they would be available.

> In spite of this lack of time their assistance was invaluable. Their disposal of the 16 men occupying the house at 945615 must alone have saved the attacking troops many casualties.

The Crocodiles deployed each used half a tank of flame fuel in this operation. 'On the next day "A" Squadron joined RHQ for a very well-earned rest.' Lieutenant Colonel Waddell's headquarters and D Reserve Squadron were still located north of the Caen-Bayeux road at Brécy in the centre of the Second Army's area and it was from here that he continued to sally forth, normally in a scout car with an accompanying jeep, to visit squadrons warned for operations.

While A Squadron was in action at Le Bon-Repos, the Luftwaffe were mounting one of their nightly raids on the cramped rear area. Another of Lieutenant Colonel Waddell's Regimental Mentions for a member of a fitter section recorded the following:

> On the night of Sunday 23rd July 1944, a heavy air raid was made on A Sqn's harbour. During the raid a camouflage net and a petrol lorry belonging to 107 RAC was set on fire. Tpr JENKINS even though the bombs were still falling rushed out from under an ARV and proceeded to put the fires out. By his prompt action and disregard to personal danger, he prevented the petrol lorry exploding and thereby putting other 'A' and 'B' vehicles in jeopardy.[13]

79th Armoured Division

It was not until September 1944 that 141 Regiment RAC formerly re-joined 31 Tank Brigade and 79th Armoured Division. As early as mid-July, however, the regiment's Crocodile holdings were already being listed in 30 Armoured Brigade's ordnance returns (see Appendix I) to 79th Division.

On D-Day the two troops had leaguered with the flails of the 22 Dragoons and after that being attached to their old formation, 31 Tank Brigade, made sense. However, with the regiment's three squadrons being deployed with various corps, it was logical for them to be routinely administered by 79th Armoured Division, whose assets were similarly dispersed.

Halfway through the campaign, Captain Bailey complained that 'although our relations with some [formations] are shall we say a little strained':

> ... a period of learning the hard way, a costly penny packet experiment over which the Regiment could have little control. During this time the CO careering over the whole front at a frightening pace, covered many hundreds of miles in his efforts to be at every action so that the hard principles from our battle experience could be extracted and hammered home to every possible arm he came into contact. Many times he was unable to be present at the planning stage and unable to rescue his troops from the whims of those who one minute had never seen a Crocodile and the next minute tossing encyclopaedists on the weapon. Nevertheless, from many costly actions, the necessary data was gathered, both positive and negative with which to

Major General Percy Hobart (left) with Montgomery and his staff later in the campaign inspecting the remains of a 'V' weapon.

buttress our old contentions, build up new ones and present a simple basic Crocodile doctrine to higher command.

The informal attachment to General Hobart's command in mid-July gave 141 RAC better protection from misuse. To ensure doctrine was actually applied, staff officers from the 79th Armoured Division were increasingly deployed to formations to assist with planning and to ensure that the 'Funnies', including the Crocodile, were properly integrated into plans and that their capabilities were used to best advantage.

2in Bomb Thrower

In addition to ten 75mm smoke rounds, the Churchill Mk VII's turret was fitted with a 2in Bomb Thrower. Fired from under cover, it used the same 2in white phosphorous bomb as the infantry's platoon mortar and provided the tank with an instantaneous smoke screen normally used to cover a withdrawal or cover from fire.

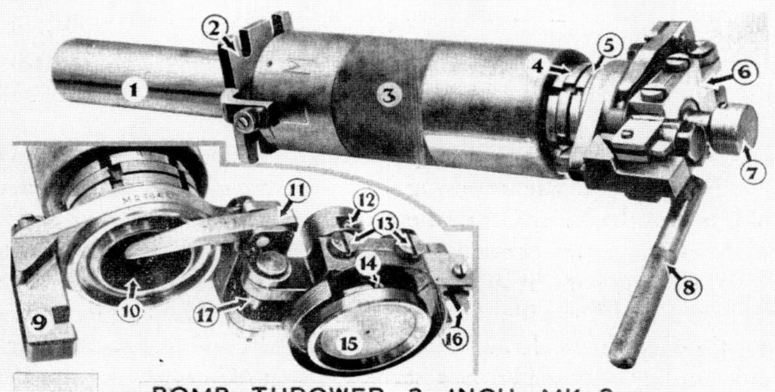

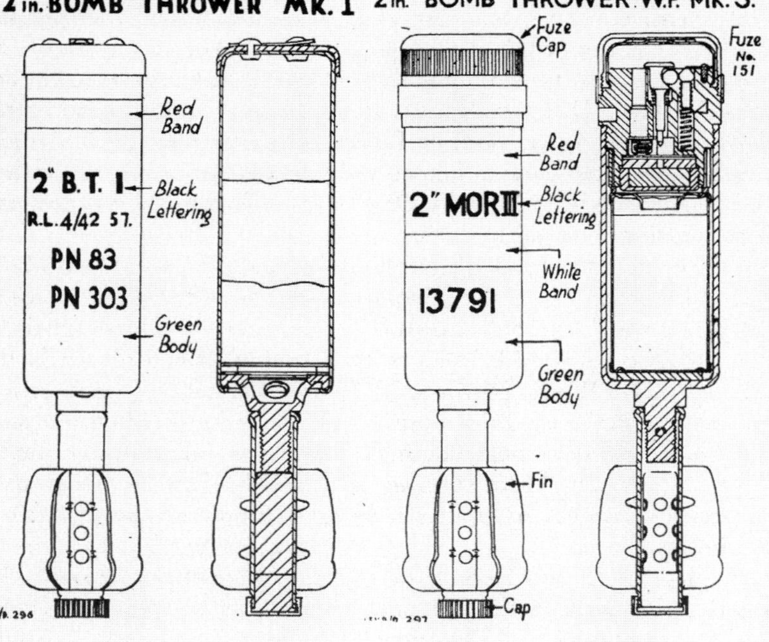

Chapter Eight

The Triangle

> Very well-planned and carried out. Continuous employment more or less for 5 hours. Crocodiles invaluable. Ideal use.[1] [51st Division]

During D+1 51st Highland Division had landed behind 3rd Canadian Division on JUNO Beach, but in the following days were transferred, still under I Corps command, east of the River Orne where the depleted 6th Airborne Division and Commandos were under pressure. All three brigades of the division held the 3-mile south-facing front from the Orne to the Bois de Bavent, via the villages of St. Honorine and Escoville. For more than a month the Highlanders were in static positions, with the large Colombelles works and chimneys overlooking them and consequently suffering a steady stream of casualties from persistent mortaring and shelling. This was not at all to the liking of this most mercurial division and, along with several failures, had a marked effect on the veteran division's morale and self-confidence.

On 18 June, the Crocodiles of B Squadron were to take part in the GOODWOOD offensive, not yet as a part VIII Corp's armoured attack but still with I Corps on the eastern flank of the operation under command of 3rd Division. They would, however, be flaming in support of 152 Highland Brigade, detached from 51st Highland Division. Along with the tanks of 27 Armoured Brigade, the 3rd Division was to thrust south to Troarn and Émiéville, widening the breach made by the armoured division immediately to their west. The rest of the Highland Division's role in GOODWOOD was to follow up behind the armoured divisions securing their gains.

With the operations already described by XII and XXX corps west of the Orne having fixed the majority of the armour in their areas, I and VIII corps and the newly-operational II Canadian Corps faced an in-position force of two German infantry divisions: the 346th Infantry and the 16th Luftwaffe Field divisions backed up by 21st Panzer Division. The Germans were deployed in a layered defence, not 5 miles as the British expected but almost 10 miles deep, stretching back to the Bourguébus ridge south of Caen. The only uncommitted enemy reserve was the shattered 12th *Hitlerjugend* SS Panzer Division which, after more than a month in combat, had only just been withdrawn to refit a day's march to the south-east.

On the night of 16 July, B Squadron joined the road move among the three armoured divisions, brigades and mass of artillery heading east towards the five bridges across the Orne. This move east was, however, on a wholly different

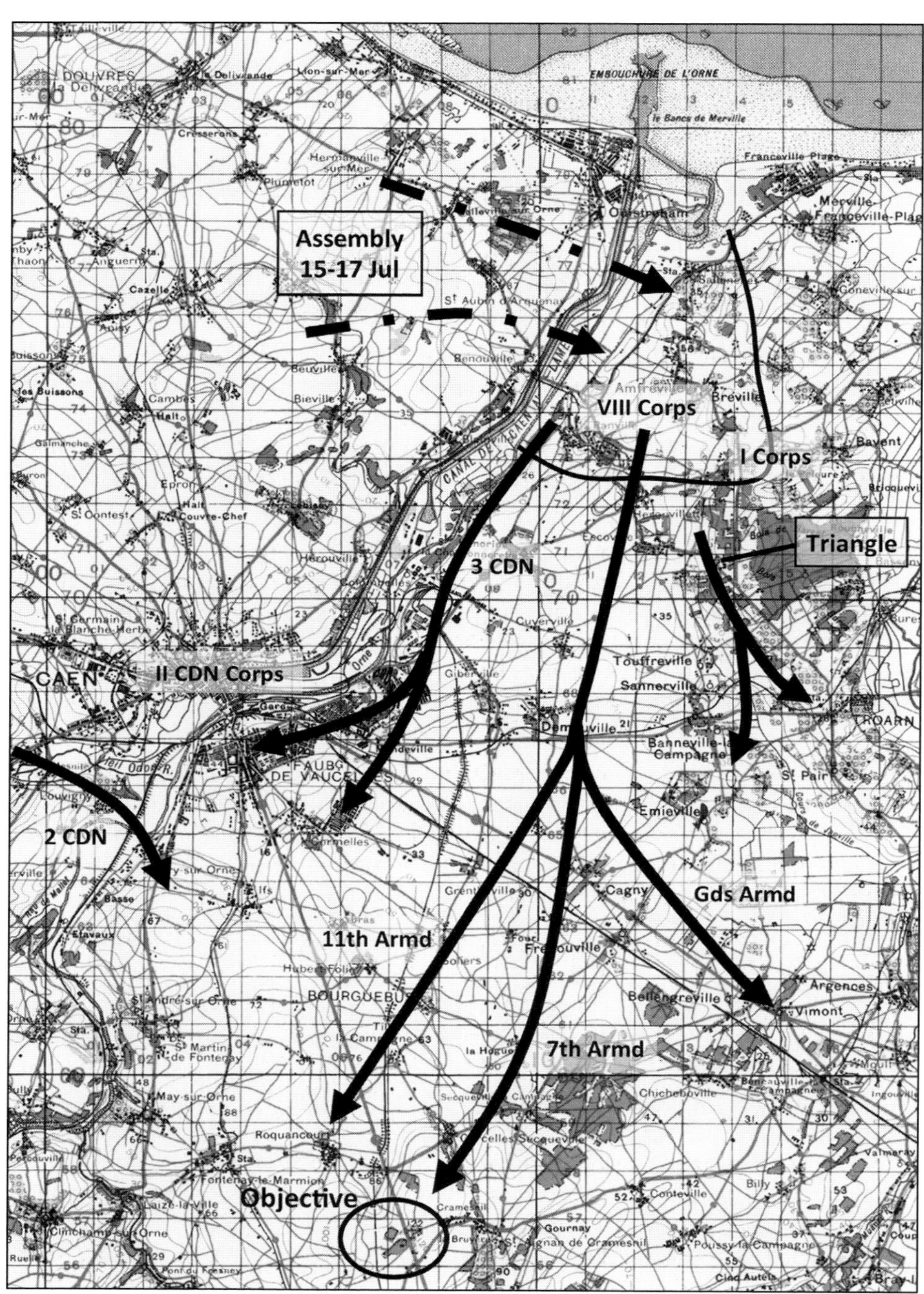

Outline of Operation GOODWOOD plan.

scale to previous redeployments, requiring detailed planning by staff officers from Headquarters Second Army down to unit level. Captain Bailey described B Squadron's move:

> There was appalling darkness, fog, dust and traffic congestion, and for a long time it looked as if they would never reach their destination before daylight, vital for security and surprise. But in some uncanny way Roy Moss as Recce Officer somehow kept them crawling and finally brought them into an orchard at 133724, about a mile north and slightly west of the Start Line, and some 200 yards from enemy positions in the east. That is all except his own tank which fell out on the way and was left in charge of Sgt Jake Morley.

Even with aircraft and artillery fire attempting to cover the sound of massed armoured movement, a squadron arriving within 200 yards of the enemy outposts can have left the Germans in little doubt over the imminence of another offensive. The squadron laid up in the orchard until the morning of 18 July, but do not at this stage mention being mortared. A recce of the operation's FUP and start line by Lieutenant Moss did, however, prompt plenty of enemy fire:

> The 'yeoman' colonel was most concerned to impress on them the need to step carefully as the ground was covered in trip wires designed to set off warning flares. 'Now you must step carefully see, use a stick and feel for them gently, or you'll set 'em off and bring all the **** in creation down. Like this, see. Teach you to be infantrymen yet, what!' At this third tentative prod of demonstration up zoomed reds, greens, whites and all the colours of the rainbow – and down came all the ****in creation.

From the Highlanders' forward positions, Lieutenant Moss, escorted by an infantry patrol, set out to recce the route the squadron would take to the start line. On reaching 'the northern edge of the orchard where they halted', Moss, a commander of tanks, found himself conducting a solo close target recce for which his training at the RAC's Officer Cadet Training Unit had not prepared him:

> 'From now on sir, it's all yours.' Now if you've got a backside like a junior barrage balloon and your Boy Scout days are long since over, you don't enthusiastically go playing cowboys and Indians in broad daylight with Germans just licking their lips at the sight of a nice bit of juicy target flesh. But Bonko [Moss] just rustled along into their lines, saw what he wanted to see, and rustled back to where the waiting patrol received him back with somewhat mild surprise.

Facing the Highland Division were battalions of the 857 and 858 Grenadier regiments of Lieutenant General Diestel's 346th Infantry Division, with a 300-strong III Battalion 857 Regiment holding the Triangle.[2] This was the name given to an area bounded by roads to the west of the Bois de Bures on the slopes of the high ground that dropped down to the plain across which VIII Corps' armoured thrust was to take place.

One of 5 Seaforths' 3in mortars. Note the No.1 is wearing an AFV crew helmet.

152 Brigade's task at the beginning of the offensive was for 5 Seaforths to attack across a few hundred yards of no-man's-land and secure the apex of the Triangle before the other two battalions of the brigade (5 Queen's Own Cameron Highlanders and 2 Seaforths) advanced through them. They were to establish positions astride the Troarn road, while 3rd Division continued the advance. It was thought that as 'the country was heavily wooded … surprise would be effected by the use of Crocodiles or even tanks in such very close country.' The task of the Crocodiles was as recorded in the war diary, and for the first time it was to be a full squadron attack:

> Lieut R. Moss (Recce Offr) was to lead from the harbour to the orchard at 136709 where the troops were to fan out right and left. Right – 6 Tp (Lt. Henderson) supported by 9 Tp (Lt. Sander). Left –- 7 Tp (Lt. Barrow) supported by 10 Tp (Lt. Mason). Both were to deal with the X-rds and support 'A' & 'C' Coys [5 Seaforths] on to these objectives. They would support 'B' & 'D' Coys, which were to come through on to the apex of the triangle.

> Owing to trailer troubles in 6 Tp slight amendments had to be made to the plan – 9 Tp took over from 6 Tp and 6 Tp later came up in support of 9 Tp.

A replacement 8 Troop had still not been formed.

At H-Hour minus sixty minutes (H-60) the Crocodiles left their orchard assembly area to drive the mile forward to join the Seaforths in the FUP out in no-man's-land within 400 yards of the enemy positions. The noise of heavy and medium bombers totalling 2,000 aircraft that had been in action over the enemy since dawn had departed and now to the sound of an artillery barrage fired by 712 guns, the Crocodiles waited for H-Hour at 0745. The attack was led by 9 and 7 troops, with 6 and 10 following in support a bound behind:

> ... with guns blazing they emerged from the orchard, advancing steadily with the infantry. Within three minutes P.W. were coming in. On the right the advance went according to plan ... Sgt Norrington stood back at

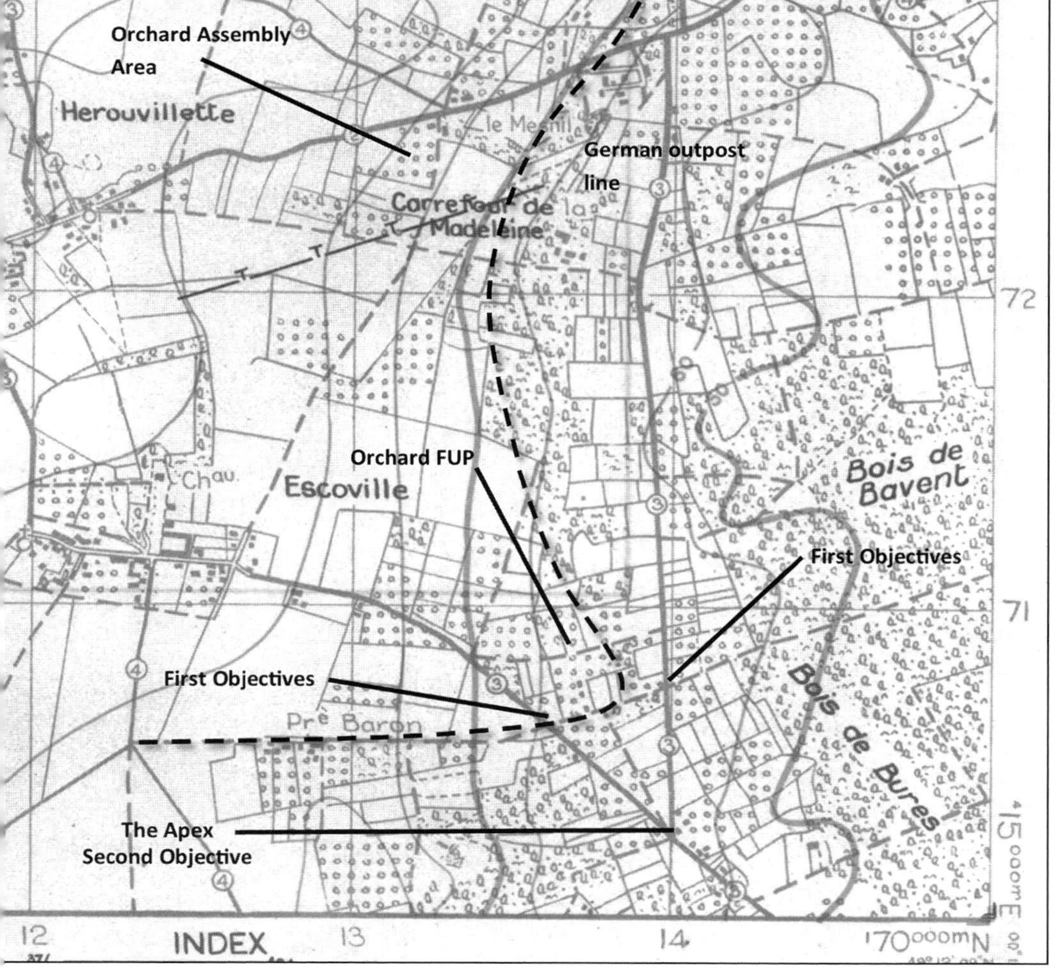

The area of B Squadron's attack on the Triangle with 5 Seaforths.

> the pond giving covering fire to Peter and Sgt Decent who went in with customary élan to flame the German positions at the crossroads, catching them in the midst of breakfast preparations. They killed many and ousted others. Pausing only to shoot up a section of Germans moving behind a hedgerow across their front, they carried on in the direction of the apex.

The Crocodiles, as with 10 DLI at Hottot, were integrated into the initial assault alongside two companies of the Seaforths and would see them onto their first phase objectives. The FUP was so sited that other than the hedgerow that marked

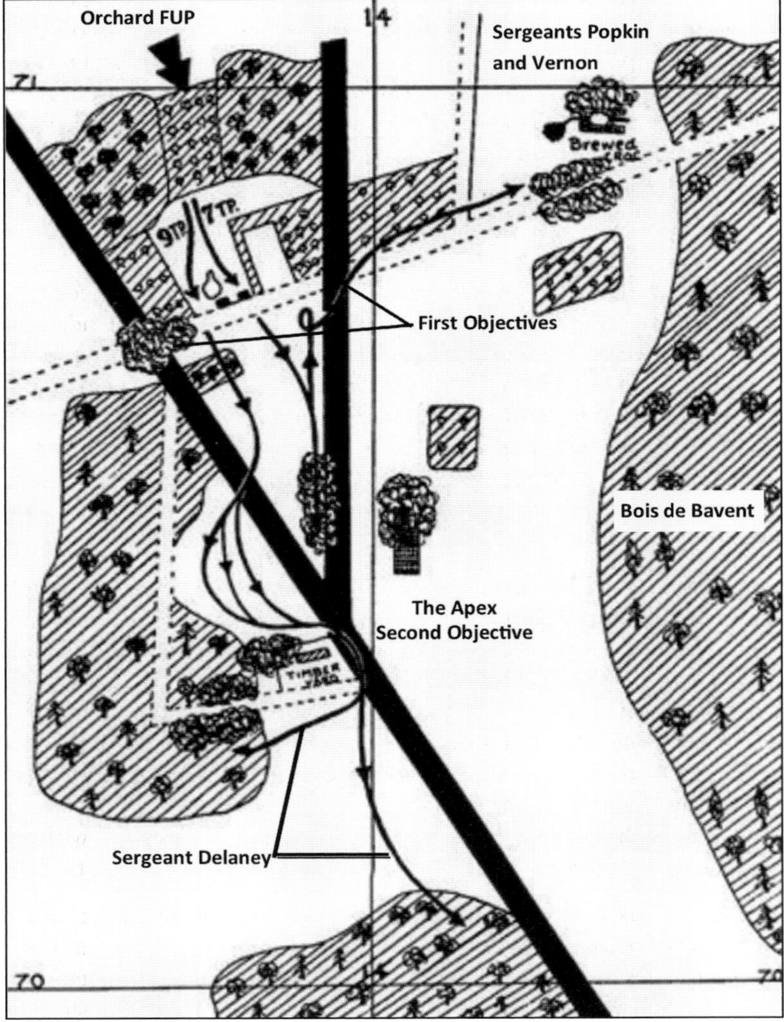

Captain Bailey's sketch map of B Squadron's action at the Triangle.

the forward edge of the FUP, the advance was a straight run at speed for 200–300 yards to the enemy outpost line. This, the first objective, was on the lateral road with its two crossroads. Here 9 Troop flamed the area around the right-hand crossroads. Captain Borthwick, the Seaforths' intelligence officer, recorded that C Company on the right met resistance on the base of the triangle: 'Two pockets of Bosch put up the biggest fight of the day; but a certain amount of dash by C Company and the appearance of three Crocodiles so impressed them that the survivors gave themselves up or went flat out for the woods.'[3]

On the left, Lieutenant Barrow took 7 Troop too far forward, missing the objective, but 'He carried on however flaming and gunning with great ferocity to the road, knocking out a 75mm anti-tank gun in the first few seconds.' In the absence of 7 Troop, Lieutenant Mason brought 10 Troop forward to flame the left crossroads, but in doing so ditched his tank, which took him out of the action.

With two fresh Seaforth companies, the advance to the second objective at the apex was resumed with 7 and 9 troops leading. At the apex they '... went in to make an absolute bonfire of the timber yard, thus establishing the infantry firmly on the final objective.' Captain Borthwick, watched the Crocodiles in action at the apex:

> ... they were beyond doubt among the more hellish contrivances of war. I watched them operating on D Company's copse. The Spandaus were blazing away cheerfully enough and then one of those horrors came waddling up. It gave them a burst of MG fire then quietly breathed on them. It was all very methodical and businesslike, just a thin jet of flame, which fanned out as it shot along close to the ground, until it arrived on the target in a great billowing cloud. Bushes caught fire everywhere. There was a pause. Again the jet of flame, the spread, the billowing cloud. The Spandaus stopped. Men ran burning.[4]

While the timber yard was being flamed, 'Sgt Decent machine-gunned further for snipers in the wood', helping the infantry significantly.

Meanwhile, with four hedgerows to clear *en route* to the second objective, 6 Troop's assistance to the infantry in mopping up behind the advance was needed as the attack carved its way quickly through III 876 Regiment's defences. Captain Bailey wrote: 'No. 6 Troop followed in a mopping-up role pumping out Besa and 75 in all directions, while the Infantry eventually reached the [second] objective led by 9 and 7 Troops.'

Following on behind them was Lieutenant Mason's 10 Troop, without their commander and his ditched tank. The other two Crocodiles were still in action:

> so [Sergeant] Pipkin carried on with Sgt Vernon in support. What happened to him then is a matter of conjecture. With strict orders not to cross the road 'Pip' nevertheless was inveigled into dashing off to flame some distant woods [to the east]. His tank hit two Tellers [anti-tank mines] and was then brewed up by bazooka fire.

Captain Borthwick, however, recorded that a B Company platoon had run into a group of Germans attempting to withdraw east through the hedgerows and woods to the Bois de Bures and 'two Crocodiles came up to help but were both knocked out.'

Sergeant Vernon's tank was the second Crocodile hit, but the driver managed to get it back to the crossroads where he 'got the wounded off to an RAP and later drove the tank back to harbour'. The bodies of Sergeant Pipkin and another crew member were brought in the following day by German stretcher-bearers.

> 7 Troop advanced to the crossroads where they found the infantry already installed in the little orchard just the other [east] side. Harry [Bailey, in a support tank] picked up a wounded infantryman and set off to take him along the lateral road. At that moment however from the other side of the cross-roads a strong body of Germans opened up and another Croc attack was put in to clear the road running north-east. Whilst 7 Troop went up the road flaming everything, Nigel [Ryle] shot up the woods and did a pincer round the back so that the position was cleared out.

Of this stage in the action, Captain Borthwick commented that '17 Platoon ... took a timber mill near the apex which the Crocodiles had breathed on and was burning hard.' 'Captain Ryle then became a little careless and strolled on unconcerned with Lieutenant Mason in search of Mausers. With startling suddenness two hefty Germans sprang out from the undergrowth in front of them – and surrendered.'

With the absence of normal gun tanks, the Seaforth company commanders asked 9 Troop to remain with them for some time, during which, probing forward, they located further Germans which they flamed as well.

In the absence of conventional armoured support, 5 Seaforths put the Crocodiles at the heart of their attack and with HE, Besa and flame from every tank in the squadron they played a significant role in a successful operation. For the Seaforths the attack on the Triangle was a welcome success that had eluded most of the rest of their division for some time. They counted eighty prisoners and fifty to sixty enemy dead, but this was at the not inconsiderable cost to themselves of eleven KIA and fifty-one wounded.[5] The losses to B Squadron were three killed and six wounded, and one Crocodile knocked out plus another badly damaged. Despite this, the regiment considered that 'The whole operation was a great success and the Squadron was congratulated and thanked by the GOC 1st Corps.'[6]

The cap badge of the 5th Seaforth Highlanders.

During the afternoon 3rd Division, supported by 27 Armoured Brigade, having been provided with a good start as the result of a successful break in battle, were fighting through the German defences towards Touffreville and Banneville.

The apex looking back towards the start line through some thick country. The timber mill is to the left of the picture, behind the hedge.

Although 152 Highland Brigade's part in the opening stage of Operation GOODWOOD, with the aid of Crocodiles, had gone well, it only partly restored their division's confidence and reputation as their previous failures had left their mark. The ensuing three weeks in the Triangle under almost constant mortar and artillery fire continued to sap the Highlanders' morale to an extent that the divisional commander, Major General Bullen-Smith, joined the growing list of senior officers being replaced.

It was not until late afternoon on the 18th that B Squadron was released and the Crocodiles drove back to their orchard, which was now 'a most unhealthy spot from every point of view':

> Though not subsequently required ten days were spent there under almost incessant mortar, artillery and indirect machine-gun fire. Units in the same field and adjacent fields were taking considerable casualties, but for a long time the luck of the Squadron held, only Tpr Gregg catching a bullet in the leg ... Sleep was impossible. Nerves were getting frayed.

When pulled back to leaguer but still within range of mortars, typically Crocodile turret crews would sleep under the Churchills in a shell rather than in the cramped confines of their battle stations. With more room, the driver and flame gunner tended to sleep in the tank's forward compartment.

By day the enemy air threat was negligible, but at night the odd squadron of German fighter-bombers was active when Allied fighters were largely grounded and anti-aircraft fire was less accurate. On the night of 26 July, it was B Squadron's turn to be located and attacked:

> It was pitch dark as they came in, flying pretty low and dropping flares till the whole area was light as day. They cruised around dropping hefty containers of deadly anti-personnel bombs all round, going for the guns.

The Bren gun with the 100-round drum magazines. Although issued as part of the Churchill's Complete Equipment Schedule, one crewman noted that his came without the loading tool, so unsurprisingly he rarely used it!

> Ammunition dumps were soon going up, adding colour to the scene. It looked as if they were going to miss this tiny little field, till a lone Bren gun tracer flickered up into the sky. Whoosh! In came the second wave with deadly accuracy.

Every Churchill tank was issued with a Bren gun with a 100-round drum magazine for air defence and it is possible that the aircraft were able to identify the

A Bren in the anti-aircraft role on its tripod mount with an AA sight.

Communications

The main radio, or wireless as it was then called, fitted to the Churchill was the WS No. 19 set that took up most of the rear wall of the turret. It comprised the following:

- The A high-frequency component with a range of up to 10 miles which was principally used for communication within the squadron and regiment.
- The B VHF component for communications within the troop or other arms. Its range was less than a mile and it was somewhat unreliable.
- An intercom system for the crew to talk to each other via microphones and headsets. There was also an emergency back-up for the commander to speak to the crew if the 19 set was damaged. The main armament loader was also the radio operator.

A second set, the WS 38, was also fitted, primarily for communicating with the supporting infantry, but it seems to have been seldom used, largely due to a lack of effective training with the infantry.

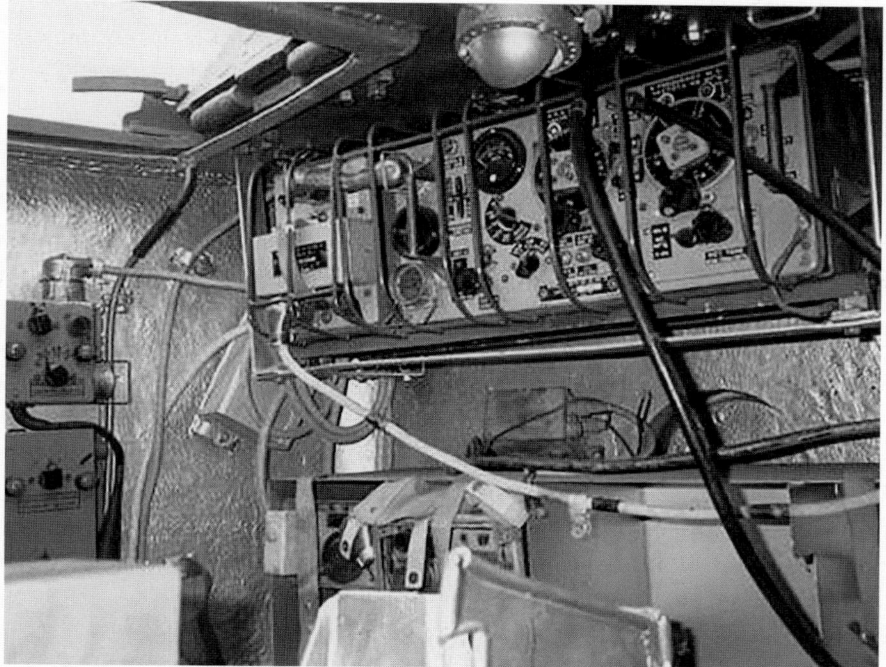

The Churchill radio fit.

A tank telephone (or I Box) was fitted to the rear of the Crocodile to allow infantry to speak directly to the crew. This, like the 38 Set, seems to have been little used due to a lack of training. It was instead mostly used by the crew to guide the driver when he was reversing to hitch up the armoured trailer.

source of the fire from the tracer rounds. With the crews diving for cover, the squadron bore the brunt of the aircrafts' attack. Ten men were wounded to a greater or lesser extent and considerable damage was done to the Crocodiles, equipment and the echelon's vehicles:

> When day broke all the trucks were found to have flat tyres, pools of FTF [flame fuel] were leaking from the punctured drums, and pools of water from the radiators. Whittingham was cursing blue murder about his precious water truck. But by and large the price had been astonishingly light.

Among the wounded was Major Spearpoint, who was evacuated to the UK, leaving Captain Ryle to take over command. The following day, B Squadron limped back to its base in the fields at Cresson.[7]

This aerial attack was probably carried out by aircraft of *Schlachtgeschwader* 10 flying the Focke-Wulf 190 F or G. This squadron was a dedicated fighter-bomber unit capable of night-flying and known to be operational in Normandy at the time. The fact that the attack was sustained rather than a single overflight is indicative of a fighter-bomber attack profile. This, coupled with the numerous explosions and the effect on men and equipment, makes the ordnance likely to have been a submunition, the 'Butterfly Bomb' (*Sprengbombe Dickwandig* 2 kg (SD-2)), which was dispersed from the AB 250-3 cluster bomb unit that could carry up to 108 SD-2 submunitions.

An unexploded Butterfly Bomb having been caught in a tree before hitting the ground and detonating.

The AB-250 cluster bomb

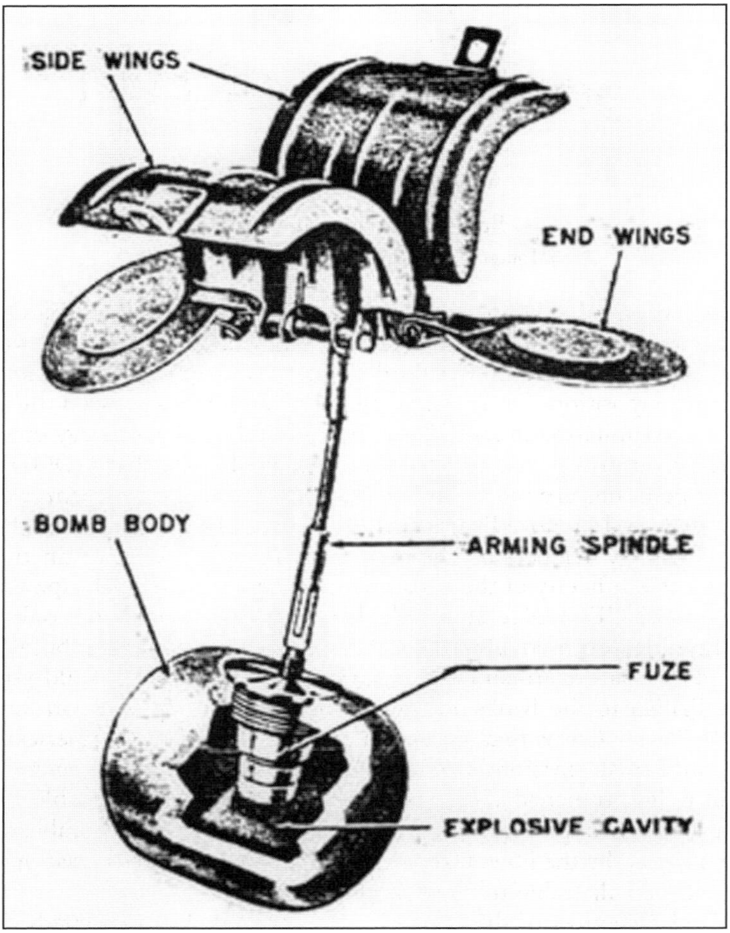

A diagram of the SD-2 Butterfly Bomb.

Chapter Nine

Operation BLUECOAT

Step on the gas to Vire.
[Montgomery to Dempsey, 28 July 1944]

After seven weeks of very slow progress in the hedgerow country, Operation COBRA, the long-awaited break-out in the west by the US First Army was finally under way on 25 July. Within days the Americans were gaining momentum south against scant opposition. On 27 July General Montgomery realized there was an opportunity to capitalize on the US success and outlined his strategy in his M515 Directive. Second Army was to take advantage of the fact that GOODWOOD and other operations around Caen had fixed six of the enemy's panzer divisions east of Noyers, and to move British formations west. In the bocage south-west of Bayeux, the enemy defences on the inter-army boundary were distinctly weaker and, despite the difficulty of the hedgerow country, were deemed ripe for attack.

Operation BLUECOAT, alongside US V Corps, would not only protect General Bradley's exposed left flank as he advanced to Avranches, but widen the breach and dissipate German counter-attacks. In addition, it would potentially place the British to the flanks and rear of the west-facing German formations of XLVIII Panzer Corps that were attempting to contain the Americans. First, however, six British divisions would have to break through the enemy's thinly spread but well-entrenched 276th and 326th Infantry divisions in a blow south of Caumont. Once through these divisions, which were sited in favourable defensive country enhanced by the liberal sowing of mines, the German formations further south would be vulnerable to envelopment.

The initial objectives of the two British corps were 10 miles south including Villers-Bocage, St.-Martin-des-Besaces and Aunay-sur-Odon (Line GROUSE). The ultimate objective 20 miles south was RUGBY on the Vire-Vassy road. On the left flank XXX Corps were to attack with the 43rd Wessex and 50th Infantry divisions, with the 7th Armoured Division poised for exploitation. Further west, VIII Corps would advance with 15th Scottish Division left and 11th Armoured right, with the Guards Armoured Division also ready to be released when the situation was ready for exploitation.

Operation BLUECOAT took the army into some difficult terrain, a wedge of high ground with two pronounced peaks. These were Mont Pinçon (Point 316) about 8 miles south of Villers-Bocage and Point 309 (Quarry Hill), some 5 miles due south of Caumont:

> The country was typical bocage but with a succession of pronounced ridges running across the southerly axis of advance. Streams run in all directions,

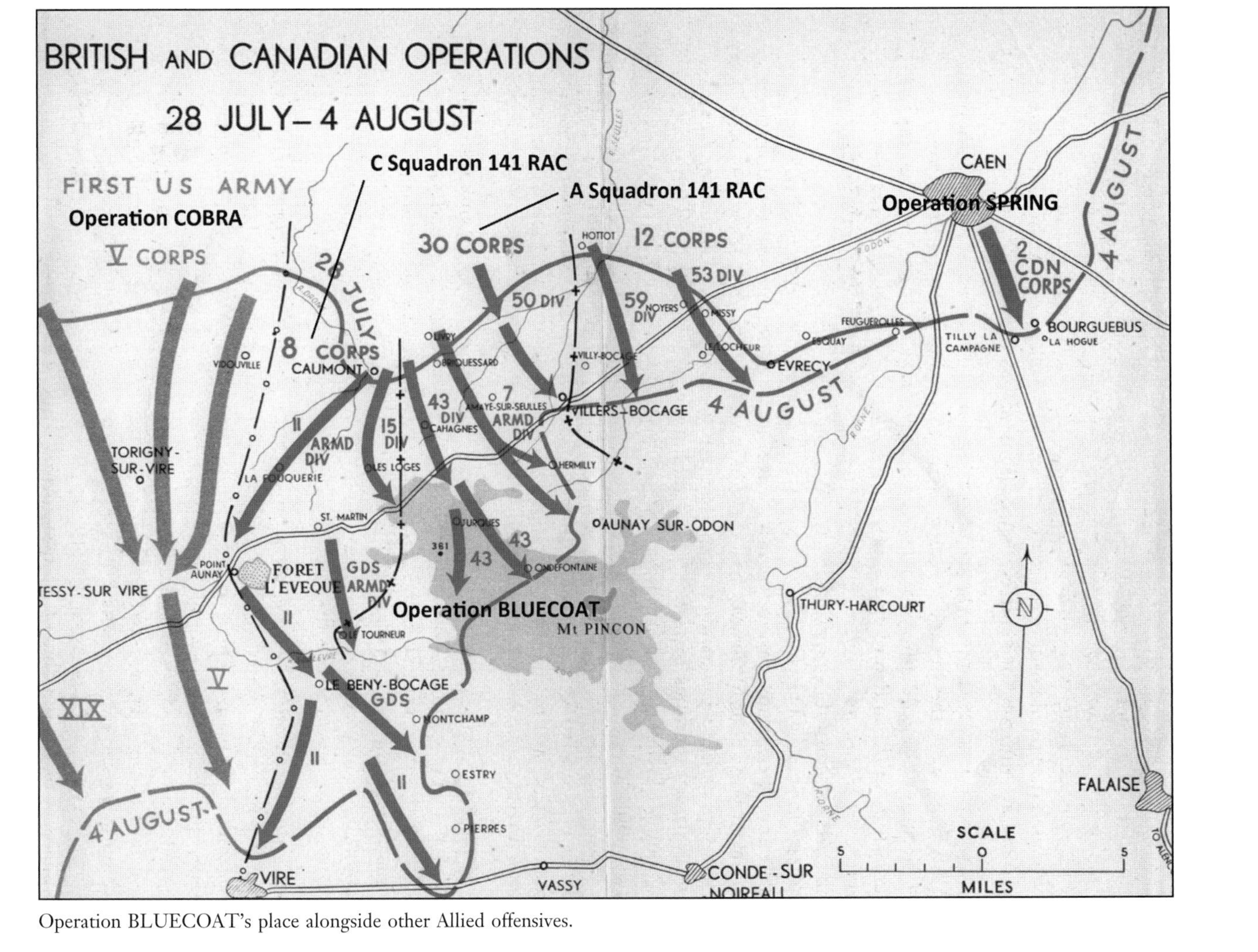

Operation BLUECOAT's place alongside other Allied offensives.

> and in many places constitute tank obstacles owing to their width, depth or marshy approaches. Decent metalled roads were few and far between, apart from the Caumont-St.-Martin-des-Besaces road, which was barely wide enough for two-way traffic. Otherwise, there were narrow farm tracks and minor bocage roads, usually wide enough for a single vehicle and were as ever tortuous, running between high banks and hedges. The area contains small villages, dispersed farming hamlets; 'the narrow tracks running through these places are difficult for vehicles, especially tanks, to negotiate.'[1]

It was more than evident to the formation planners that the advance was bound to be slow, with the bocage country 'hampering the bringing up of reserves, restricting the cross-country movement of tanks, carriers and other vehicles, and hindering supply and replenishment. In spite of the existence of certain view-points, the closeness of the country prevents detailed ground observation, or the accurate locating of opposition.'

The original D-Day for Operation BLUECOAT was 2 August, but with the American spearheads forging south, launching the attack from the area of Caumont was brought forward to 30 July. Consequently, on 29 July, 141 RAC's A and C squadrons joined the rear of a short-notice and enormously complicated lateral passage of lines from Brécy and La Paumerie respectively. They were to regroup with formations of VIII and XXX corps for the opening phase of the operation.

As an example of the difficulty of the march west, a young military police officer of the 43rd Wessex Division manning a traffic control point at a crucial road junction had to squeeze two lanes of traffic down a narrow embanked and hedged road:

> A cavalry officer at a head of a column ignored my men's hand signals, stopped and climbed down from his tank. Looking at the road we were directing him down, he said, 'It can't be done' and refused to move. Eventually, with my NCOs behind me, handcuffs in hand, I drew my revolver and said, 'It must be done!' Muttering about 'B***** red caps,' he climbed back into his tank and it was done.[2]

Both of 141's squadrons were not at their full strength, so were organized into four troops rather than five as a result of continuing repair, replacement and mechanical problems. There was, however, a new issue: battle casualty replacements that were in increasingly short supply.

While the Crocodiles of A and C squadrons were rushing west to support the British divisions' advance south, B Squadron, following its ten days under mortar fire and the air attack, spent the last week of July undertaking some serious refitting. While at Cresserons, well to the rear, they were 'indulging in their well-kept secret of the delights of Lion-sur-Mer'.[3]

Due to the rapid redeployment west in just forty-eight hours via insubstantial roads, it was impossible to mass the accustomed level of fire support for

Infantry carriers from a motor battalion and field artillery quads on the march to BLUECOAT.

BLUECOAT. In this case only 8 AGRA with four medium and one heavy regiment (fifty-six guns) was available to supplement the divisional gun groups. Therefore, the British and US bomber barons provided 700 heavy and 650 medium aircraft to deliver strikes on nine target areas in depth across the front of the two corps. These strikes would be followed up by the fighter-bombers of Second TAF taking on targets including Lutain Wood and opportunity targets further to the rear.

For this operation A Squadron was placed under the command of VIII Corps. Captain Strachan and two troops were attached to 6 Guards Tank Brigade, operating under 15th Scottish Division and the remainder of the squadron with Major Cooper went to 11th Armoured Division. As usual, C Squadron remained with XXX Corps and was back with 50th Infantry Division.

Almost on the inter-corps' boundary stood the ruins of Caumont, which had been taken by the Americans during the early days of the invasion, but had subsequently been just behind a static front and suffered badly: 'The Start Line for the advance ran just South of CAUMONT. This small town stands on the top of a ridge which gives good observation over the area of the advance but is itself dominated from the final objective (Point 309).'[4]

C Squadron: XXX Corps

While the Crocodiles were driving to General Bucknell's XXX Corps' assembly area east of Caumont, Major Duffy went ahead to attend 50th Division's orders group. Here he established that two of his troops would support the infantry brigades and that for the first time they would be working with 8 Armoured Brigade. H-Hour was to be at 0600 hours and the enemy was the by now significantly reduced regiments of 276th and 326th Infantry divisions. The squadron war diary records that:

> In this operation 'C' Sqn with two tps under Capt Barber allotted to 50 Div, thence sub-allotted 14 Tp (Lieut Grundy) to 231 Bde and 11 Tp (2/Lt. Wareing) to 56 Bde. The remainder under Major Duffy were u/c 8 Armd Bde and moved to LA PAUMERIE [as a reserve]. No protests at this splitting were of any avail – everyone must have a little bit 'just in case'.

On his way back from the O Group to his half-squadron's harbour area:

> ... Major Duffy had his celebrated night out. Having given orders for his portion of the Sqn to move to a given location he carried on liaising with the thousand and one personages and institutions which at any given moment will provide you with a hundred and one 'perfect jobs for the Crocodiles old boy'.
>
> In the darkness Major Duffy, enthroned in his scout car, set off to find his Sqn. For hours this search went on until from out of those electric whiskers there proceeded an obscenity and 'We'll kip here for the night.' At first light the 10.5cm under whose very muzzle he had unbeknowingly parked his car opened fire – the car was given an initial impetus of some 12 yards and never stopped moving.

Lieutenant Colonel Bredin of 1 Dorsets of 231 Brigade provides an insight into one aspect of battle procedure of which Captain Barber was a part:

> The Commanding Officer's 'O' (or Orders) Group on the 29th was typical of the enormous size to which these time-honoured gatherings had swollen – besides all the representatives such as company commanders and specialist platoon commanders from within the Battalion, our supporting arms representatives included the armoured squadron commander (of the 13th/18th Hussars), the commander of two troops of Crocodiles, the commander of the troop of flails (Westminster Dragoons), the guns (of 124th Field and

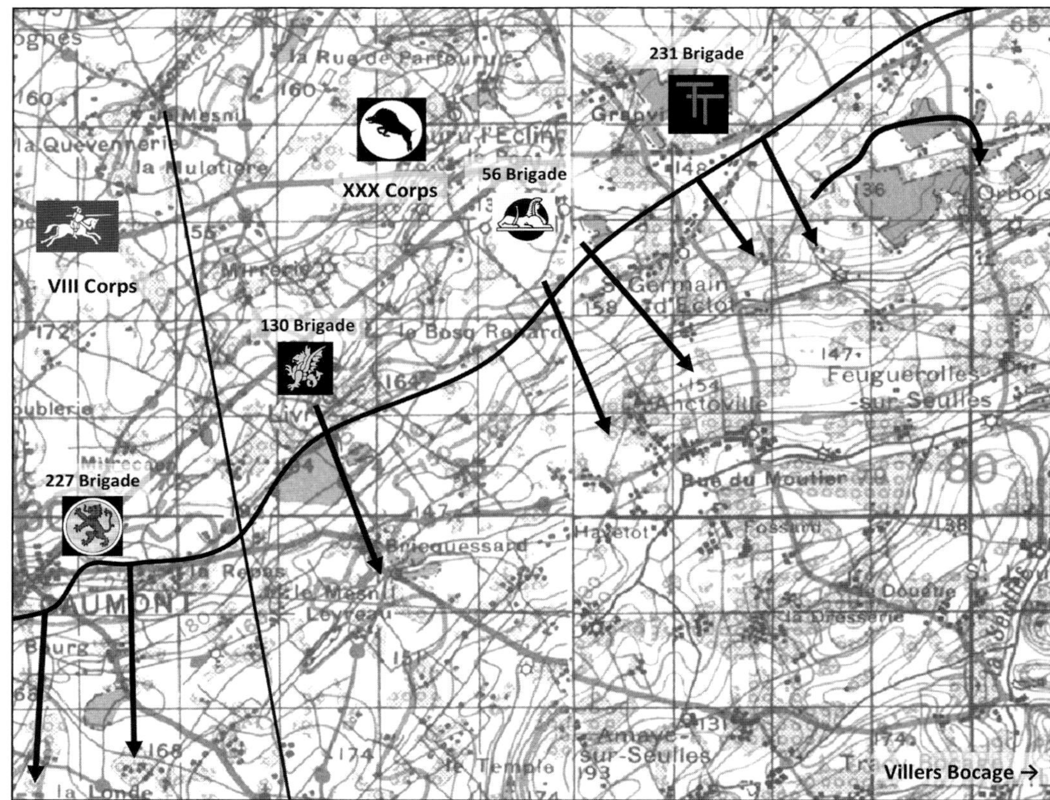

XXX Corps' Operation BLUECOAT: 30–31 July 1944.

> 99th Anti-Tank Regiments), the sappers (of 295th Field Company) and the machine-gunners (of B Company, 2nd Cheshires). Later, the squadron Commander of our supporting armoured regiment was usually put in charge of all the 'funnies' like the Crocodiles and flails.[5]

56 Brigade: St.-Germain-d'Ectot

At 0800 hrs on 30 July, 11 Troop, under Lieutenant Wareing, was scheduled to cross the start line with 2nd South Wales Borderers (2 SWB) but he 'found himself with not a single trailer fit for action':

> The route to the start line was too tough for them. The infantry Bn without success launched three attacks on MGs in the orchard at 768624 [see map SW of St.-Germain-d'Ectot] taking heavy casualties. At 2000 hrs Lieut. Wareing was once more ready and assaulted with 'D' Coy 2 SWB and one Tp 13/18 Hussars.

At the end of the flame shoot, as was often the case, the infantry, seeing flame in action for the first time, held back:

> Lieut Wareing noticed the infantry some distance away in the lee of a bogged Crocodile thoroughly enjoying the fireworks display. With Northumbrian

> forthrightness he dismounted, went back and took them 'by the ears' on to the objective. The MGs had been driven off without casualty either to infantry or Crocodiles.

Colonel Waddell recorded in a Regimental Mention that the success of the attack 'was entirely due to 2/Lieutenant Wareing's coolness and courage under fire'.[6]

Wareing's leadership is, however, not acknowledged by 2 SWB who noted 'that in taking the final orchard on the ridge, D Company with bayonets fixed, actually trod in the flames of the Crocodiles supporting them.' They had not, however, completely secured the area of St.-Germain-d'Ectot; they had established a hold on the ridge, but not the village. The following day Lieutenant Grundy and 14 Troop, having been released by 231 Brigade, joined 11 Troop for

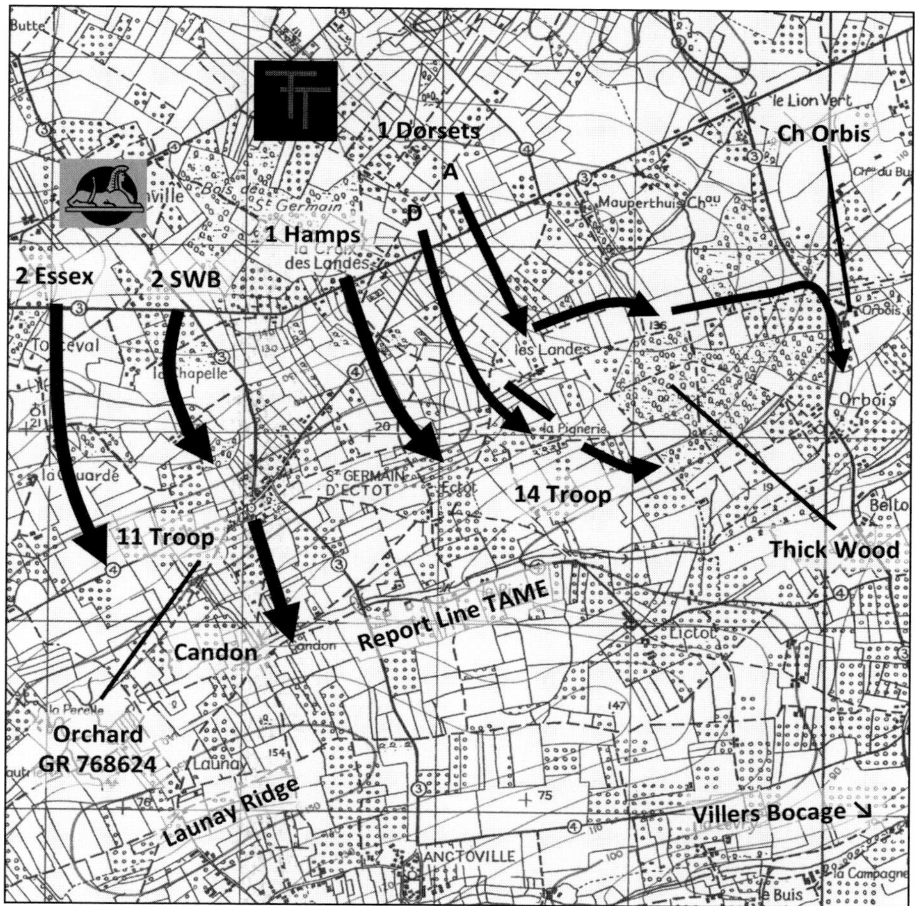

Operations of 56 and 231 Infantry brigades during 30 and 31 July 1944.

The brigade sign (centre) and cap badges of 56 Brigade's assault battalions 2 Essex and 2 SWB.

another attack on the strongpoint south-east of the village. An entry in the squadron war diary reads:

> On the morning of 31 Jul 11 Tp flamed the orchard and house at 768624 (first tackled by the AVREs), assisting 'D' Coy of the 2 SWB after a concentration of mediums in the village. This time the infantry showed no hesitation and were on to the objective almost before the flaming had ceased. The evening twilight overtook 11 & 14 Tps strolling arm in arm under the paternal eye of Capt. Barber in the walk-through advance of the 2 Essex to LAUNAY.

This advance of 1,000 yards took the Essex down into the valley beyond St. Germain to the hamlet of Candon at the foot of the Launay Ridge, which was eventually taken on 2 August by 2 Essex and 2 Devons.

231 Brigade

On the morning of 30 July 231 Brigade was to advance in a south-easterly direction towards Villers-Bocage across successive parallel ridges. The first of these was the one that ran north-east from St.-Germain-d'Ectot and included Les Landes, Ectot, La Pignerie ('The Piggery') and Orbois, as well as a feature known as 'Thick Wood' between Les Landes and Orbois. The Dorsets recorded that 'each of these ridges afforded the enemy O.P.s ample view of our advance.'

The role of Lieutenant Grundy's troops was once again to be in reserve awaiting the call of the infantry, in this case 1 Dorsets. The war diary records that during 30 July he had a 'trying time with 231 Bde ... in a deluge of purposeless requests and none of the logistic support needed by Crocodiles'.

One of these requests during the afternoon resulted in 14 Troop being sent forward to support the brigade's attack that had stalled. The Dorsets, with 1 Hampshire on their right, had advanced south on a two-company frontage with the tanks of 13/18 Hussars initially largely confined to a track in the centre. With mines and the thick bocage being overlooked by German artillery OPs on the Launay Ridge, as well as enemy infantry in advantageous and deeply-dug positions that had survived the preliminary bombardment, going was inevitably slow. As a result of the threat from mines and *Panzerfausts*, the Hussars struggled to keep up with the infantry in their first battle in the bocage. As the ranks of both his leading battalions thinned significantly, Brigadier Stanier halted the advance, but with an open flank to the east 1 Dorsets' fighting for the day was not over.

The Crocodiles of 14 Troop had been with B Company in reserve, following as the Royal Engineers and Dorsets' assault pioneers cleared numerous mines, but after hours of waiting, they were called to support C Company in an attack on 'Thick Wood' as part of an advance on Château Orbis.[7] Lieutenant Colonel Bredin recorded in his battalion's history:

> Next came the clearing operations on our left flank. We were first of all asked to make use of our Crocodiles in this direction. Accordingly, with No. 13 Platoon of C Company as escort, the Crocodiles were sent out from B Company to deal with any opposition found in the south-western corner of Thick Wood. But, as we found now and later, the whole wood and its vicinity was heavily mined. Several casualties were caused to No. 13 Platoon by S mines, and the Crocodiles were unable to continue owing to Teller and other mines. So, the Crocodile patrol had to come back without having accomplished very much.

This is more than a little ungenerous. The presence of the Crocodiles and their accompanying platoon making their way around the enemy's main defences that were sited along the northern edge of Thick Wood helped 'unhinge the German

Looking further ahead in the campaign, a B Squadron Crocodile fitted with a Culin cutter, a hedgerow attachment, while operating with US infantry. Photographic evidence suggests that gun tanks were not so equipped.

The divisional sign (centre) and cap badges of 231 Brigade's assault battalions 1 Dorsets and 1 Hampshires.

defences'. Even though they could not close to within flaming range, they had engaged and burned several hedges and fired HE and Besa into the flank and rear of the wood. It is worth bearing in mind that 13/18 Hussars' ability to manoeuvre and provide close support to the infantry was similarly impeded by mines.

That evening, as already recorded, Lieutenant Grundy was released and rejoined Captain Barber and his logistic vehicles to replenish his Crocodiles for the following day's action with 56 Brigade. Meanwhile, Major Duffy's half of C Squadron remained in reserve '. . . frenetically moving the remainder of his sqn from one planned attack to another.' Typical of the incidents in this period is one recorded in the squadron war diary:

> On 2 Aug he moved NE of CAUMONT, preparatory to an attack on CAHAGNES under command of SR [Sherwood Rangers Yeomanry] and in sp of 43 Div. As the Crocodiles lumbered down to the SL, they were stopped by a hot-foot Brigadier who declared our own tps were already in CAHAGNES from another direction.

A Squadron: VIII Corps

The task of VIII Corps was to break through the similarly well-established defences of 326th Infantry Division in what had hitherto been a quiet front held by the US V Corps. The Germans were deployed with two regiments (751 and 752) holding a line of some 9 miles with six infantry battalions. Their third regiment was in reserve with some armour in the form of Marders and *Sturmgeschütz* IIIs.

Once again, despite their assembly they found themselves split up, with Captain Strachan's two troops of Crocodiles joining 6 Guards Tank Brigade to spearhead the attack of the 15th Scottish Division, and the other two troops under Major Cooper joining 11th Armoured Division.[8] While the Crocodiles were driving the 20 miles from Brécy to the assembly area north of Caumont, Major Cooper and Captain Strachan had gone on ahead to attend their respective divisional orders groups. The two halves of the squadron were ready for an 0655 H-Hour the following morning. Major Deakin, second-in-command of

4 Tank Grenadier Guards, provides an insight into the battle procedure in which the officers of A Squadron would have been involved:

> The battalion had moved up to the assembly area during the night 28/29 July and 29 July was spent in 'O' Groups and joint recces with the infantry. The recces were carried out under some secrecy as it was essential not to let the Germans realise that there were tanks opposite them. Black berets were not allowed to be worn and the time spent in recce was limited.[9]

In preparation for the guardsmen's first action in the bocage:

> It was not fully appreciated during this recce that the thickness of the banks in each hedgerow would tend to split up the tank/infantry formations so much. However, the confidence was due to the fact that we had lived and worked together for a considerable period in ENGLAND, and without this period together there is no doubt that the operation would have been much more difficult, much slower, and more costly in men and materials.
>
> The FUP, just behind the CAUMONT ridge, was reached at last light on 29 July and the infantry married up with their tanks at about 0300 hours on 30 July.

Churchill Mk IVs of 4th Tank Grenadier Guards. Note the rear tank has its turret reversed covering the rear of the column.

227 Highland Brigade: Lutain Wood

Captain Strachan's half-squadron was to assist with the first phase of being grouped with 2nd Battalion, The Gordon Highlanders:

> On 30 Jul after very careful though hurried planning the day before Capt Strachan's party (2 and 3 Tps under Lieut McCulloch and that very dashing and able young officer Lieut Tonbridge) attacked the Northern edge of LUTAIN WOOD, south-east of CAUMONT as first stage in the drive south. The assault was made with 2 Gordons and the Grenadier Tank Guards. On the way to the Start Line owing to fluctuating Crocodile strength Capt Strachan had twice to re-organise his plans (commencing with 6 from the harbour, plunging to the lowest depths with 3 just before zero and actually doing the attack with four).

The hurried road move and a lack of time for maintenance almost certainly contributed to the number of breakdowns on the morning of the attack.

The brigade's plan was for Cameronians to attack the village of Sept-Vents and 2 Gordons the hamlet of Montdant along with the adjacent Lutain Wood, which was believed to be held by two or three companies of 752 Grenadier Regiment. Both battalions were supported by a squadron of Grenadier Guards' Churchills. Once these features were secure, the brigade's break in battle would be completed by another two battalions, 2nd Argyll & Sutherland Highlanders (2 A&SH) and 10 HLI, with an advance through the centre. Lieutenant Colonel the Earl of Caithness described his plan for 2 Gordons' battlegroup in greater detail:

> My plan was for A and B Companies to lead the attack, each supported by two troops or tanks. A Company on the Right was to capture the orchard area on the West of LUTAIN WOOD, B Company on the Left was to capture the orchard area on the East of the Wood. D Company was to follow A and B Companies and take LIEU MONDANT, supported by one troop of tanks. When this had been done, C Company was to come up on D Company's Right and these two companies were to attack right through the wood mopping up any enemy they found in it, and hold positions on the far side. They were to be supported by CROCODILES up to the forward edge of the wood and these were to flame the hedges leading up to the wood and the front edge of it. Once the four companies were in position round the wood, I could then set about any further clearing of the inside of the wood that might be necessary. It was not thought that there would be much enemy opposition.

Major Deakin of the Grenadiers added some detail on the armour's part in the operation:

> The tank allotment was two troops and one 95mm tank with each leading company. Each tank group was commanded by a Captain, one was the Squadron 2IC, the other the Squadron Recce Office, each in his 95mm tank.

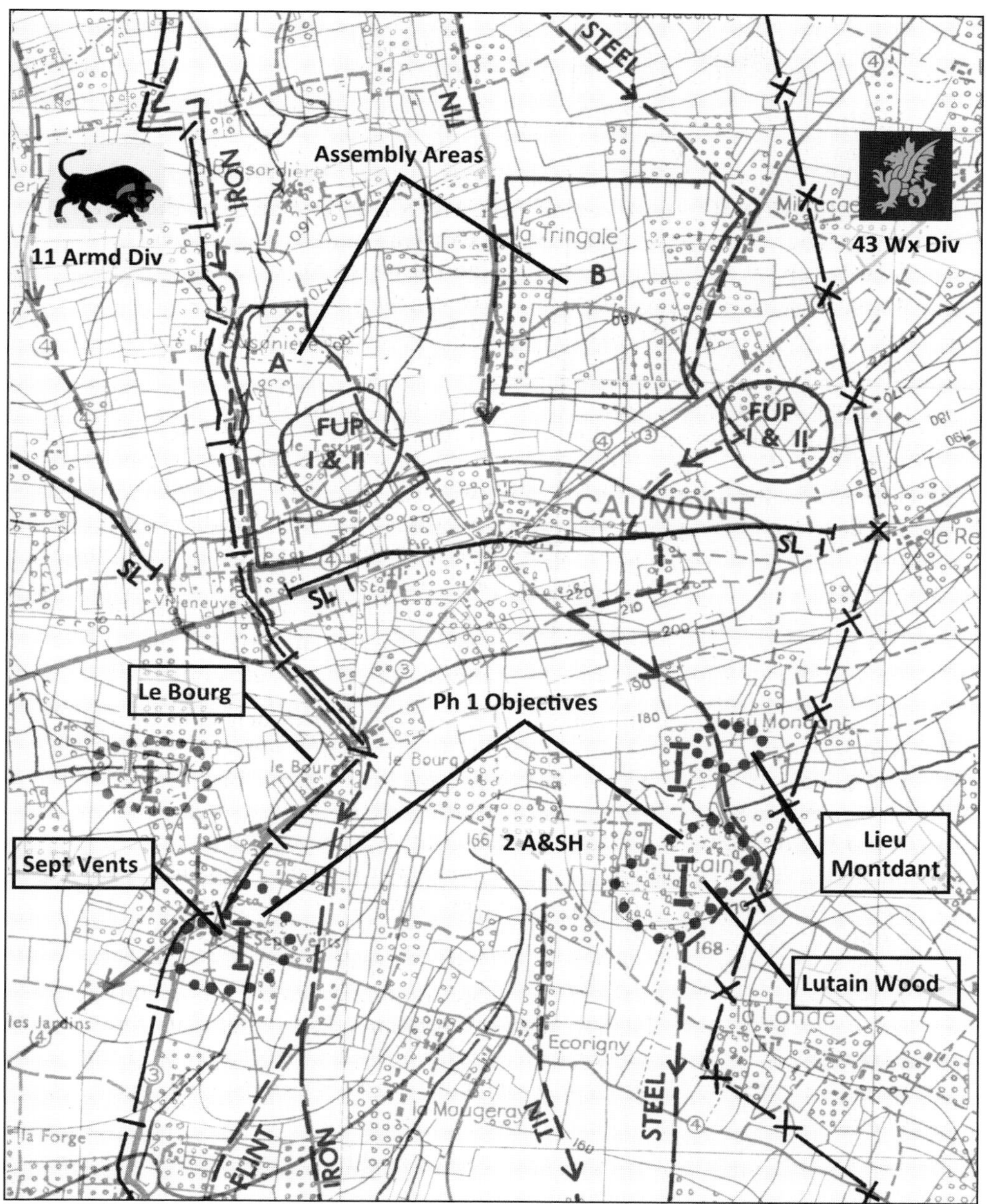

227 Brigade's plan for the opening phase of Operation BLUECOAT: 2 Gordons' right assault and the Cameronians' left.

> Squadron HQ and the reserve troop remained with the infantry battalion Tac HQ.

The first phase went according to plan and, with the leading companies and squadron having broken through the German outpost line, Captain Strachan's four operational Crocodiles then moved forward on Route STEEL towards Lutain Wood with C Company. Major Deakin again:

> During the second phase of the attack, which was the advance of C and D Companies, the CROCODILES were brought into use since they were the only weapons which could deal with the deep pits the Germans had dug. They advanced with their companies but were unable to actually flame the edge of the wood, although they did a good job flaming the hedgerows approaching it from the North.

The Gordons' commanding officer makes it plain that the Crocodiles' part in his plan did not work in its entirety:

> C Company then went forward on D Company's Right and started its attack through the wood. The Boche was holding the forward edge of the wood quite strongly but the companies attacked very well and succeeded in killing or capturing many of the Germans holding these posts while others, not so brave, as soon as our troops got near them, retreated into the wood. The CROCODILES proved rather a failure, as, although they flamed the hedges leading up to the wood, they were stopped by a high bank from getting right up to the edge of the wood. However, we found out from a prisoner afterwards that their morale effect was fairly great and that the Boche didn't like them much.

The substantial embanked hedge that halted the Crocodiles was particularly steep and crossing it was way beyond the tolerances of their trailers' towing gear.

Of their part in this phase of the battle, A Squadron's war diary is somewhat dismissive: 'The operation was quite successful, but it is doubtful if there was any enemy there other than a few snipers.' In reality, with the Churchills enveloping the wood and the Crocodiles flaming to their front, the enemy infantry abandoned their positions and surrendered to the Gordons in large numbers. Advancing on route TIN into the 1,000-yard gap between the Cameronians at Sept-Vents and Lutain Wood, 2 A&SH found themselves in battle approximately 1,500 yards short of their FUP. Having previously fought in more open country further east, the 15th Division had clearly not appreciated the detailed clearance of ground necessary in the bocage.

Having aided the fight through the enemy position, Captain Strachan's half-squadron was released by the Gordons and 227 Brigade. They motored back 3 miles north of Caumont to replenish flame fuel, gas cylinders and ammunition, but 'was not used again in this show'. By 1030 hours, having broken through 15th Scottish Division, led by the stellar performance of 6 Guards Tank Brigade

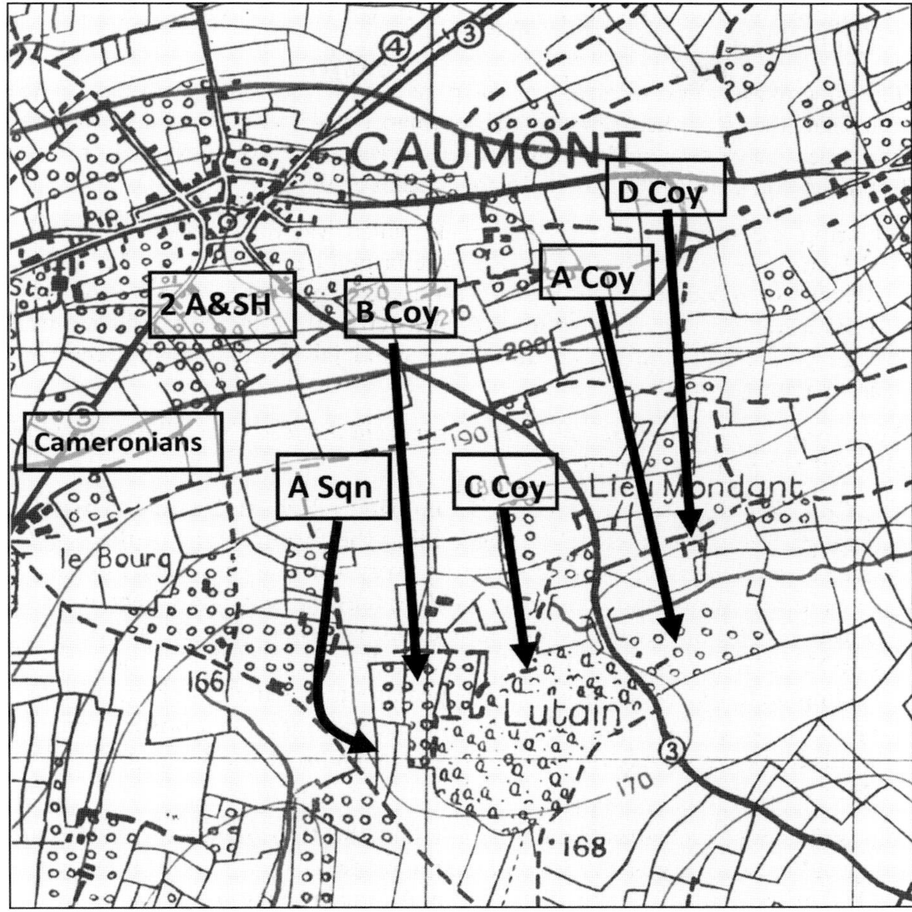

The action by 2 Gordons' battlegroup at Lutain Wood on the morning of 30 July 1944.

and the bomber strikes generating momentum, the leading squadrons reached their objectives 5 miles deep in enemy territory by 1900 hours. Overnight the tanks were joined by the Scottish infantry.

Major Deakin notes several lessons, two of which were that detailed planning and recce was required during the break in battle with the Crocodiles, but once through the first layer of defences '... the tanks must push on to their objective, if necessary without their infantry. We found later that this paid tremendous dividends both physical and psychological from both arms' point of view and should be considered a point of honour as well as a tactical doctrine.'

In contrast with the way in which Major Deakins' Churchills were able to 'take the hedgerows full steam ahead', the Crocodile with its trailer had difficulty verging on mechanical impossibility of coping with the ups and downs of

Tanks of 6 Guards Armoured Brigade pass a Sherman Crab that had just beaten its way through one of the extensive anti-tank and anti-personnel minefields south of Caumont.

hedge-crossing and still having a serviceable flame gun. Major Deakin continued: 'The most dangerous time was when the tanks stopped moving; firstly, because the tanks were bazooka'd and secondly, because the enemy Spandaus and mortars regained their confidence which was shaken when tanks were on the move, and came to life to deal with our infantry.'

11th Armoured Division: In Reserve

The fate of A Squadron's other half-squadron is summed up very well in the squadron war diary, albeit somewhat cynically:

> Major Cooper with two tps under 11 Armd Div had original instructions to allot one tp to each Bde axis – moving down the road behind the advance [of the advance guard]. This had most unexpected consequences – even for a disillusioned Cooper. Lieut Andrews was solemnly ordered to provide a flying flank patrol to the armour, and Lieut Brereton found himself attached to a RA OP.
>
> Obediently the two tps waddled along their two roads but were told so firmly and so frequently by personages in high places to get off the 'bloody road' that finally they took them at their word and retired to the harbour S.W. of CAUMONT. Here they remained as the battle (such as it was)

> rolled forward some 20 miles. Peace reigned. Major Cooper sipped a double whisky.

A Squadron remained on call for six days before being summoned east for Operation TOTALIZE with the Canadian First Army.

Le Bon-Repos (again)

For a third time Le Bon-Repos was to be attacked alongside the 53rd Welsh Division and 107 Regiment RAC, this time by Captain Barber's half of C Squadron consisting of 11 and 14 troops. At 1540 hours on 2 August, the Crocodiles were harboured 25 miles to the west and were informed that they would be attacking with the Welsh Division and needed to join them by 1730 hours:

> The affair was to be a repetition of Storrar's foray in July with the same object – a raid on LE BON-REPOS with Crocodiles and inf (again 4 Welch), moving astride the road from Les VILLAINS to capture PW. A Sqn who knew this terrain backwards were doing nothing at the time –

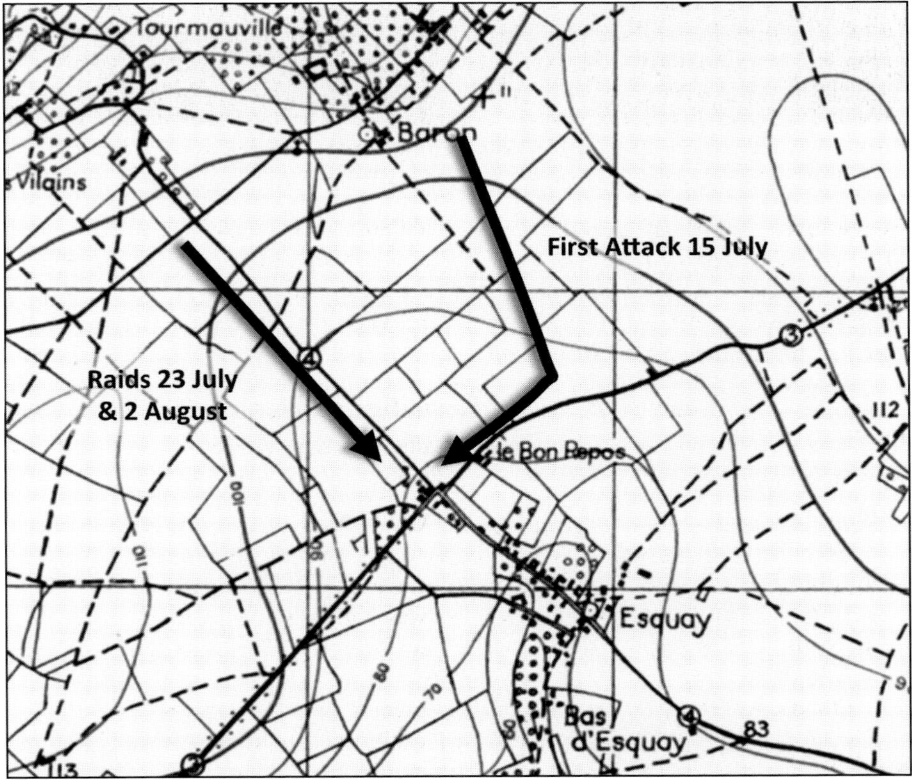

An extract of the 1:25,000 map showing the area of the attack and raids on Le Bon-Repos.

> an irrelevant remark. Phlegmatic to the end, and a little curious, Capt Barber motored off to investigate the show, leaving Lieut Grundy (a little caustic by now) to bring up the Crocodiles. It was not until 1640 hrs that the move order was decoded and off went the Crocodiles, arriving at 1930 hrs after sundry directions of very doubtful value from an LO in MONDRAINVILLE.

Once again with just thirty minutes to be briefed, lieutenants Grundy and Wareing had only a sketchy idea of their part in the raid, though it is conceded that 'the big plan was quite sound'. However, as they moved to the FUP the rush 'manifested itself with trailer after trailer having problems'. H-Hour was at 2100 hours and as dusk settled about half the squadron advanced with the tanks and infantry:

> The flaming expedition was in fact a success and 17 PW were brought in, including one offr. Everyone was happy except Capt Barber. One Crocodile went on a mine (presumably enemy) near LE BON-REPOS and had to be destroyed by 107 RAC. Another went on a mine (presumably British) almost on the SL. Yet a third lost a bogie possibly from mortar fire. A fourth developed a broken turret ring from an HE hit. The remaining two stuck to the more mundane routine of extensive trailer trouble. What remained of the Crocodile force limped into harbour at CHEUX that night.

Villers-Bocage: C Squadron

Back on 6 June XXX Corps had planned to dispatch 8 Armoured Brigade to form a patrol base on Point 213 overlooking Villers-Bocage, but having been much delayed in heading south, the tanks were halted on Point 103. After weeks of fighting in villages that were familiar to C Squadron such as La Senaudière, La Belle Épine and Hottot, Operation BLUECOAT had finally broken the German line. This was exactly what senior German commanders had repeatedly warned Berlin would happen, and even though the enemy was still fighting hard on XXX Corps' front, the British had by 3 August closed in on Villers-Bocage. Lieutenant Wilson recalled that after several days of waiting, Major Duffy's half of C Squadron was called forward, but it proved to be another day of frustration:

> Now there was to be a big attack, preceded by an air bombardment. The Crocodiles were to mop up strongpoints in the wake of an armoured division [*sic* 50th Infantry Division and 8 Armoured Brigade]. They took up position in a field about three miles away. It was a fine, warm day, with just a little mortaring.
>
> The RAF Lancasters came over towards evening. No one was quite prepared for them. They were used to seeing daylight raids by American bombers, flying high up in faultless formation with their silver wings glittering in the sun. But the Lancasters – night-bombers – did it their own way. There was a rumble of engines as the first bunch appeared, lolloping and

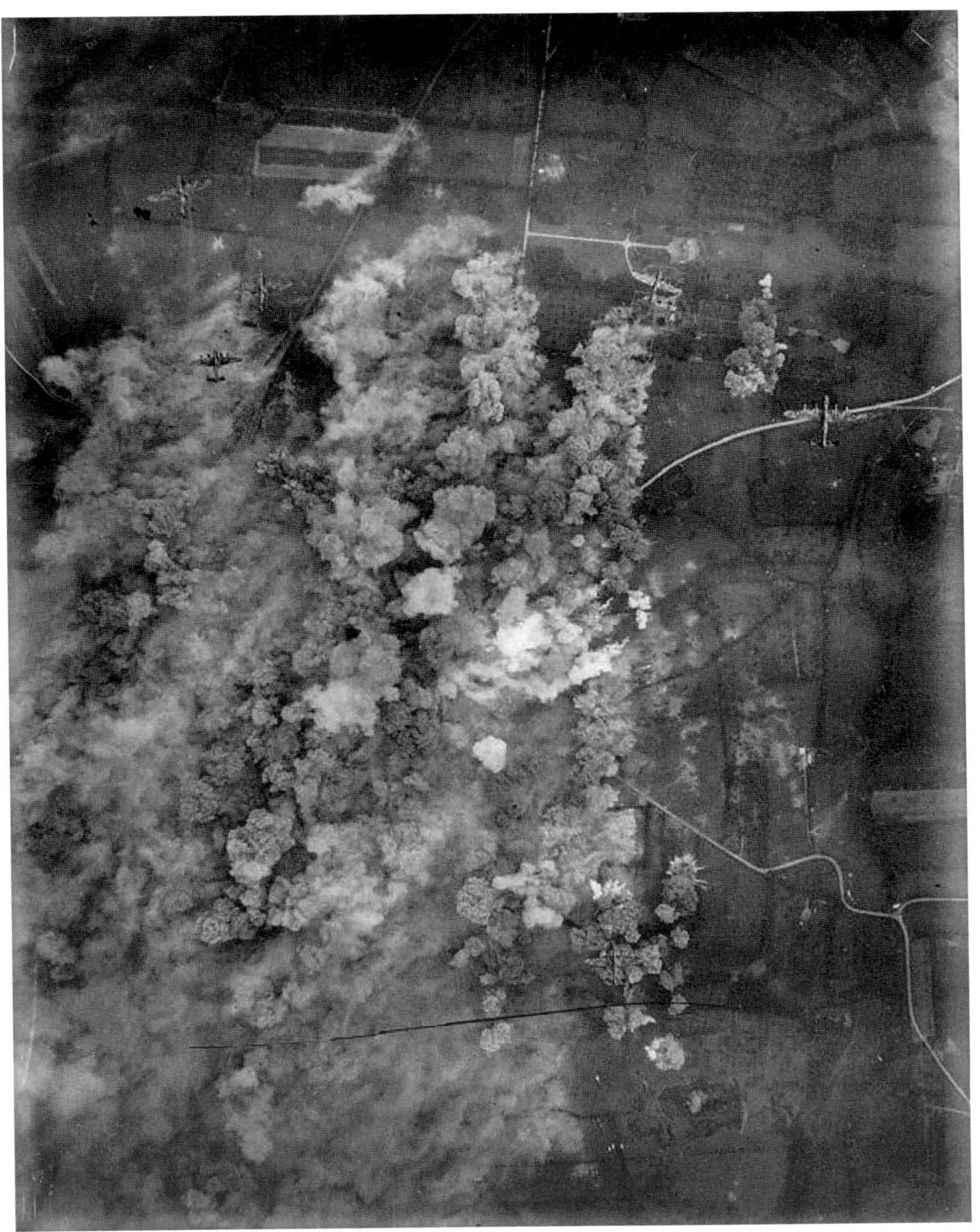

Bombs falling on Villers-Bocage during the evening of 30 July 1944. Several Lancasters at low level can also be seen.

swaying like big black crows above the woods. They made a short circuit and went into the German flak. The bomb-doors opened and you could see the sticks of bombs falling.

The next lot came. It wasn't a formation, but more like a flying circus. They circled round and round with wingtips almost touching, until it was their turn to go in . . . the earth shook continuously and a big yellow cloud of smoke and dust arose. When the last went home, it was impossible to believe that a single German soldier was left to resist.[10]

On the morning of 4 August, with the Crocodiles standing by to pressure up, 'From the fields ahead came the sounds of battle, and the Crocodiles waited for the order to advance. But it never came.' The reason was that immediately before the bombing, as a part of the methodical withdrawal, the enemy had abandoned their main defences north of Villers-Bocage[11] and had prepared a new position south of the town. Patrols mounted by 1 Dorsets 'entered the ruins later that day without opposition, rounding up a handful of disorientated prisoners.'

Following the capture of Villers-Bocage C Squadron regrouped with 7th Armoured Division that was fighting its way forward just to the west. The next significant town, Aunay-sur-Odon, was another 'name on the map that had suffered the same fate at the hands of the air forces.'

The XXX Corps' plan had always been to release 7th Armoured Division between 50th and 43rd Infantry divisions towards Aunay as soon as they had broken through what they believed to be a crust of defences. Released at 1500 hours on 1 August, the division, however, 'made little progress'.[12] By 3 August some ground had been made, but three German counter-attacks brought the Desert Rats' advance to a halt. Eventually, the ruins of Aunay were bypassed to the north without the services of C Squadron's Crocodiles being called for.

Estry

Having been warned for several operations that were either cancelled or overtaken by events, Major Duffy was on the afternoon of 8 August conducting training in lieu of likely action. Finally, the Crocodiles of C Squadron were called forward to support an attack on the village of Estry the following day. They were to fight alongside battalions of 44 Lowland Brigade from 15th Scottish Division and the Churchills of 6 Guards Tank Brigade.

Estry consisted of a hamlet on the Aunay-Vire road, with the main body of the village clustered around the church. It was stoutly defended by 326th Division and had resisted capture during the previous days. The two assault battalions were 6 King's Own Scottish Borderers (6 KOSB), left, and 6 Royal Scots Fusiliers (6 RSF), right, with 10th Highland Light Infantry in reserve. The Crocodiles of C Squadron would be fighting alongside 3 Squadron of 4 Tank Grenadier Guards and two troops of AVREs from an Assault Regiment RE:

Quite wisely it was decided to keep the Crocodiles concentrated, two tps of AVREs being given to the left. 12 Tp (Lt McFarlane) was to take the right in

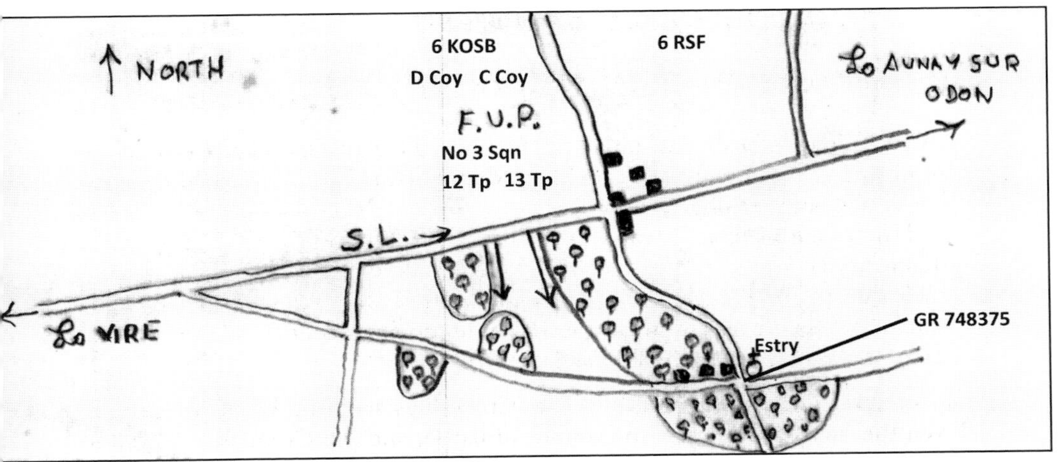

A map of the attack on Estry on 9 August from C Squadron's war diary (annotated).

> support of D Coy. 13 Tp (Lt Sutherland-Sherrif) in sp of C Coy on the left were to flame the orchards running SW from the lateral road as far as a track junction at 748375 [see diagram]. The Crocodiles were to go first with a section of in behind each tp and two sections mopping up.

There was, however, a problem. The start line for 6 KOSB's part of the attack was a sunken lane that the troop commanders had not had the opportunity to recce with their knowledge of the Crocodiles' gap-crossing capability:

> Major Duffy pointed out that he could not guarantee to cross the sunken rd; only the leading Crocodile would be able to tell if it were possible. SL was to be the main AUNAY-VIRE lateral road and during the move up ESTRY was to be bombarded by Div, Corps and AGRA arty. The REs reported a rise on the lateral road of 3′ to 3′ 6″ which would give hull down to the village. This proved erroneous. In view of the presence in the village of a Tiger which had the lordly habit of patrolling up to the crossroads, this was quite important. In effect it meant that if gun tks were to give effective support to the Crocodiles, they must cross the lateral road.

The attack had been delayed from 1000 hours to 1200 hours, but in the difficult country even getting to the FUP was challenging, and 'The action started off on the wrong leg':

> The route to the start line had been recced and prepared by bulldozers but one of the Gds tks (who were leading) bogged and there they stayed for some time. Sutherland-Sherrif and McFarland on foot at last managed to find a detour arriving on the SL some twenty minutes late and only with great difficulty finding the inf who had gone to ground in a shower of arty fire. Lieut McFarlane was wounded in the wrist and his trailer turned upside down by blast, so that both tps now had only two Crocodiles as they moved over the SL. So far is known the Gds tks never did cross the SL.

The Grenadiers' war diary seems to support this possibility: 'The attack began reasonably well but later the impossible country for tanks held up all types &

The start line on the Aunay-Vire road today. It has been widened and the right hedge removed. The advance was from right to left.

heavy losses amongst the flame throwers & petard tanks forced their withdrawal with little done.'[13]

The Grenadiers' account is only partly correct, as recorded in a detailed account from C Squadron's war diary:

> The right hand tp quickly came to a halt after dealing with one target, stopped by the sunken road and were released by the inf. Sutherland-Sherrif however with 13 Troop was in for a little excitement. In the first field he was busily flaming the hedges in the orchard when he saw a flash from the vicinity of the church. Five times the gun shot at him, missing every time, before transferring its attentions to Sergeant Webb. Sutherland-Sherrif, panicking a little now, stopped as the gun emerged into full view some 200 yards to the left in the shape of a full-blown Panther. There's only one way to treat Panther – to hit it! Which the gunner did first shot on the turret ring – and the turret crew bailed out with more haste than dignity. The gunner switched to Besa . . . the gun jammed but far from behind Sgt Webb had already bagged two of the crew. Meanwhile, still occupied by the dvr the Panther did a smart right turn and disappeared.
>
> The flaming was resumed and at the same time MGs in the barn nearby were destroyed by Besa. For some unknown reason it rapidly became obvious the infantry [had] started to retire and Sgt Webb, looking around with more than average curiosity spotted a Tiger on the left. 20 rounds of smoke and the Crocodiles were out of it. Sgt Webb claimed one hit on the Tiger without effect; he also fired several shots into the smoke for luck.

An air photograph of the Estry crossroads taken before the battle.

The adjutant of 6 KOSB highlighted the failure of the armour in his battalion's war diary:

> Owing to the close nature of the country both tks and Crocodiles were unable to make headway and the inf were required to go on by themselves. C Coy on the left succeeded in reaching limited objectives; D Coy on the right met with less success. The 6 RSF on the left succeeded early in reaching the line of the rd running EAST and WEST through ESTRY. Orders were accordingly received to consolidate on this line and after considerable confused fighting this was effected by the evening.

Of an operation that left the Scots holding the start line, Major Duffy, in addition to his earlier comments about effective recce, concluded:

> In actual fact there had been nothing at all in the hedgerow flamed. Indeed, although the attack was planned in very careful detail, it seems reasonable to

> say that it lacked direction, lacked correct appreciation of the enemy by the inf and lacked aggressive protection by supporting gun tks.

The Adventures of Lieutenant Wilson

During the weeks of waiting for the break-out, 141 RAC, in moving backwards and forwards across the tight confines of the beachhead, were increasingly familiar with the country's geography and the approximate location of the fighting. Now, as Lieutenant Wilson was to find out, the army was advancing into unfamiliar terrain.

While C Squadron was once again on the move behind BLUECOAT, Lieutenant Wilson went back to RHQ at Brécy to collect a new Crocodile and a replacement officer. Before departure he visited the headquarters and was given a grid reference for the new harbour area by the signal sergeant. The new location was west of Villers-Bocage, but 'it didn't surprise him, as in the last few days ... the war was beginning to move':

> They went out on one of the 'tank tracks' which had been marked out across country. Wide and straight, they cut for miles through open fields and led

A regular task of squadron echelons was filling jerry cans at RAOC fuel points along the pipeline that followed the road from Port-en-Bessin via Bayeux to the N13 and the road to Tilly-sur-Seulles.

> the tanks swiftly from the beach area to the front . . . All the fields which had been packed with troops and vehicles were empty. It was very quiet. You couldn't even hear gunfire any longer.
>
> The Churchill VII did thirteen miles per hour. It was twilight as they got near Villers, and dark when they entered it. There were no buildings and no streets – just a bulldozed canyon through a pile of rubble which stretched for half a mile, and over it all the bitter taste of dust and charred wood.

Having driven south to Aunay, where some sappers were 'working their bulldozer with shaded headlamps' to clear the way between similar piles of rubble:

> Beyond Aunay the road went up a steep hillside, and at the top there were some infantry with anti-tank guns. Two miles further on Wilson halted the tank at a crossroads. 'This is it,' he said. But there was no sign of the squadron and they pulled the tank into the yard of a deserted farm and took it in turns to mount guard but they had withdrawn.

At daylight they cautiously went on to a village, which 'was eerily empty'. A figure in a cassock appeared and Wilson dismounted to speak to him and found out that he had been parked up for the night in no-man's-land in close proximity to the Germans: 'Wilson turned the tank around and they started back towards the British lines. He hoped the [anti-tank] gunners' identification charts had been brought up to date. In case they hadn't, he reversed the turret and hung out the red-white-and-blue recognition flag.'

After they had gone a mile back to their lines, they met the first infantry advancing in open order astride the road. A bewildered captain held up a hand to stop them. 'Where the devil have you come from? The captain beckoned to his wireless operator and spoke with his battalion headquarters':

> 'You're luckier than you think,' he said, 'you've just missed being at the wrong end of a divisional artillery shoot.'
>
> The squadron was in a small village at the foot of Mont Pinçon when he found them. They were all very busy, getting ready to join in the general advance; there wasn't even time to tell his story, which was a pity, because it seemed to him a very good story.

Uniform

Tank crews were issued with two sets of brown serge 1940-pattern (economy) battledress (BD) consisting of a short blouse with two chest pockets and trousers with a map pocket and one for a field dressing, as well as normal hip and seat pockets. One suit was for daily use and a second kept for 'best' with full regimental and formation insignia and their normal rank badges. Crewmen were also issued with green denim overalls, to be worn over BD but frequently worn instead in warm weather. They had strengthened shoulder epaulettes to assist in lifting an injured crewman from a tank.

Three of these tank crewmen are wearing BD, one denim overalls and two the leather jerkin.

Left: a lieutenant's badges of rank with the yellow pips of the RAC and the red bar of 141 RAC. Right: An early other ranks' epaulet slide with the green diablo of 31 Tank Brigade.

Working on the layer principle, a woollen jumper and shirt were issued, along with a string vest for wear under BD as the weather dictated.

Calf-length greatcoats were issued, and although somewhat impractical within the confines of a tank, they were useful as an extra blanket. In addition, there were the practical and popular sleeveless leather jerkins, which were often worn over BD or overalls, providing some protection from the weather and a wipe-clean surface.

Footwear was the standard ankle-length 'ammunition boots', but without metal studs in the soles to avoid slipping. Crews often wore issued plimsoles or crepe-soled footwear such as the 'desert boot' for comfort and grip on slippery armour.

The black RAC beret was the usual headgear, worn with a silvered RAC version of the Buffs' cap badge. Crews were also issued with a special RAC helmet, using the shell of the airborne forces' helmet without the lip on the Mk 2 helmet as a practical solution for wearing inside an AFV. These, however, had the disadvantage in general wear away from the tank due to their resemblance to those worn by German soldiers.

Once on campaign, with Montgomery leading the way, as army group commander he allowed officers to adopt virtually any practical form of dress when they landed in Normandy.[14]

The Ack Pack or 'Lifebuoy' flamethrower

The man pack flame thrower of the Second World War was primarily used in the Far East, but was held by RE units in north-west Europe. It was known as the Ack Pack and consisted of a ring-shaped container with 4 gallons of fuel; in the centre was a pressurised gas container. From the bottom of the fuel tank a hose led to a flame gun with a pair of pistol grips and a trigger. Around the nozzle was a revolving cylinder with ten ignition cartridges. On the release of fuel, the next cartridge would ignite the flame, which had a range of approximately 120ft.

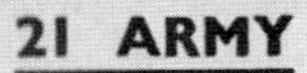

21 ARMY GROUP

PERSONAL MESSAGE FROM THE C-IN-C

(To be read out to all Troops)

1. At this time of great opportunity I feel that I want to speak to the officers and men of the Allied Armies in France. We are a great team—American, British, Canadian, and also the soldiers of Fighting France and of Poland—all knit together into one fighting machine, and all working to one plan.
2. We have been through some difficult times since D Day and, on occasions, great patience and confidence were necessary if we were not to falter. When the struggle was in its most critical stage there were some who had doubts as to whether we would win through. But you and I had no doubts—not one; we knew that so long as we did our duty all would be well; and to-day, all is well.
3. What a change has come about in the last few weeks. The whole of the Cherbourg peninsula is in our hands, and most of Brittany also; our armies are moving relentlessly eastwards into France; many hundreds of towns and villages have been liberated. The prisoners taken are well over 100,000, and great quantities of enemy equipment and war material have been captured or destroyed.
4. And, best of all, the great bulk of the German forces in NW Europe are in a bad way; we are round behind them in many places, and it is possible that some of them will not get away. They will fight hard to avoid disaster; that we know.
But let each one of us make a tremendous effort to "write off" this powerful German force; it has caused us no small trouble during the last two months; let us finish with it, once and for all, and so hasten the end of the war.
5. Across the water in England, the starting point for this great adventure, our families and friends are playing their part and are bearing up well against the flying bomb nuisance and other troubles. Our thoughts are with them; we are all in this business together, we all bear the burden equally, and we are all determined to see the matter thoroughly finished.
6. In these hot August days, amid the dust of the battlefield, it is not always too easy to keep up the pressure.
But these are momentous days and complete victory lies ahead, and is certain—so long as we do not relax.
7. Let us therefore continue the battle with renewed and ever greater energy; and we must remember to give the honour and praise where it is due.
Before the battle of Bosworth Field, the Earl of Richmond used these words as part of his prayer:—

> "O Thou! whose captain I account myself,
> Look on my forces with a gracious eye;
> Make us Thy ministers of chastisement,
> That we may praise Thee in Thy victory."

8. Good luck to you all.

B. L. Montgomery
General
C.-in-C.,
21 Army Group

11th August 1944.

General Montgomery's message to 21st Army Group, 11 August 1944.

Chapter Ten

Operation TOTALIZE

With the US armies in the west finally surging south into central France and Brittany, the Canadian First Army had been activated in the east and Montgomery's M516 directive ordered General Crerar to attack south from Caen:

> The time has now come to deliver the major attack towards FALAISE, which has so long been the fundamental aim of our policy on the eastern flank. I planned that the Canadians should drive South East from CAEN to gain as much ground as possible in the direction of FALAISE, in order to get behind the enemy forces facing the Second [British] Army, and to continue the process of wearing down the enemy formations in the sector. I envisaged this operation as a prelude to subsequent exploitation of success.[1]

After days of waiting A Squadron was 'On 6 Aug roused out of their delightful but non-productive vegetation by having to move across the whole bridgehead to just south of Caen' where they were grouped with the Canadian 2nd Division. This mechanically fatiguing march of some 25 miles probably contributed to the squadron becoming non-operational in the middle of the month. B Squadron, having spent ten days at Cresson, was also committed to TOTALIZE, but with a much shorter march reached Cormeilles where units joining 51st Highland Division assembled for the operation.

During their period of refit B Squadron had undergone some changes. Captain Storrar had come across from A Squadron as 2iC and 8 Troop had been re-formed under Lieutenant Ward and Sergeant Morley, bringing the order of battle back to five troops. With the arrival not only of replacement Crocodiles but officers, there was a shuffle around of subalterns in time for the squadron's next operation.

Following operations GOODWOOD and those that followed, SPRING and EXPRESS at Maltot, the majority of I and II SS panzer corps were fixed against the Second Army and now the Canadians, but with the Americans spilling out of Normandy, Hitler intervened. Following the 20 July bomb plot, the Führer no longer made any pretence of listening to the professional advice of his generals who, in the prevailing climate of fear, had little stomach to do anything other than obey orders; in this case, to mount a counter-stroke against the US First Army.[2]

Hitler reasoned that with the situation in the west of Normandy rapidly deteriorating, this was the main threat and one that he had to deal with. He ordered Commander of Army Group B, *Generalfeldmarschall* von Kluge, to launch

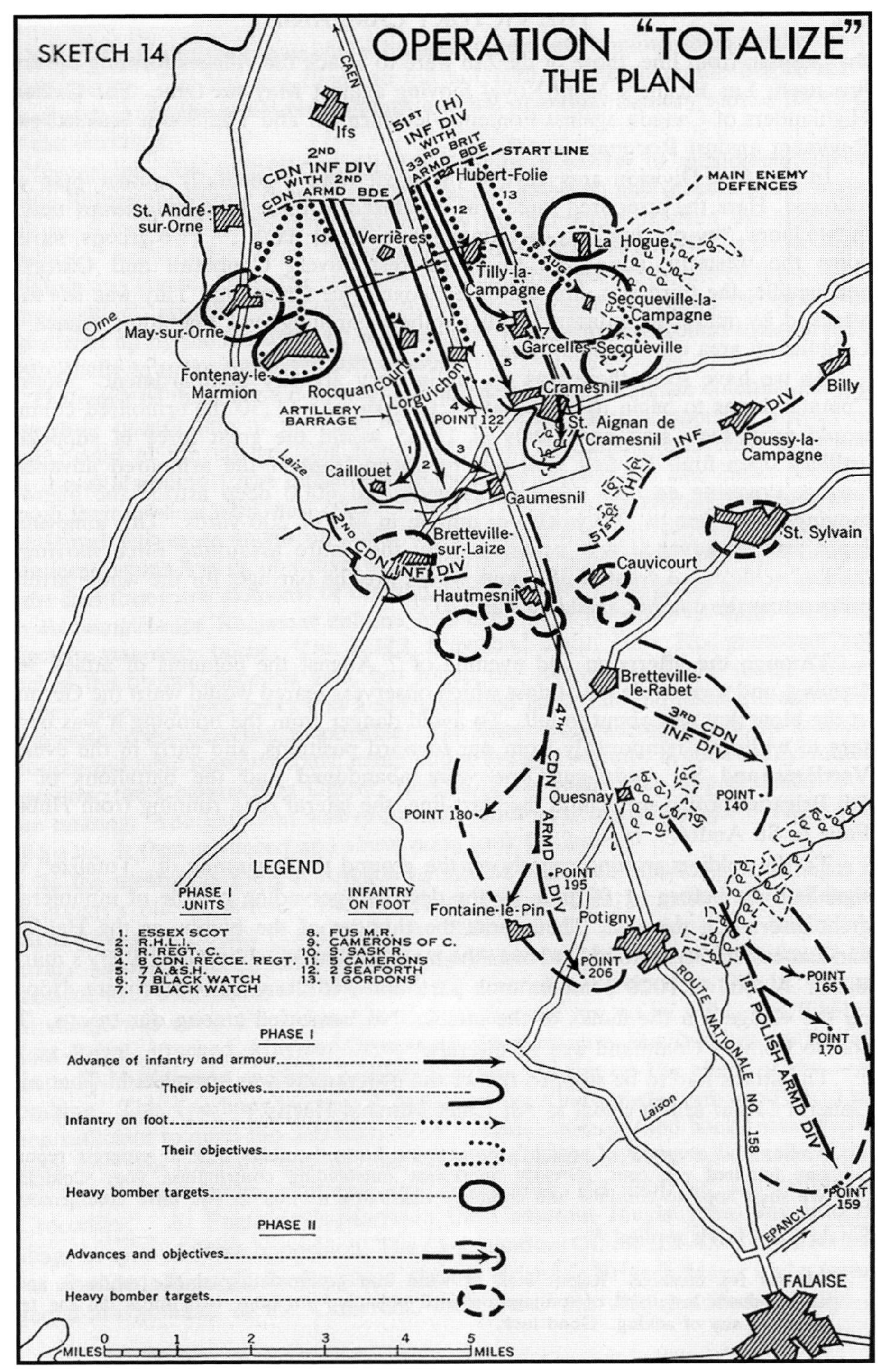

Operation TOTALIZE: the plan. (Colonel Stacey, *The Victory Campaign*)

'an immediate counter-attack between Mortain and Avranches', despite von Kluge's strong advice that there was no prospect of success. On 4 August Hitler emphatically ordered that Operation LÜTTICH was to be launched.

Thanks to decoded ULTRA messages, the British were able to monitor German intent and the weakening of I SS Panzer Corps as the panzer divisions departed west. Sepp Dietrich's corps that had successfully contained the Allies around Caen for three weeks was now left with the 89th Infantry Division defending the road south to Falaise. The *Hohenstaufen* and the *Leibstandarte* marched on the night of 4/5 August, having handed over their defensive positions to the 89th. However, in preparation for their march west, the 12th *Hitlerjugend* SS Panzer Division, though still with the corps, had been pulled back into reserve prior to joining the march west for LÜTTICH.

Lieutenant General Guy Simmonds' II Canadian Corps had in previous weeks been stalled before the Verrières Ridge and, having been given a warning order on 29 July, he knew, having seen GOODWOOOD and suffered his own reverse in Operation SPRING, that he had to adopt a different approach to fighting south. Conducting a formal estimate and analysing previous failures must have been a salutary experience. In this process he stated that his objective was 'to break through the German positions astride the CAEN-FALAISE Road', and considered the by now well-known strengths of the German position and concluded that:

> The ground is ideally suited to full exploitation by the enemy with the characteristics of his weapons. It is open, giving little cover for either infantry or tanks and the long range of his anti-tank guns and mortars firing from carefully concealed positions provides a very strong defence in depth. This defence will be most handicapped by bad visibility – smoke, fog or darkness, when the advantage of long range is minimized. The attack should therefore be made under these conditions.

His solution was to drive 5 miles into the enemy's layered defences in Priests, self-propelled guns with the guns and racking removed to produce an armoured personnel carrier.[3] This advance into the depths of the German positions would be followed by dismounted infantry to clear bypassed enemy positions. The Crocodiles were to be available to the two assault divisions for this task.

Canadian ingenuity led to a careful examination of the Crocodile by the commanding officers of Brigadier Young's 6 Canadian Infantry Brigade on the morning of 7 July and some careful thought about the role of flame in the forthcoming battle. This refreshing occurrence was novel enough to be recorded in some detail in A Squadron's war diary:

> TOTALIZE was to begin as a night operation on 7/8 August and it was suggested that the Crocs be used at night also. The CO himself carried out tests in firing the flame by night and came to the conclusion that once the target was found it was not impossible for the front gunner to take aim,

Before: a 105mm Priest and gun crew earlier in the campaign, and …

> especially if a high shot was tried first. There were, however, very serious snags – the Crocs would have to be led almost right up to their objective (range of some 80 yards) by the inf. Once the first shot had been fired, the inf would be fully illuminated on the gd [ground], thus giving the enemy all the advantages of daylight whilst he himself retained invisibility. This would be accentuated should a Croc 'brew up' as it would illuminate the objective all night and present the enemy with an admirable aiming mark for mortar and artillery fire.[4]

Consequently, A Squadron, which had been brought back to four troops following losses at Estry, was once again to be split in two and would move forward at H-Hour, but would wait on the brigade's start line just north of Trotreval Farm until called for if needed after dawn. In Phase Two when the armoured divisions were to be released, the squadron was to move up to the second start line and again await call.

By August 1944, thanks to the already well-established practice of splitting the squadron in two due to rarely having a full establishment of Crocodiles or crews,

. . . after: a 'defrocked Priest' or Kangaroo being used as an armoured personnel carrier on a 51st Highland Division route south of Caen.

going into action with four troops of four tanks became the normal order of battle for 141 RAC's squadrons. Each half-squadron had a Mk IV command and a Mk V support tank.[5]

As was by now customary, II Canadian Corps' attack began with a bomber strike.[6] Captain Bailey described the fireworks and their move forward the following morning:

> From Cormeilles that night they watched the superb night-bombing of the RAF, then the Bofors tracers that soared gracefully through Monty's Moonlight down the axis of advance and the great flashes of artillery at the sending and receiving ends. At 1000 hrs on the 8th the Crocs moved out to a position of readiness just west of the rubble that had been Le Bras, where the little shell-scarred Calvary still stands.

A Squadron: May-sur-Orne

Following behind the armoured columns of 2 Canadian Armoured Brigade, 6 Canadian Infantry Brigade were on foot. The clearance task they had was complicated by the fact that the bypassed villages had numerous mine workings in which the German defenders sheltered from the bombing and barrage. During the night the twin villages of St.-André-sur-Orne and St.-Martin-de-Fontenay were finally fully in Canadian hands, but Les Fusiliers Mont Royal (FMR) had failed to secure the next village of May-sur-Orne.

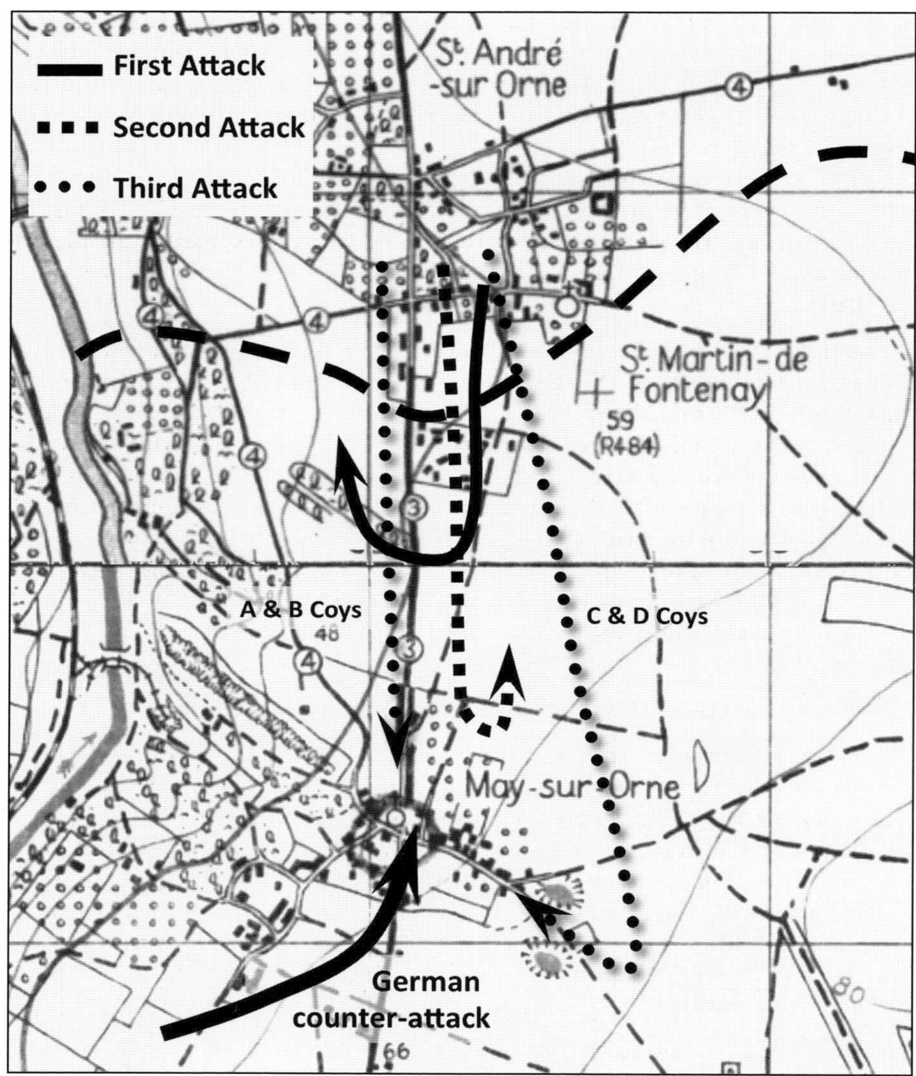

The attacks of the Fusiliers Mont Royal on May-sur-Orne.

The German defenders of May who had also sheltered in the mines, and deep dugouts held the Fusiliers' first attack. A vigorous counter-attack then threw the FMR back from a toehold they had established in the woods north of the village and they withdrew to the area of La Cité de la Mine ('The Factory') where they continued to be subjected to machine-gun, artillery and mortar fire and required assistance. Brigadier Young brought up another squadron of the 1st Hussars, but this second attack was also rebuffed. Finally, by early afternoon with only the reserve squadron of Shermans left to add to the attack, the brigadier called on the Crocodiles of A Squadron, which had earlier motored forward from the suburbs of Caen to Trotreval Farm. Major Cooper for the first time prevailed on the Fusiliers' commanding officer to use the whole squadron to flame May rather than a single troop.

The attack was to be launched from the area of La Cité de la Mine. Following a short but heavy five-minute bombardment, screening smoke shells burst to the flanks of the axis of the renewed attack. The Crocodiles' part in the plan is summarized by Captain Storrar, the new second-in-command, in A Squadron's war diary:

> The plan was to attack with four Tps up on the village, with one Tp right of the main CAEN-MAY-SUR-ORNE rd and three Tps left of the rd. FUP behind the mine bldgs, which were held by us. SL the line of the Mine bldgs. H-hr when the Crocodiles crossed the SL. The four comd tks were to give covering fire and smoke from the area of the mine bldgs. The length of the adv being some 600 yds. Arty concs went down on the village, and subsequently on the back of the village to prevent any enemy getaway.
>
> The Crocs pressured up a mile from the FUP and 2 Tp had to be dropped because of their trlr and gun troubles. The attack then went in at 1505 hrs with 1 Tp right and 3 and 4 Tps left as per diagram.

As Trooper Cox moved up to the start line, he noted that 'The Canadian Infantry … were in high spirits they had been in the cider factory':

> The attack went on as planned with us firing 75mm HE and Besa to make them keep their heads down and leave our infantry alone. As soon as we were into flame range about 80 yards everyone let fly. Anyone in the houses had no chance. The other troops were smashing down garden sheds, toilets, greenhouses, fences to flame the backs of the houses; no one was going to get out of there. We thought of those targets back at Ashford, but this was real.

The diagram from A Squadron's after-action report to illustrate their flame assault.

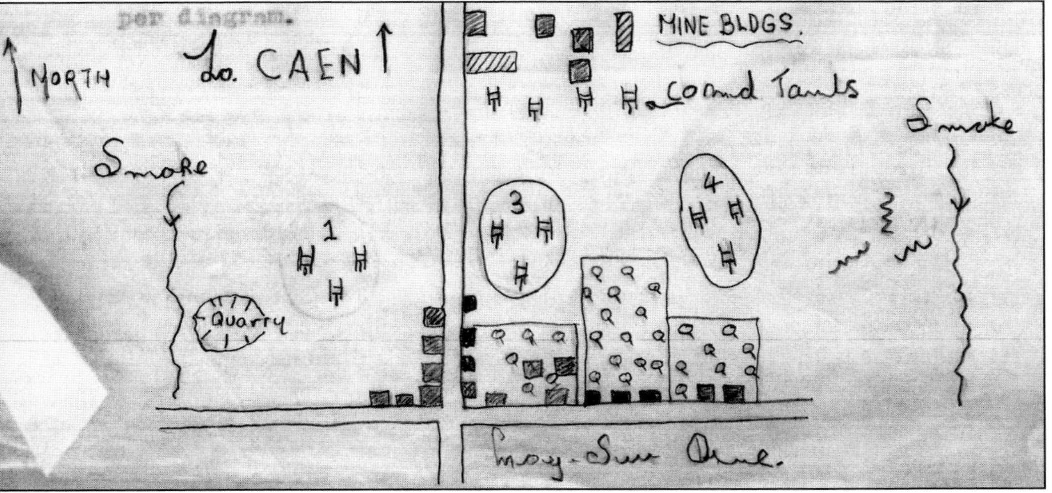

German soldiers were in these houses, but it was them or us. The Canadians thought they were at a rodeo, we could hear them yelling and yahooing from inside our tanks; they thought it was a field day. Some of the German soldiers must have seen what was happening to their mates and got out quick and about a hundred were rounded up by our Infantry. The Canadians hadn't lost a man.[7]

A report produced by Headquarters II Canadian Corps provides more detail:

The general plan was that behind each tank would move two sections following very closely on the [flame fuel] trailer behind the tank. As the tank approached a house it would fire, knock a hole in the house [with its 75mm], then squirt the liquid flame into the opening thus created. Immediately the section directly behind the tank would dash for the doorway and clear the house as quickly as possible.

The tank meanwhile moves forward down the line to the second house and turns its turret against it. Gun and flame-thrower repeat their actions and the second section of infantry following the tank is available for clearing this house. These two sections thus alternate in entering the buildings set ablaze by the tank and the sections of the reserve platoon following further in rear occupying the buildings already searched.[8]

Canadians clearing May-sur-Orne after the fighting.

Even though many of the enemy had fled, it took the Fusiliers more than an hour to work through the village and secure it, in the process rounding up more than 100 prisoners.

The Crocodiles had made all the difference and the village or at least the rubble of it was finally in Canadian hands. Captain Storrar wrote 'The dream of a whole squadron being used together materialised' and B Squadron's conclusion was that 'This attack bore out the contention that the effect of flame is increased out of all proportion when used *en masse*'.[9] Trooper Cox observed that

> It must have been quite a sight up on that ridge for all to see. A leading BBC correspondent described the attack in his report. Of course, our unit could not be mentioned. Our unit stayed the night on the ridge where our trucks could reach us and the usual job of re-arm and re-fuel went on quite late after dark.

A perennial complaint of the infantry is that when tanks pull back out of action as it gets dark 'they are leaving us to it'. Once harboured, however, the work for the crew begins with 'bombing up and refuelling the tanks', starting with the 75mm ammunition. Trooper Cox complained:

> The way they were packed one would think every shell was perfect. In packs of three, in a wooden crate bound with steel bands, the shell was sealed in a heavy cardboard container, with an end cap sealed with tape. We cursed them, usually undoing all this wrapping in the dark; it took ages. Next was petrol, oil, water, food, nitrogen, bottles and general servicing of our tanks. After that everyone took turns on guard. One of us had to be awake at all times, which didn't give us much time to sleep and when we did, the artillery barrage would wake us up. We invariably started an attack tired.

B Squadron: Secqueville-la-Campagne

At 1000 hours B Squadron's Crocodiles motored forward from Cresson to the ruins of Bras, leaving the trucks of their logistic echelon at Cormeilles. They were not called into action despite some stubborn defence of villages and the imminence of a major counter-attack by the *Hitlerjugend* Panzer Division. They were still waiting when the air strike by the USAAF that preceded TOTALIZE's second phase was under way. The war diary noted: 'Later in the day CORMEILLES was to be well and truly "stoked" by the "precision bombing" American Fortresses giving close sp to our fwd tps precisely 10 miles away. As it was, B Squadron's echelons lost 1 OR killed and three ORs wounded.'

Captain Bailey described the misbombing in more detail:

> From here looking back that morning they saw a great force of Forts come round the flank of Caen – then, no it couldn't be possible, wheel slowly round and drop the most colossal load of bombs on Cormeilles itself. The echelon of course was still back there. They dropped them on the line of guns at the bottom of the echelon's field, causing absolute havoc.

> Tpr Humphrey, left out of battle as the survivor from Lt. Brooke's tank, was killed. Tprs Hartfield and McDougall were wounded ... One fuel truck was burning fiercely and the heated bottles were being shot out just like torpedoes. Regardless of everything Sgt Little, who later got the MM, and L/C Knight first backed away the petrol truck, parked close behind, then drove off the truck in front. Another fuel truck was burning at the hood – Sgt Little drove it off while L/C Knight got up behind and fought the fire out. It's not nice to play around with fire when you've got a load of FTF on board. The grass was all alight so they drove the whole echelon into another field and got cracking on the flat tyres. And that evening Speedy's echelon was at the appointed spot to meet the Crocs and fill them up.[10]

This misbombing by an element of the US force hit numerous units and headquarters, including the Polish translator section, essential for the integration of the Polish Armoured Division in the second phase of TOTALIZE.

It wasn't until the afternoon that Major Ryle's B Squadron received a warning order for an attack and they moved forward from Bras to Garcelles. They were, however, not to attack Secqueville-la-Campagne with the 5th Seaforths as planned, but with 1st Gordon Highlanders of 153 Brigade. Consequently 'The

B17 Flying Fortresses in action bombing from altitude during a daylight raid.

plan was ready-made but the change-over was very hurried and naturally a bit confused':

> Major Ryle went to tie up with the Inf Comd at 1400 hrs but owing to a protracted O Group he was not himself able to hold one until 1610 and with a 1630 H-hr the Tps were not able to mate up properly with their opposite numbers. This may account for some of the subsequent confusion.[11,12]

Lieutenant Colonel the Honourable Cumming-Bruce's plan to take Secqueville was rushed as he was under pressure to complete the clearance of an area through which the Polish armoured division was to pass. The colonel explained: 'Time was very limited and no detailed reconnaissance was possible except by myself [the commanding officer]. 1 GORDONS moved on foot to an assembly area at LORGUICHON Wood and eventually joined up with the tanks and Crocodiles on the start line at GARCELLES-SECQUEVILLE as the attack started.'

Without a detailed recce and a well-formed plan, there had been inevitably time-consuming questions from junior commanders during the O Group. Other than Major Ryle these commanders included those from the Shermans of 148 Regiment RAC and a platoon of 4.2in mortars from the divisional machine-gun battalion. Of the German 272nd Infantry Division, there was a fair amount of intelligence:

> The enemy was known to be holding the village and was also dug in between the latter and GARCELLES-SECQUEVILLE. Reports during the morning had shown considerable enemy movement in the vicinity of SECQUE-VILLE and the woods to the East, and stiff opposition was expected. Luckily the heavy enemy shelling of GARCELLES slackened as the battalion formed up, and only sporadic fire and one particularly accurate defensive fire concentration were met during the advance.

The plan was for two companies of Gordons, with a squadron of Shermans in close support, to advance astride the road and go straight into the village, leaving D Company and the Crocodiles to mop up patches of wood in front of the houses. The other two squadrons of 148 Regiment RAC were to provide flank protection and direct fire support as necessary.

Major Martin Lindsay, the Gordons' second-in-command,[13] was leading the battalion forward to join the CO and the company commanders in the woods at Garcelles-Secqueville. He wrote:

> As soon as I could I turned off [the road] and across a field, 500 fighting men well dispersed following behind me. Then I heard the awful groaning of Moaning Minnies and looked around to hear the crack and see the burst as some twenty smackers landed just about where we had left the main road. But as luck would have it, they came down between two companies.[14]

Separately, the Crocodiles came forward across country to Garcelles-Secqueville, 'swung right by the church, the tracks grinding horribly through the rubble

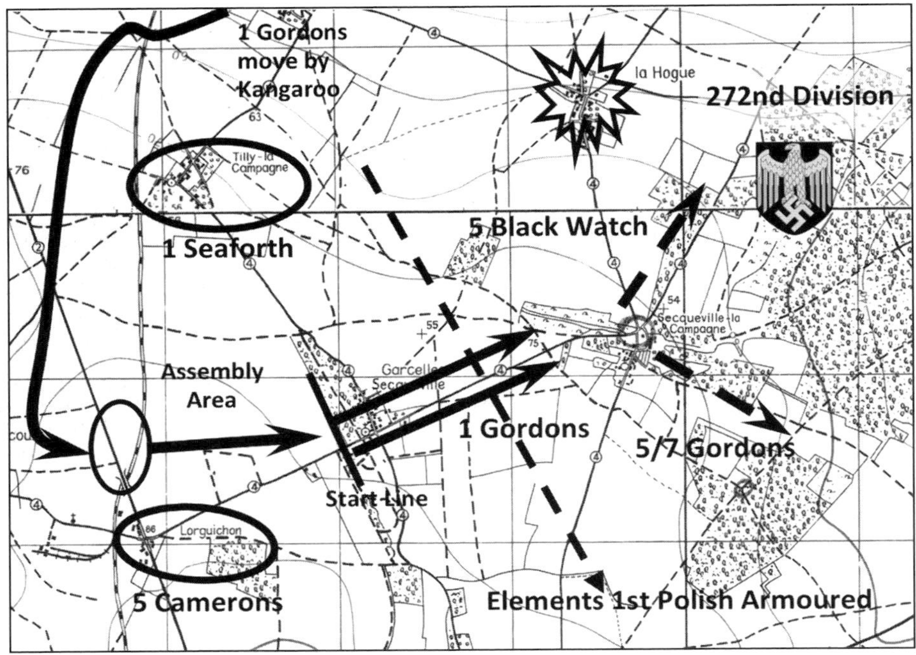

1 Gordons' attack on Secqueville-la-Campagne.

threatening every minute to come off' and formed up behind a ridge south-east of the village. With the enemy 'having been subjected to everything that war can devise', the attack got under way:

> As usual the Germans were where the defence overprint [map] was blank, and as the Crocs topped the ridge in their advance the first 95mm brought out a dozen of them just ahead. Not finding 'D' Company, 7 and 8 troops found themselves supporting the forward companies instead. The attack went too far right.

Without any form of regrouping having taken place, lieutenants Barrow and Ward had missed D Company, but Lieutenant Ward's 7 Troop was able to flame; however, his Crocodile became stuck while manoeuvring and he had to abandon his trailer. In the meantime, 10 Troop had come forward to the left to take 8 Troop's place.

To add a level of confusion, while B Squadron was attacking east the Polish Armoured Division was advancing south across the same ground. Major Ryle's war diary describes the resulting 'general melee':

> The Poles chaffing at the leash had been released over their start line ... and off they went gleefully rubbing their hands in anticipation, so the whole attack was a gleeful pandemonium of Polish tanks, 148 RAC and Crocodiles

The road to Secqueville was the axis of the attack. In 1944 there were far more hedgerows such as that on the right of the picture that needed flaming.

> milling around with the infantry 'hither and thithering' with the greatest calm and gaiety!

Meanwhile, the *Hitlerjugend* had launched a counter-attack against the forward elements of the two Allied divisions, spearheaded by the surviving Tigers of 101 *Schwere* Panzer *Abteilung* under *Hauptsturmführer* Michael Wittmann. To screen their continued activity around Sequeville, Colonel Waddell 'had detached himself with the self-appointed job of OC smoke':

> with Tigers being suspected in the east. Now Herbert Waddell with true Scottish conservancy did not intend to waste that smoke. So, having first placed his tank for all the German world to see, in a long discussion on the air he took Roy, the gunnery king, into advisory partnership ending thus: 'Now look here young man, ah don't propose to argue any further on the "A" [radio set], just come over to my tank.' An excellent plan was finally agreed and carried out by both.

Meanwhile, Major Lindsay was waiting in Garcelles to bring up the Gordons' anti-tank guns and mortars and passed the scene of the Crocodiles' action:

> There seemed to be a good deal of shelling coming both ways and I couldn't tell what was happening. So I nipped back and got a carrier and ran up to see Harry [Cumming-Bruce]. I found him with his Tac HQ at a hedge junction just short of Secqueville. The earth all around was burnt out by our flame-throwers. He told me that all the companies except one were on their objectives except one and that I should bring up the anti-tank guns.

A pre-operational photograph of almost half a platoon of infantry in a Priest Kangaroo.

Colonel Cumming-Bruce recorded that:

> The support from the artillery concentrations, mortar fire and Crocodiles was very effective, and although the enemy in the village fought hard, all objectives had been captured by 1800 hours, an hour after the attack started. Sixty-five prisoners from 1055 GR were captured and many more had been killed during the action. Patrols pushed out along the tracks through the woods to the East, but few enemy were seen.

Following the Gordons' attack, the brigade's other two battalions moved up in the available Kangaroos and cleared the small wood to the north-east of Secqueville-la-Campagne and occupied La Hogue and the wood south-east of the village. By 2100 hours 153 Brigade was secure and B Squadron was released to drive back to harbour at Cormeilles.

Despite the problems, the attack was later summed up as having a 'Good plan. Strong artillery and tank support. Good Inf who followed up well. Enemy had been heavily bombed. Attack overwhelmed a weak defence (51st Div).'[15]

In the aftermath of the USAAF misbombing, B Squadron returned to find its echelon devastated by friendly fire. Trooper Smith was among a salvage party sent forward from D Squadron:

> The echelon had been harboured in a copse south of Caen, together with a Polish AA battery and a troop of 17-pounder anti-tank guns. We had lost three men, the Poles fourteen, while the casualties of the RA were not

> reported; all their guns and quads were wrecks. In fact the whole wood covering several acres was gutted trees and undergrowth had crumbled into ashes which still smoked as we scuffed through to find our lorries. These were twisted wrecks of brown and red metal smelling horribly of burnt rubber. Some of the gas bottles had blown open but the real messes were the ammo trucks which had simply blown apart.

So comprehensive had the destruction been that the salvage party returned empty-handed. Smith added that it was not just the bombers that worried them: 'If the fighter-bombers were in action within 5 miles we would be distinctly nervous. I never spoke to a tank crew that at one time or another had not been attacked by them. They made more of a mess than damage.' The way the liberal deployment of yellow smoke grenades is frequently mentioned in other memoirs indicates that there was a very real fear of attack by their own fighter-bombers.

Operation TOTALIZE had run out of steam by 10 August, with II Canadian Corps having advanced some 10 miles.

B Squadron: Operations EGG and TEMPEST

Having been released during the evening of 8 August, B Squadron was placed under I Corps, which as an adjunct to TOTALIZE was preparing to advance east of the railway in the area of Vimont and out of the tight confines of the Orne bridgehead. Major Ryle and Captain Storrar were called to Headquarters 49th Division to receive orders for a 'renewed association with 31 Tank Brigade'. The fighting would be through some light bocage country studded with the usual strongly built and easily defensible villages initially astride the railway.

Returning to the squadron that was waiting to move at Cormeilles, Major Ryle led the troops forward to harbour amid the unsalvageable tanks knocked out during Operation GOODWOOD:

> Nigel [Ryle] leading the Crocs to where he had proudly discovered the perfect harbour for the tanks just NW of Cagny at 097648 [Le Mesnil Frementel].[16] Two minutes later the place was being shelled by 88s ... The whole of that area was overlooked from the high ground west of Troarn and the slightest movement anywhere brought stonks down.[17]

During 9 August, the OC and 2iC spent the day on recces. They travelled 'in a scout car, unpleasantly exposed on skylines to 88s which had not the slightest hesitation in potting at them whenever they appeared, travelling about to various "O" Groups.'

Eventually it was confirmed that the Crocodiles were to support the Hallamshire Battalion of 146 Brigade along with C Squadron 9 RTR. However, as noted in the war diary of 9 RTR:

> At the time this plan was made the situation was very fluid and obscure; the enemy were fighting local actions, but there was a general belief that they were withdrawing.

> Operation EGG was never given a definitive H-Hour and will only be put into operation if a definite defence centre round Vimont was encountered. Consequently, various phases of Operation EGG were completed by troops other than those given the task and there appeared to be no coordination at all.

The Hallams and two troops of C Squadron 9 RTR attacked Chicheboville on 9 August, but by nightfall had only reached the outskirts of the village. The following day they completed consolidation of the village before attempting to secure the woods east of the village and Bénouville, but mortars and shells exploding in the trees drove the infantry back to Chicheboville. For B Squadron it was also regular mortaring while they waited to support the Hallams during 10 August. The following day it was a repeat with the Leicesters of the attack on Bénouville. Later that day crossing the railway:

> A troop was asked for to go into the rubble of Vimont but after a Wasp was brewed by an 88 firing straight down the road, rapidly followed by a tank in

The plan for Operation EGG and the area of the subsequent days' fighting.

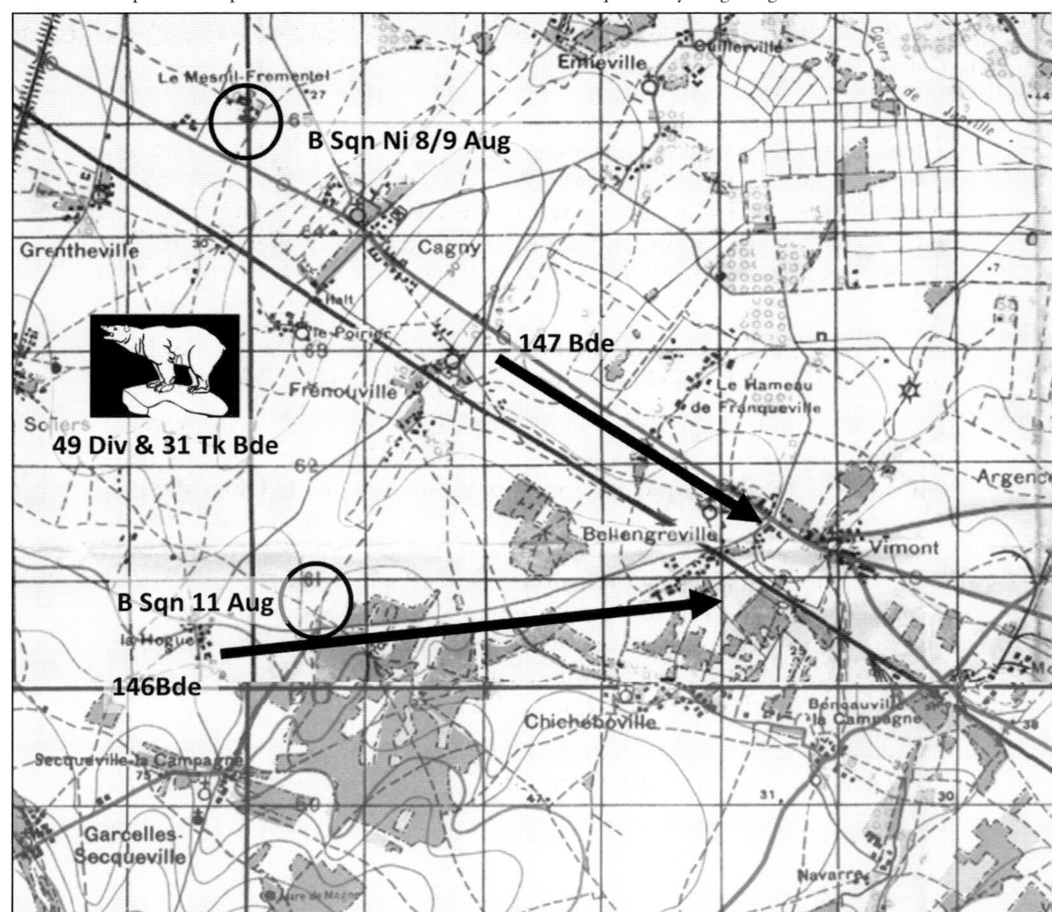

The road into Vimont was covered by well dug-in anti-tank guns and infantry, both in the village and to the flanks.

> the same manner the idea was given up. Still being potted at by 88s, the scout car survived next as far as Chicheboville where a plan was laid on to attack Bénouville [La Campagne] in Operation TEMPEST on the next day and then work up to Vimont from the south. This Nigel tied up with the 9 RTR, beautifully timing his arrival at the harbour to coincide with another hefty stonk.

A flavour of the time spent waiting in the woods just north-east of Secqueville-la-Campagne before being called into action is provided by Captain Harry Bailey:

> ... the Squadron spent three most unpleasant days in these woods. Sgt Decent bowled up from Workshops during daylight with his tank and from then on, the place became a very favourite spot for German shoots. Picky Preston, the padre, came along and the tanks were formed into a crescent whilst he gave a service; it was an extraordinary thing but during that service not a single shell came over. As soon as it was over it all started up again. On the 12th of August all the best people back home began to shoot grouse. But in the woods at Secqueville the Boche was going out for different game and that day he winged five – Sgt Wetherell, Cpl Grant, Cpl Wallace, Tpr Bewsher and Tpr Walsh.

On 13 August B Squadron left I Corps on the eastern flank and were regrouped with II Canadian Corps for Operation TRACTABLE alongside A Squadron.

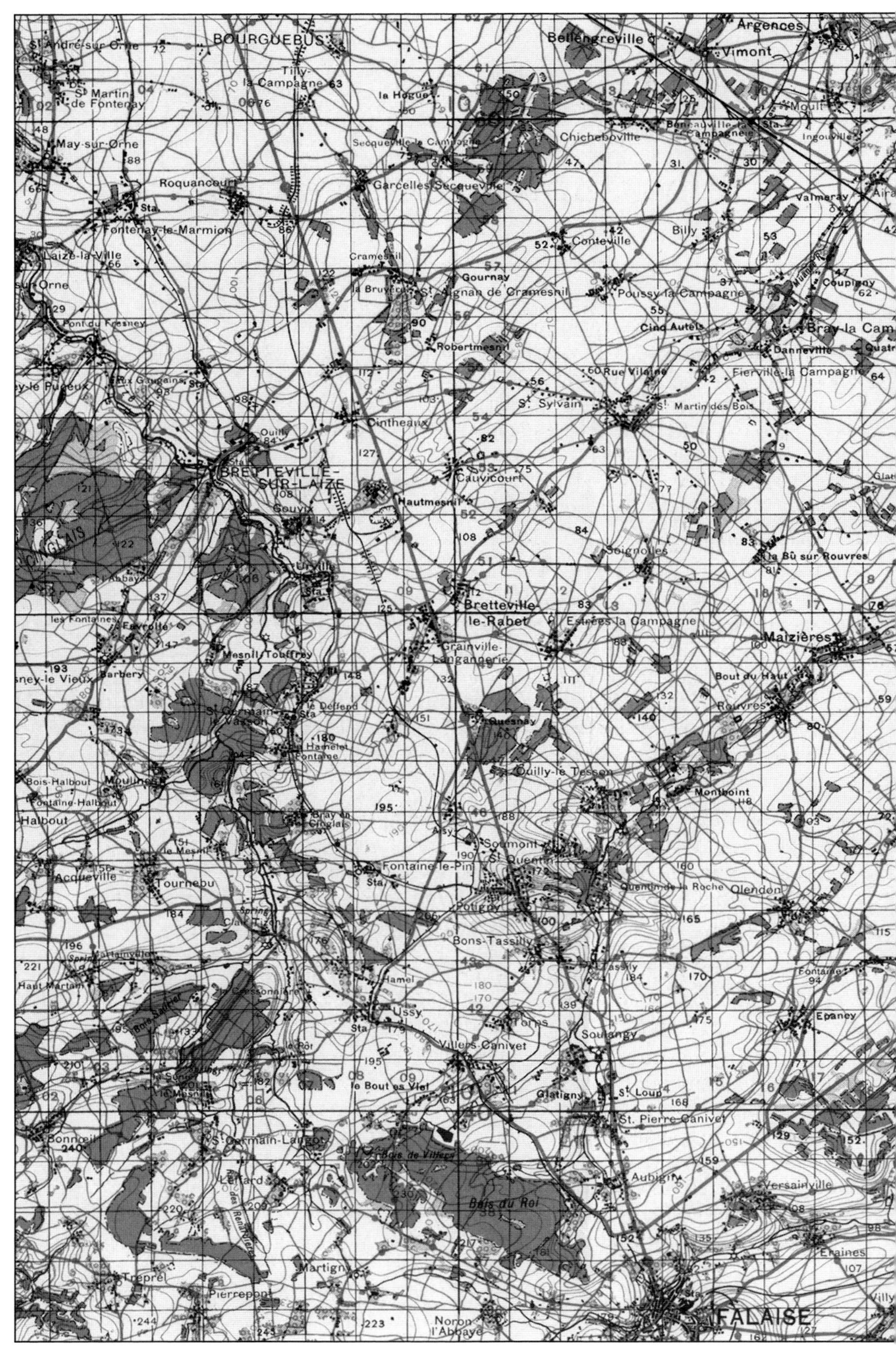

BOURGUEBUS
Bellengreville
Argences
Vimont
St. André-sur-Orne
St. Martin de Fontenay
Tilly-la-Campagne
la Hogue
Chicheboville
May-sur-Orne
Secqueville la Campagne
Roquancourt
Garcelles Secqueville
Fontenay-le-Marmion
Conteville
Billy
Valmeray
Laize-la-Ville
Cramesnil
Gournay
la Bruyère
St. Aignan de Cramesnil
Poussy la Campagne
Coupigny
Pont du Fresney
Cinq Autels
Bray-la Cam
Robertmesnil
Danneville
Rue Vilaine
Fierville-la Campagne
St. Sylvain
St. Martin des Bois
Cintheaux
BRETTEVILLE-SUR-LAIZE
Cauvicourt
Hautmesnil
Gouvix
Soignolles
la Bû sur Rouvres
Urville
Bretteville-le-Rabet
Estrées la Campagne
Maizières
les Fontaines
Fresney-le Vieux
Barbery
Mesnil-Touffrey
Grainville-Langannerie
Bout du Haut
Rouvres
St. Germain-le-Vasson
le Deffend
Quesnay
Hamelet
Fontaine
Bois-Halbout
Moulines
Fontaine-Halbout
Ouilly-le Tesson
Monthoint
Bray en Cinglais
Aisy
Soumont
St. Quentin
Acqueville
Tournebu
Fontaine-le-Pin
Quentin de la Roche
Olendon
Potigny
Bons-Tassilly
Tassilly
Haut Martain
Hamel
Ussy
Epaney
Fontaine
Villers-Canivet
Soulangy
le Bout es Viel
Glatigny
St. Loup
St. Pierre-Canivet
St. Germain-Langot
Bonnoeil
Bois de Villers
Aubigny
Leffard
Bois du Roi
Versainville
Eraines
Martigny
Treprel
Pierrepont
Noron l'Abbaye
FALAISE

Chapter Eleven

Operation TRACTABLE

After the attack on May-sur-Orne on 8 August, A Squadron followed the advance over the next three days, moving from command of one formation to another, but was not called upon. Finally, when TOTALIZE ran out of momentum with the armoured divisions having advanced just 5 miles, preparations were made for Operation TALLULAH, subsequently renamed TRACTABLE, which was to be launched on 14 August.

Captain Bailey described the concept for the attack across a ridge of high ground down to the initial objective, which was crossings of the River Laizon:

> TALLULAH was to be a repetition of TOTALIZE methods [i.e. armoured columns with the infantry in Kangaroos] in order to seize the controlling ground north and north-east of Falaise – the famous Falaise pocket was in the making. 2 Canadian Corps was to attack on a two Div front with right 3 Canadian Inf Div and left 4 Canadian Armd Div. Again two armoured columns were to lead: right 2 Canadian Armd Bde, left 4 Canadian Armd Bde; these in turn followed by Priest-borne battalions of 9 and 8 Canadian Inf Bde responsible to clear the River Laizon once the armour had crossed. This time, however, the operation was to be done in daylight with extensive smoke on the flanks and heavy bombers.[1]

The Crocodiles were to be in action with 3rd Canadian Division, with A Squadron allocated to 9 Brigade and B Squadron to 8 Brigade. The role of both squadrons was to follow the initial advance up onto the ridge above the Laizon and assist the infantry in clearing the river valley once the Shermans of the armoured brigades had crossed the small but muddy watercourse.

The Crocodiles would, however, not be the only flame weapon system deployed in the operation. The Canadian infantry battalions had been issued the carrier-based Wasp and were to use it for the first time in TRACTABLE.

The bomber strike by fifty-three medium aircraft on the positions of 85th Infantry Division began at 1140 hours and was followed by a barrage of mixed smoke and HE fire by the corps' artillery. The armour began its advance to the high ground overlooking the Laizon valley at 1142 hours, with the Canadian Corps HQ giving the order 'Move now'. Fifteen minutes later both Crocodile squadrons followed their respective assault troops. 'On the appointed day "B" Squadron formed up at St.-Aignan-de-Cramesnil and after crossing the Start Line just to the south, went flat out in tactical formation', but moving into the smoke and dust of the bombardment proved to be chaotic. As described by the

The Wasp Flame-Thrower

The first recorded use of a flame-thrower mounted on a carrier was in 1940 when a projector was tested by the Welsh Guards. Further development resulted in what became known as the Ronson. Little interest was shown in the UK, however, due to its short range of 40–50 yards, but Canada maintained their interest and made arrangements for twenty of these flame devices to be sent to the US Marine Corps in the Pacific where they were mounted on M3A1 tanks. This weapons system became known as 'Satan'.

The Wasp Mk I was the first version to be produced with an improved flame projector with a range of up to 100 yards. The flame projector was mounted over the left front side of the carrier. This made its purpose very conspicuous. Some 1,000 of these weapons were completed by November, but were only used for training.

The flame gun of the Mk I Wasp.

The next version was the Wasp Mk II with a redesigned projector mounted in the machine-gun housing of the carrier, giving a much lower profile. This projector gave a much more concentrated burst of flame when hitting the target. It was also much easier to use. The fuel was stored in the two rear compartments of the carrier, one with 60 gallons of fuel and the other with 40 gallons. It was planned to have six Wasps issued to each infantry battalion in their carrier platoon.

The Wasp Mk II with the internal flame fuel tanks.

The Mk IIC Wasp with its external flame fuel tank.

The first time these formidable weapons were used was by the 1st Battalion, the Royal Highland Fusiliers in support of D Company, the 2nd Royal Monmouth Regiment in an attack on Étréville, Normandy on 29 July 1944. As these battalions were from different brigades within the 53rd (Welsh) Division, there was clearly much flexibility in the division's planning and confidence in how the new weapon would perform.

The next version to be produced was the Wasp Mk IIC with the C meaning 'Canada', the country responsible for its development. This was another improvement on the basic design where only one 75-gallon flame fuel tank was carried but at the rear of the vehicle, leaving the interior free for another crew member and provision for a Bren or a 2in mortar to be carried. Canadian troops first used this version in August 1944 during operations TOTALIZE and TRACTABLE. The Wasp could now be used as a normal carrier when not flaming and this flexibility, recognized by the British Army, meant that all Wasp production was switched to the Canadian variant and by early 1945 the Mk IIC was the standard issue with the earlier mark being modified to have the flame fuel tank at the rear. Plastic armour was fitted to the front of Wasps as proof against 7.92mm armour-piercing ammunition and 20mm fire.

Canadian report, the columns 'gradually disappeared behind the continuous screen of dust into which the white puffs of smoke had merged':

> Almost at once drivers found it impossible to keep direction; they could merely press on with accelerator pedals pushed to the floor. Running blind behind their clumsy fascines, the Churchills began to stray stupidly among a welter of Shermans, carriers, Crocodiles and Flails, each trying desperately to get back on to the required direction, the heavier monsters fighting to keep up with the head of the column. Units lost formation, and in less than an hour, the almost ceremonial array of the forenoon had degenerated into a heterogeneous mess pouring down into the smoke-filled valley ... In spite of the dust which obliterated landmarks and made visibility extremely poor, obstacles were surmounted, minefields marked and bypassed; and after each brief halt to check direction, the lumbering vehicles lurched forth again to disappear with a roar into the mist like smoke, acrid with the stink of engines and cordite.[2]

German anti-tank guns of 85th Infantry Division were deployed in a screen on slightly higher ground south of the Laizon and fired, often speculatively, into the smoke, which added to the confusion and, along with mines, knocked out about twenty tanks from the two armoured brigades.[3]

The squadrons eventually arrived at the first objective, the high ground from which the enemy outposts had been driven. There they waited, overlooking the Laizon and the Germans' main position for the call from the Canadian infantry. Up on the ridge clear of the smoke the Crocodiles of B Squadron 'came in for a good deal of direct anti-tank fire', as recalled by Captain Bailey:

> ... from the other side of the river and a Flail brewed at the side of Tony Ward. Nigel saw the AP spurts near Tony's Croc and told him to pull back as he was being fired at. Back came the young man's answer, 'You're telling

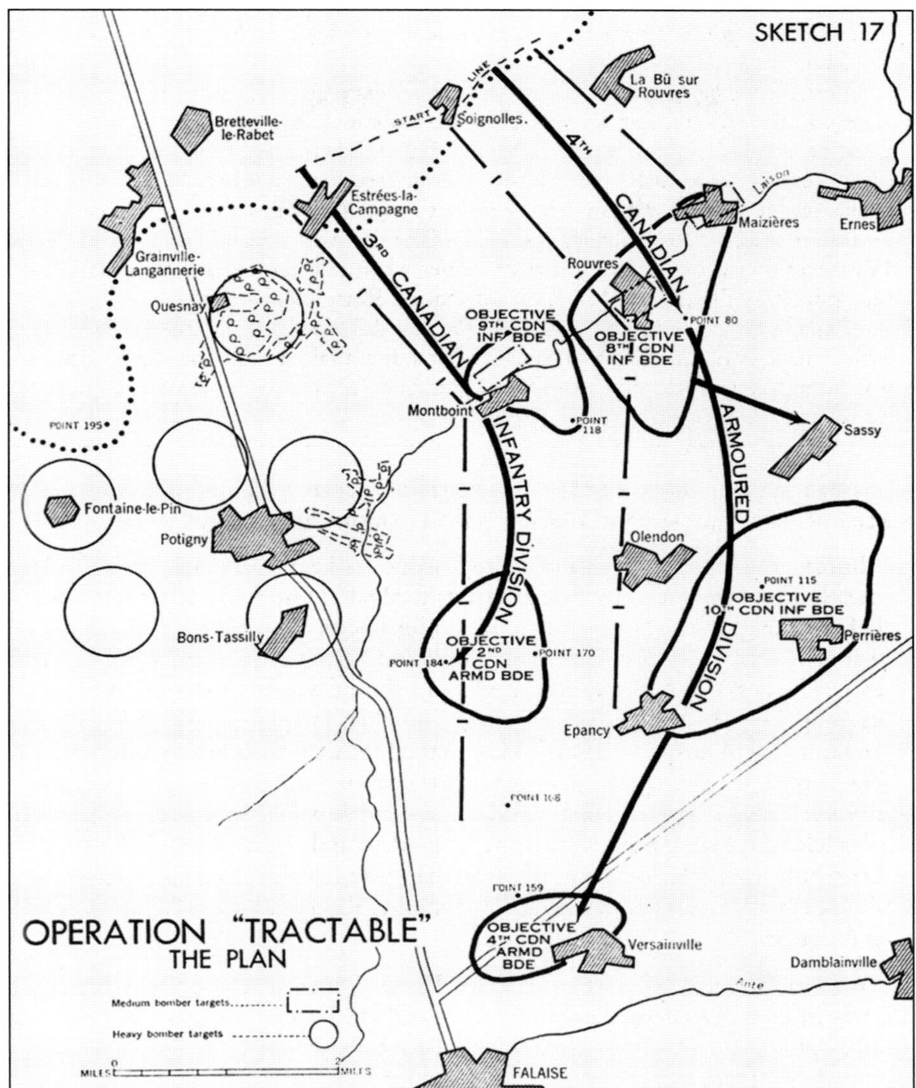

The Canadian OH map showing the TRACTABLE plan.

> me.' By use of extensive smoke the Squadron managed to get into more reasonable positions. Peter claimed one anti-tank gun.

From conversation over the radio net, it was soon apparent that the infantry of 8 Canadian Brigade had captured their objective at Rouvres, had cleared it on their own and that the assistance of the Crocodiles was not required. Major Ryle spoke to his squadron LO, Captain Shearman, back at brigade headquarters who

Shermans of the Fort Garry Horse and 79th Armoured Division assault vehicles waiting for H-Hour.

'apprised the Brigade Commander of this. Having lost all communication with his battalions due to the intervening high ground, the Brigadier was pleasantly surprised more than somewhat and used the Crocodile communications to give orders to his other two battalions to advance, as he was not in touch with them either.'[4]

The squadron consequently remained on call in the forward assembly area, relaying messages until 8 Canadian Brigade established their own communication on the high ground. Having been shelled throughout the afternoon, B Squadron was eventually released back to harbour at Garcelles late in the evening without having come into action.

A Squadron

In the area around Assy, the infantry of 9 Canadian Brigade mounted in Kangaroos appears to have arrived in front of the positions before the leading columns of Shermans after what the Stormont, Glengarry & Dundas (SG&D) Highlanders' diarist described as 'an armoured charge of the Light Brigade.' A Squadron had followed this advance and also arrived at the first objective, the hill between Points 140 and 132:

> Onward we went about six miles since we went cross-country, probably about thirty minutes driving. By now about three miles inside the German lines yet still we had seen no one. We found the road and at the exact spot, it was deserted, we thought it would be packed with Germans trying to escape but not a sign.

A mix of carriers, M10 Tank Destroyers, AVREs, Shermans and a Crocodile waiting in the Forward Assembly Area during Operation TRACTABLE.

> The Infantry [the North Nova Scotia Highlanders] came up digging into the ditches either side of the road, plenty of cover, high trees and hedges on both sides. Our troop took up its position in a wheat field along the side of the road, the other troops either on or over the road; theoretically the road was secure.
>
> The sun blazed down the tanks, becoming uncomfortably hot. We sat there for a while switching on the fans which just circulated the hot air, the sweat ran into our eyes, our clothing soaked up the moisture until it could hold no more, we began to strip off. Not a wise decision; tanks had a habit of catching fire.
>
> For quite some time little seemed to be happening. We knew that being this far into enemy lines would provoke some kind of action sooner or later; while we thought about it the call came through.

Advancing across the hill, the Highland Light Infantry of Canada (HLI of C) and the SG&D Highlanders pressed on down to the next objectives: the western part of Rouvres and Assy and the crossings of the Laizon. Here they encountered a battalion of 1053 Grenadier Regiment with the forward edge of their main defences dug in along the Rouvres to Ouilly-le-Tesson road, some 500 yards north of the river line.

Two troops, 2 and 4, were called forward into action. 2 Troop flamed some hedgerows west of Rouvres for the HLI of C and 4 Troop was called sometime after 1300 hours to help the SG&D in the hamlet of Assy, where the German infantry of 6th Company were holding out.

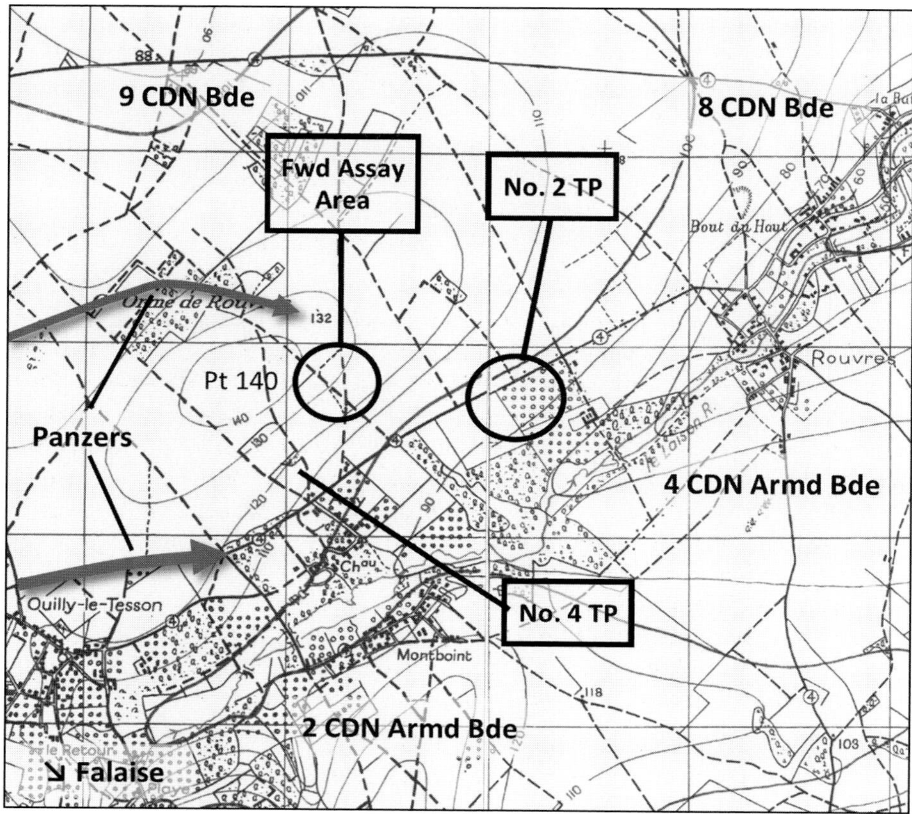

A Squadron's area of operations on 14 August 1944.

The Crocodiles of 2 Troop advanced to flame some tight country and a defended farm on the western outskirts of Rouvres just south of the road. Trooper Cox was driving that day:

> Our Troop was selected to go forward and flush them out with flame. The Troop Leader called us to report when ready; once we confirmed the call came to advance. Moving along the hedge we came to a gate and followed the Troop Leader through. Two Tiger tanks blocked the road; both had their 88mm guns depressed almost to the road. This gave the impression they were knocked out or abandoned; we knew they had fuel supply problems. There was no sign of life. The Troop Officer paid them no heed. We crossed the road not 10 feet from them and carried along a track, the ground climbed in front of us and to our right a thick hedge, against this in the shadow, another Tiger. We couldn't see which way he was facing, at a range of about 800 yards there was no point in taking him on with our pop gun. That would be like putting a hand in a hornets' nest, you would only get

> badly stung and we just prayed he hadn't seen us. At that moment the order came over the air to pull right. Simultaneously our three tanks burst through the hedge, finding ourselves in an apple orchard. We could see the farm and buildings through the rows of trees and started up with our Besa to keep their heads down; no point using 75mm HE amongst the trees. We gave the farm and buildings a thorough hosing of flame, getting carried away in the process and using all our flame fuel. We received our recall and returned the way we came past the two Tigers still sitting there and back to the starting point.[5]

Following TOTALIZE, the number of operational Tigers had been reduced to a handful and these were operating alongside the surviving Panthers and Panzer IVs of *Obersturmbannführer* Max Wünsche's 12th SS Panzer Regiment. The fifteen Panthers of 2nd and 3rd companies had been amalgamated and were providing armoured support to 85th Division. They were thinly spread in five separate platoons on TOTALIZE's right flank as well as south of the Laizon. The panzers north of the river had advanced east from hides in the Quesnay Wood area and around the high ground of Point 140. The North Novas of 9 Brigade digging in on Point 140 reported panzers north of the feature and C Company SG&D Highlanders' forward company near Assy reported Tigers advancing on the road from Ouilly-le-Tesson and that the OC's carrier was knocked out. It would seem that 4 Troop's flame attack had been just before the Tigers advanced east along the road. The war diary notes:

> These Crocs came under 88mm fire almost immediately from a Tiger concealed at the bend in the rd. The Tp Sgt's tank was hit twice and the

The original caption states 'Tiger 211 abandoned south of Potigny'. This is just to the west of 4 Troop's action and the Tiger was probably abandoned as a result of mechanical failure.

> Tp Ldr's once, whereupon they were ordered to withdraw. A Tiger appeared on the right flank and the Crocs took up posn to engage it should it come within effective 75mm range to engage it should it affect our own infantry moving up to the village south of the road [Assy-Montboint].

Of 2 Troop, the war diary continues:

> One Croc (comd by Lt McCulloch) in an attempt to get a favourable viewpoint from the high ground to the north of the road was hit by an 88mm shot which penetrated the driver's front plate. The Croc was set on fire and only the Comd and co-driver escaped. A second tank following the Croc was also hit but was able to take cover immediately.

This action that takes only a few lines to summarize is expanded by Trooper Cox in a harrowing and very personal story:

> ... it seemed strangely quiet, something wasn't right. No shell fire, no mortars, no rifle or machine guns, yet here we were several miles into the German lines, a lone Sherman tank sat away from the hedge about 60 yards away in the wheat field ... the smoke was moving away slowly, we made our way up the hill. The troop officer [Lieutenant McCulloch] leading, then ourselves a little lower and to his side the Sergeant's tank a little further back. Another 200 yards we would be able to see over the crest, I kept an eye on the Troop Leader to help keep formation, suddenly his tank stopped, smoke and flame billowed out, our officer was fighting to get out, the flames licking up around him. His headphones had tangled up; he finally got out, fell onto

A Churchill Crocodile at Bayeux. A recognition feature of the Mk VII Churchill was the round escape hatches, which replaced the square hatches on earlier marks.

> the track, then to the ground. At the same time we saw the escape door on the side opened, the tank leaning to one side helped it open. The Flame Gunner lay half in and half out of the tank. This had only taken a few seconds. Dickie looked over to me; nothing was said. Simultaneously we both threw open our hatches and leapt down. I dashed over and dragged out the Flame Gunner, pulling him by his arms to the shelter of our tank. Dickie tried to help our officer but his leg was smashed, how he got himself out I'll never know, just willpower. I went back to the escape door; it was an inferno in there, no one else would be getting out. The ammunition was starting to explode and we had to back off, we had good mates in there ... I went over to Dickie; our officer had passed out which was a blessing. His shin bone poked out of his torn trouser leg, his eyes were still open though could see no pupils; it was as if they had rolled backwards with black web-like burnt skin over them. We laid him across the front of our tank ready to take him back down off the hill and to the medics.
>
> Suddenly everything went black and little specks danced before my eyes. I recall running three or four steps, falling, then nothing. I have no idea how long I laid there, but when I did rally round, I was on my own, the troop leader's tank blazing a few feet away destroying itself as the shells exploded. No sign of my own tank. I felt very exposed and stood up in a daze.

Cox was on his own and when he moved, he came under machine-gun fire, but he eventually escaped using the cover of a burning haystack. On foot and alone, he was passed by 4 Troop's Crocodiles that had survived their encounter with the Tigers on the road below:

> The Sergeant's tank stopped and asked me if I was alright, I said I was. Some Canadian anti-tank gunners with 6-pounders were pushing their guns forward. They asked me if I'd seen any German tanks; I knew it wasn't the two Tigers on the road, the shellfire was from further back. When I told them this off they went on their Tiger hunt, I walked back along the road.

Cox reached his own Crocodile on the edge of woods near the top of the hill.

Meanwhile, the SG&D's 6-pounder anti-tank guns had come forward and were firing the new Armour-Piercing Discarding Sabot (APDS) ammunition and claim to have knocked out one of the two Tigers on the Rouvres to Ouilly-le-Tesson road.

Having re-joined 'Stallion', fortunately for Cox, he was still out of the tank when the tank and empty trailer were hit by an AP round. The Crocodile, however, did not burn:

> I climbed into the turret, what a mess, the 88mm armour-piercing shell had passed between Dickie and myself [driver and flame gunner positions] just catching the top of the hull. It ricocheted up [through the roof of the driver's compartment] into the gun mantlet tearing the gun and mantlet from its mounting, ramming it back through the radio into the back of the turret.

> By the look of it perhaps it was better that I was outside at the time! How Ray escaped sitting down on his gunner seat I'll never know. I began to get the shakes at the thought of it. I had to get out, I couldn't stand it in there; once outside I felt better, we began to talk about it.[6]

Meanwhile, despite being 'unable to go right flanking because of the Tigers', the two SG&D Highlander companies along with some Shermans had followed up 4 Troop's attack and broken into the village. The German defenders started to surrender in large numbers and Montboint was reported in Canadian hands at 1340 hours. The surviving Crocodiles of A Squadron, along with the Highlanders' 6-pounder anti-tank guns remained in action covering the open right flank, but suffered further losses. The war diary continued:

> During a long period of waiting for an attack to come in from the right flank a command tank was hit whilst in posn in a hedgerow. The crew bailed out and the tank was hit a further three times. There is no indication of the direction from which these shots were fired.

Trooper Cox and the rest of his crew were all wounded and needed patching up, so they walked back to a Canadian aid post, where they waited to be taken back to a dressing station. While they were there:

> Another of our casualties came in; he was the gunner of our Sergeant's tank, he had gone 'bomb happy'. I felt so sorry for him and tried to console him, but he kept on crying. I'd known him a long time, always a cheerful smile and full of life, now a wreck unable to control his emotions. He'd given his best and could take no more.[7]

For A Squadron, the Canadian armour and 79th Armoured Division's 'Funnies', the cost of the advance had been heavy in terms of lost tanks and soldiers killed or wounded. The panzers had only conducted limited counter-attacks during

The Tiger's view of the advance of the SG&D Highlanders and 4 Troop on Assy.

14 August and concentrated on containing the Canadian advance, which on the same day, took the line 9 miles forward and at its furthest point reached 3 miles south of the Laizon. Falaise, 5 miles further south, was in Canadian hands two days later.

Meanwhile A Squadron, having flamed, was still fighting its conventional tank action and 'Stallion's' de-horsed crew were on their way back through the Canadian medical chain 'going cross-country dodging bomb craters and blazing vehicles. Guns were sticking up at strange angles, the whole area in a turmoil. Apparently, it was the RAF's turn to bomb our own troops; someone who should have known better had created another SNAFU.'

What had actually happened was that an RAF bomber strike, beyond the Laizon in advance of the second phase of TRACTABLE, took place at 1400 hours. Six targets were attacked by 417 Lancasters, 352 Halifaxes and forty-two Mosquitos of Bomber Command that dropped 3,723 tons of bombs. Sadly, seventy-seven of these aircraft, forty-four of them RCAF, misbombed through a mixture of a failure to take navigational precautions[8] and confusion over target-marking. This was because the recognition signals used by Allied ground troops when aircraft were overhead was yellow smoke, and yellow smoke was on that day being used by the pathfinders to indicate targets: 'Unhappily, neither SHAEF nor Headquarters Allied Expeditionary Air Force had advised the RAF Bomber Command of this procedure. Thus, the yellow smoke burned

The misbombing of Haut Mesnil on 14 August. This village was adjacent to Cox's route back to a Canadian dressing station.

by the units under attack had the reverse effect to that for which it was intended, merely attracting more bombs.'[9]

The war diary records that:

> This was not A Sqn's lucky day. The RAF were giving close heavy bomber sp to the fwd tps but many of them entirely misjudged their target and bomb after bomb rained down on the area 0956 [St.-Aignan-de-Cramesnil], where A Ech of A Sqn and many other Echs (including the Poles) were harbouring. The tragic result for A Sqn was loss in vehs of 6 3-tonners [trucks], 4 half-tracks, 1 water truck, 1 M/C, and of personnel, Lieut Walters killed, 1 NCO died of wounds, 1 NCO missing and 4 other personnel wounded.

In addition, six Crocodile crewmen are listed as being killed, and all but one of them are commemorated on the Bayeux memorial to the missing. The loss of four tanks in battle and most of the others damaged to a greater or lesser extent left the squadron inoperable.

The diarist concludes that 'in this sorry state A Sqn harboured for the night.' Following their long trek on their tracks from BLUECOAT and the mileage involved in TOTALIZE and TRACTABLE, A Squadron was sent to Tilly-sur-Seulles. Here the Crocodiles were 'given a complete overhaul and refit by 1 Aslt Tps Wksp', while the squadron's crews had a few days in a Canadian rest camp. After a week in the rear area, including a visit to the delights of Lion-sur-Mer, on 26 August the squadron was returning to the front.

The Wasp Flame-Thrower in Action

A brief return to 14 August is warranted by the first use of the Crocodile's smaller cousin, the Wasp flame-thrower, by the Canadians. Very few Wasp flame actions in the latter part of the Normandy campaign are recorded in any detail, if mentioned at all. SG&D Highlanders, having secured Château d'Assy several hours earlier, reorganized and resumed the battle with an attack by B Company on enemy positions near a bridge across the Laizon, 400 yards west of the château: 'The unit was stopped by frontal fire within a stone's throw of its target . . . The answer to this irritating problem of infantry tactics will long be remembered by the Highlanders.' At 1700 hours:

> A section [three] of these terrible weapons, waiting at battalion headquarters, was called forward to the leading company, which lay at the foot of the copse across the road from the orchard. Using routes selected by the commander of the carrier platoon, they were brought up to within 30 yards of the nearest of the enemy's diggings. Then the flame-throwers saturated both men and weapons in this and three other positions and routed the seared and screaming survivors. Elated by the proof of a horribly superior weapon, the Canadians took possession, and for three more hours held off numerous isolated tanks which continued to worry them. Gradually these gave way to snipers, and the sound of firing died away before 2000 hours.[10]

Rations

When in the squadrons' static locations, regimental cooks would provide central catering. Normally the crews of Crocodiles were in isolated locations, committed to battle or on the move, so food was issued to crews to prepare for themselves. In north-west Europe this was usually in the form of tinned Composite Rations (compo), which included powdered milk/tea/sugar mixtures, breakfast, snack and main meal menus, also four sheets of toilet paper per man per day ('one up, one down, one around and one for shine'), boiled sweets, what passed for chocolate and seven cigarettes per man. Fresh bread was very rarely available, so the compo ration included the traditional 'hard tack' biscuits ('Biscuits AB' were 'Alternative to Bread' or 'anal blockage').

Tank crews could normally have hot food simply by wedging tins between parts of the engine while on the move.

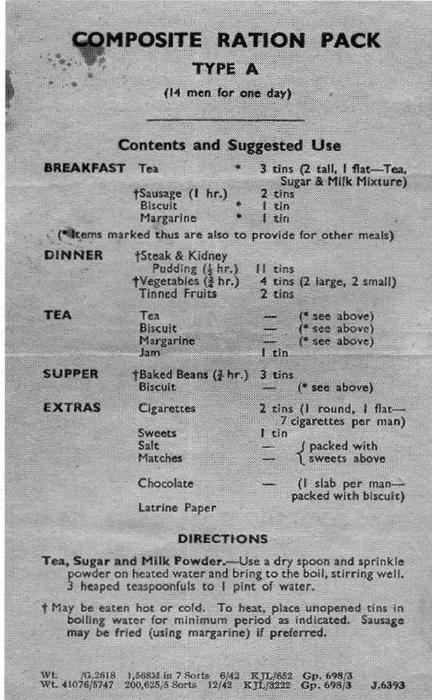

COMPOSITE RATION PACK

TYPE A

(14 men for one day)

Contents and Suggested Use

BREAKFAST	Tea *	3 tins (2 tall, 1 flat—Tea, Sugar & Milk Mixture)
	†Sausage (1 hr.)	2 tins
	Biscuit *	1 tin
	Margarine *	1 tin

(* Items marked thus are also to provide for other meals)

DINNER	†Steak & Kidney Pudding (½ hr.)	11 tins
	†Vegetables (¾ hr.)	4 tins (2 large, 2 small)
	Tinned Fruits	2 tins
TEA	Tea	— (* see above)
	Biscuit	— (* see above)
	Margarine	— (* see above)
	Jam	1 tin
SUPPER	†Baked Beans (¾ hr.)	3 tins
	Biscuit	— (* see above)
EXTRAS	Cigarettes	2 tins (1 round, 1 flat—7 cigarettes per man)
	Sweets	1 tin
	Salt	— } packed with sweets above
	Matches	— } packed with sweets above
	Chocolate	— (1 slab per man—packed with biscuit)
	Latrine Paper	

DIRECTIONS

Tea, Sugar and Milk Powder.—Use a dry spoon and sprinkle powder on heated water and bring to the boil, stirring well. 3 heaped teaspoonfuls to 1 pint of water.

† May be eaten hot or cold. To heat, place unopened tins in boiling water for minimum period as indicated. Sausage may be fried (using margarine) if preferred.

Wt. /G.2618 1,568M in 7 Sorts 6/42 KJL/652 Gp. 698/3
Wt. 41076/5747 200,625/5 Sorts 12/42 KJL/3222 Gp. 698/3 J.6393

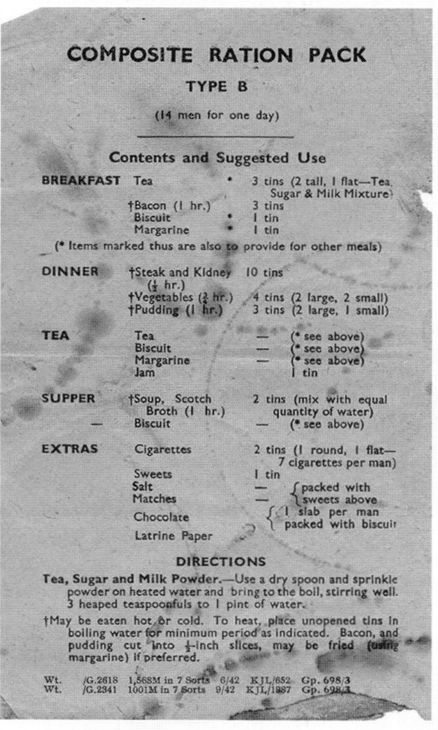

COMPOSITE RATION PACK

TYPE B

(14 men for one day)

Contents and Suggested Use

BREAKFAST	Tea *	3 tins (2 tall, 1 flat—Tea, Sugar & Milk Mixture)
	†Bacon (1 hr.)	3 tins
	Biscuit *	1 tin
	Margarine *	1 tin

(* Items marked thus are also to provide for other meals)

DINNER	†Steak and Kidney (½ hr.)	10 tins
	†Vegetables (¾ hr.)	4 tins (2 large, 2 small)
	†Pudding (1 hr.)	3 tins (2 large, 1 small)
TEA	Tea	— (* see above)
	Biscuit	— (* see above)
	Margarine	— (* see above)
	Jam	1 tin
SUPPER	†Soup, Scotch Broth (1 hr.)	2 tins (mix with equal quantity of water)
—	Biscuit	— (* see above)
EXTRAS	Cigarettes	2 tins (1 round, 1 flat—7 cigarettes per man)
	Sweets	1 tin
	Salt	— } packed with sweets above
	Matches	— } packed with sweets above
	Chocolate	{ 1 slab per man packed with biscuit
	Latrine Paper	

DIRECTIONS

Tea, Sugar and Milk Powder.—Use a dry spoon and sprinkle powder on heated water and bring to the boil, stirring well. 3 heaped teaspoonfuls to 1 pint of water.

†May be eaten hot or cold. To heat, place unopened tins in boiling water for minimum period as indicated. Bacon, and pudding cut into ½-inch slices, may be fried (using margarine) if preferred.

Wt. /G.2618 1,568M in 7 Sorts 6/42 KJL/652 Gp. 698/3
Wt. /G.2341 1001M in 7 Sorts 9/42 KJL/1887 Gp. 698/3

The compo menu.

Various menus were available, and the one including steak and kidney pudding was much prized. Less so was that other staple of army rations, 'Preserved Meat', which was known to one and all as 'bully beef'. A brisk trade, particularly of the less popular compo tins such as haricot bean stew and sardines, was maintained with civilians in Normandy for milk, bread, eggs, butter and of course cider and the

A fourteen-man compo ration box.

fiery calvados apple brandy. Rations were often supplemented with livestock taken from abandoned farms. One Normandy veteran wrote as follows:

> Living on 'compo' rations is all very well for a little while, but biscuits, soup and tinned food are not much to keep a healthy young man of nineteen going. Many of us were often hungry, so the addition of some fresh horsemeat and spring onions cooked in freshly made Norman farmhouse butter was something that tasted out of this world! Cooked in a billy-can all mixed up together, it did not look all that appetizing, but to us it was a feast, washed down with strong army tea all out of the same can. Nectar, sheer nectar, never had anything like it since.[11]

Chapter Twelve

Pursuit to the Seine

With the Germans having at Hitler's insistence so stoutly resisted the attacks of Montgomery's armies, when they finally gave way it was clear that the end of the battle of Normandy was approaching. The distance being covered by the Americans, now organized as 12th US Army Group, was significant against negligible opposition. General Hodge's First US Army having broken out was swinging east with a prospect of enveloping the Germans emerging, while Patton's US Third Army drove south to the Loire and west into Brittany. In 21st Army Group General Dempsey's Second Army was fighting its way east and south-east towards Falaise, which was captured by the Canadian First Army before turning to drive the enemy to the south-east.

After the mid-August battles the squadrons of 141 RAC were all out of the line. A Squadron, after its mauling during TRACTABLE, was in rest camps while their Crocodiles were being rebuilt and B Squadron had been withdrawn into army reserve. Trooper Cox had been released from hospital and completed his recuperation in a camp run by the Canadians where he was well looked after:

> Apart from a couple of days earlier on we had not been out of the line since landing. The camp albeit a makeshift one had been set up and run by the Canadians. We were their guests, and they did everything they could for us. The rest of the squadron had been there four days and it had been a tonic. The camp was right on the beach at Lion-sur-Mer which had long since been cleared of mines and the debris of war. There were several landing ships that had been sunk, they would take longer to clear and were in no one's way. By now it was safe to swim in the sea and quite a few were taking advantage of the opportunity, but the water was not too clean with oil and other flotsam. My wounds had just about healed, and I didn't fancy infection, so I spent the afternoon sunning my snow-white body. It felt so relaxing; the war went on but to us it belonged to someone else, but at the back of my mind and I take it everyone else's, we knew we would soon have to start again where we left off. The Canadians fed us well and couldn't do enough for us; anything you want just ask.[1]

Towards the end of the month Cox and the rest of the squadron's soldiers were collected by transport 'that had been begged borrowed and stolen to re-form the [logistic] transport section' and were taken to Marcelet. Having collected their Crocodiles, A Squadron was reassembled in the same field near St. Manvieux with the six unexploded bombs still in place. Other things, however, had changed.

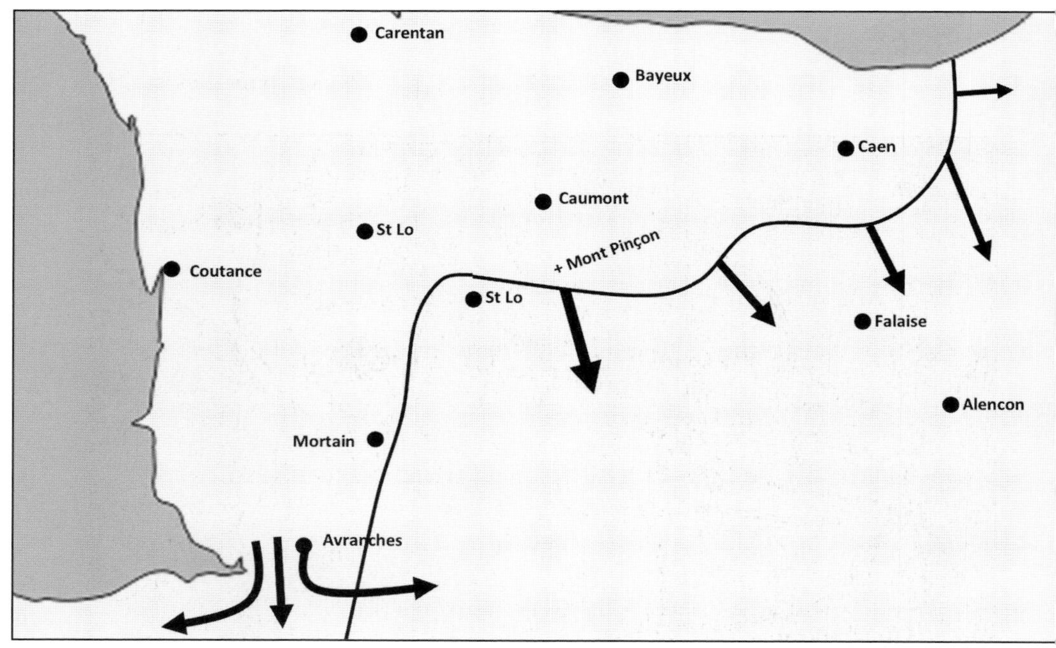

The breakout in early August and the general lines of advance.

While they had been away, 'The dead cattle had been buried or at least an attempt had been made, big pits had been dug and the carcasses pushed in and covered up leaving the odd leg sticking out here and there. Most of the smell had gone too, thankfully.'

Cox noted that 'Some Crocodiles had been repaired mainly by cannibalising, by taking parts from other tanks to make one good one. Our own tank would take longer to repair, so we had a new one and had to find a signwriter to put our name "Stallion" back on our new mount.' There were also a replacement personnel for 3 Troop:

> We had a new Troop Officer, several new faces in the troop; one had to feel for the new chaps. We knew what to expect, how to exist, how to survive, we'd had to learn all these things. I don't know why it would be any different for them; perhaps we had started as innocents, came in for the first act, they had seen it but had not yet performed. The Troop Officer seemed alright and made himself known amongst us; we didn't anticipate he would require a lot of 'moulding'.

All the troops of A Squadron had new crewmen brought up through the replacement system and needed bringing into the team, but in doing so, the Buffs' character of the regiment was changed:

> Now we had new accents to deal with; most of us came from London or the South-East, cockney being the main language with all its slang. We did have one 'Taffy' but he too was born and bred in London, but with the name of Jenkins it was as natural as 'Chalky' White or 'Dusty' Miller. Now we had Geordies, Scouses, Jocks, Mancunians, they came from everywhere, 'bloody

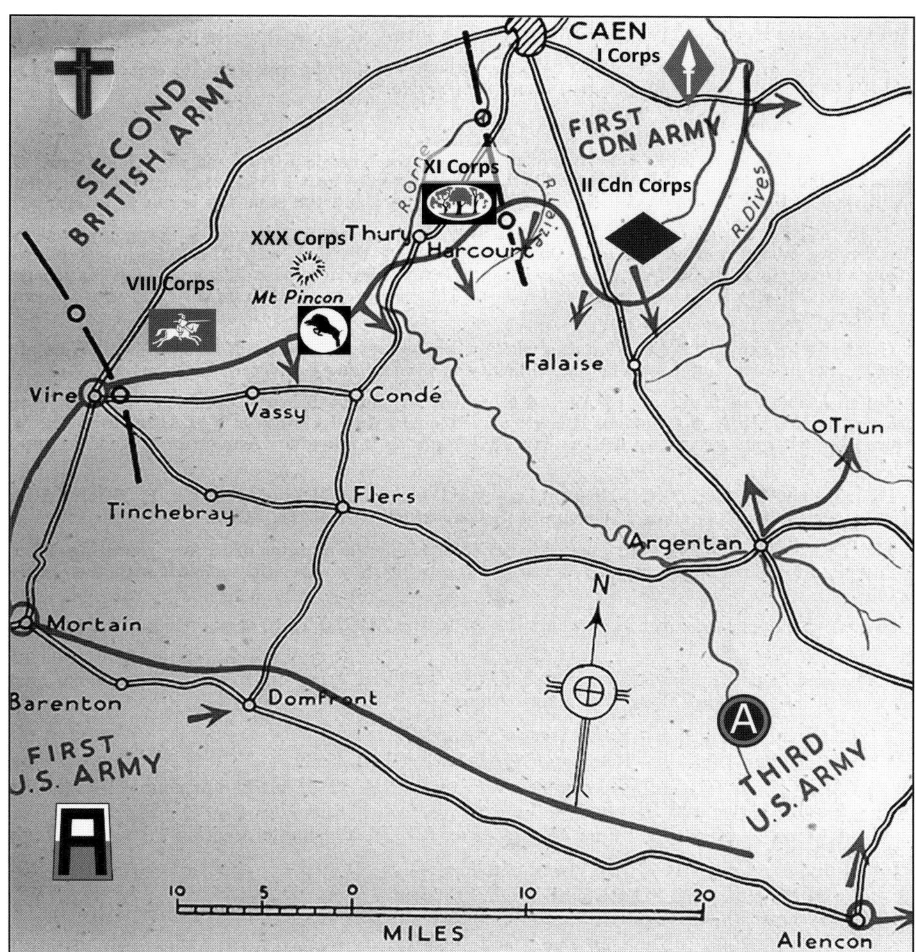

The forming of the Falaise pocket.

foreigners'. They got their legs pulled, it was good to find out about each other and make the new lads feel they were welcome. We didn't talk about what had happened during the previous weeks; that came under shooting a line these chaps would know soon enough. We looked into these new faces, yet saw the faces of the people they replaced; for a teetotal party it was a great success, time to turn in.

C Squadron

Meanwhile, only C Squadron was immediately ready for operations, and in the days following their action at Estry they moved east to join XII Corps on 10 August. They were to work with 59th Division and were under command of

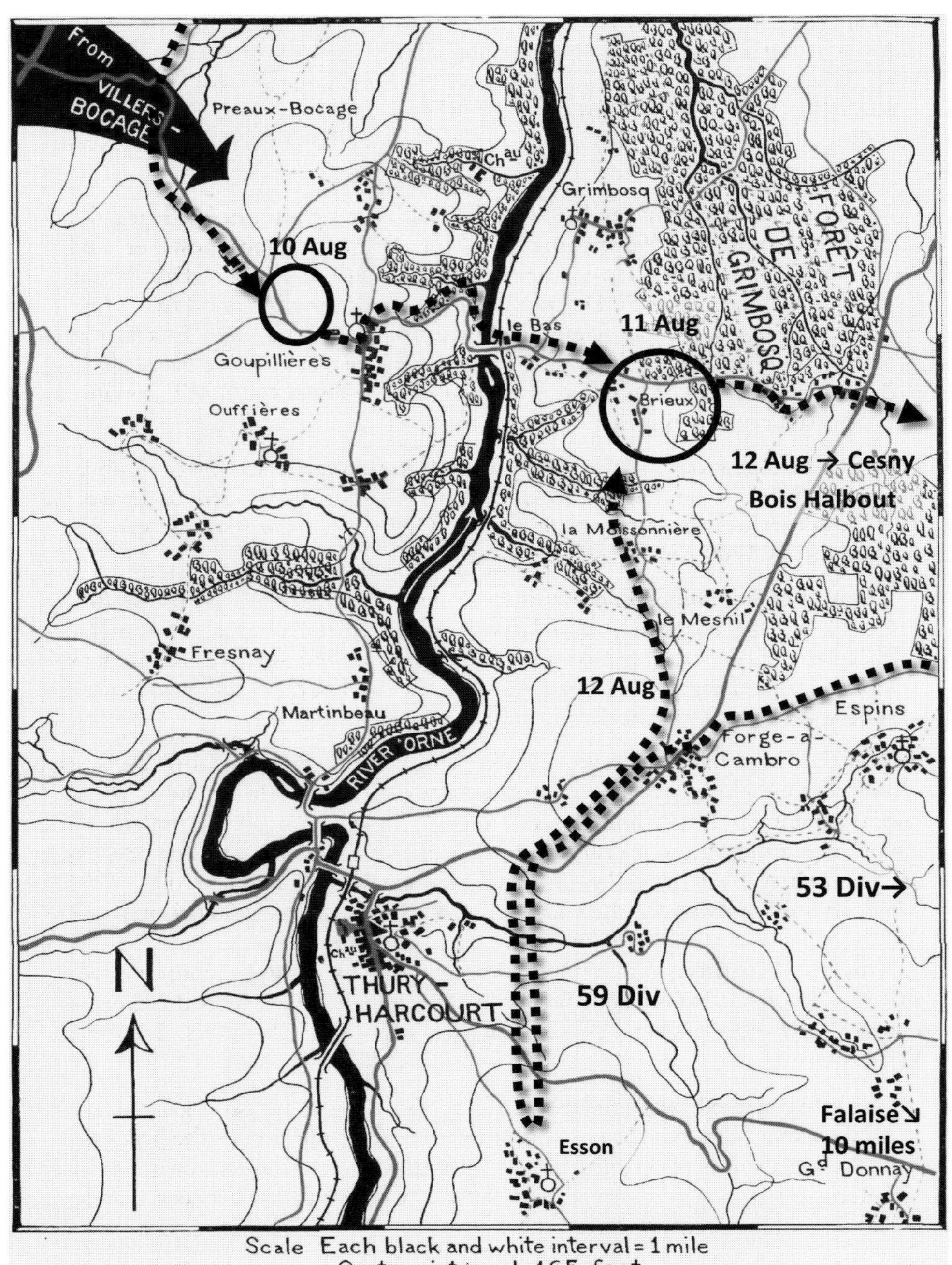

The peregrinations of C Squadron, 10–12 August 1944.

34 Tank Brigade. Their task was to cross into the newly-won Orne bridgehead and push south of the Forêt de Grimbosq. The war diary recorded that 'For C Sqn life was certainly becoming a war of movement' and that on 11 August they crossed the river at 1000 hours and harboured at Brieux. The following day, attached to 153 Regiment RAC, the squadron 'strolled on behind 2 E Lancs to sp them if necessary':

> Major Duffy offered his services when, whilst listening into the battle [on the radio], he heard the Wasps being called for. At that moment, however, OC 153 RAC ordered the Sqn to move to Esson and report to 53 Div. Major Duffy duly reported to 53 Div where he was sent to 56 Bde of 50 Div. Here the BM [Brigade Major] strongly advised him not to move to Esson as it happened to be strongly held by the enemy and that they had in fact wanted the Crocodiles earlier in the afternoon at THURY HARCOURT. Finally, C Sqn returned to Brieux.[2]

Over the next few days Major Duffy drove from one O Group to another as I Corps advanced on Falaise. On the 15th he was summoned to orders at 1530 hours and was promptly told that 'the Crocodiles were required two miles further east at 1700 hrs' for an attack on Leffard:

> It was of course impossible. Another 15 mins was squeezed out of the Bde Comd and the corps arty would give another 10 mins grace. The inf bn doing the show was the 2 Mons ... and the bn with which the unit had looked forward eagerly to since the days of Eastwell Park ... Everything possible was done to get the Crocs there on time.

To get the Crocodiles into action, Lieutenant Colonel Brown of 147 RAC personally went back to get the trailers pressuring up, while Major Duffy went on with the planning. It was, however, not to be. C Squadron arrived in time to act as a reserve, but the Monmouthshires took the objective in their stride unaided, and so it continued over the following days. Captain Bailey remarked that 'Things were certainly cracking for the Germans in the Falaise pocket and prisoners were rolling in.'

Now the squadron, still under command of XII Corps, alongside other British, Canadian, Polish and American troops were enveloping the Germans in a 15-mile-long pocket between Falaise, Trun and Chambois. Lieutenant Wilson wrote:

> Until they arrived there, nobody had any idea what the Falaise gap meant. All they knew was that the remains of thirty or forty divisions – the best part of the German army in the West – were suddenly being encircled by the American advance in their rear. The only way of escape lay between Falaise and Argentan, twenty miles to the south.[3]

The Germans, however, were fighting desperate delaying actions as they struggled to escape encirclement. Wilson described C Squadron's last action helping to

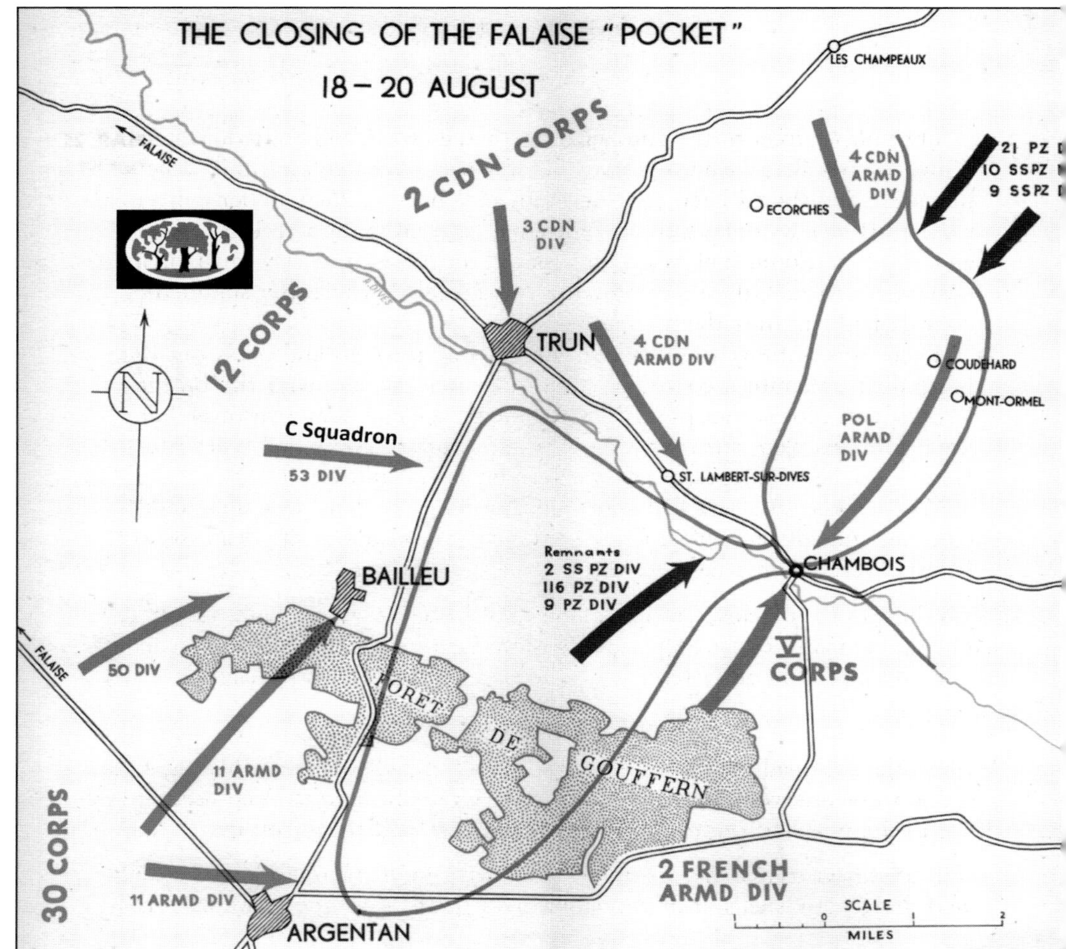

Closing the Falaise pocket.

compress the pocket, advancing with 53rd Division south of Falaise in the direction of Nécy, cutting the Argentan road in the process:

> Next day at first light the squadron moved on. The battalion they were supporting was pursuing a panic-stricken mass of infantry and transport, whom the enemy command had abandoned.
>
> About midday there was a momentary check. The battalion came under a storm of mortar fire at a village in a close little valley between wooded hills. No one could get through. A Bren-gun carrier with a load of ammunition had been hit, and the squadron waited in an orchard, listening to the explosions of the burning ammunition.
>
> Then they were called forward. The village was strewn with wreckage. The driver of the carrier was slumped over the steering-wheel like a charred sack. Wilson tried to avert his eyes, but next moment his attention was caught by a scene of almost unbelievable horror.

> The village street turned into a narrow sunken road, and the road was full of dead – not British, but Germans. It was part of the column they'd been pursuing, and they'd been caught, jammed tight, in a 25-pounder concentration. Men and horses were mangled and crushed in the wreckage of guns and vehicles. Some had been pressed like transfers into the earth banks beside the road. Others lay bloodily spreadeagled where the stampeding column had run over them.
>
> There was nothing to do but to force a way through and press on. But beyond, the shambles continued. The road was blocked with the burning wreckage of motor transport. Some of the trucks had been overturned and their contents were strewn by the wayside – office stores and typewriters, crates of wine, bandages, rations, eiderdowns and suitcases.
>
> Many of the suitcases had split open, spilling out pink women's underclothing and silk stockings. They lay on the grass among the dead, slowly being covered with a layer of ash.

With the gap finally closed at Chambois on 18 August and a break-out attempt led by the remnants of the SS panzer divisions largely contained, B Squadron was halted and placed in army reserve on the edges of the Falaise pocket.

A Squadron

Meanwhile, A Squadron was on the move again, avoiding roads which as far as possible were reserved for wheeled vehicles. They also had to keep their speed down as the new and refurbished Crocodiles were still being run in:

> Travelling on tracks was a slow business with frequent unexplained stops. Bert and I took spells at driving about two hours at a time as we motored

Destruction in the Falaise pocket.

> towards Falaise. I sat on top of the turret, as we passed through the town, not a house standing, the place an absolute shambles. All those weeks, all those dead, for what? A pile of ruins, in just a few short minutes we were through it. As we progressed so the signs of war began to diminish; the Germans had passed through in a hurry not to get trapped this side of the Seine where it was thought they would make a stand.
>
> Our little column progressed steadily towards the river; at this stage we had no idea what our task would be. The main front was miles away and racing forward; at our rate of progress we would never catch them up. Our tanks were going well and mechanical problems few.
>
> We had been on the road now for two days, and we began to see more French people who came out to wave. In towns and villages French families in crowd proportions lined the sides of the road. Ray was a great mimic; he sat on the turret giving a royal wave to the left and right.[4]

Even once clear of the detritus of war there were sights that the Crocodile crews did not like at all or understand:

> One thing that did not impress us was these so-called resistance people. Once a town was liberated, they would creep out of the woodwork, pick up a

New or refurbished tanks and trailers had to be run in at gentle speeds and tracks etc. were adjusted at every halt.

> discarded German rifle and put on a red, white and blue armband. Their next act of bravery would be to shave off the hair of women who had gone out with German soldiers. They would parade these women for our benefit as we passed. It seemed petty and achieved little. We showed our disapproval with reverse victory signs.

After several more days of motoring, A Squadron reached the Seine and harboured in an orchard on the outskirts of a village short of the river, where the routine of engine maintenance and 'track bashing' kept the crews busy: 'As the infantry divisions made their assault crossings, rumours about the future of the war and our next task were passed from tank to tank.'

B Squadron

B Squadron was the last element of the regiment to be on the move east and was still at seven days' notice to move in a field between Caen and the coast. On 20 August they were called forward by I Corps:

> At 0230 hrs on that same night an LO made a most unwelcome appearance with orders for the Squadron to move at first light to the area Les Authieux-Papion 4080 (Sheet 7/F4), whilst the squadron commander with an LO were to report forthwith to HQ 7 Armoured Division under whose command they now came.[5]

Captain Bailey commented rather acidly that 'seven-day notice or any other notice falls among those many chimera designed solely to feed the ever hungry bumf-machine, an exquisite device fashioned that there may not exist widespread unemployment in the Staff':

> Major Ryle and Captain Moss accordingly set off and by good fortune alone hit on the correct location of 7 Armoured Division after a very ambiguous map reference which could have referred equally to two places fifty miles apart. A wet and miserable column of tanks set out under an even more wet, grim and miserable Storrar. Not before Lieut Sander had armed himself, however, for the journey with an empty 75mm shell case for he was suffering more than somewhat from diarrhoea.[6]

Amid the logistic traffic heading south-east, Captain Storrar led the Crocodiles, gun tanks and the squadron's echelon towards St.-Pierre-sur-Dives through persistent rain:

> Beyond St. Pierre the column was stopped by a very irate DAQMG of the Highland Division who informed George that he knew nothing of the Crocs, wanted nothing of the Crocs and would the Crocs damn well get off his axis or else. Well George [Storrar] is a Scotsman too and in best Gaelic English retorted it would be a pleasure, or something to that effect, and pulled into an orchard at 296510 NE of St.-Pierre-sur-Dives. Nigel burst into this serene atmosphere from 7 Armoured Division with the news that

One of B Squadron's Crocodiles on the march during the Normandy campaign.

> the Squadron's move was a mistake anyway. True, they had a vague recollection of a passing mention some few days ago that the Crocs would have been useful on a certain strongpoint, but that was all over and done with long ago. Sorry and all that. George's language is a little strong at times.

After another two days of waiting, B Squadron was on the move again in the rain:

> 7th Armoured Division were making a concerted drive east through Lisieux and 'B' Squadron were kept in reserve to deal with stubborn pockets that might crop up, moving on the 23rd to 442786 and thence to 506680 (7/F4) just SW of Lisieux. But the advance along the whole front was now proceeding at a pace which made it impossible for the Crocs to keep up and be put into operation against any strongpoint before it was quickly reduced by normal arms alone.
>
> Eastwards and ever east. Past the roadside havoc that had been a German Army. The dead horses by the road, the long lines packed tight with overturned and burnt-out trucks, guns and tanks, the river valleys chock full of the German impedimenta of war.

Passing beyond the Falaise pocket towards the Seine, the detritus of war reduced, and even though warned to assist an assault crossing of the River Risle under command of 33 Armoured Brigade, there was to be no action. On 29 August the squadron finally halted just north of Bourg-Achard from where they expected to be shortly crossing the Seine, but again they found themselves waiting, this time in an 'equestrian and pastoral world of prosperity' complete with their own milking cow.

While waiting to cross the Seine, the Crocodiles of 141 RAC laid on a flame demonstration.

Spoils of War

At the end of the month B Squadron was still waiting to cross the Seine and spent time rummaging through the vast amount of equipment and vehicles abandoned by the Germans on the approaches to the river: 'Here the Squadron liberally endowed itself with high-powered German motor cars and other things conducive not only to a pleasant life but operational efficiency as well, which later higher authority saw fit to take away.'

C Squadron had been halted on the outskirts of the Falaise pocket where, amid the grim destruction of the German Army, they had richer pickings. Lieutenant Wilson recalled:

> At first they came back with the usual German helmets, which would be hung around the tank for a few days and then thrown away. Then word went round that there was better stuff to be had. The rugger coach came in with a battered Opel two-seater, and someone else with an amphibious Volkswagen. Sherrif's crew arrived, riding on a half-track. It became a kind of competitive treasure hunt. MacFarland, who was in charge of squadron transport now, came in with a big bus, painted in yellow Wehrmacht camouflage and full of *Panzerfausts*.
>
> 'What the hell do you think you're going to do with that lot?' said Duffy, regarding them like children on a Sunday-school treat.
>
> 'Take them along with us,' said Sherrif.
>
> 'Oh no, you won't – not if the regiment knows anything about it.'

An Opel Blitz bus. These vehicles and others were often found in divisional and corps headquarters as mobile offices or staff transport.

After some negotiation, a resolution: 'All right,' said Duffy resignedly, 'but nothing else. Not another frigging thing.' Just then there was a heavy rumbling. Something quite enormous was pushing its way through the trees. Sergeant Pye and his fitters appeared, roaring with triumph, sitting on a Panther. Sadly for the squadron, it proved to be impossible to keep these enhancements to the transport section away from the eyes of authority, with even the best concealed vehicles being taken away from them by the military police while they waited to cross the Seine bridges.

Chapter Thirteen

With US VIII Corps at Brest

With the Allies having broken out from the confines of the Normandy beachhead, the campaign was entering a new phase with a different character. The slow-moving Crocodiles had already experienced the war of movement during the dash to the Seine, but for all three squadrons their next battle would be against the enemy in fixed port defences.

The Allied armies needed ports to handle the vast tonnages of supplies that were perforce coming ashore across the beaches and via the surviving Mulberry Harbour. To compound the logistic problem with the headlong advance to the River Seine, the distances covered by transport in loops from the Rear Maintenance Area to the forward troops and back were getting longer and longer. In addition, supplies were becoming increasingly thinly spread as the armies expanded to some thirty-seven divisions and it was calculated that during September they would require 26,000 tons of supplies a day. Against this logistic background, the only significant port captured by the Allies had been Cherbourg, but it was so badly damaged that a month later it was still barely making a useful contribution.

Unable to throw the Allies back into the sea, the German high command resorted to limiting the scope of their operations by making the logistics equation of distance and consumption impossible to reconcile. The Germans calculated that if they denied the Channel and Atlantic ports to the Allies, they could rely on the deteriorating autumn weather to choke off the supplies to Normandy that were necessary to keep their armies moving. This, they argued, would at the very least buy time for the Reich's V-weapon programme to bear fruit. Consequently, Hitler declared that all major ports were to be 'fortresses' that were to be defended to the last.

In Brittany the fortress ports were Saint-Malo, Lorient, Saint-Nazaire and Brest. The Allied planners' intent had been that after the first phase of the campaign these ports, as had been the case during the First World War, would be the US theatre entry points for manpower and logistics direct from the USA. Together it was intended that these ports would handle US logistics and further formations that would bring the US Army up to its planned strength. To capture Brest, the most significant of these ports, 6th US Armoured Division was tasked by General Patton to dash into Brittany. Virtually unopposed, it reached the environs of the port on 8 August but was halted by its defences. Saint-Malo fell on 17 August, but its relatively low-capacity port facilities were again badly damaged. Meanwhile, Brest was invested and in a battle for the port that lasted

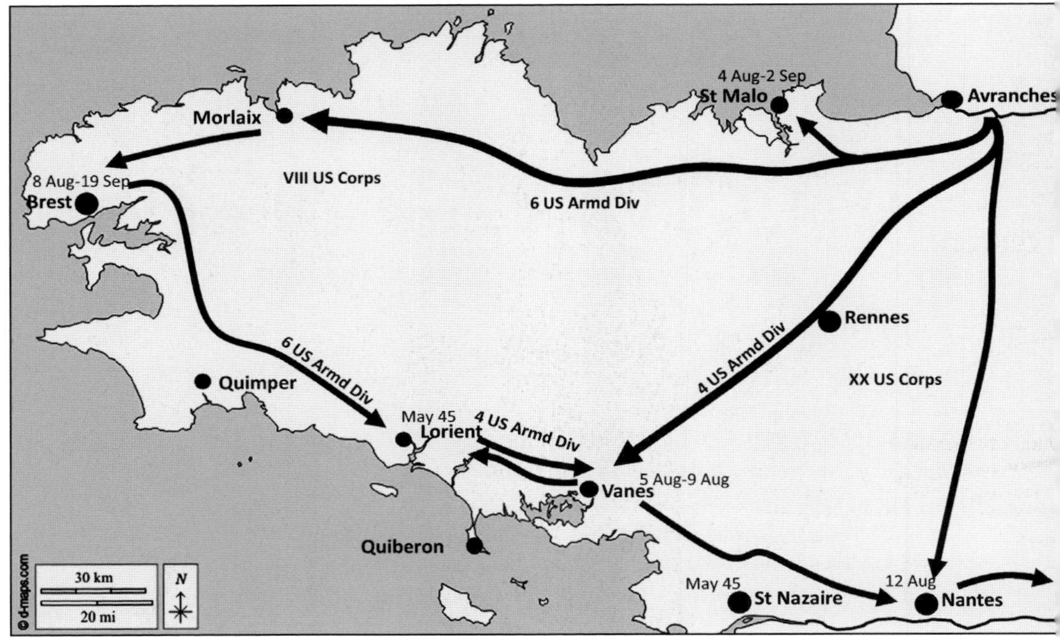

The fortress ports and the US Third Army's advance into Brittany.

more than a month, General Middleton's VIII US Corps, numbering 75,000 men, employed three full infantry divisions and 5th US Rangers to take the city and the badly-damaged docks.

Under the veteran *Fallschirmjäger* commander General Ramcke, the German garrison of Brest numbering almost 40,000 men was well prepared. The outer defences 3 miles from the port were a shield of conventional field defences, consisting of mutually supporting bunkers and entrenchments. The inner defences used the nineteenth-century inland port ramparts as its basis, with additional casemates, pillboxes and trenches, all of which were enhanced by extensive minefields. Weapon systems ranging from numerous machine guns through flak guns to coastal artillery and dismounted naval guns were well protected in concrete bunkers and field positions.

The hard core of the fighting troops that put up a remarkably stout defence were highly-motivated *Fallschirmjäger* and Marine *Stosstrupp* ('shock troop') companies of naval infantry. In addition, there were largely ad hoc *Kriegsmarine* units consisting of redundant U-boat, ships' crews and dockyard personnel. Finally, there were the soldiers of a disbanded Luftwaffe Field Division.

During the first two weeks of the battle the US forces assembled, isolated Brest and mounted probing attacks, while the Germans continued to work on their defences. Facing strong enemy resistance, General Middleton prepared to assault with the 2nd, 8th and 29th Infantry divisions, and after some preliminary attacks, artillery bombardment and air strikes, he launched his assault on 26 August. The Americans were, however, repulsed and suffered heavy casualties.

Middleton changed tactics from all-out assaults on the enemy positions to smaller but bloody bite-and-hold attacks, taking one strongpoint at a time, which

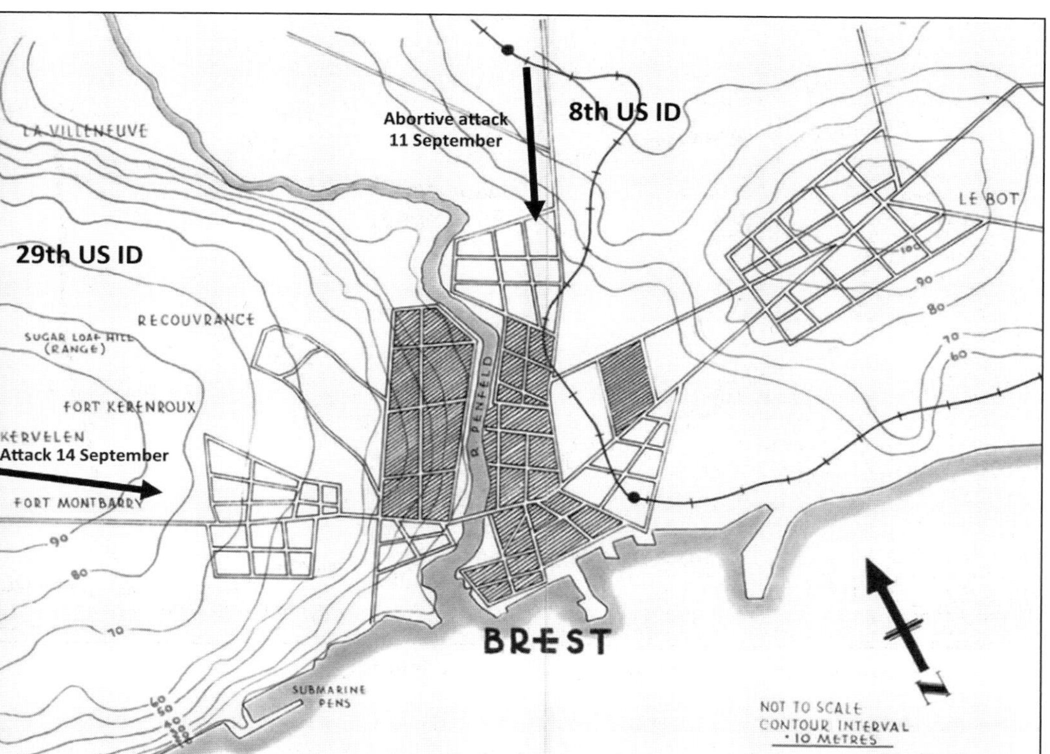

The Battle for Brest, 7 August-20 September 1944.

then had to be held against German counter-attack. Fighting through the outer defences was a slow process with a mounting list of casualties. Against this background, the Americans requested the help of British assault armour.

At the beginning of September, the men of B Squadron were still enjoying their 'bucolic existence' on the banks of the river Seine, complete with horses and a cow,

> when out of the blue came the thunderbolt that B Squadron had been detailed by some mysterious power to join the Americans in front of Brest, and moreover would proceed forthwith. The Colonel knew nothing about it and the Brigadier very little else … That evening the transporters roared into life and B Squadron was off, taking in tow [a platoon of an] RASC Company and a Medical Section of 31 Tank Brigade Light Field Ambulance.

During 7 September the first five Crocodiles completed the 300-mile journey and arrived in the assembly area east of Brest. By late afternoon of the following day the last of the stragglers had arrived 'and the Squadron was hard down to it preparing for action.' Initially they were under command of 1st Battalion, 13 US Infantry Regiment for operations in the Lambézellec area where pressure from the GIs had driven back the Germans from the outer defences towards the main fortifications. Major Ryle had been recceing 'the best possible country over which to employ the Crocs and it wasn't too promising. Here was bocage at its

Tank Transporters and Movement of Crocodile Flame Fuel Trailers

In the early part of the campaign, before the arrival of tank transporter units in July, the Crocodiles did some fairly long and mechanically wearing marches on their tracks. Now, with 21st Army Group fully deployed, tank transporter units were available to help move the Crocodiles to where they were required. Trooper Cox describes the process of loading the squadron onto transporters for a road move:

> The tanks were no sooner ready when tank transporters arrived to pick us up to be taken who knows where ... It was our first experience of transporters. The tractors were heavy Diamond 'T' trucks of American origin and the trailers were built in Canada, which together made a heavy multi-wheeled affair. Our [flame fuel] trailers had to be detached and towed by trucks. The transporters moved up the road each followed by a tank until the whole squadron was lined up. The ramps were lowered, and the tank was directly behind, and in low gear began to climb the ramp, climbing forever skyward. The driver could see nothing until the point of balance was reached, at which stage the tank would come crashing down, hopefully square on the trailer. Once the tank was shackled on the transporter the convoy closed up ready to move off. Some of the crews rode in the tanks or in a small cabin on the back of the tractor; this cabin sat on top of a steel box about eight feet square and three deep which was full of iron weights to give the driving wheels more traction. No one seemed to know our destination.[1]

From early in the campaign, it had become normal procedure for the flame fuel trailers to be towed separately from squadron bases to assembly areas. Without

An M19 Diamond T of 21st Army Group's Tank Transporter Company RASC (862) with a Churchill tank on its Canadian-built trailer. Interestingly, even though the company was an army group asset, the vehicle has the green patch of 31 Tank Brigade with the white diagonal line and the number 862.

brakes or suspension other than the balloon tyres, a road move of the 6.4-ton armoured trailer of any distance was bad practice mechanically. Towing behind the Churchill caused wear to the tank's transmission and wear on the all-important elbow joint, resulting in breakdowns of the tank or failure of the Crocodile system. To ensure that the maximum numbers of Crocodiles were fit for action at the beginning of the operation, it became usual practice to tow the flame fuel trailers behind trucks. For shorter moves this was often 141's own trucks, but they were relatively low-powered vehicles so this was a challenge. Consequently, borrowing Royal Artillery AEC Matador 4x4 prime movers to help the squadron deploy from the rear to operational assembly areas became normal procedure. These were most probably vehicles issued to anti-aircraft batteries to tow the 3.7in gun, which with a reasonably static role, were the most readily available towing vehicle man enough for the job. For longer moves tank transporters were used, with three flame fuel trailers per vehicle being a typical load.

An AEC Matador truck in its normal role towing a 3.7in anti-aircraft gun through the ruins of Caen.

very worst – minute fields bounded by banks 8–10 feet high and the same width.' Not only that, but

> Here the defences were well-nigh impregnable, situated as they were behind a colossal minefield, a moat 40 feet wide and 20 feet deep, then a wall some 60 feet high banked on the German side with earth to a distance of 80–100 feet. The whole area in front covered by guns and mortars of every type and calibre – 15cm bows, hordes of 88s, 40mms, 20mms and dozens of just plain ordinary MGs. In one of the recces you could see Jerry setting up yet another 88.[2]

Attacks on Brest were supported by air strikes that reduced much of the city to rubble.

By 11 September the VIII US Corps had fought its way a mile into the defences, but during the Battle for Brest there was a perennial supply problem. While Middleton's corps had the heaviest US Army artillery available, being out on a limb they lacked what was normally considered sufficient ammunition for the task:

> Such artillery as there was on this occasion was designed to breach the wall by direct fire from the 240mms covered by smoke and HE from the 155s. An all-out assault by the Crocs would then flame the gun positions and pillboxes on and in front of the wall, whereupon the infantry would be launched through a corridor of flame into the breach to a *sauve qui peut* ['run for your life!'].
>
> At the appointed hour the Crocs rolled to a standstill and switched off behind a small hill some 300 yards short of the fort, then watched from ringside seats the extraordinary spectacle of a great 240mm in full view pounding away at the fort from a mere 100 yards ... All day long it pounded away, the crews taking one hell of a packet. But did it make the slightest dent? Did it hell!
>
> After two days the whole show was declared off in favour of an entirely new approach on Brest. On the 12th of September the Crocs pulled out and ... joined up with the 29th US Infantry Div who were attacking Recouvrance

(the western and most important half of Brest, holding as it did the giant submarine pens) from the west. Fort Montbarey, key to the defences, barred the way.

29th US Infantry Division: Fort Montbarey

> 29 Div was for 'B' Squadron a superb impression of the American Army; the 'Let's Go' boys were the sort of guys with whom you were proud to scrap.
> [Harry Bailey, *The Playboys*]

Major Ryle and a battalion commander of 116 US Infantry Regiment were soon taking part in some hair-raising recces of the approaches to the German fortifications:

> Every recce brought down heavy fire from mortars and 40mms firing direct, but time after time the Croc recce groups got away with it.
>
> Right away Nigel and 29 Div got down to the technical and tactical problems of the Crocodiles in this bocage stuff. On the technical side there resulted the astonishing feat of designing, making and fitting a Rhinoceros-type hedge-cutter to every tank within three days.

It was clear from the recces that getting the Crocodiles within flaming range of objectives was a considerable problem, 'the outer defences of the dominating fort being extremely strong.' Firstly, there was a deep minefield of very large naval

A US 240mm gun in a direct-fire engagement during the Battle for Brest.

A pair of Crocodiles fitted with the culin or 'Rhino' hedgerow-cutter. The design and build of the hedgerow-cutter was adapted for the Churchill. Captain Harry Bailey noted 'drive, enthusiasm and the superiority of services which manpower helped to give them. Not one welder but two whole teams working 24 hours long by shifts.'

shells in front of the defences extending north-east to Fort Keranroux and beyond. 'Against these, even had there been any, flails would have been blown sky-high.' The only way through was for the American engineers to breach the minefield manually, relying on suppressive fire to protect them. After the minefield the attackers would have to negotiate a wide anti-tank ditch and there were no AVREs to lay fascines or bridges across it. Then there were three lines of defence, heavily defended by machine guns and 40mm and 20mm anti-aircraft guns in the ground role, many protected in concrete bunkers:

> The whole of this area was so cratered to hell as to be almost impassable by ordinary tanks, never mind Crocs. Finally, the kernel of the position, the fort itself, hedged in by sunken roads, surrounded by a moat forty feet wide and twenty feet deep and walls so loopholed that the garrison could fire into the moat from either side.

While the recces were under way the Crocodile crews were training in the use of flame alongside the American infantry of the 1st Battalion 116 Infantry.

An attack by the 115 Infantry Regiment to close in on Montbarey had begun at midnight on 11/12 September, but they were unable to get near the fort due to heavy German fire, and approximately 200 defenders remained in the fort during the following days. Now it was the turn of Major Tom Dallas' 1st Battalion 116 Infantry and the Crocodiles.

> On the night of the 13th September, masked by artillery fire, the Crocs were crawling up to the Start Line at a mere 2mph ready to go in next day. First light found the four HQ tanks and a platoon of M10s, guns blazing away all out, covering an assault company of infantry as they secured a footing on the anti-tank ditch. In the wake of the infantry with superb courage the engineers were clearing a path through the minefield and carrying forward prepared charges for the ditch. Casualties were high but they carried on. By midday this phase was complete. The assault infantry had penetrated to within about 200 yards of the fort but were now completely stopped and

> pinned down. The time had come to put . . . 8 Troop to wipe out the outer defence north and north-east of the fort.
>
> Captain [Harry] Cobden made a plan with the [1st Battalion's] reserve company but first had to go on foot with Sgt Humphreys as far as the anti-tank ditch to check a possible crossing. He found one spot and one only where it was just feasible that a Croc might go and only just thanks to a fortuitous conjunction of craters that had torn down the walls. Though a heavy toll was taken of the sappers, Humphreys and Harry somehow made it there and back. Very creditable. At 1400 hrs 8 Troop and its attendant gun tanks rolled into action and Tony, ably assisted by the superb driving of Tpr Clare, was already winning his Silver Star.

Three of the squadron's gun tanks led their way up to the gap that had been cleared through the minefield alongside the three M10s. Here they gave covering fire while Lieutenant Ward's 8 Troop picked their way through the craters and into the minefield gap, staying within the limits of the cleared path, firing as they went. One Crocodile, however, set off one of the 300lb shells that had not been cleared by the engineers 'with most fearsome results. There was a colossal explosion, and the whole track wrapped itself over the turret.' The driver was killed outright and the remainder of the crew were badly injured. The knocked-out Crocodile completely blocked the minefield gap and under covering fire of the tanks and M10s the American engineers cleared a new path around the shattered Crocodile, suffering a dozen casualties in the process. Lieutenant Ward of 8 Troop sometime after midday led the way in his Crocodile:

> through the minefield and on to the tricky anti-tank ditch, over it by the skin of his tracks, then a very pretty game of in and out the craters, scything his

Two of B Squadron's Churchill gun tanks in the command role photographed during operations at Brest. They are either up-gunned Mk IVs with the 75mm gun or the Mk VI. The lead tank has lost its left-hand mudguard and has appliqué armour in the form of Sherman tracks to defeat hollow-charge weapons such as the *Panzerfaust*.

An oblique air photograph of Fort Montbarey taken from the attackers' perspective.

> burning track of death through the rich harvest of MGs and light AA/AT guns. Driving and commanding were and had to be superb. The infantry were following up and a steady stream of prisoners now flowed back. Right up to the sunken road on the north side, from where he flamed and shot the infantry into the German positions along the whole length of the wood surrounding the fort. Then over to the left and round the corner, flaming and blasting until the doughboys were in possession of the eastern wooded fringe as well drill working famously, infantry right up behind and cashing in 100 per cent. Tony [Ward] got 'proper mad' at a 50mm firing at him from a pillbox where the sunken road meets the main road and sent a 75mm crashing through the slit into the ammunition inside. The top blew right off and with fragments of the crew sailed way up. Another 50mm firing from the SE never recovered from the same medicine.

While the remainder of 8 Troop stayed between the minefield and the fort and the American infantry attempted to advance, Lieutenant Ward stormed off in his Crocodile on a 900-yard rampage, 'using up all his HE and twenty belts of Besa. Disdainfully giving the KO to a 10.5cm field gun and its crew, he was flinging stuff at everything rash enough to show its head, finally coming to the houses and giving them a look of glaring derision.' Realizing he was out on his own

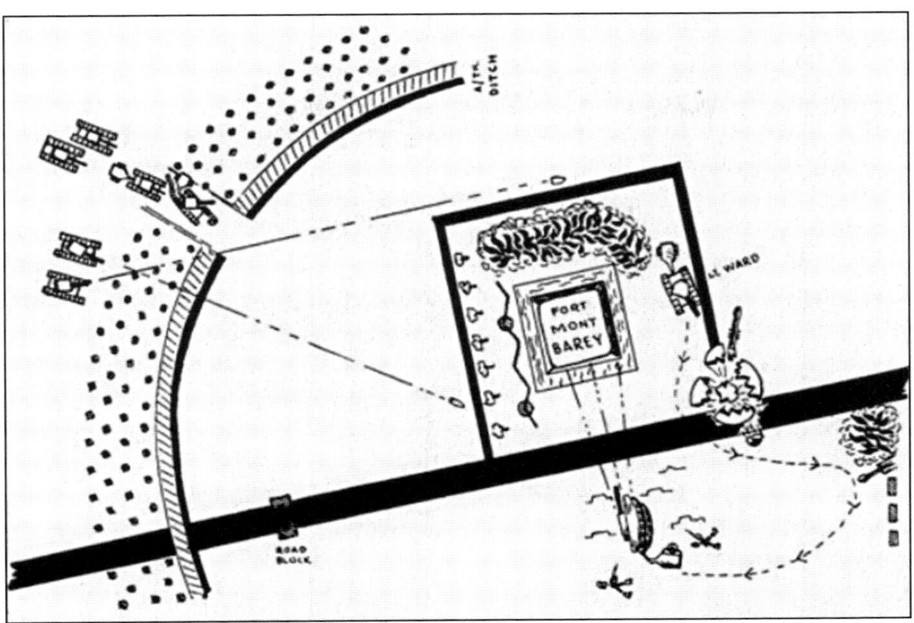

Captain Bailey's sketch map of his squadron's flame action at Fort Montbarey. Note the gun tanks giving covering fire to the Crocodiles in the minefield.

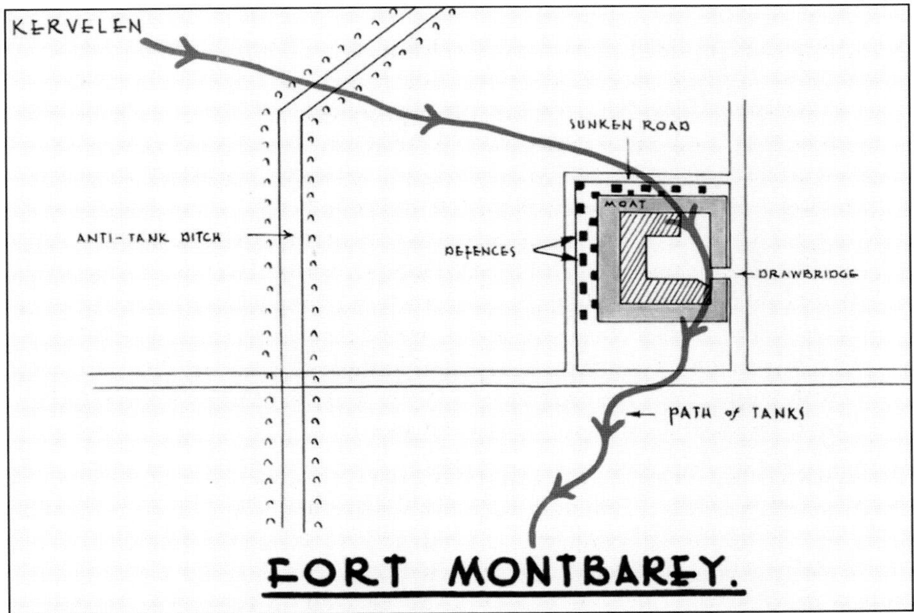

The diagram from the 29th US Division's report showing further details.

approaching the edge of the town, Lieutenant Ward turned to head back to the southern edge of the fort. He was almost back when:

> he was somewhat perturbed when the Croc suddenly heeled over on its side and crashed down into a bunker full of Germans. White flags momentarily appeared and just as rapidly disappeared as they realised the entry was unrehearsed. Tony shut down quickly to have a quiet think. This wasn't helped any by the pair of steel blue eyes which tried to peer at him through the periscope, and a staring match now began.

Calling for help over the radio did not work, 'the Germans, crafty sods, had whipped his aerial.' With the tank filling with petrol fumes and a methyl bromide fire extinguisher having gone off, Lieutenant Ward was forced to open his hatch 'and in best Yorkshire German yells "*Hände hoch*!" ("Hands up!")':

> At which unexpected display of awfully bad behaviour ... the Germans duly '*hoched*' their hands. Before they could recover their *sangfroid*, the rest of the crew were already out and Tony, making a grab at the Bren, was testing it with fearsome abandon. So the Germans lined up, all thirty-nine of them.

Although fired at by the Germans, Lieutenant Ward, his crew and prisoners made it back to the safety of the American infantry who were advancing to meet them. At the same time some of the other Crocodiles that had hitherto so adroitly navigated craters, sunken lanes and moats also ran out of luck: 'Cpl Briggs dropped himself well and truly in the, well in the mire. His Croc capsized into a concealed cesspool, tilted over until the foul stuff was lapping round the turret. At which precise moment Harry Cobden's tank went off its tracks and Lieut Hare went down a crater.'

A total of three Crocodiles and a gun tank had been disabled. Under fire from flanking light anti-aircraft guns, Lieutenant Ward managed to extricate himself from the collaapsed bunker and Captain Cobden's tank was towed back onto its tracks. Meanwhile, Corporal Briggs used a Bren gun to cover his crew out of the tank and keep the Germans away. Eventually Lieutenant Hare's tank went forward to rescue Briggs' Crocodile, 'whilst with sleeves rolled up, they plunged deep into the liquid excrement, "eyes down, look in", and hooked up the tow-rope. And that's how 8 Troop got its present name.'[3] Unfortunately, as they were moving back through the minefield gap, Lieutenant Hare's Crocodile was blown up by one of the naval shell mines and in the massive explosion it was wrecked with its turret being blown off. The driver and flame gunner were killed, but the turret crew, although injured, amazingly survived.

Despite the rampage and penetration of the defences by a Crocodile, the commander of the fort refused to surrender and the battle continued, and majors Dallas and Ryle started planning another attack. With B Squadron having lost two Crocodiles and their crews being either killed or wounded as a result of the buried naval shell, they 'insisted upon the minefield gap being completely cleared and the approaches bulldozed to the fortress.' Under fire from various German

A Crocodile at Breast threading its way through shell holes, flaming as it advanced.

guns, this took the US engineers and their armoured bulldozers most of the next day, 'whilst the three remaining HQ tanks whiled away the time by plastering up the fort.' Despite the dangers, Major Ryle took each Crocodile commander forward on a recce up to the edge of the moat.

The attack was resumed on 16 September. This time 9 Troop was to lead the flaming part of the attack with the gun tanks in support:

> They fanned out on the northern side at the edge of the moat and sent 75s and 95s crashing into the fort. The troop emptied its trailers in the moat and across the other side in one glorious conflagration of flame and smoke. Then from a shelter in the moat emerged 'Hermann the German'. [Major] Dallas sent him back into the fort to demand its surrender at the pistol point. But that modernised mediaeval fort was just as tough as ever. Out came 'Hermann the German' to tell Dallas that the commandant's orders were to remain there and fight to the bitter end – and unless they produced a damn sight more flame and destruction so he would.

Major Dallas retorted 'He wants it, well we've got it', and ordered all available weapon systems to deluge the fort with fire. Major Ryle sent 10 Troop to flame,

One of B Squadron's Crocodiles flaming at Brest.

'who used up the whole of their HE and flame in one mad outburst', and were replaced by '6 Troop who piled in just as heavy':

> At the same time all available firepower, infantry mortars, phosphorus shells and heavy weapons crashed down. Two 105mm close-support Hows lined up into action against the gate itself ... [10 Troop] pounding away with them. The outhouses were now a blazing inferno and a truly Walt Disney nightmare of flame, smoke, flying metal, sound and fury. Gradually the weight shifted its point of impact as a task force of infantry jumped into the moat and placed charges against the wall. The little force returned and blew the charges. Straight away into the hole charged the infantry, covered by an absolute crescendo of flame, 75s, Besa and smoke. 10 Troop even used up their smoke grenades. Straight through the outhouses, capturing en route 30 PW too asphyxiated by the flame and smoke to surrender. A sharp spell of hand-to-hand fighting and the show was over, the remainder of the garrison left alive surrendering – 78 ORs, 3 Officers, a WO and an officer cadet.

The fall of Fort Montbarey tore a breach through the Germans' main fortifications and the Americans were now able to infiltrate successfully into Recouvrance. The next day the two half-squadron commanders, Captain Cobden and Lieutenant Barrow, recced and planned a battle inside Brest in support of 115 US Infantry Regiment, while Major Ryle planned with the 5th Rangers. Everything was ready for the 18th, but now the German defences began to crumble and they 'packed in here without waiting for the Crocs', which stood by, largely unemployed.

On 19 September, General Ramcke, having ceremonially fired the last shell, surrendered the port to General Middleton after completing demolition of its facilities, which could not be repaired in time to be a theatre entry point as planned. The Battle for Brest had wider ramifications for the Allies for both logistics and reinforcement. The cost of some 10,000 casualties in overcoming the defenders of Brest resulted in Eisenhower making the decision in the second half of September to invest and isolate the other German fortress ports, avoiding the necessity of storming them in set-piece battles. Most of the remaining Brittany ports surrendered on 9 May 1945, the day after VE Day. One of the exceptions to this general rule was Le Havre, where the Crocodiles of A and C squadrons were in action with I Corps under the First Canadian Army.

Having salvaged what they could from the knocked-out Crocodiles, enjoyed the hospitality of the US Army and some of the locals, B Squadron was spared the long journey back east on transporters. Instead they, their echelon and a number of 'acquired vehicles' embarked on two Landing Ships Tank to sail them back to re-join the Second Army that had now advanced out of Normandy. Leaving Brittany, the LSTs sailed via the Solent where members of the squadron were lucky enough to have some shore leave before the last leg of their journey to

The level of destruction of Brest and its port through demolition, bombing and shelling was remarkable. Seven months later, the port had made a negligible contribution to the Allied logistic effort.

Ostend in Belgium, arriving on 6 October. B Squadron's war diary for September summed up the lessons of Brest:

> CONCLUSIONS
>
> The flame-thrower tanks were a very important factor in the capture of Fort Montbarey. Their successful use in this operation can be attributed to the following factors:
>
> (1) The splendid co-operation between the infantry battalion commander and Major Ryle, the flame-thrower Squadron Commander, and the great pains which they took in recce and detailed planning for the operation.
>
> (2) The great courage displayed by the British flame-thrower unit and the American infantry which took part in this attack.
>
> (3) The skilful employment of the flame-thrower effectively upon the vulnerable parts of the fort. Also the effective use of their 75mm gun and machine guns against the enemy in the fort and outlying positions.
>
> RECOMMENDATIONS
>
> It is believed that the flame-thrower tank has a very definite usefulness in support of the infantry in hedgerow or similar country where the terrain is favourable to the enemy in defence, but where it will permit operation of the tanks. Also where the infantry is confronted with defensive installations which can be attacked effectively by the flames such as were found at Fort Montbarey. It is believed that one or two battalions of these flame-thrower tanks might well be assigned to the Army and held as troops for employment where needed.[4]

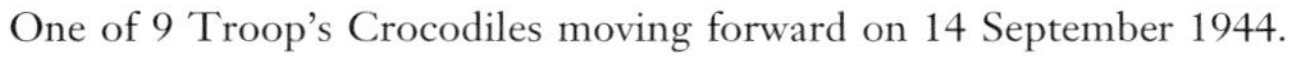

One of 9 Troop's Crocodiles moving forward on 14 September 1944.

Chapter Fourteen

Le Havre: Operation ASTONIA

On 4 September 141 Regiment RAC ceased to be categorized as army troops and re-joined 31 Tank Brigade, which itself was now titled 'armoured', coming under command of 79th Armoured Division. Thus the Crocodiles were now formally under the wing of Hobart's 'Funnies', with 7 RTR due to begin conversion to a Crocodile regiment. Trooper Cox noted that 'The division sign, a yellow inverted triangle with a bull's head in the centre, was now on all of our tanks.'

The newly-promoted Field Marshal Montgomery's direction for 21st Army Group in the next phase of the North-West European Campaign was 'to destroy all enemy forces in the Pas-de-Calais and Flanders and to capture Antwerp.'[1] However, for A and C squadrons of 141 Regiment RAC, there were fortress ports to be captured and further east the cross-Channel guns to be reduced. For these operations they would be under command of First Canadian Army, which had reached the Seine on a front between Rouen and the sea. General Crerar's orders were that having crossed the Seine, 'I Corps will be turned westwards into the Havre Peninsula to destroy the enemy forces in that area and to secure the port of Havre.' Based no doubt on the ongoing US experience of attacking the Brittany ports, Montgomery stressed that 'No more forces will be employed in this task than are necessary to achieve the object. The main business lies to the north, and in the Pas-de-Calais.'

The sign of 79th Armoured Division.

Trooper Ernest Cox of A Squadron 141 RAC.

A Squadron was to support 2nd Canadian Division at Dieppe, but with that port quickly in Allied hands the squadron was available for re-tasking. Consequently, both A and C squadrons were to remain under command of General Crocker's I Corps, which was operating on the left flank of the First Canadian Army. For Trooper Cox of A Squadron, his mind was on practical matters as the Crocodiles made their way to Elbeuf and across the Seine in heavy rain:

> The weather was moving from summer to autumn and continuous rain made life very

As I Corps closed in on Le Havre, the Germans began the demolition of the port facilities.

> unpleasant; we never seemed to dry out, the nights too began to have a bite. There was little we could do about it, knowing as the year progressed it certainly would not improve.
>
> Major Stoddard, newly promoted, was a welcome return and he now commanded the squadron. He had been our Troop Officer when he joined the Regiment; he had a bit of a soft spot for our troop.[2]

Trooper Smith of C Squadron recalled the road move across the Seine amid 'a long line of carriers and trucks. The skies were grey again, the steady drizzle blanketed the landscape and the hammering tracks steamed on the wet tarmac. The turret crews were wrapped in waterproofs, gloved and scarved, smoking damp cigarettes and trying to stop the moisture seeping into the turret.'[3]

On 1 September, the two divisions of I Corps were across the Seine about 25 miles east of Le Havre. Initially the 51st Highland Division would strike north to St.-Valery-en-Caux[4] and then south-west along the coast to Le Havre. Meanwhile, the 49th West Riding Division was to turn west and follow the Seine estuary directly to the port, where the outposts of the German defences on the River Lézarde were reached on 3 September. With both divisions having closed in on Le Havre, they were instructed to 'continue to drive in the enemy outposts and by vigorous patrolling intimidate him and learn everything possible about his dispositions. If the enemy showed any sign of weakness and if presented the opportunity, penetration of his main positions was to be made.'[5]

On the 4th the fortress and its 11,000-plus garrison was invited to surrender, but *Oberst* Wildermuth refused. He later confessed to his interrogator that he:

> appeared to have had a vain hope that it [an assault] might not come and that a siege would be attempted instead. This hope stemmed from the fact that the Allies probably knew that the harbour had been made unserviceable, and that Le Havre as a port had, for the time being, been destroyed. But it was a forced hope, and later Wildermuth admitted that in his heart of hearts he realized that a siege at that stage of the campaign was unlikely.[6]

On 5 September the process of softening up the port and its defences began with 15in naval gunfire from the monitor HMS *Erebus* and the battleship *Warspite*. This was followed by medium and heavy bomber strikes over subsequent days.

With insufficient fuel available to 21st Army Group to keep more than the armoured spearheads dashing east to the Pas-de-Calais and on to Brussels, there was plenty of artillery support for the attack on Le Havre. The Crocodiles joined the columns of traffic from the two infantry divisions, corps' troops and the guns of two AGRAs, as well as the tanks of a pair of armoured brigades.

Employing slave labour and consuming vast amounts of concrete, steel, wire and mines, the Germans, as Hitler had declared, had created a fortress that was every bit as strong as those on the Atlantic coast and elsewhere in the Channel. The First Canadian Army report described the physical defences:

> The assaulting forces were faced with a difficult task, for Le Havre was strongly protected from ground attack, both by the nature of the ground and by man-made defence works. Water protected three sides of the port: on the west the open Channel, on the south the Seine estuary, and on the east the flooded valley of the Lézarde River. It was obvious that the attack would have to come from the north. But here again the topography aided the defenders. Hilly ground around Octeville, about two miles north of the city and half a mile inland from the sea, commanded the northern approaches to the city, and to the north-east, on the west side, or the Lézarde valley, were two high plateaux. This high ground was protected by a belt of wire and minefields running from the Lézarde valley at La Rive near Montivilliers to the coast near Octeville. Air photos revealed running between the minefields, along the northern slope of the natural feature, was an anti-tank ditch, 20 feet wide and about 10 feet deep.
>
> Numerous concrete strongpoints for the employment of machine guns and anti-tank weapons studded the outer defence positions to the north. Eleven of these were spotted (and their positions confirmed by deserters) on the northern plateau west of the Lézarde. In the port itself were twenty-eight artillery positions, nominally of four guns each. The majority of these, however, could only fire out to sea. Within the city two forts, Fort St. Adresse and Fort Sanvic, together with roadblocks, pillboxes, fortified houses and concrete shelters, completed the defensive system behind which the enemy awaited the assault.

No. 90(A) - LE HAVRE (FRANCE) Troop Concentration. 1st. Wave of the daylight attack on the 5th. September, 1944 showing T.I. falling at 18.08 Hours and bombing concentration at 18.42½ Hours.
(1,3 & 8 GROUPS)

CONFIDENTIAL.

Photographs from a report on the 5 September bomber strike.

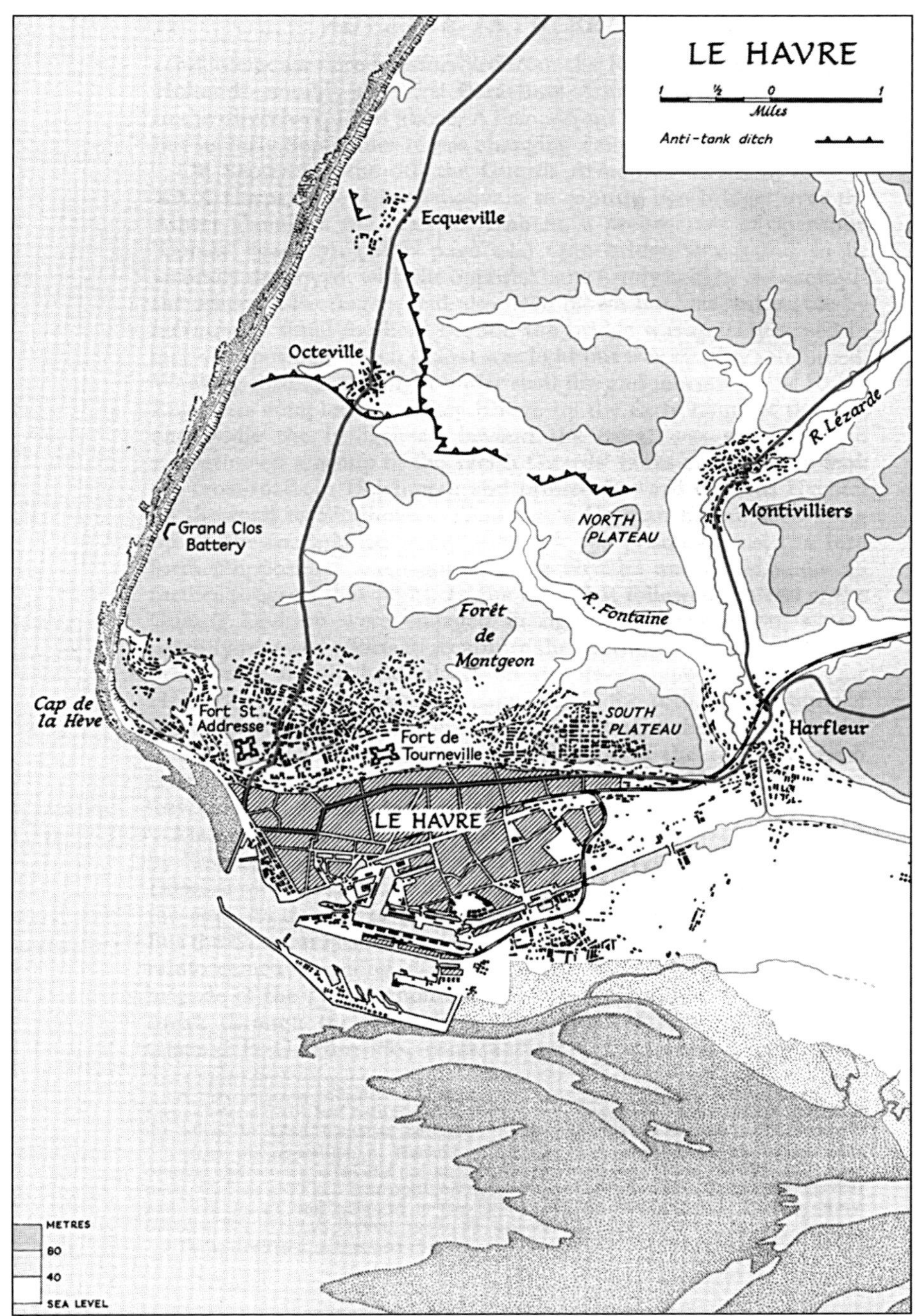

Map of Le Havre and its environs.

An extract from the 1:50,000 scale map (Special Sheet 7E 4&8 E3) used during operations in the Le Havre area.

Based on *Oberst* Wildermuth's post-war interrogation reported by the Canadians, he went on to describe the defenders:

> He was pleased with the conscientiousness and ability of his staff of elderly reserve officers. He had about 4,500 infantry of varying quality. He considered that his best troops were a battalion of 245 Inf Div. These men were well trained and knew the problems of the defence. Battle-experienced men on leave from the eastern front, hastily banded together into two battalions, had not yet shaken down into a smooth-working team. The men of 81 Fortress Unit, and two battalions of 5 *Sicherungs* Regiment (Security Regiment) were infirm and of small fighting value. The fortress commander, having considered the quality of his troops and the facilities for defence, had reported to the commander of Fifteenth Army, so he alleged later, that the fortress could be held against an assault for 24 hours in unfavourable circumstances, or 72 hours if circumstances favoured the defence.

Planning and Preparation

The first draft of the plan for Operation ASTONIA was produced on 3 September. Le Havre was to be captured in an assault by I Corps' two infantry divisions, both supported by a tank brigade, assorted 'Funnies' from 79th Armoured Division, divisional artillery and six medium and two heavy regiments RA. For the first time the Crocodiles were grouped with 30 Armoured Brigade alongside the other 'Funnies' of 79th Armoured Division and from there they were put under operational command of the two assault divisions.[7]

Lieutenant General Crocker's plan for I Corps' assault in Phase One was for both divisions to create three gaps each of two or three lanes through the enemy's protective wire and minefields. The 49th (West Riding) Division was to break through the outer defences to secure the Northern Plateau, cross the Fontaine stream and seize a toehold on the Southern Plateau. In Phase Two, the 51st (Highland) Division was to secure positions north of the Forêt de Montgeon while 49th Division expanded its grip on the Southern Plateau. The 51st would then attack the enemy defences around Octeville and Fort St. Adresse and advance into the north-western part of Le Havre. The final phase would see both divisions attacking from the high ground into the city and port.

A Squadron was to attack with 49th Division and the Churchills of 34 Tank Brigade and C Squadron was to fight alongside 51st Division and the Shermans of 33 Armoured Brigade. This deployment meant that 'Colonel Waddell was again denied his ambition to command his whole regiment in action as one unit.'

Not many of the infantry battalions had worked with such a large assembly of assault vehicles from 79th Armoured Division and as a sensible measure, a rehearsal of the breaching phase was laid on. It did not reassure all of those watching, including Major Lindsay of 1st Gordons:

> After supper I drafted the orders of march for our advance. We are to have Crocodiles, AVREs, tanks and flails. All very complicated, too complicated in fact, and I have been trying to persuade Harry [Lieutenant Colonel Cummings-Bruce] to leave some of this menagerie behind as I fear they will get stuck in the woods we have to go through. We were up early for our rehearsal with the funnies. It has been raining for days and the flails and AVREs got stuck in the mud, and the Crocodiles did not do much better.[8]

According to Trooper Smith:

> The flails pounded a patch of earth into a slightly stickier consistency; the Shermans chugged across the valley with the infantry wading behind knee-deep in wet grass. We stood about in the rain and got soaked. I could not see that anyone was better off for the exertion but the officers seemed happy.

C Squadron's display of the Crocodile's capability, however, met with approval:

> The Squadron gave a flame demonstration to troops of 51st Highland Division. It was the first time this particular battalion had worked with a flame

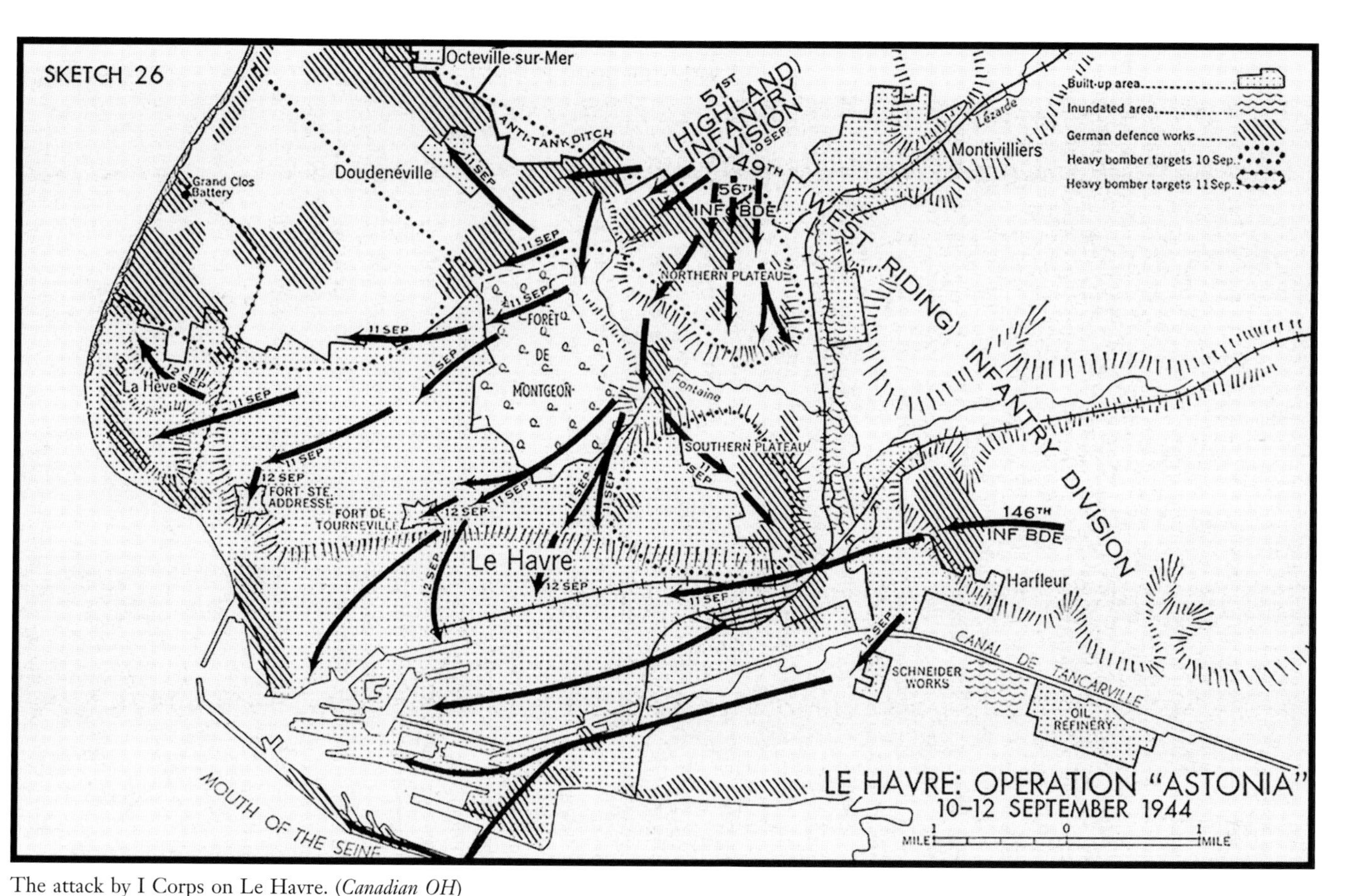

The attack by I Corps on Le Havre. (*Canadian OH*)

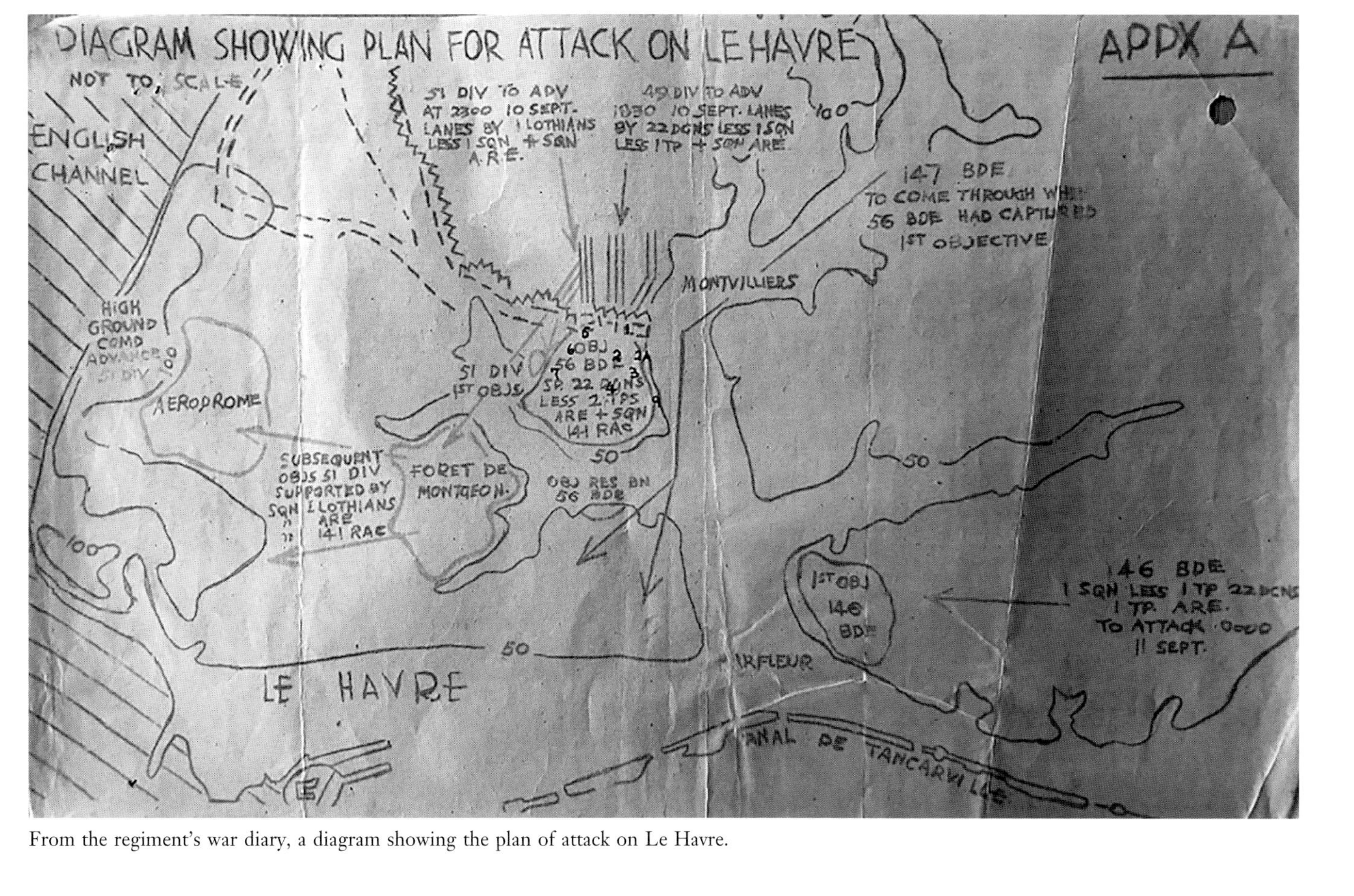

From the regiment's war diary, a diagram showing the plan of attack on Le Havre.

> regiment, and they were alleged to be more afraid of us than the Germans. In any case, the 51st had a reputation for not liking tanks. To dispel these feelings, they were given a preview of the show.

The attack was originally planned for 9 September, but 'preparations for the attack were hampered by consistently bad weather. The frequent downpours of rain soaked the clay soil, so that the passage of even a few vehicles reduced it to a quagmire. As a result, D-Day ... was postponed 24 hours.'

A Squadron: 10 September 1944

The 49th Division, with 56 Infantry Brigade delivering the initial attack, was to make three gaps through wire and minefields and, in the case of the central gap, bridge an anti-tank ditch. To achieve this the brigade had the flails of the 22 Dragoons to deal with mines, AVREs to bridge the ditch, and the Churchills of 7 RTR to engage the enemy strongpoints beyond the minefields and wire. Finally, there were additional AVREs and A Squadron's Crocodiles to reduce the enemy defences for the infantry of 56 Brigade.

The attack, delayed by twenty-four hours, eventually had to go ahead on 10 September, but there had been little improvement in the going. The Canadian report recorded that 'Fortunately, the weather cleared, but the heavy state of the ground was seriously to affect the operation, particularly the performance of the flail tanks.' Having moved forward into their FUP overnight to avoid enemy observation, Trooper Cox and the crew of 'Stallion' had a short, uncomfortable and wet night:

> On the 10th September orders came to move towards the start line. H-Hour was to be 1745, to us a rather odd time. The RAF was to bomb [the Southern Plateau] at 1645, hopefully this time they would drop their bombs on the Germans.[9] This to be followed by half an hour of artillery barrage so we didn't want to be late on the start line; the squadron moved out in good time. The weather had improved; the rain had stopped though the ground was very soft as we moved up cross-country. Several tanks became bogged down including our own, the recovery tank doing trojan work along with a Scammell truck from REME using trees as anchors and winching tanks out. Everyone made the start line just in time to have a grandstand view of the bombers pounding the town and the heavy guns still ranging from the beachhead.
>
> Time now for I Corps' artillery to take over where the bombers had left off. Laying down half an hour's intense barrage, as this crept forward the signal came to move forward. Reconnaissance had shown extensive minefields as the first line of defence behind which the enemy were well dug in forming hedgehog positions. On our attack maps these had all been marked and numbered 1 to 11. The whole area was well covered by 88mm anti-tank guns, plus heavy artillery. The flails had the task of clearing the minefields; not an easy task proceeding over open ground. The German defenders were

A Sherman crab flail tank in action.

> surprised to see tanks entering the minefields in such a bold way. The flails began to take casualties from both anti-tank guns and from mines their chains had missed.

In creating the gaps nicknamed – from north to south – LAURA, HAZEL and MARY, the problem for the A Squadrons of 22 Dragoons was that flailing the sodden earth reduced the effect of the beating of their weighted chains. The result was that one after another, virtually all the Crabs hit mines:

> The flails went into action in the left gap at 1825 hrs. By 1940 hrs three lanes were completed, at a cost of four flails. The centre gap was very difficult, as it involved bridging an anti-tank ditch. Here, even after tremendous effort, only one lane was successfully completed. The eastern gap was meant to consist of two lanes, but it was only possible to open one as three flail tanks were destroyed after only 50 yards of operation. The gapping cost altogether 29 flails and two command tanks – most of which were disabled by mines – and six AVREs.

In gap LAURA, four flails were lost to mines, with the troop's surviving Crab widening the lane to 20ft but it was enough. Following the flails and Churchills of 7 RTR through the various lanes were 56 Brigade's leading battalions, the 2nd Gloucesters and 2nd South Wales Borderers (2 SWB), each with two troops of A Squadron's Crocodiles and another squadron of flails in support. Captain Hall and 4 and 5 troops were to support the Gloucesters and Major Bryant's 1, 2 and 3 troops 2 SWB.

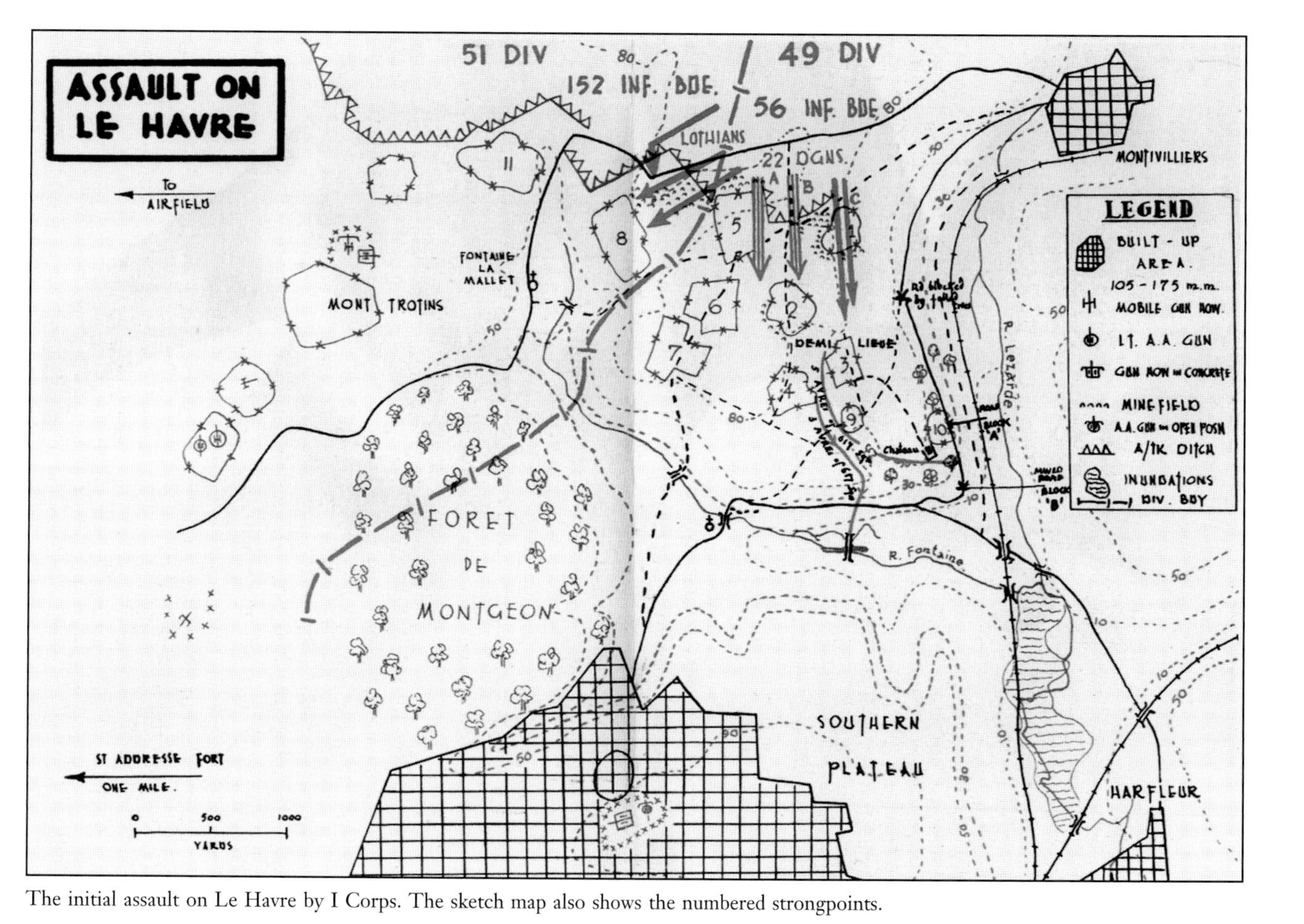

The initial assault on Le Havre by I Corps. The sketch map also shows the numbered strongpoints.

Crocodiles of A Squadron waiting to go through gap LAURA. Strongpoint 5 is the wood in the distance on the far side of the minefield.

The force's task was to capture the seven forward strongpoints consisting of concrete and field defences, surrounded by wire and mines, while 2nd Essex followed mounted in Kangaroos ready to take their objectives, strongpoints 9 and 10 sited in depth. Trooper Cox continued his account of Major Bryant's half-squadron in support of 2 SWB:

> It was time for us to follow in their wake. Immediately losing a tank from anti-tank fire. It was quite harrowing as we proceeded, wondering if all the mines had been blown. The answer was not long in coming: a Mark IV of our HQ in front of us blew up on a mine. No injuries to the crew other than a shaking. We gingerly pulled out to pass him. The flails became fewer and fewer as one after the other they stopped, victims of the mass of mines. Our infantry from the South Wales Borderers followed in our wake, making use of what cover our tanks afforded. Not for them the luxury of steel protection from the mines or shell fire. The last of the flails succumbed to the mines still 150 yards short of our first objective [strongpoint 5]. No turning back now, we had our infantry to think of; without tank support they would be in the open to be cut down like standing wheat. Being the junior tank, we were ordered into the lead, pulling out past the last of the flails. How far did the minefield go? Now was the time to find out. The rest of the tanks followed in our tracks, and we held our breath; by now five more of the squadron had been disabled on mines, again fortunately without casualties to crews.

The two A Squadron troops had lost a Crocodile on the start line and a tank in the minefield and the remainder were able to use a combination of 75mm HE, Besa and flame against the enemy positions, with Major Bryant's Crocodiles attacking strongpoint 5, alongside the Churchills of 7 RTR. The AVREs of 617 Squadron RE fired their demolition guns and the Crocodiles are recorded as flaming 'with gusto, and strongpoint 5 gave in after eleven minutes'.[10] The war diary was altogether more effusive: 'The Crocs went through a gap with the inf and absolutely soaked posn 5 with flame. It was a magnificent and awe-inspiring sight and the inf entered immediately afterwards. It was from here that a PW subsequently remarked that "It is not British".'[11]

Nonetheless, the 2 SWB suffered heavy casualties in fighting through Objective 5 and a fresh company was brought up to clear 6 and 7. Even with the assistance of assault armour, the infantry had to get into them through gaps in the wire that surrounded the defences and on through the largely uncleared anti-personnel minefields that surrounded strongpoints. Once inside the perimeter there were deep dugouts out of which the Germans had to be winkled, having survived bombardment and flame. The company attacking No. 6 suffered sixty casualties, mostly in a single platoon, mainly caused by flanking fire from No. 8, which had yet to be captured.

On the left flank breaching the minefield was also costly, but A Squadron's other two troops and one of AVREs were through the single lane to support the

The result of a typical mine strike to a Churchill: broken track and the loss of running gear. Trooper Cox, however, noted that 'The tanks soon became operational once the tracks were repaired and the damaged bogies replaced.'

The Crocodiles, followed by assault infantry and an AVRE fascine, go through the minefield gap.

Gloucesters whose objectives were numbered 1–4. The advance of Captain Hall's half-squadron was stalled before it began. The war diarist noted that 'On the left there was only one unmarked gap that the Crocs couldn't find. After milling around for some time, Captain Hall's party was in a minefield dilemma. However, some nearby flails noticed his plight, came forward and cleared a gap in front of him.' In addition to a Crocodile that had become stranded in a sunken lane on the way to the start line, despite the best efforts of the flails a further two Crocodiles were lost to mines. However, 'Lieut Mackie and Sgt Roskelly pushed through and were onto strongpoint 2 with the inf almost before the enemy were aware of it.'

Strongpoints 1 and 2 soon fell to the attackers 'and at 2035 hours the Crocodiles flamed No. 3 which went up in smoke; but the Crocodiles got off course and missed No. 4 which, however, fell later.' Now in darkness at 2200 hours, Major Bryant's surviving Crocodiles had almost certainly followed the Essex towards the château and down towards the River Fontaine. However, the bombing, shelling and rain had 'so disturbed and cut up the ground that movement by foot or vehicle became a major problem. The woods became an absolute tangle; even with the help of artificial moonlight, it was most difficult to advance.'[12]

Consequently, the Essex abandoned the Kangaroos and with the support of the Crocodiles set out to take on strongpoints 9 and 10. Captain Hall's three Crocodiles made a solo attack on No. 9 under Lieutenant Mackie, as the infantry had not arrived. It was noted that 'long afterwards the inf bde were debating whether it would be possible to use Crocs against this position, not knowing that it was already taken.'

The Northern Plateau was in the hands of the 49th Division, but the Essex had only been able to 'push patrols over the bridges and onto the high ground

A squadron flaming strongpoint 5.

beyond'. They were unable to establish a secure bridgehead across the Fontaine simply because the necessary support weapons could not be brought forward.

Even though remarkably they had not suffered any casualties, the trials of the night were not over for A Squadron:

> This action took place far too late for comfort and in complete darkness. Major Bryant was faced with the problem of getting together his Crocs on the enemy side of a vast and almost unmarked minefd and getting them to the other side without jamming the exit of the other arm trying to do likewise. Nevertheless, it was done and the Sqn replenished very late that night near LE VASSEUR and by 0500 hrs was ready to support 147 Bde, no mean feat.

51st Highland could not launch their part of the operation to capture the westernmost part of the Northern Plateau in daylight as the area they were to attack was overlooked by the high ground of Mont Trotin, the village of Doudeville and further west the airfield defences. Their H-Hour was to be at 2300 hours, when they would advance with the benefit of three searchlights playing on the clouds to provide them with Monty's Moonlight.

With a later start, C Squadron was still preparing for battle as the fighting began some distance forward and to their left. Trooper Smith recalled:

> I sat in the sun and watched the echelon jolting across the field to bring us petrol. A little to the east a group of Engineers argued around a bundle of fascines they were trying to hoist on to their AVRE. Over Le Havre great clouds rose in the air and we climbed on the tank to watch through

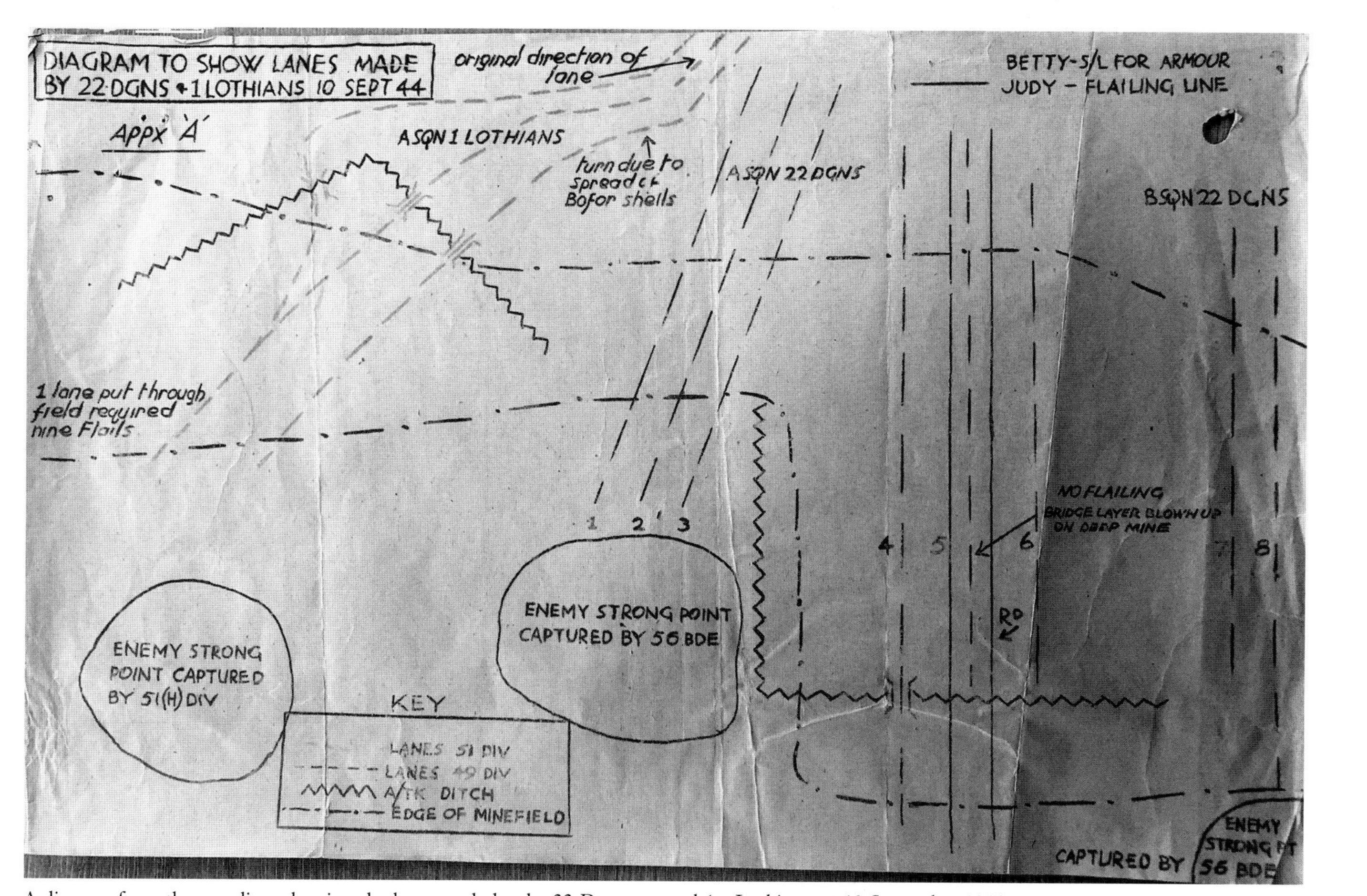

A diagram from the war diary showing the lanes made by the 22 Dragoons and 1st Lothians on 10 September 1944.

> binoculars as the Halifaxes and Lancasters, bomb doors open, flew steadily in, undeterred by furious flak, until the bombs tumbled down out of our field of view.

Major Lindsay, second-in-command of the Gordons, was responsible for the FUP and mustering the battalion's supporting assault armour and tanks, and was clearly not placated by the rehearsals the previous day, noting in his diary that:

> It is going to be very difficult to control this zoo. We shall have fifty-four vehicles and they are all being lined up tonight (9 Sep). I hope to goodness they mark the route well, and especially the minefields so that we cannot go wrong in the dark. Our column is being led by a sapper, Sergeant Whitefield, in charge of a scissors bridge to put across the first anti-tank ditch. It seems a great responsibility to give an NCO.

Trooper Smith also had doubts:

> Le Havre looked dodgy. 152 Infantry Brigade were on the right flank. There was an anti-tank ditch to be crossed at point Rum, strongpoints marked as numbers 8 and 11, the village of Fontaine-le-Mallet, the Forêt de Montgeon and strongpoints to the right of Mont Trotin. For our part, 13 Troop were to emerge from the Forêt and attack on the right flank of some 88mm guns situated on the southern part of Mont Trotin, flaming two 20mm and a barracks on the way. 14 Troop had the left flank while Shermans of the East Riding Yeomanry made a frontal assault. We consulted the oracle and Jack [the driver] was of the opinion that if we did, after all, go in with 13 Troop then we were in for something definitely dodgy.

The Canadians noted, however, that 'The use of sand tables and cloth models of the minefield breaching operation and the areas to be assaulted proved valuable, and particularly so to 5I (H) Inf Div, which was to assault in darkness.' The plan for 'Major Duffy with two troops was with C Sqn 144 RAC to sp 5 Black Watch and Capt Barber was with B Sqn to sp 1 Gordon Highlanders' of 153 Brigade. Smith described the move forward to the FUP and the wait:

> Artificial moonlight. Searchlights spread low across the fields. A line of men and carriers moves down the side of the hill, silhouetted against a pale violet glow. We lurch off the road, giving way to a long convoy of trucks. Gun flashes stab the blackness – blackness doubly intense in contrast to the searchlights. Fires are burning, winking patches of red on the hillside towards Le Havre. Beyond the hill [the Northern Plateau] the flickering of exploding shells.

As a result of the soft going on the approaches to the minefield across which the tracked vehicle carved 2ft-deep tracks, coupled with poor visibility and the resulting difficulty in keeping direction, the gapping teams took an hour instead of the estimated thirty minutes to reach the anti-tank ditch. They had not been helped by misdirection of tracer fired by Bofors light anti-aircraft guns on a fixed line as an aid to direction-finding in the dark. By 0240 hours, however, work was reported being 'in progress' in all three lanes and that bridges had been launched across the obstacle. Just before 0500 hours 'one lane was complete, swept of mines, and in fit condition for vehicles to use.'

The work of the flails to breach the minefield proved to be as costly on 51st Division's flank as it was on the 49th's front, but sufficient lanes were created to get the Highlanders through to attack the enemy positions. Probably because of the widely shared concerns over armoured traffic jams in the gaps, 51st Highland decided that they would only call on the Crocodiles in case of need. Consequently, with the battle progressing well, C Squadron waited on the home side of the minefield. Smith recalled:

> Then there is the faint glow of dawn. Dim shapes become trucks, tanks, carriers and jeeps. I doze and when I wake it is almost day. We stand on the side of a hill behind a squadron of flails. The Lothians are moving their tanks about and we are emboldened to sit on the engine-deck and warm hands and feet on the exhaust.
>
> There is a line of ragged, dirty figures coming over the brow of the hill and down the slope towards us. Prisoners. They are unshaven and bleary-eyed, bewildered and miserable old men for the most part, but one tall blond fellow is bomb-happy, laughing and singing and falling over the ruts. Or he is drunk. There is only one Tommy as escort and he looks ill. His face is grey and strained and he holds his Sten as if it were trying to get away from him.

152 Brigade's assault teams waiting in their FUP, early evening of 10 September 1944.

An officer of 141 Regiment RAC wearing a crew helmet.

As the Highlanders advanced towards northern Le Havre, the time came for the Crocodiles to move forward through the gaps in the minefield in order to be able to make a timely response to a call from the infantry:

> Over the hill and it looks like time to close down. There is a long grass slope down to a wood, with thick [anti-glider] poles at intervals, and the tanks spread out, each troop making its own road. About a mile ahead a water tower is being shelled. Rising above the greenery of the woodland, the white stonework gleams in the sunlight and the shell bursts are black patches on the clear blue sky. We do not know if they are British or German. I ask if the wood is the Forêt de Montgeon.

> A few hundred yards ahead mortars are bursting in a corn field, great gouts of black and red against the golden wheat. They disturb the columns of prisoners that trudge along the track to a house – at every explosion a ripple of alarm runs along the line as those nearest start to run but are gradually stopped by those in front.

C Squadron is listed as being present during the reduction of the enemy defences during the day, but with the attack going well, the support of Major Duffy's Crocodiles was not required. However, they remained on call, following up close behind the fighting throughout 11 September as 51st Highland Division closed in on battery positions and to within 1,000 yards of the city and port of Le Havre.

The Fall of Le Havre: 11–12 September 1944

Not having been called into action by 51st Highland Division, C Squadron was during 12 September ordered by First Canadian Army to be regrouped with II Canadian Corps at Boulogne. In haste, they were soon on the road north-east. This left A Squadron to support the final phase of the assault on Le Havre.

During 11 September A Squadron worked as usual in half-squadrons: one would accompany the infantry of 146 Brigade into the town and the other head east of the River Lézarde with 147 Brigade to clear the enemy defences.

East of the River Lézarde the infantry had some hard fighting in the orchards surrounding strongpoint Oscar. C Squadron 22 Dragoons had beaten a lane through a mined orchard by 1030 hours, having detonated some fifty mines in the process, and the infantry attacked again at 1215 hours: 'The Crocodiles of A Squadron 141 RAC sealed the enemy's fate and the position fell by 2 o'clock.'

Meanwhile, the other half of the squadron was in action on the approaches to the city. Second Lieutenant Wareing described the more flexible organization of the 'Funnies' for this phase of the assault: 'An attack group consisted of two of each type of tank' (that is a pair of Crocodiles and two each of flails and AVREs):

> I was put in command of one such group and led them down into the town. We started about 5 miles out and had to deal with some small skirmishes on the way. It was late in the day when we got down to the harbour and docks, but we managed to set up a suitable position for defence or attack … whatever might be needed. We found that we were in the town square and conditions were quite good with plenty of fresh water, etc.
>
> At daylight the following day [12 September] we got ready for anything that might happen. We put out our white flag to liaise with the enemy and soon afterwards three Germans came to see us. We told them that for them the war was over and to go back and tell their officers to surrender unconditionally. They returned very quickly and told us that they would not surrender.
>
> With this information, I instructed my sergeant to bring his tank and trailer up to us and fire a burst of flame against the garrison wall. He did so and this brought all the enemy out to us with hands on their heads including

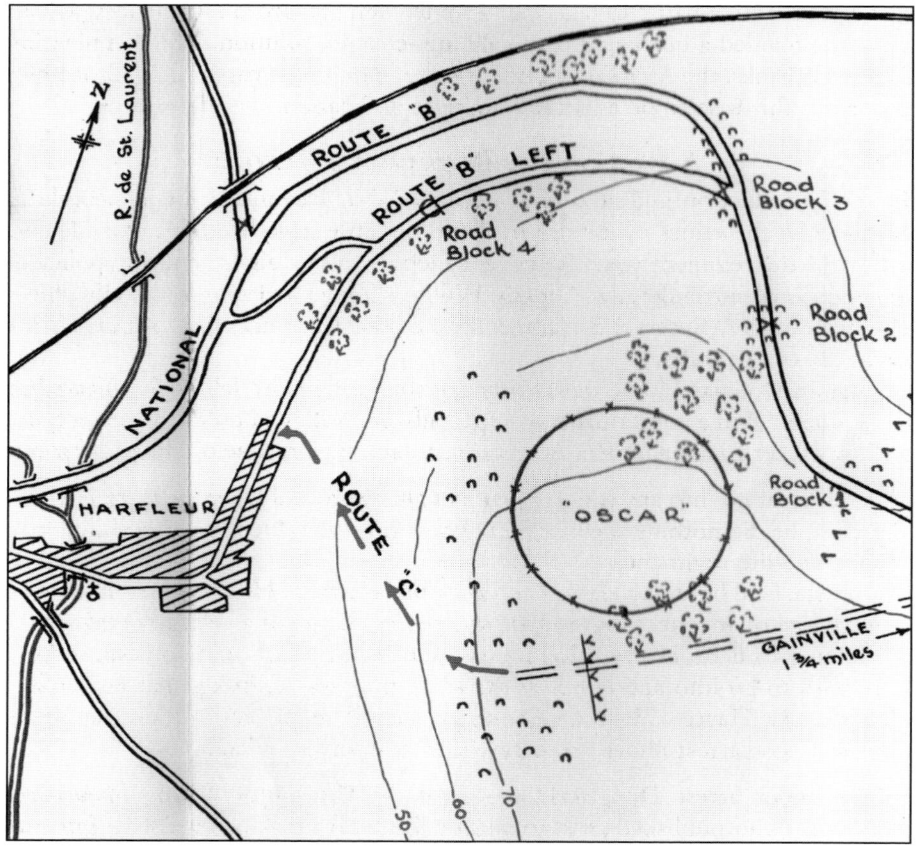

Defences east of the River Lézarde, 11 September 1944.

some of the officers. We accepted their surrender and started to organise it officially. I relieved an officer of his pistol and binoculars. The latter are still in my possession.

After settling down we began to realise how big the operation had been. We had captured the main HQ for the area which held provisions, ammunition, mail and horse-drawn vehicles. The loss of so much equipment made them helpless and useless. In all 12,000 men including 3,000 sailors surrendered after 2 days of fighting.

Lieutenant Colonel Waddell came up and congratulated us on a great job before ordering us to prepare for the next operation which could be the capture of the cross-Channel guns which were about 140 miles away near Calais.[13]

The success of the assault on Le Havre stands in stark contrast to the costly and protracted battle fought by the Americans at Brest, and it is reasonable to conclude that in a battle to take well-manned and resourced fix defences, assault armour provided a quick and relatively low-casualty solution. The combination of the flail tanks, the AVRE in all its variety of equipment carried and Crocodiles proved in this case to be a battle-winning combination.

A Blot on the Regiment's Record

In the Introduction and at several points in this account of the Crocodile in Normandy, the ethics of the use of flame in battle have been questioned. One officer of the regiment who always had such concerns, along with the policy of unconditional surrender, was Captain William Douglas-Home, nominally officer commanding D (Reserve) Squadron, one of the few remaining officers in the regiment of 7th Buffs.[14]

Captain Douglas-Home was clearly not soldiering material. Such officers had to be tolerated in a conscript army, especially one who had political connections. Fellow officer Lieutenant Wareing wrote a damning critique of Douglas-Home:

> He did not go into any action as far as I am aware and when we were not in action, he did nothing. I really don't know how he came to be there at all in such an elite regiment.
>
> In the field he ate by himself and slept under a tank. He did not seem to be in charge of anyone. However, he was put in charge of a group of tanks for the attack on Le Havre. This created something of a situation because he refused to go into action but at the same time was claiming that he could capture Le Havre without firing a single shot. The CO accordingly put him under close arrest under the supervision of another officer.[15]

While under arrest Douglas-Home wrote to the editor of the *Maidenhead Advertiser*, who published an exclusive on Le Havre that could not be ignored. After a court martial, he was sentenced to imprisonment.

A Final Note

With all three squadrons of 141 Regiment RAC heading north-east out of Normandy, the regiment had come of age. As our story has demonstrated, under Lieutenant Colonel Herbert Waddell, the mostly wartime serving officers and men had taken a barely-tested weapon system and with it had been pitched into battle with little more than a theoretical knowledge of its capabilities. They had learned 'on the job' to understand the strengths and weaknesses of the Crocodile's mechanics and how to use flame in battle. They had also provided that essential human element of determination to succeed, which resulted in the Crocodile becoming an effective weapon system. In particular, the regiment produced a tactical doctrine for the use of flame on the battlefield alongside the stresses and strains of units and formations in combat. This was a significant achievement under the leadership, guiding hand and sheer hard work of Colonel Waddell, which has to be fully recognized. The blighting of his career in the

A Crocodile flaming.

army thanks to the political influence at play in the Douglas-Home incident was a travesty.

Such was the demand for Crocodiles as a part of overcoming stout German defence that by the end of the Normandy campaign, a decision to bring 31 Tank Brigade into 79th Armoured Division had been taken. First 7 R was converted to flame-throwers and later 2 Fife and Forfar Yeomanry joined the re-titled 31 Armoured Brigade with Crocodiles.

Appendix I

Tank Numbers

Listed below are the asset numbers of the tanks and armoured cars of 141 RAC listed in the war diary of 30 Armoured Brigade's Ordnance Field Park for July 1944 as appendices to a letter dated 16 July 1944. It is clear, therefore, that the regiment's attachment, if only in terms of replacement equipment-holding, pre-dated the formal inclusion of the regiment in the 79th Armoured Division during September 1944.

* * *

APPENDIX 'A'

INITIAL SCALINGS REQUIRED – 'A' VEHICLES

W.D. NO. Description. Total Vehicles held by 141 Regt. RAC (The Buffs)[1]

W.D. NO.	Description	Total
REC.31705B REC.68347B REC.68169B REC.32032B	Churchill ARV.	4
T.172514B R.69135B	Churchill IV. (O.P.)	2
T.68831B: T.32193B: T.32151B T.68788B: T.32387B: T.32420B T.68078B.	Churchill IV.	7
T.172911B: T.172930B: T.172931B T.172916B: T.172917B: T.173211B	Churchill V.	6
T.173264H: T.173265H: T.173266H T.173152H: T.173262H: T.173267H T.173183H: T.173153H: T.173269H T.173157H: T.173151H: T.173271H T.173155H: T.173156H: T.173272H T.173285H: T.173154H: T.173270H T.173282H: T.173278H: T.173161H T.251648H: T.173167H: T.173162H T.173176H: T.173168H: T.173274H T.173177H: T.173169H: T.173275H T.173178H: T.173170H: T.173276H	Churchill VII.	56

T.173179H: T.173172H: T.173277H
T.173180H: T.173281H: T.173163H
T.173181H: T.173283H: T.173280H
T.173182H: T.173284H: T.173166H
T.173174H: T.251651H: T.251652H
T.173173H: T.173185H: T.173187H
T.251649H: T.251656H: T.173184H
T.251654H: T.251653H.

APPENDIX 'D'

SUPPLEMENTARY SCALING REQUIRED – 'A' VEHICLES
WD NO. Description. Total Already Scaled. Increase to Total.

WD NO.		Description	Total Already Scaled / Increase to Total
F.195601:	F.195673	Car, Scout, Humber MkI.	12, 31, 43
F.195687:	F.195528		
F.195928:	F.195924		
F.195918:	F.195889		
F.195899:	F.195727		
F.195870:	F.195860		

From the data above it can be seen that the 141 Regiment RAC held the establishment of seven Churchill Mk IVs as command tanks (two per squadron and one for RHQ) and six Churchill Mk V support tanks (two per squadron). From the number of references to the commanders firing the 95mm guns, it would seem that in practice there was not a neat division between command and support tanks.

At the stage of the North-West European Campaign covered by this book, some Mk VII Churchills may have been older versions upgraded to meet Mk VII specifications, particularly the command and support tanks.

* * *

Named Tanks of 141 Regiment RAC[2]

Stallion, A Squadron, 3 Troop
Steed, A Squadron
Standard, B Squadron Headquarters
Sabre, ARV B Squadron, 7 Troop, T.68434C
Support, B Squadron, 95mm gun tank
Scimitar, B Squadron, 7 Troop
Sword, B Squadron, 7 Troop
Sheridan, B Squadron
Sudan, B Squadron
Squirt, B Squadron
Sandgate, C Squadron, 13 Troop
Sandling, C Squadron, T.173174
Sublime, C Squadron, 14 Troop
Superb, C Squadron, 14 Troop
Supreme, C Squadron, 14 Troop
Samovar
Sandwich
Sidcup
Skipper
Stalin
Stalingrad
Sultan, CO's tank, RHQ

Appendix II

Operational Use of the Churchill Crocodile

Flame-Throwers in NW Europe, June–October 1944[1]

Set out below are the conclusions and summary which appear at the end of a report produced by Headquarters 141 Regiment RAC. The author, Captain Harry Bailey (?), appended the following: 'NOTE: The analysis of actions is based on personal experiences and collected notes. It is not official or necessarily comprehensive.'

* * *

<u>RAC USER OFFICER'S SUMMARY</u>

1. On only two occasions have the Crocodiles failed to get our Infantry in and either rout, kill or force the surrender of the Germans no matter whether SS or normal troops. Of those, 'Château le Landel' was badly planned and executed in the early days. The other, east of Tilly, was a 'mess-up' and no-one came with Crocodiles.
2. They always operate with those divisions which are leading the army attack and therefore have not yet the intimate co-operative which comes from fighting regularly with the same Infantry, tanks and gunner.
3. The retention of the 75mm gun (or better) is essential versus the Germans.
4. Their use by the Canadian 3rd Division was unusual and unorthodox. The weak morale of the enemy in the Channel ports proved this to be justified. The more normal employment by the 2nd Army at the end of October gets full use of the flame.
5. There is still a tendency to 'give a few' to each Division and this prevents the employment of whole Squadrons, or even the Regiment on worthwhile objectives with full support of other arms. Two Squadrons of Crocodiles flaming at once on a relatively narrow front would strike terror in anyone's heart.
6. There is no real connection between Crocodiles on the one hand and 'flails' or 'AVREs' on the other. Crocodiles can be used almost endlessly and always with Infantry. The other two are only required on special occasions.
7. Technical troubles have been decreased by recent modifications and will improve even more. Spares are the main difficulty.
8. The trailer has been 'holed' on occasion, and has also suffered from mortar bombs, but on the whole it has been rarely hit, and no extra armour appears

vitally necessary in the light of experience to date versus the Germans in NW Europe.

9. The link has been excellent.
10. The Quick-Release gear has rarely had to be used. If the tank has been properly hit by the 88mm, 75mm or Bazooka fire it has 'brewed-up' so quickly that the trailer could not be released. Only recollect two cases of a trailer going on fire and being released. Would not be without Quick-Release gear, nevertheless.
11. A longer range of shot is still to be desired.
12. An increased arc of fire for the flame-gun is still desired, but not at the expense of the 75mm gun. For the real street-fighting the present Crocodile is not much good with its present small 'arc of fire' and the difficulty to manoeuvre with the trailer in the street often full of debris. For jungle fighting an all-round traverse for the flame gun might well be essential. It would also be helpful in street-fighting. Crocodiles when flaming have to point the entire tank at their objective.
13. Only recently has the capacity of the trailer been really used. Anticipated that the next few months will show that the full 400 gallons has been required over and over again.

GENERAL COMMENTARY

The value of the Crocodile is greatly enhanced by the tremendous effect of flame on enemy morale. It combines the armour and hitting power of the Churchill tank with the additional threat of death by flame.

In the 31 actions herein described the casualties inflicted on the enemy are given as 154 killed by flame to 5,425 who gave themselves up. In many of the actions the opening flame caused the early collapse of enemy resistance and its use must therefore have saved our troops many casualties. This is especially marked, of course, where the enemy is of poorer quality and it follows that as the strain on German manpower increases, the value of the flame attack will also increase. Again, the earlier in action this threat is applied, the fewer casualties will be suffered by the attacking troops.

Perhaps the main disadvantage under which the Crocodile has to work at present is that in order to apply its flame it must close to within 80–100 yds of the enemy. It follows therefore that longer range would be a great asset. This necessity for closing with the enemy also demands close support from Tanks and Artillery to ensure that the Crocodiles can advance to fighting range, with the Infantry right up to take immediate advantage of any break in enemy resistance.

The greatest value appears to be achieved when 'combat team' technique is applied. This requires training and working together which obviously cannot be done when the few Crocodiles available have to be transferred from formation to formation. The unit whose actions are described has been used in action with every formation in the British and Canadian Armies and several times with the U.S. Army.

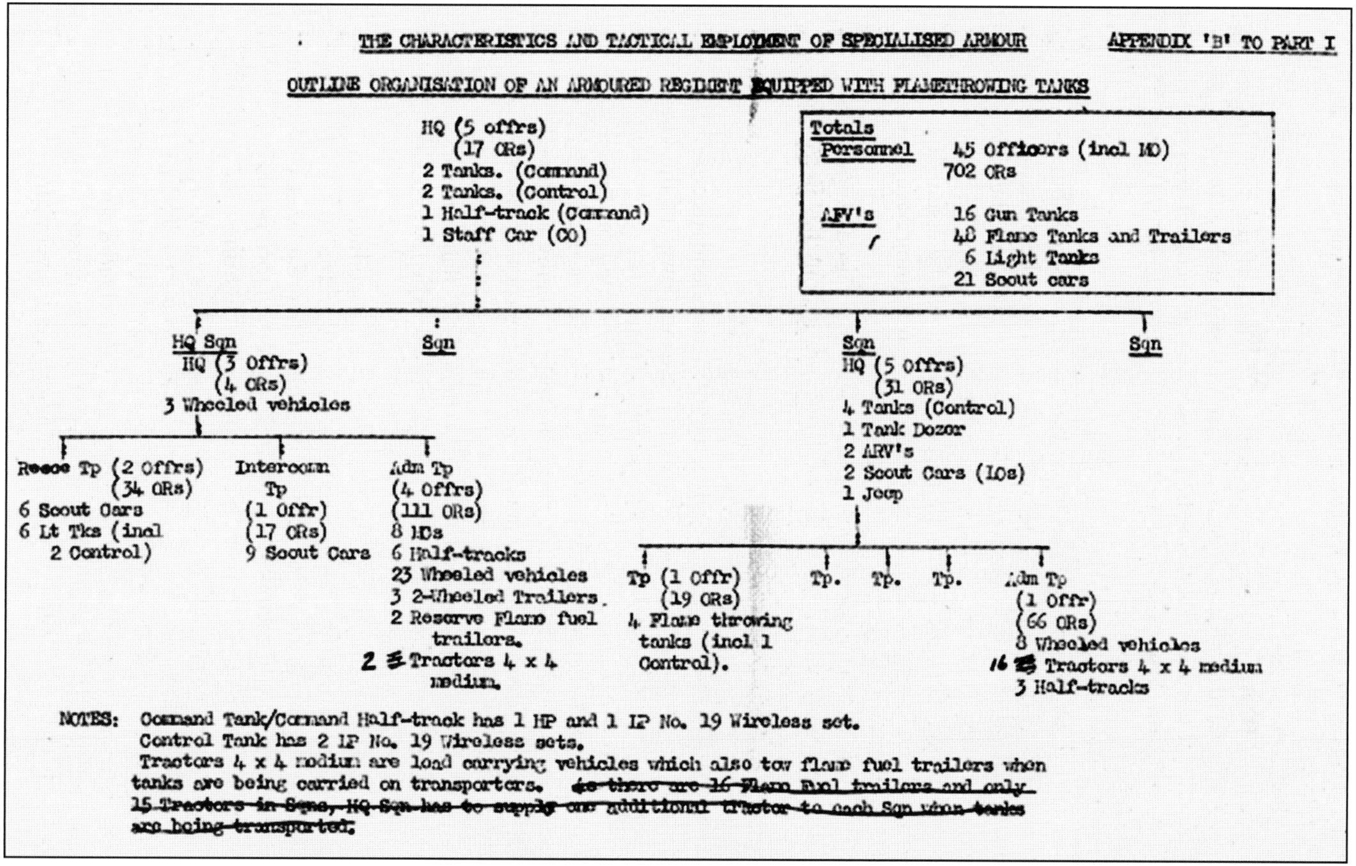

THE CHARACTERISTICS AND TACTICAL EMPLOYMENT OF SPECIALISED ARMOUR — APPENDIX 'B' TO PART I

OUTLINE ORGANISATION OF AN ARMOURED REGIMENT EQUIPPED WITH FLAMETHROWING TANKS

Totals

Personnel: 45 Officers (incl MO); 702 ORs

AFV's: 16 Gun Tanks; 40 Flame Tanks and Trailers; 6 Light Tanks; 21 Scout cars

HQ (5 offrs) (17 ORs)
- 2 Tanks. (Command)
- 2 Tanks. (Control)
- 1 Half-track (Command)
- 1 Staff Car (CO)

HQ Sqn

HQ (3 Offrs) (4 ORs)
3 Wheeled vehicles

- Recce Tp (2 Offrs) (34 ORs)
  - 6 Scout Cars
  - 6 Lt Tks (incl 2 Control)
- Intercom Tp (1 Offr) (17 ORs)
  - 9 Scout Cars
- Adm Tp (4 Offrs) (111 ORs)
  - 8 MCs
  - 6 Half-tracks
  - 23 Wheeled vehicles
  - 3 2-Wheeled Trailers.
  - 2 Reserve Flame fuel trailers.
  - 2 ~~3~~ Tractors 4 x 4 medium.

Sqn

Sqn

HQ (5 Offrs) (31 ORs)
- 4 Tanks (Control)
- 1 Tank Dozer
- 2 ARV's
- 2 Scout Cars (LOs)
- 1 Jeep

- Tp (1 Offr) (19 ORs)
  - 4 Flame throwing tanks (incl 1 Control).
- Tp.
- Tp.
- Tp.
- Adm Tp (1 Offr) (66 ORs)
  - 8 Wheeled vehicles
  - 16 ~~15~~ Tractors 4 x 4 medium
  - 3 Half-tracks

Sqn

NOTES: Command Tank/Command Half-track has 1 HP and 1 LP No. 19 Wireless set.
Control Tank has 2 LP No. 19 Wireless sets.
Tractors 4 x 4 medium are load carrying vehicles which also tow flame fuel trailers when tanks are being carried on transporters. ~~As there are 16 Flame Fuel trailers and only 15 Tractors in Sqns, HQ Sqn has to supply one additional tractor to each Sqn when tanks are being transported.~~

The organisation of the Crocodile regiment, in common with other armoured ORBATs, was subject to continual change. This table comes from a report by 79th Armoured Division in September 1944 for circulation to all formations in 21st Army Group.

As the advance east continued, the Crocodiles of 141 RAC took part in Canadian operations at Boulogne. As can be seen from this photograph, the cost was significant.

It would also appear that the employment of Crocodiles in small numbers does not get the full use out of the weapon. This would no doubt be obviated and improvement in training and working together be able to be made when further Crocodile units become available.

FT equipment in the Crocodile comes out of the report with flying colours and it is interesting to note that the trailer with light armour is seldom destroyed by penetration and the main use of the jettisoning gear is to enable the Churchill to go off and fight as a gun tank occasionally.

Apart from the question of longer range already mentioned, the most urgent requirement appears to be wider traverse for the flame gun. This difficulty may be aggravated in jungle warfare where it may be more difficult to manoeuvre the Tank.

Notes

Introduction

1. TNA SUPP 15/37, Report on the use of Flame-Throwers in the Opening Stages of the Campaign in Normandy (D to D+55).
2. Smith, John G., *In at the Finish: North-West Europe, 1944–45* (Minerva, 1995).
3. Ellis, Joseph (Oral History), IWM 80014484.

Chapter 1. Conversion and Experimentation

1. Bailey, Captain Harry, *In All Innocence* (141 Regiment RAC, Regimental Association).
2. Cox, Ernest, *Out of the Frying Pan into the Fire* (private memoir).
3. 10 RTR was subsequently renumbered 7 RTR when the original regiment of that number was destroyed during the Battle of Gazala in June 1942.
4. Cox, Ernest, *Out of the Frying Pan into the Fire* (private memoir).
5. Head-to-head trial at Chertsey in 1943 between a Churchill and a captured Panther provided by the Red Army.
6. Barclay, Brigadier C.N., *The History of 53rd Welsh Division in the Second World War* (MLRS reprint).
7. They were named OKE after a member of the design team Major J.M. Oke.
8. Even though development of the Crocodile equipment formed a part of 79th Armoured Division's remit, the regiment did not at this stage actually join the division.
9. Wilson, Andrew, *Flamethrower* (William Kimber & Co., London, 1956).
10. Bailey, Captain Harry, *In All Innocence* (141 Regiment RAC, Regimental Association).
11. The Combined Operations Staff Handbook 1945, Part IX gives the figure of 286 hours' work to waterproof a Churchill tank.

Chapter 2. The Invasion and Early Days

1. Two of the twelve LCTs type 3 of 15th LCT Flotilla, JIG Beach.
2. There are numerous claims to have knocked out the casemate at Le Hamel, but that of the AVRE is most likely.
3. Two of the twelve LCTs type 3 of 12th LCT Flotilla, KING Beach.
4. Bailey, Captain Harry, *In All Innocence* (141 Regiment RAC, Regimental Association).
5. TNA WO 171/877 (141 RAC War Diary, August 1944).
6. *Ost* battalions were formed from former Soviet prisoners, mainly from Eastern republics of the Union. They were of dubious quality, despite including German officers and senior NCOs.
7. *30 Corps, 50th (Northumbrian) Division and 7th Armoured Division – Planning, Appreciations and Operations* (Cabinet Papers, MLRS Books, 2005).
8. TNA WO 171/877 (141 RAC War Diary, June 1944).
9. 2nd County of London Yeomanry (Westminster Dragoons). Having joined 79th Armoured Division, the regiment was converted to flails in early 1944 and landed with 6th Assault Regiment RE on KING Sector.
10. The 8th Hussars were 7th Armoured Division's Recce Regiment, equipped with Cromwell tanks.
11. Most of the flails had been knocked out on D-Day, where they invariably led the breaching teams off the beaches.

12. The Germans had soon learned that a withdrawal out of close contact by the British heralded a bombardment or air attack. By moving forward, they not only avoided the fire strike, but were able to deploy outposts with which to disrupt the subsequent advance.
13. There are no records of Panzer *Lehr* having armed Panzer IIIs. They were often used as unarmed OP vehicles and there were command variants listed in other divisions. The tank may have been a misidentified Panzer IV.
14. Later models of Panther had a distinct lip at the bottom of their gun mantlet to prevent this dangerous downward ricochet.
15. TNA WO 171/877 (141 RAC War Diary, August 1944).
16. Cox, Ernest, *Out of the Frying Pan into the Fire* (private memoir).

Chapter 3. Into Battle

1. Cox, Ernest, *Out of the Frying Pan into the Fire* (private memoir).
2. Second Army Operation Order No. 1 dated 21 April 1944.
3. Bailey, Captain Harry, *In All Innocence* (141 Regiment RAC, Regimental Association).
4. Armoured squadron fitter sections were commanded by a REME Technical Sergeant and consisted of four regimental fitters.
5. Meyer, Kurt, *Grenadiers* (J.J. Fedorowicz, Canada, 1994).
6. The squadron 2iC would normally be mounted in one of the squadron's two command tanks, accompanied by one of the 95mm support tanks.
7. Reporters from the division's propaganda company along with others in search of good news 'wrote up' events for consumption at home, *viz* Michael Wittmann's 'second attack' at Villers-Bocage.
8. Three weeks into the campaign the *Hitlerjugend* had lost most of their Pak 40 anti-tank guns thanks to Allied artillery and being vulnerable in a large open gun pit, even when well dug in.
9. Quoted by Meyer, Hubert, *The History of the 12 SS-Panzerdivision Hitlerjugend* (J.J. Fedorowicz, Canada, 1994).
10. Possibly Trooper H.H. Peck, aged 20, the youngest of the crew. He is commemorated on the Memorial of the Missing at Bayeux. The ultimate fate of a crew member assumed to be missing must be treated with caution.
11. The 12th SS Panzer Regiment had been containing 49th Division's MARTLET attack, but with the attack by 15th Scottish and 11th Armoured divisions the Panzer IVs of 2nd Battalion were sent to blocking positions around Le Haute du Bosque. The Panthers remained on the Rauray Spur. Both 2nd Vienna Panzer Division and II/12 SS Panzer Regiment did, however, send Panther reinforcements to that area during the morning of 27 June.
12. Brigadier Carver, commander 4 Armoured Brigade, banned the word 'sniper' to counter the 'phobia' that had developed, insisting on the use of 'isolated riflemen', which was in many cases what they were.
13. There is frequently confusion in contemporary accounts, reports and histories between Château de la Londe and Château du Landel. The former was the objective of Operation MITTEN, and the area of the latter was already in Allied hands.
14. German divisional headquarters had very effective radio intercept platoons, which noted an increase in radio chatter when attacks were imminent and were able to triangulate the source of the signals to generate target data for mortars or artillery.
15. 1947 Staff College battlefield tour papers.

Chapter 4. D (Reserve) Squadron

1. These Churchills would have been knocked out during EPSOM, and probably be of the earlier marks still in service with the tank brigades at this stage of the campaign. The Crocodiles were based on the Mk VII Churchill which was significantly up-armoured.
2. Wilson, Andrew, *Flamethrower* (William Kimber & Co., London, 1956).
3. The 24th Lancers have a very good account from EPSOM of how they were unable to knock out Panthers, but by firing HE against frontal armour they could drive them off. TNA WO171/601.

4. Smith, John, *In at the Finish* (Minerva Press, 1995).
5. The Crocodile had smoke dischargers that were fired from within the tank mounted on the rear of the turret to cover withdrawal from flaming.

Chapter 5. The Battle for Caen

1. A *Hohenstaufen* return on 2 July lists the loss of six Panthers, sixteen Panzer IVs and ten *Sturmgeschütz*; a total of thirty-two AFVs (*Fürbringer*). This is an unusually close correlation of claims.
2. The units of 70 Brigade earned the battle honour 'Rauray' and from the Germans, via Lord Haw-Haw, the nickname 'The Butcher Bears'.
3. Wilson, Andrew, *Flamethrower* (William Kimber & Co., London, 1956).
4. Meyer, Kurt, *Grenadiers* (J.J. Fedorowicz, Canada, 1994).
5. Bailey, Harry, *Playboys: The Story of B Squadron 141 RAC* (Apple iBooks, 2014).
6. Captain Bailey makes the point that 'Because of its trailer a Croc will get ditched or bogged long before any other tank.'
7. It is always unpopular when officers take over another tank or APC from one of their NCOs.
8. The National Archives, WO 171/877.
9. Some 15 per cent of the bombs had delayed-action fuses timed to detonate at the Allied H-Hour of 0420 the following morning.
10. The French population was not so lucky. Even though the majority of them had left the city, it is estimated that between 300 and 400 French civilians were killed.

Chapter 6. The Bocage

1. Strong forces were still being held by Fifteenth Army in expectation of a second landing at the Pas-de-Calais thanks to the continuing effect of Operation FORTITUDE's deception.
2. Spelled 'Granville' on Allied maps. This was one of many mistakes made when printing plates were engraved for the 1:25,000 GSGS 4347 and 1:50,000 GSGS 4250 series of maps from French originals. The correct name of the village was Crauville.
3. To the mix of weapons should be added the hollow-charge *Panzerschreck* and *Panzerfaust*, which were highly effective weapons at close range in the bocage country.
4. The 276th Infantry Division had arrived from southern France where it was raised in January 1944. It consisted of six battalions of infantry in 986, 987 and 988 Grenadier regiments.
5. TNA, WO 170/27. The report was captured and translated and published as Weekly Int Sum No. 42.
6. The German version of the armoured flame-thrower was highly unpopular with its crews and thoroughly dangerous and as a result was rarely used in action.
7. Because of the long track base the arc of fire from the flame gunner's position was further restricted by the tracks stretching forward.
8. Army Group B in the weekly report of 17 July stated that losses in Normandy to date totalled 100,000 men.
9. Zetterling, Niklas, *Normandy 1944: German Military Organisation, Combat Power and Operational Effectiveness* (J.J. Fedorowicz, Canada, 2000).

Chapter 7. Hill 112 and the Second Battle of the Odon

1. Saunders, Tim, *Hill 112: The Key to Defeating Hitler in Normandy* (Pen and Sword, Barnsley, 2022).
2. TNA, WO 216/986, *The Operational Effectiveness of the Flame-Thrower Tank (Crocodile).*
3. On taking over command of Panzer Group West, General Eberbach issued a directive implementing Hitler's instruction to hold the current line in depth and prepare a counter-offensive for the end of the month. This latter aim was, of course, overtaken by the US break-out.
4. Point 213 was a D-Day objective of 8 Armoured Brigade where they were to form a patrol base. It was also where 4th County of London Yeomanry came to grief at the hands of *Hauptsturmführer* Wittmann during Operation PERCH.

5. This was 107 RAC's first operation, having recently arrived in Normandy with 34th Tank Brigade.
6. Foley, John, *Mailed Fist* (Harper Collins, 1975).
7. 107 RAC lost six Churchills and fourteen men killed, wounded and missing during the latter stages of the operation.
8. Cox, Ernest, *Out of the Frying Pan into the Fire* (private memoir).
9. Verey lights were fired by a signal pistol and were used for signalling or providing short-lived instant illumination and came in red, green and white cartridges. The Germans had a similar system, and at the risk of often giving away their own position as in the case at Le Bon-Repos, would fire them in an attempt to disorientate the enemy.
10. Wilson, Andrew, *Flamethrower* (William Kimber & Co., London, 1956).
11. TNA, WO 171/877. War Diary Annex to 141 RAC's war diary, July 1944.
12. Ibid., August 1944.

Chapter 8. The Triangle

1. TNA 15/36, Analysis of operational use of Churchill Crocodile flame-throwers in NW Europe, June-October 1944.
2. This battalion was assessed as having a strength of 300–350 men, of whom only 60 per cent were German, with 24 per cent being ethnic Polish and 15 per cent Russians.
3. Borthwick, Captain Alistair, *Sans Peur: The History of the 5th (Caithness and Sutherland) Battalion, the Seaforth Highlanders, 1942–1945* (Eneas Mackay, 1946).
4. Borthwick, Captain Alastair, *Battalion: A British Infantry Unit's Actions from El Alamein to the Elbe, 1942–1945* (Baton Wicks, London, 1994).
5. The infantry formed just 14 per cent of the Second Army and had been expected to take 70 per cent of the army's casualties, but in Normandy the figure was 85 per cent. Staff planning rates for casualties for the campaign were established as 'Normal' and 'Intense', but a third category had to be introduced which was 'Double Intense'.
6. TNA SUP 15/37, Report on the use of Flame-Throwers in the Opening Stages of the Campaign in Normandy (D to D+55).
7. Major Spearpoint, having later recovered from his wounds, commanded a squadron of Churchills in 107 Regiment RAC.

Chapter 9. Operation BLUECOAT

1. G (Trg), *Battlefield Tour: 8 Corps Operations South of Caumont 30–31 July 1944 (Operation BLUECOAT)* (HQ BAOR, June 1947).
2. Author's interview with Lieutenant Blake, 43rd Divisional Company, Military Police.
3. TNA, WO 171/877, War Diary Annex to 141 RAC's war diary, July 1944.
4. Ibid.
5. Bredin, Lieutenant Colonel A.E.C., *Three Assault Landings* (Gale & Polden, Aldershot, 1946).
6. TNA, WO 171/877, War Diary Annex to 141 RAC's war diary, August 1944.
7. Château Orbis had been the site of Panzer *Lehr*'s divisional headquarters for most of June 1944.
8. 6th Guards (Independent) Tank Brigade had originally been a part of the Guards Armoured Division, but when the ORBAT was changed to a single armoured brigade it left the division training under VIII Corps alongside 15th Scottish as a tank brigade having been re-equipped with Churchills.
9. G (Trg), *Battlefield Tour: 8 Corps Operations South of Caumont 30–31 July 1944 (Operation BLUECOAT)* (HQ BAOR, June 1947).
10. Wilson, Andrew, *Flamethrower* (William Kimber & Co., London, 1956).
11. In this case elevated positions for OPs from which the British assembly could be seen and heard and the work of radio intelligence sections warned the Germans of the forthcoming attack.
12. Headquarters Second Army, *An Account of the Operations of Second Army in Europe 1944–1945* (Headquarters Second Army, August 1945).
13. TNA, WO/171 12554; Tank Grenadier Guards war diary, August 1944.

14. The Duke of Wellington was similarly relaxed about uniform during the Peninsular War, although he did draw the line at his staff using ladies' parasols during the Waterloo campaign.

Chapter 10. Operation TOTALIZE

1. Montgomery, *Normandy to the Baltic* (British Army of the Rhine Stationary Services, April 1946).
2. *Generalfeldmarschall* von Kluge, commander Army Group B, had warned Hitler on 22 July that German forces in Normandy were verging on collapse, but he was ignored and instructed to stand firm.
3. Seventy-two 105mm Priest self-propelled guns had been issued to 3rd Canadian Division for D-Day, but were now to be returned to the US Army. The Americans readily agreed to removing the guns and racking, or as it was known 'defrocking' the Priests and blocking the opening with a steel and sand sandwich. See Saunders, *Battleground Totalize*.
4. TNA WO 170/27, A Squadron war diary.
5. Cox, Ernest, *Out of the Frying Pan into the Fire* (private memoir). With serviceability issues, even this neat arrangement was not always possible.
6. The Bomber Barons, who saw providing support to the army a distraction from their strategic bombing campaign, complained that 'The army is not fighting its own battles.'
7. Cox, Ernest, *Out of the Frying Pan into the Fire* (private memoir).
8. Historical Section (GS), Report No. 65, *Canadian Participation in the Operations in North-West Europe 1944, Part III: Canadian Operations, 1–23 August* (Army Headquarters, 1953).
9. The comments about penny-packeting reflect those of the *Schwere* Panzer battalions who also advocated using their Tigers en masse, but as in 141 RAC, they were usually parcelled out by company.
10. Bailey, Harry, *Playboys* (Apple iBooks, 2014).
11. An enduring rule of battle procedure is that a commander takes one-third of the time available for his planning and orders, leaving two-thirds for his subordinates down the chain of command for their own planning and preparations.
12. TNA WO 170/27, B Squadron war diary.
13. Major Lindsay had been commanding officer of 8 Para, but prior to D-Day he had left Bigot top secret papers unattended while he went to the lavatory. He was reported by his second-in-command Terrance Otway, sacked and replaced by Otway. Major Lindsay served with distinction throughout the campaign with the Gordon Highlanders.
14. Lindsay, Martin, *So Few Got Through: The Diary of an Infantry Officer* (Collins & Co., 1946).
15. TNA SUPP 15/36. Analysis of operational use of Churchill Crocodile flame-throwers in NW Europe, June-October 1944.
16. Scene of wholesale destruction of the Fife and Forfar Yeomanry during Operation GOODWOOD.
17. Bailey, Harry, *The Playboys* (Apple iBooks, 2014).

Chapter 11. Operation TRACTABLE

1. TNA WO 170/27, A Squadron war diary.
2. Historical Section (GS), Report No. 65, *Canadian Participation in the Operations in North-West Europe 1944, Part III: Canadian Operations, 1–23 August* (Army Headquarters, 1953).
3. It is believed that the Germans captured a map showing their identified anti-tank positions and moved them overnight. As a result they were largely missed by the bombing and bombardment.
4. HQ 8 Brigade was on the low ground north of the ridge and the battalions were in the valley of the Laizon, with the high ground that defeated VHF radio communication in between. Once the brigadier's tactical headquarters was static up on the ridge with a shorter range and line of sight, comms would have improved.
5. Cox, Ernest, *Out of the Frying Pan into the Fire* (private memoir).
6. Talking among fellow soldiers is one of the accepted ways of reconciling what has just happened to them and another way is in writing it all down, in which this memoir may have been the aim.

7. 'Exhaustion' cases were not listed as casualties. Few returned once they had passed the point of breakdown, but as the campaign went on units became better at spotting the signs of exhaustion, and soldiers, if sent back to echelon or a special rest camp, returned to their units more frequently.
8. The Canadian OH notes 'The incident was fully investigated on the orders of Air Chief Marshal Harris. The technical reasons which led to it need not be explored here, but Bomber Command considered that a blameworthy aspect was the failure of the bomber crews to carry out orders which required them to make carefully timed runs from the moment of crossing the coast. This precaution would have prevented the errors. Disciplinary action was taken against individuals whose responsibility could be established. Two Pathfinder Force crews were re-posted to ordinary crew duties, squadron and flight commanders personally involved relinquished their commands and acting ranks and were re-posted to ordinary crew duty, and all crews implicated were "starred" so as not to be employed upon duties within 30 miles forward of the bomb line until reassessed after further experience.'
9. Stacey, Colonel C.O., *The Victory Campaign*, Vol. III (Ministry of National Defence, Ottawa, 1966).
10. Historical Section (GS), Report No. 65, *Canadian Participation in the Operations in North-West Europe 1944, Part III: Canadian Operations, 1–23 August* (Army Headquarters, 1953).
11. ww2talk.com, Compo Rations.

Chapter 12. Pursuit to the Seine

1. Cox, E. (private memoir).
2. TNA, WO 171/877, C Squadron war diary, August 1944.
3. Wilson, Andrew, *Flamethrower* (William Kimber & Co., London, 1956).
4. Cox, Ernest (private memoir).
5. TNA, WO 171/877, B Squadron war diary, August 1944.
6. Bailey, Harry, *Playboys* (Apple iBooks, 2014).

Chapter 13. With US VIII Corps at Brest

1. Cox, Ernest (private memoir).
2. Bailey, Harry, *Playboys* (Apple iBooks, 2014).
3. The nature of that nickname is unknown, but the area of speculation is obvious.
4. TNA, WO 171/877 B Squadron war diary, September 1944.

Chapter 14. Le Havre: Operation ASTONIA

1. Directive M520.
2. Cox, Ernest (private memoir).
3. Smith, John, *In at the Finish* (Minerva Press, 1995).
4. St.-Valery-en-Caux was where the 51st Highland Division had been forced to surrender in 1940. At the same time 2nd Canadian Division had been directed to Dieppe, the scene of their disastrous raid in 1942. By such moves ghosts were laid.
5. Historical Section, *Report No. 184, Canadian Participation in the Operations in North-West Europe 1944. Part V: Clearing the Channel Ports, 3 Sep 44–6 Feb 45* (Canadian Military Headquarters).
6. Special Interrogation Report, Colonel Eberhard Wildermuth, quoted in CMHQ Report 184.
7. 'In view of the nature of the defences, specialized armour from 79 Armd Div was made available. This included 44 armoured personnel carriers (Kangaroos) of the newly organized 1st Canadian Armoured Personnel Carrier Squadron, a unit formed as a result of the successful use of "unfrocked Priests" on 7/8 Aug and 14/15 Aug.' (CMHQ Report 184).
8. Lindsay, Martin, *So Few Got Through* (Pen & Sword, Barnsley, 2000).
9. 'Daylight attacks were made by heavy bombers on 5, 6 and 8 Sep, during which 1,000 aircraft dropped over 4,000 tons of bombs upon the town and surrounding defences. To prevent any repetition of the tragic errors of 14, forward troops were withdrawn 3,000 yards during these attacks, but the bombs were dropped with extreme accuracy and were well concentrated upon their proper target.' (CMHQ Report 184).

Churchill Crocodiles were also deployed in other theaters. This one is photographed in Italy in 1945, with a New Zealand infantryman.

10. Anon, *The Story of 79th Armoured Division* (Germany, 1945).
11. This statement has been attributed to a number of German prisoners at different places and different times during the attack on Le Havre.
12. Elliot, Lieutenant Colonel G.G., Personal campaign notes, 2nd Battalion, the Essex Regiment.
13. Lieutenant Wareing, personal account, 1993.
14. Brother of Alex Douglas-Home, future prime minister of the UK.
15. BBC, *People's War*.

Appendix I. Tank Numbers

1. TNA, WO 171/30.
2. https://mikesresearch.com/2018/06/10/141-rac-regiment-crocodiles.

Appendix II. Operational Use of the Churchill Crocodile

1. TNA, SUPP 15/36.

21 ARMY GROUP

PERSONAL MESSAGE FROM THE C-IN-C

(To be read out to all Troops)

1. On the 11th of August I spoke to the officers and men of the Allied Armies in NW France. I said we must "write off" the powerful German force that was causing us so much trouble; we must finish it, once and for all, and so hasten the end of the war.
2. And to-day, ten days later, it has been done.
The German armies in north-west France have suffered a decisive defeat; the destruction of enemy personnel and equipment in and about the so-called "Normandy pocket" has been terrific; and it is still going on; any enemy units that manage to get away will not be in a fit condition to fight again for months; there are still many surprises in store for the fleeing remnants. The victory has been definite, complete, and decisive.
3. As soldiers, we all want to pay our tribute to the Allied Air Forces. I doubt if ever in the history of war, air forces have had such opportunities, or have taken such good advantage of them. The brave and brilliant work of the pilots has aroused our greatest admiration; without their support, we soldiers could have achieved no success.
4. Where all have done so well, it is difficult to single out any for special praise.
As a British General, I can speak for all the soldiers of the Empire, and can express our high admiration for the brave fighting qualities of the American Armies in the opening stages of the "break-in" battle on 25 July and following days; and we followed with tremendous enthusiasm their great achievements during the wheel of the right flank almost to the gates of Paris. We never want to fight alongside better soldiers.
As an Allied Commander, and the overall commander of the land forces under General Eisenhower, I can praise the fighting qualities and tenacity in battle of the British, Canadian, and Polish troops on the eastern flank; they fought the enemy relentlessly, and took heavy toll of him during the whole of this great battle.
5. But surely it matters little who did *this* or *that*.
All that matters is that it was well and truly done by the whole Allied team.
The proper motto for Allies should be:
"One for all, and all for one."
And that is our motto. I want to thank you all for the way you responded to the call.
6. The victory in NW France, south of the Seine, marks the beginning of the end of German military domination of France.
Much still remains to be done, but it will now be done the more easily.
7. And what next?
Having brought disaster to the German forces in NW France we must now complete the destruction of such of his forces as are still available to be destroyed. After knowing what has happened to their armies in NW France, it is unlikely that these forces will now come to us; so we will go to them.
8. "The Lord mighty in battle" has given us the victory.
The news is very good from the war fronts all over the world.
The end of the war is in sight; let us finish off the business in record time.

France, 21 August 1944.

B. L. Montgomery

General
C.-in-C.,
21 Army Group

Montgomery's message to 21st Army Group in the immediate aftermath of Falaise.

Index